BERGESEN'S BRITISH CERAMICS PRICE GUIDE

BASED on a far-reaching survey of British ceramics available on the market, in antique shops, fairs and elsewhere, this unique book provides a reliable and accurate guide to every major type of collectable British pottery and porcelain. Clearly set out with over 1,500 photographs, it ranges from a 6th-century cremation urn to modern studio pottery. The collector, whether beginner or expert, as well as the dealer and valuer, the buyer or seller, the cataloguer or the casual owner of a few family treasures, will find the work an indispensable tool.

An extensive introduction explains manufacturing techniques, ceramic marks and guides to dating, and gives warnings on fakes and reproductions, as well as sound advice on the effects of damage etc. Every section has a helpful introduction, with suggestions for further reading. Each item is illustrated and described, with details of mark, size and period, and notes of any faults.

Victoria Bergesen has drawn on the advice of a team of leading specialist consultants, one of whom, Geoffrey Godden, aptly sums up the work: 'More than a price guide, more than a reference book.'

VICTORIA BERGESEN is an American writer and lecturer who has lived in Kent since 1984. She is the author of Majolica: British, Continental and American Wares 1851–1915 and the Encyclopaedia of British Art Pottery, both published by Barrie & Jenkins. Her articles on a wide variety of British ceramics have appeared in many magazines and journals. As an inveterate collector and erstwhile dealer she has a wide knowledge of the antiques trade both here and in the United States.

CONSULTANTS

PAUL ATTERBURY is the author or editor of some ten books in the field of art and antiques, including *The Dictionary of Minton* (1990) with Maureen Batkin and *The Pottery of William and Walter Moorcroft* (2nd edition 1990). He is a past editor of *Connoisseur* magazine and Historical Adviser to the Royal Doulton Group. He is well known as a member of the BBC 'Antiques Roadshow' team of experts, and is a frequent contributor to the specialist journals. In 1989 his part in the rescue of a Gilbert Bayes ceramic freize, now in the Victoria & Albert Museum, won him a National Art Collections Fund award.

CHRIS BLANCHETT has been a member of the Tiles and Architectural Ceramics Society since 1982, and a member of the committee since 1984. He has been editor of the Society's newsletter since 1988, and has contributed a number of articles on tiles to various magazines and books. He is a major contributor to the travelling exhibition 'Fired Earth, 1000 Years of Tiles in Europe', and co-author of its catalogue. He is currently collaborating in the publication of a new book on the history of tiles.

GEOFFREY GODDEN, Hon. D.Litt. (Keele), FRSA, joined the family antique business at Worthing in the mid 1940s, and has been engaged in the trade for nearly fifty years. He quickly made an International name in the field of British ceramics, and his *Encyclopaedia of British Pottery and Porcelain Marks*, first published in 1964, is regarded as the last word. He has written over thirty other books, and is currently preparing two new ones on Continental porcelain. His experience, as both a collector and a major dealer over many years, in correctly identifying, dating and valuing British ceramics is unique.

DR R. K. HENRYWOOD worked for twenty years in engineering and computing, but is now a freelance author and lecturer. He started collecting English pottery when he was a student at Imperial College, University of London, and has put together a major collection of 19th-century earthenwares and stonewares. He contributes frequently to the specialist magazines, and his books include *The Dictionary of Blue and White Printed Pottery 1780–1880*, written with A. W. Coysh, and *Relief-Moulded Jugs 1820–1900*.

JONATHAN HORNE, pottery specialist, developed an early interest in his subject through archaeology. He started dealing in 1968 and quickly established his reputation. By 1976 he was exhibiting at Grosvenor House; and he is now regarded as the foremost authority in his field. At his premises at 66c Kensington Church Street, London W8, outstanding, as well as inexpensive, examples of English pottery can always be seen. Jonathan Horne also publishes a number of specialist books on ceramics.

BERGESEN'S
Price Guide

Victoria Bergesen

BARRIE & JENKINS
LONDON

First published in Great Britain in 1992 by
Barrie & Jenkins Ltd
20 Vauxhall Bridge Road, London SW1V 2SA

A catalogue record for this book is available from the British Library.

ISBN 0 7126 5382 1

Typeset by SX Composing Ltd, Rayleigh, Essex
Printed and bound in Great Britain by Butler and Tanner Ltd, Frome and London

While every care has been exercised in the compilation of this guide, neither the
author nor the publishers accept any liability for any financial or other loss incurred by
reliance placed on the information contained in *Bergesen's British Ceramics Price Guide*.

CONTENTS

PREFACE

THE study and collection of British ceramics is a very exciting field. This activity is now open to anyone with a little time and less money, but approaching the subject for the first time can be very confusing. There is such a wealth of information that one does not know where to begin. This guide is meant to serve as a lifeline to the beginner, but it should also be useful for those with a long-standing interest.

We have made an attempt in this guide to portray a good cross-section of British ceramics for sale today. Some items are very rare and only likely to be found in the shops of specialist dealers; some are quite common and similar examples may be found in a sweep around any town with a number of general antique shops or a large antiques and collectables fair. Even though 1,500 illustrations at first seemed an enormous number, the incredible variety and ingenuity of British potters has made it impossible to cover everything. However, with a systematic approach we hope in succeeding years to build on this, the first edition. If your favourite pots have been slighted or ignored, do let us hear from you. There is always next time!

VICTORIA BERGESEN

ACKNOWLEDGEMENTS

THE world of pottery and porcelain collectors has changed significantly in the past thirty years. Even thirty years ago, reference books spoke of connoisseurs, whereas today they speak of experts and collectors. The rarefied atmosphere has largely dispersed and knowledge once closely guarded is freely shared among large and enthusiastic groups of collectors and scholars, both professional and amateur, from all walks of life.

The most significant event which set off the avalanche of interest in collecting pots was the publication of Geoffrey Godden's *Encyclopaedia of British Pottery and Porcelain Marks* in 1964. There had been mark books before, but never one so comprehensive and up-to-date. Geoffrey Godden has since published many monographs and general works on ceramics, whose standard has served as a bench-mark for all of us who have chosen to write about the subject. A new level of professional but accessible scholarship has been established.

Long before I had the opportunity of knowing Geoffrey, his work served as an inspiration to me. He was instrumental in the development of this work, and during its preparation has been a valued adviser in all respects.

Paul Atterbury, Chris Blanchett, R. K. Henrywood and Jonathan Horne are all distinguished in their fields. They have shown unfailing patience with my inquiries and made many valuable suggestions. While I am responsible for any fallings of this volume, its merits are due to their careful reading of the portions of the text which I have submitted to them.

The dealers who have allowed me to set up my studio in the midst of their premises are listed at the end of the book. I thank them all for their hospitality and patience and for the useful information which they provided.

Other people who have offered information, time, advice and encouragement are: Robert Copeland; Audrey Dudson; Jonathan Gray; Leslie Hayward; Tony Herbert; Robin Hildyard, Victoria & Albert Museum; Joan Jones, Minton Museum, Royal Doulton Tablewares Ltd; Barry Lamb, Reference Works; Kathy Niblett, Stoke-on-Trent City Museum and Art Gallery; Paul Rice; and Michael Whiteway.

HOW TO USE THIS BOOK

IF you want to get the most out of this book do read the Introduction and What is it Worth? Most of us tend to skip over introductory matter, to get to the 'good' part of a book, but these two chapters are the frame of reference on which the rest of the book is based. The Introduction explains many technical terms used in the entries and is essential reading.

Every attempt has been made to make this book easy to use. First you must recognise that the chances of any one particular pot being in this volume are small: the number of patterns and shapes used by British potters runs into the millions. Yours may be one of the 1,500 illustrated here, but if not it will still be possible to learn more about it. If you have a pot with a factory mark, check the index for references to the firm. If the pot is not marked with the factory name or the firm has not been mentioned in the index try to find pots which look similar. Wares have been grouped by type and period. The photographs are along the outside margins of the pages, which makes it quick and easy to flip through until you begin to see wares which resemble the pot you want to identify.

Now examine your pot carefully. Try to determine whether it is pottery or porcelain. You can usually determine this simply by holding it before a strong electric light: if the pot is translucent it is almost always porcelain. How is the pot decorated: relief-moulded, painted, printed etc.? Various techniques are described in the Introduction. Look carefully for any marks. There are many types of marks and most are useful indicators for the collector.

Entries describe each illustration, giving maker, type of body, shape, method of decoration and approximate date. Pattern and shape names in *italics* are known to have been used by the manufacturer. Pattern names in quotation marks have been assigned by scholars and collectors, and are in general use. Pattern names in lower-case letters are descriptive, but not names in general use.

Any damage or flaws in the items illustrated are noted. Remember that these affect the value, and if you have a perfect example yours will be worth more. Conversely, if you have a damaged pot, the value will be less than a perfect example shown. All marks, including among others factory marks, pattern or shape numbers, registration numbers, and date cyphers or codes, are also noted. The size is given, followed by the code of the dealer and the retail price. Dealers' full names are listed at the end of the book.

Further reading sections list books which are particularly useful if you want to learn more about an individual factory or type of ceramic. Works referred to by author only will be found in full in the further reading lists of the relevant chapter or factory. With a few exceptions very rare and costly reference works have been omitted, and where possible I have listed works which are readily available. Enthusiasts are reliant on specialist dealers, who keep a good stock of out-of-print books on ceramics. Their catalogues are reference books in themselves. It is always useful to check the shelves of general second-hand book dealers, but be sure that the volume you buy is the most recent edition. When ceramics reference books are reprinted they often incorporate new research, which may make the previous edition obsolete. A complete bibliography includes all works referred to anywhere throughout this book. Unless otherwise noted, all books have been published in London.

INTRODUCTION

B RITISH ceramics are without doubt the most varied in the world. Nearly every type of ceramic has been made at one time or another. Some techniques, such as the tin-glazed earthenwares commonly referred to as delftware, were brought from other nations. Others are British innovations, and it is these innovations, such as bone china, which have brought to Britain an unparalleled international reputation for its ceramics.

Many of the terms and processes described here may be unfamiliar to the reader, but it is necessary to understand how a pot is made in order to identify it and value it. Also included are a general section on the types of marks used on ceramics, and some recommendations on where and how to purchase pots and on how to expand your knowledge of the field.

BRITISH POTTERY CENTRES

The largest centre for pottery and porcelain production in Britain since the 18th century has been the Staffordshire Potteries (sometimes just referred to as the Potteries). The availability of coal to fire the kilns and good quality clays (often dug as a by-product of coal-mining) made it an ideal location for potteries. Lead and salt for glazing were brought from nearby Derbyshire and Cheshire. Canals and later railways made the local availability of clay and coal less important, and as the industry grew, the increasingly skilled local workforce became the predominant reason for remaining in the region. Today most of the clay used is imported from Cornwall or the West Country.

Other major centres of ceramic production have been Bristol, Derbyshire, Devon including Bideford, Barnstaple, and Torquay (in the late 19th and early 20th centuries), Glasgow, Liverpool, London, the Scottish East Coast, the Severn Valley, South Wales and Yorkshire. However, pottery has been made nearly everywhere in the nation at one time or another. The industry in most of these centres declined during the 19th century, and if it exists today is usually dominated by one firm. The trade began to refer to these as the 'out-potters', that is those outside the Staffordshire Potteries, now the only major centre for production of pottery and porcelain.

The centre of the Staffordshire industry is the Five Towns. In fact there are six towns, but in his novels about the region Arnold Bennett called them the Five Towns, and the name has stuck. The six towns are Stoke, Hanley, Tunstall, Fenton, Longton and Burslem. These were federated as Stoke-on-Trent in 1910, although the towns have maintained a certain degree of individuality. For example, Longton has long been a centre for china manufacture; Stoke is dominated by Minton and Spode; Burslem by Royal Doulton. Today a visit to the area is a must for those interested in British ceramics. The industry still thrives, and there are many opportunities to tour factories and museums.

BODIES AND PASTES

The *body* is the mixture of clays and minerals of which the pot is actually made. The term *paste* is generally used when speaking of porcelains. The mixture of materials in the body determines the colour, strength, texture and translucency of the finished pot.

Bodies are generally divided into two groups: pottery and porcelain. With very few exceptions, pottery is opaque and porcelain is translucent. However, there are many types of bodies within each of these two groups.

Pottery is made of clay, or a mixture of clays. Without the addition of metallic oxides, clay generally fires white, buff or red. The types of wares obtained from clay depend on the mixture of the clays and the ways in which they were fired. *Terracotta* is an unglazed clay (most often red) fired at a low temperature. *Earthenware* is a coarser, more open body which requires a glaze to make it watertight. *Stoneware* is fired at a very high temperature which vitrifies the silica in the body, giving it great strength. Some very fine stonewares are slightly translucent, the only exception to the rule that pottery is always opaque. Stoneware is usually salt-glazed or smear glazed (see below). *Dry-bodied wares* are unglazed stonewares. They include *basalt* (stained black), *cane ware* (a buff ware also known as *bamboo ware*) and *jasper* wares (stained with metallic oxides, most often cobalt). *Ironstone* or stone china is a feldspathic stoneware, which was glazed and decorated in the manner of ordinary earthenware. Feldspar (or felspar) is a mineral used in bone china or ironstone which can be used to replace Cornish stone, which itself contains some feldspar. Ironstone is *sometimes* translucent. It is also sometimes called *semi china* or *opaque china*.

Porcelain is a very strong body made with china clay (kaolin to the Chinese) and china stone (petunse to the Chinese); various other ingredients such as feldspar or calcined bone may be added to make the body whiter and stronger. This is fired at a very high temperature, which vitrifies the pot, rendering it translucent. Porcelain was first made in China. The first European porcelains were made in the eighteenth century at Meissen (c.1710) and Vienna (from 1719) and after 1740 its manufacture spread throughout the Continent. The first English porcelains were made by Chelsea and Bow in London c.1745; these were soft-paste wares, unlike Meissen and most of its continental imitators which were hard-paste.

The difference between *hard-paste* and *soft-paste* porcelain can seem bewildering to the novice. The oriental porcelains and most of the Continental porcelains were hard-paste. The 18th-century soft-paste bodies include powdered glass or frit, which does indeed give them a glassy texture. Although these wares were fired at a lower temperature than hard-paste porcelains, the rate of kiln loss was very high, and by 1800 soft-paste had been abandoned in favour of bone china or hard-paste type porcelains. Early soft-paste porcelains are rare, and one is not likely to come across them at the local flea market. The only real way to learn to distinguish them from hard-paste porcelains is by handling. Many seminars and classes will offer examples of both types for handling and inspection.

Bone china is a very fine white porcelain obtained by the addition of finely ground calcined bone (animal bones which have been made brittle by baking in a kiln) to a body made of china clay and Cornish stone. It is neither a true hard-paste nor soft-paste porcelain, but in a category of its own. Josiah Spode II is credited with inventing bone china c.1800. Although the patent granted to Thomas Frye at Bow in 1749 used bone ash, his was a soft-paste porcelain.

Parian, also known as Carrara or statuary porcelain, is a highly vitrified, often unglazed, fine-grained feldspathic porcelain which was first introduced by Copeland & Garrett and by Minton in the mid 1840s. It was principally used for figures and busts, but also for relief-moulded jugs and tablewares.

Semi-porcelain is not porcelain at all, but a name given to earthenwares in the 19th and 20th centuries.

MANUFACTURING METHODS

The body or paste having been mixed, it must be shaped into a pot. This may be done using one of several methods. The simplest (or most difficult depending on the skill applied) is to *model* the plastic clay with the hands. This can be used to make simple pinch pots, of the sort children make at school, or to sculpt elaborate figures or ornaments., *Throwing* is done on a wheel, which by centrifugal force enables the thrower to create a pot.

Throwing requires considerable skill, and has been largely replaced in the industrial potteries by slip-casting (see below). It is the preferred method of 20th-century studio potters. *Turning* is a method used for giving the wares a smooth finish or to apply banded decoration with a lathe.

Upchurch Pottery earthenware vase decorated with matt boracic based glazes.

c.1928. Incised mark 'Upchurch'; glaze code painted in black 'PB/BC'. 16.5 cm height   CG

£45

Note the prominent bands made in the course of throwing the vase. These would have been obscured if the vase was turned after throwing.

Moulds can be made of fired clay or, after its introduction c.1740, of plaster of Paris. *Press-moulding* is pressing the plastic clay into the mould. *Slip-casting* is pouring slip (liquid clay) into a mould. After the mould has absorbed most of the moisture, the *leather-hard* pieces are removed and joined with slip. Slip-casting increased in viability in the 19th century with the introduction of deflocculants, which when added to a thick mixture of clay and water increase viscosity. This reduced the amount of water necessary to make the slip pourable, and so reduced the amount of time needed for the moisture to evaporate to produce a leather-hard piece.

The shaped ware is then allowed to dry and is subsequently fired. This first firing is known as the *biscuit firing*, and the unglazed ware resulting is known as *biscuit ware*.

SHAPES

Pots are divided into two categories, *flat ware* (shallow articles such as plates, saucers, or meat plates) and *hollow ware* (such as cups, jugs, and teapots). Each of these is described using a terminology with which most people are familiar.

Flat wares have *rims* and *centres*. Their bases have *footrims*, upon which the item rests. Sometimes a few small marks may be found on the rims. These are known as *stilt marks*, which are left by the small stilts placed between the wares in the kiln to prevent them from sticking together. After firing the stilts are knocked off, and the remains ground off, always on the face, and sometimes on the reverse.

Different hollow ware shapes have their own body parts. Henry Sandon has remarked that the body parts of a jug are like those of a human body. The jug has a spout or a lip, the body itself has a neck, a shoulder and a bottom. The handle is rather like an arm. Teapots have spouts, handles, and lids with knops or finials. Another important characteristic for identifying teapots is the strainer inside the pot, which prevents the tea leaves from blocking the spout.

In the descriptions that follow the reader will find continual mention of shapes. Shape is the surest guide to placing a pot within a period of time. Perusal of *An Anthology of British Teapots* by Philip Miller and Michael Berthoud or *A Compendium of British Cups* by Michael Berthoud will show the reader how shapes changed with decorative periods and influences. Although a large factory might have produced hundreds of new patterns each year, shapes are used repeatedly. This is because of the enormous expense of introducing a new shape. Some common shapes are shown below.

Top left: typical 18th-century coffee cup shape, in imitation of Chinese export porcelain.
Top right: Bute shape bone china cup, c.1800–15.
Bottom right: London shape bone china cup, c.1815–25.
Bottom left: Glasgow shape bone china cup, c.1845.

To create a new shape, the designer must first draw each item required in the new shape, for example, a teapot with lid and stand, sugar bowl, cream jug, tea and coffee cups, saucers, slop bowls, bread and butter plate for a tea service. Then each item must be modelled in plaster or clay. As there is a reduction in size during the biscuit firing, the model must be at least 6 per cent larger than the finished item. The mould, usually made of plaster of Paris (or at the present time of a resin material), is then taken from the original. This first mould is called a *master* or *block mould*. A shape is then cast from this mould, and another mould, the *case mould*, taken from the item. A further *working mould* taken from the case mould is the one actually used for production. The master and case moulds are preserved for use in making other moulds.

Plaster of Paris moulds have a short life, and soon the moulded features become less crisp. Moulds could also be made of fired earthenware. These moulds lasted for a longer time, but caused further complications because when they were first fired, they would naturally shrink, after which they would still need to be larger than the finished item. They were also non-absorbent which prolonged the time necessary to fire the ware to a leather-hard state.

One may often see the mould lines under the handles or along the spouts of jugs. These may be obscured by *sponging*, which is rubbing down the mould marks with a damp sponge before biscuit firing. *Relief-moulding* refers to a raised pattern created by using a mould.

Brownhills Pottery Co. relief-moulded smear glazed stoneware teapot painted with polychrome enamels.

c.1881. Painted pattern number 1469/4. 19 cm height   AF

£45

Some items such as teacups were *jollied*. In this process the cup would be thrown on a wheel inside a plaster of Paris mould, thus creating a smooth interior. Flat ware is *jiggered* by throwing a pad of clay on to a mould, and lowering a *profile* to shape the back of the plate and make a foot rim.

METHODS OF DECORATION

Methods of decoration are largely determined by two factors, the properties of the material being used and the cost of the finished item. Decoration may be divided into three groups: methods applied to the pot while in a leather-hard state before biscuit firing;

methods applied to biscuit ware; and methods applied after glost (or glaze) firing (on top of the glaze).

Starting from the inside and working out, the simplest form of decoration is by tinting or staining the body itself. The *dry-bodied wares*, such as black basalt or jaspar, have stained bodies, which need no glaze to colour them. *Agate wares* are made by mixing slices of two or more coloured clays, to form a pattern, which is then sealed under a clear glaze. Agate ware is also known as onyx ware or pebble ware – in the United States scroddled ware or lava ware.

Even very primitive wares are often *embossed*, or impressed with relief stamps or rollers while the clay is still in a leather-hard state before firing. During the 19th century printers' type was sometimes used to impress inscriptions. Leaves and fern fronds were sometimes impressed into wares, leaving a pattern when the vegetable matter burned away in the kiln. Pieces of fabric, especially lace, could be employed in the same manner (see Doulton & Slaters Patent, p. 215). An embossed effect can also be created by a mould.

Engine-turned decoration is done on a lathe when the ware is in a leather-hard state. This creates a band of uniform decoration, often geometric, diced or fluted. Sometimes the ware was coated in slip so that the turning revealed the differently coloured body beneath.

Pierced decoration is created by cutting through the ware in a leather-hard state. This can be quite crude, or exquisitely fine, as in the case of George Owen's vases made for Worcester Royal Porcelain Co. (see p. 486). *Incised* decoration is created by drawing on the leather-hard clay with a sharp, pointed instrument.

SLIPS

Some of the earliest decoration was done with slips (clay diluted in water). The simplest technique is *sgraffito*, where for instance a red-bodied pot is dipped in a white clay slip. When the slip has dried to a leather-hard state, a design is then scratched in the white slip revealing the red body below. The entire pot is then covered with a honey-coloured galena (lead) glaze. The *intaglio* technique actually cuts away sections of the slip to reveal panels or larger sections of the body beneath. These two techniques were often employed together on the same pot. *Barbotine* is a method of painting the ware with coloured slips, giving the texture of an oil painting.

Slip-trailing uses a slip the consistency of cake icing. This was placed in a container with a nozzle and the design squeezed on to the surface of the pot. *Tube-lining* is a refinement of the slip-trailing process introduced in the 1890s, using a much finer nozzle to produce delicate raised lines. The areas between these lines were then filled in with coloured glazes. This technique was widely used by art potters, the most famous example being the wares designed by William Moorcroft for James Macintyre at Burslem, and later at his own works. It is believed that Harry Bernard introduced the technique at Macintyre's. It was also widely used by members of the Rhead family, at various other Staffordshire works. Tube-lining is most often found on tiles, where it was an effective way of putting sinuous art nouveau designs on the flat rectilinear tiles. However, the technique required considerable skill, and soon manufacturers reproduced the effect with relief-moulding.

Combing is a decorative technique where the pot (usually flat ware) is coated with slip, which is allowed to dry slightly. The slip is then 'combed' to make a pattern over the surface of the ware. Traditionally the combs were made of leather or wood, but later potters have used rubber, cardboard or even plastic.

Feathering is achieved by coating the ware with a coat of slip, followed by a second coat of slip in a contrasting colour, which is trailed into the first coat. A sharpened quill or similar instrument is then drawn across the surface to break the slip into fine hair-lines.

Marbling is achieved by pouring two or more coloured slips into a leather-hard dish or bowl. These are swirled about to create a marbled effect.

13

Pâte-sur-pâte uses slips to build up the pattern on the body of the ware, always porcelain. The technique was brought from France and developed by Marc Louis Solon, who worked at Minton. While Minton introduced the ware to Britain, they were soon copied by other manufacturers.

Mocha wares are decorated with a band of coloured slip, often, blue, greenish-grey or tan. The potter then created the mocha decoration with 'tea', a mixture of tobacco juice, urine and manganese. This was applied while the slip was still damp. The decoration fanned out on the slip in a pattern resembling trees. Bands of black were then used to finish off the decoration.

APPLIED DECORATION

Applied decoration refers to decoration made of clay and then fastened to the pot with slip. In some cases this may be *modelled*. The most common method of applied decoration is *sprigging*, as often found on jasper wares. Clay is pressed into small moulds, and when leather-hard it is carefully lifted from the moulds and fastened to the pot with slip. The finest sprigging, on early Wedgwood jasper wares for example, was carefully cut away resulting in transparent areas, for instance in the flowing draperies of classical figures.

UNDERGLAZE PAINTING AND COLOURS

These are wares painted or dusted with metallic oxides before the biscuit firing. The wares are then glazed and glost-fired. As the decoration is beneath the glaze, it cannot be scratched, washed or rubbed off. However, as the colours must be able to withstand the heat required for biscuit firing, the palette is more limited than that of enamel colours (see Painting below).

GLAZING

Glazing is necessary to keep the body watertight, but it also offers an easy method of decoration which can be carried out by less skilled workers. The glaze is actually a glass-like coating containing silica which fuses to the body of the ware. Coloured glazes are obtained by the addition of metallic oxides. Wares are most often dipped into the glaze, but glaze can also be painted on or, in modern times, applied with an aerograph (a jet gun powered by compressed air). It is usually poured into hollow wares like vases or jugs and swirled around, then the excess is poured out. The ware is fired in a *glost kiln*, where the temperature is lower than that used for the first or biscuit firing.

One of the earliest methods of glazing was *salt-glazing*. Salt glazes are different from the glazes described above in that the glaze is not applied to biscuit ware and then glost-fired. Salt-glazed wares are once-fired during which process salt is literally thrown into the kiln when the fires are at their height. The sodium chloride vaporises, and when cool again the wares are found covered with a hard shiny glaze formed by the reaction of the clay with the sodium in the salt. This can only be done at a very high temperature, and so only stonewares, which can survive a temperature of up to 1600 °C, are ever salt-glazed. Other bodies would collapse under the heat.

The greatest limitation on salt-glazed stonewares is the palette. Colour is obtained by painting the pots with coloured oxides before firing, but few oxides can withstand the high temperature. Doulton Lambeth expanded the palette considerably during the intensive period of experimentation after the creation of their art pottery studio. Walter Martin, of the Martin Brothers, was also successful in devising new colours for salt-glazing. None the less these are largely sombre shades of brown, blue and yellow. The technique has been used on stonewares since the early 18th century, and today is popular with studio potters.

Smear glazing is used on vitreous bodies such as Parian or stoneware. A soft glaze is placed in a crucible within the saggar with the unglazed wares (or the walls of the saggar itself are coated with the glaze). At high temperatures the glaze becomes a volatile mist which settles as a very fine coat of clear glaze on the wares. This is the preferred method for relief-moulded stoneware or Parian, as the very thin coat of clear glaze does not obscure the finer details of the moulding or colour of the tinted body.

Tin-glazed wares include Italian maiolica, French faience and the English and Dutch delft-wares. These were low-fired earthenwares with a white glaze that chipped easily, the body also crumbling once broached. The wares were twice-fired: the biscuit-fired pots were dipped in the tin glaze and decorated before the second firing. The decoration was created with a slurry from coloured oxides mixed with powdered glaze. This was a difficult process, as once the mixture touched the tin-glazed surface, it could not be wiped away.

Dublin delftware meat plate painted in blue.

c.1750. Crack. Painted mark S. 35.7 cm length   JH

£575

Lead has long been an important element in glazes. Lead glazes are fired at a relatively low temperature, which affords a wider range of colour. A clear, brilliant lead glaze is easy to achieve and was much favoured by British manufacturers.

Even in the 18th century potters were aware that lead poisoning was an industrial hazard. As knowledge of the dangers of lead poisoning increased, potters devised various ways of minimising the danger. During the early 20th century, some artist potters developed leadless glazes, but these were not adopted by many of the industrial manufacturers at that time. It is now known that lead also offers a danger to the consumer, as acidic food on very low-fired wares can cause the lead to leach into the food. Today increasingly strict legislation has almost eliminated lead from glazes.

Galena glazes were used in medieval pottery and continued in use at country potteries into the 20th century. As this requires the dusting of lead powder on to the surface of the pot, it was terribly dangerous and has been abandoned.

Underglaze colours were widely used in the second half of the 18th century. The coloured oxides were sponged or sprinkled on the biscuit ware and then covered with a clear lead glaze. These wares are often inaccurately called Whieldon wares, though Thomas Whieldon (1719–95) was only one of many manufacturers who produced wares of this type. The palette is fairly limited to mottled or streaky browns, yellows, blues and greens, which are usually subdued. Specks of undissolved colour may sometimes be seen beneath the glaze. Creamwares are white earthenwares with a greenish or yellowish tint to the glaze, introduced c.1740. Pearlwares were introduced c.1770, when it was discovered that using a glaze with a slight blue tint made the ware appear much whiter. The tint of the glaze can be seen where it pools inside the footrims of most items. In the case of pearlware it is not unusual to see an occasional fleck of undissolved cobalt in the glaze. Pearlwares painted

15

with high-temperature underglaze colours are known as Prattware or Pratt type wares. These should not be confused with the multicolour printed wares such as pot lids, which are also known as Prattwares.

Prattware type earthenware jug portraying the Duke of York.

c.1795. Restored. 19.8 cm height   JH

£680

The next great development in glazes was the *majolica* glaze developed by Léon Arnoux for Minton in the middle of the 19th century. These lead glazes had a brilliance of colour hitherto unknown. The wares were soon copied by many manufacturers throughout Britain and on the Continent. Although a few special pots were embellished with scenes painted in enamels, most majolica was relief-moulded and then highlighted by painting with the majolica glazes. The cheaper pieces were simply dipped in glaze and spattered with other colours to create a mottled effect.

The chemist potters of the late 19th and early 20th centuries devoted themselves to creating glazes known to the Chinese, but along the way developed many striking original effects.

Sang de bœuf glaze, literally ox-blood glaze, is a reduction copper oxide glaze (produced in a kiln atmosphere starved of oxygen) with variations caused by kiln conditions. The Chinese perfected this technique in the late 17th and early 18th centuries. It was revived by the French art potters in the 1880s. In early 20th-century England, Bernard Moore perfected this glaze, which was also made by William Howson Taylor at Smethwick ('Ruskin' pottery), Howsons at Hanley and Royal Doulton at Burslem who marketed them as *rouge flambé*.

Matt glazes became popular in the 20th century. The glaze is devitrified to remove the glassiness. A number of different minerals or compounds may be added to the glaze to achieve this.

The great challenge to the potter is to create a glaze which fits the body. Like all other substances, bodies and glazes expand and contract with changes in temperature. A glaze which fits the body correctly will expand and contract at the same rate as the body. If the glaze fits poorly, the ware will *craze*. Crazing is the fine cracking seen across the surface of many old pots. Crazed pots are often stained, as the fine cracks admit dirt and food, which then stain the body beneath. High-fired glazed wares such as stoneware and porcelain are less prone to crazing than the lower-fired earthenwares.

Since the last century some potters have experimented with *crackle* or *craquelé* glazes. These are usually doubled-glazed wares, on which the top coat of glaze is deliberately crazed to reveal the different colour of the glaze beneath. Crazing is sometimes deliberately induced to make reproduction Staffordshire figures appear older than they are: it is in this case a form of faking.

PRINTING

Printing from engraved copper plates is one of the most common methods of decoration on British ceramics. The earliest prints were *on-glaze*, applied over the glazed pot. The first to use this method on ceramics in any quantity were Sadler and Green of Liverpool c.1756, who printed tiles using the *bat-printing* method, an on-glaze technique whose origins are uncertain. A gelatine 'bat' or pad is used to lift the pattern in oil from an engraved copper plate. The bat is then applied to the pot, leaving the oil behind. Powdered colours are then dusted on to the oil which retains it. The surplus is cleaned away leaving the desired design. Bat-prints are fairly small, as it would be too difficult to manipulate a large gelatine bat. The prints are often black, as that achieved the clearest results, but occasionally other colours and even gold were used. The prints are exceptionally fine, and were used on tin-glazed tiles, 18th century creamwares and the best porcelain tea wares. A number of examples by different English factories are illustrated in this book.

Later the technique of *underglaze* or *transfer-printing* was developed. An engraved copper plate is coated with a mixture of pigment and oil, the excess is scraped off, leaving the oil in the impressions. A press then transfers this design to a piece of strong tissue-like paper. The paper is placed on the ware and rubbed on. The ware is then placed in a tub of water, where the paper floats off leaving the oil and pigment behind on the surface of the pot. The pot is then fired in the kiln to harden-on the design and burn off the oil, leaving the pigment behind. The pot is then glazed and fired for the final time, unless enamel and/or gold decoration is to be added. Underglaze prints will not wash or rub off as they are fixed beneath the glaze. The most popular colour for underglaze prints was blue, because cobalt was the most stable pigment in the kiln.

Flow blue wares are underglaze printed wares where a flow powder has been added to the glaze to achieve a blurry print. The flow powder creates a chlorinated atmosphere in the kiln, which is particularly effective with cobalt. This method was popular in the late 19th and early 20th century, when many of these wares were exported to the United States.

Ackeying was an early two-colour underglaze printing technique introduced by Spode by 1819, involving coating areas of the ware with a thick substance, ackey, which was impervious to oil and yet soluble in water. The first print was laid on the ware, coated with ackey for protection, and then the second print in a different colour was laid on. The ackey was washed off with water. Ackey was also used to coat areas of ware which were meant to be left bare of decoration.

Pluck-and-dust printing is an on-glaze technique where oil without pigment was transferred from an engraved copper plate by way of paper rather than a glue bat. Powdered pigment was dusted on afterwards. The pigment adhered to the oil and was dusted from the remainder of the surface. With this technique larger areas can be printed than is possible with bat printing.

Lithographic transfers were introduced in late 19th century. Until the First World War most of these were imported from Germany. Printed in polychrome colours, they have largely replaced hand-painting in the industry today. The transfers are printed on sheets, and when moistened they are slid off and applied to slightly warmed biscuit or glazed wares.

OVERGLAZE PAINTING

Overglaze enamels are a mixture of fat oil, turpentine and pigments. The fat oil is made with pure turpentine. Each painter has a 'fountain' filled with turpentine; as the turpentine evaporates, the fat oil residue is left behind. One of the problems of the painters is keeping the colour 'open', that is wet enough to manipulate. This is achieved by adding aniseed oil (or sometimes oil of fennel or lavender) to the coloured oxides. Visitors to painting studios will often notice the characteristic liquorice smell.

Different colours need to be fired at different temperatures. Thus successive firings in a small *muffle kiln* are required for polychrome paintings. The colours needing the highest temperature are fired first, followed by those needing progressively lower temperatures. Very elaborate paintings have been known to require as many as twelve firings. There is also a risk of kiln damage with each firing, so the cost of manufacture can be high with this process.

Jewelled or raised enamel decoration consists of thickly applied enamels, most often white, coral or turquoise, which are meant to give the impression of semi-precious stones. This technique is usually found on better quality porcelains.

Raised paste decoration is a method of building up the surface with an enamel paste, which is then cut with a sharp tool. This requires considerable skill and is only found on better quality porcelains. The raised ground is normally gilt.

Clobbering originally referred to Chinese export porcelains which had decoration added in England at a later date. It has since been used to describe transfer-printing with additional enamel decoration. This second definition is confusing as the enamel decoration was added at the original factory, and the use of the term should be avoided.

Banding or lining is the painting of bands of colour using a banding wheel. The pot is rotated on the wheel (a turntable) and the painter holds the brush steady, creating a perfect band of colour. This technique when observed at the Wedgwood factory, where it is still used for rims of quality wares, appears very easy. In fact is is very difficult, and a highly skilled task. Banded tablewares were very popular from the late 1920s through the 1930s. Although some firms continued in the 1950s, the technique was largely abandoned as being too expensive.

Aerography applies colour or glaze with a spray gun and compressed air. The technique first appears in the late 19th century, and is very widely used today.

GILDING

Gilding is the most expensive decorating technique and was reserved for the best wares. Gilding is expensive not only because 22-carat gold was used, but because the gilding mixture of mercury, fluxes and pure gold must be applied by the most skilled of decorators. The ware then requires an extra firing.

As mentioned above in the discussion on overglaze painting, there is a risk every time the pot goes back to the kilns. A polychrome enamel-decorated piece may have already visited the kiln from five to twelve times. Each time it survives the kiln, it becomes more precious. By the time the pot reaches the gilding process, the potter has invested considerable time and money in it.

After firing, the gold was usually burnished using a pointed agate or bloodstone (for deeply embossed areas) and fine, sharp polishing sand, sometimes called silver sand. This is also a highly skilled occupation. Occasionally the gold was left unburnished, that is dull and matt, rather than shiny. This is most often found on pieces which are meant to be reproductions of shapes from antiquity, e.g. Greek or Roman.

Acid etching was introduced in 1863 and is still used today. The technique involves etching an intricate pattern into glazed whiteware, and then laying gold over the entire design. The raised areas are burnished and the rest is left unburnished, resulting in a contrast between shiny and dull gold.

Raised paste gilding is gold mixed with slip to give it a thick and raised effect.

Raised gold is gilding applied over a relief-moulded pattern.

Bright gold or *liquid gold* has been used since the late 19th century on cheaper wares. It is actually a form of gold lustre, and it emerges from the kiln shiny, eliminating the need for burnishing (which requires a very skilled worker). It is very brassy in appearance in comparison with burnished gold. It is also very thin and wears away easily.

Bone china coffee cup and saucer painted with grey and pink enamels and raised paste gilding.

Dated 1896. Saucer inscribed 'TO MISS HALES from FRANK, 1896'. Cup with painted number 1566. Cup 7.3 cm height; saucer 14.2 cm diameter   AF

£18

LUSTRE

Lustre can refer to several types of metallic decoration. The first lustres were produced by painting metallic oxides on the pots. These are fired in a reducing atmosphere (starved of oxygen) in the kiln, leaving a metallic deposit of iridescent effect, depending on the thickness of the painting. These lustres were introduced in Persia, and Hispano-Moresque lustres were later produced in Spain. These and the Italian lustres were 'rediscovered' by William De Morgan in London in the 1870s. The technique has since been used by art and studio potters.

The most commonly found lustres are a uniquely English invention c.1805. These are items coated with a thin film of pigment containing gold (for a copper or pink lustre) or platinum (for a silver lustre) and fired in a low-temperature oxidizing atmosphere. 'Splashed' pink or purple lustre was obtained by dropping oil on a wet gold lustre.

Coloured lustre glazes were produced by adding metallic salts or carbonates to the glaze and firing in a low-temperature reducing atmosphere. They were popular in the early decades of the 20th century.

During the late 19th century, commercially prepared liquid lustre became available. This was painted overglaze on the pot to create a mother-of-pearl sheen, which has been widely used in the 20th century.

Henry Tooth & Co. Caliph Ware earthenware vase painted in green, purple and orange enamels and covered with liquid lustre.

c.1926. Impressed marks 'BRETBY' with rising sun; 'MADE IN ENGLAND'; shape number 6670. 19 cm height   AF

£30

MARKS

Marks can be baffling to the novice, but are the most easily mastered technique of identification. There are several ways in which marks can be applied and one pot may have marks of different types.

Impressed marks are stamped into leather-hard clay.

Incised marks are scratched into leather-hard clay.

Applied or *pad* marks are made from tiny bits of clay pressed into a small mould and then stuck to the body of the pot with slip (liquid clay).

Moulded marks are part of the mould on slip-cast wares.

Painted marks are painted in the same way as the pot, either overglaze or underglaze.

Printed marks, sometimes called *backstamps*, are transfer-prints, or in more recent times lithographic transfers. Sometimes during the 20th century they are simply applied with a rubber stamp.

Paper labels may be found on pots of the 20th century. These have usually been removed by the original purchaser or have come off when the item was washed. If you should buy a pot with a paper label, *do not* remove it even it is tattered. Labels added subsequently by collectors should also be preserved as they are a part of the pot's history and may help in determining its provenance.

The information which can be gleaned from these marks varies. It may include:

Manufacturer's name, initials or *device*, sometimes with pottery name and address. Initials must be treated with caution, as the same set may have been shared by several firms. For example, at least eight firms used the initials J.B. in their marks. Devices can be confusing as some popular ones such as anchors, garters and Staffordshire knots were used by several different potters.

Retailer's name, often with address. In the late 18th and early 19th century these names often appeared without the manufacturer's marks. This is presumably so that the customer wanting further pots could not by-pass the retailer and order directly from the factory. By the mid 19th century it was common for both retailers' and manufacturers' marks to appear together.

Signatures and *initials* of artists, designers, decorators or very occasionally potters may appear on the face or reverse of pots.

Date marks. Some manufacturers had date codes or ciphers to identify their wares, meant for internal use, and not for the public. These are generally impressed marks, applied before the biscuit firing, and as wares may have stayed in the warehouse for a period of time before being decorated they only represent the date of biscuit manufacture. Some special pots may be dated by the artist, and art pottery sometimes has dates, usually incised.

Size numbers. Jugs in particular often bear impressed size numbers, generally ranging from 2 for the largest to 64 for the smallest. These refer to the number of items in a 'potter's dozen', which was a wholesale pricing unit; e.g. for 10 shillings the retailer could buy 2 of the largest jugs or 64 of the smallest.

Shape numbers. These are usually impressed, although they may be part of a mould. They served mainly as a reference to the retailers placing orders with the manufacturers.

Pattern names. Transfer-printed pattern names found on transfer-printed wares after 1810, and usually much later. They can sometimes be helpful in identifying pots, but some names (e.g. Asiatic Pheasants) were used by many different makers.

Pattern numbers. These are usually painted marks. Again, they served as a reference for the retailers placing orders with the manufacturers.

Workers' marks. Many of those employed in the potteries were paid on a piece-rate. Thus the worker would place his mark on each pot which passed through this hands, so that a tally could be kept. The nature of the mark is generally related to the task performed. For instance transferers would place a small transfer-printed mark on the ware. Painters would paint their mark, usually in one of the colours employed in the decoration. Gilders' marks are often in gold. Glazers' marks, most often found on majolica, are relatively large and crude, being quickly painted on with a dark coloured glaze.

Registration marks. In 1842 the British Government instituted a system whereby designs could be registered for many different classes of goods. In the case of ceramics, the designs were for shapes or patterns. The designs registered were then protected for a period of three years. However, it was not uncommon for the registration marks to continue in use after the protection had expired. This is particularly the case when the mark is part of the mould.

From 1843 to 1883 the registration was noted with a diamond registration mark. The table below shows how to decipher these marks.

DIAMOND REGISTRATION MARKS

KEY	1842–67	1868–83
	a class	a class
	b year	b day
	c month	c bundle
	d day	d year
	e bundle	e month

YEAR CODE

1842	X	1848	U	1854	J	1860	Z	1866	Q	1872	I	1878	D
1843	H	1849	S	1855	E	1861	R	1867	T	1873	F	1879	Y
1844	C	1850	V	1856	L	1862	O	1868	X	1874	U	1880	J
1845	A	1851	P	1857	K	1863	G	1869	H	1975	S	1881	E
1846	I	1852	D	1858	B	1864	N	1870	C	1876	V	1882	L
1847	F	1853	Y	1859	M	1865	W	1871	A	1877	P	1883	K

MONTH CODE

January	C	April	H	July	I	October	B
February	G	May	E	August	R	November	K
March	W	June	M	September	D	December	A

NOTES

(i)   In 1857 the letter R was used 1–19 September.
(ii) In 1860 the letter K was used for December.
(iii) From 1–6 March 1878 the following mark was issued:

instead of

From 1884 every design, regardless of class, was numbered consecutively beginning with 1. The following table lists the years and the design numbers which were assigned for them.

TABLE OF REGISTRATION NUMBERS 1884–1987

1 = 1884	116648 = 1889	224720 = 1894
19754 = 1885	141273 = 1890	246975 = 1895
40480 = 1886	163767 = 1891	268392 = 1896
64520 = 1887	185713 = 1892	291241 = 1897
90483 = 1888	205240 = 1893	311658 = 1898

21

331707 = 1899	742725 = 1929	891665 = 1959
351202 = 1900	751160 = 1930	895000 = 1960
368154 = 1901	760583 = 1931	899914 = 1961
385180 = 1902	769670 = 1932	904638 = 1962
403200 = 1903	779292 = 1933	909364 = 1963
424400 = 1904	789019 = 1934	914536 = 1964
447800 = 1905	799097 = 1935	919607 = 1965
471860 = 1906	808794 = 1936	924510 = 1966
493900 = 1907	817293 = 1937	929335 = 1967
518640 = 1908	825231 = 1938	934515 = 1968
535170 = 1909	832610 = 1939	939875 = 1969
552000 = 1910	837520 = 1940	944932 = 1970
574817 = 1911	838590 = 1941	950046 = 1971
594195 = 1912	839230 = 1942	955342 = 1972
612431 = 1913	839980 = 1943	960708 = 1973
630190 = 1914	841040 = 1944	965185 = 1974
644935 = 1915	842670 = 1945	969249 = 1975
653521 = 1916	845550 = 1946	973838 = 1976
658988 = 1917	849730 = 1947	978426 = 1977
662872 = 1918	853260 = 1948	982815 = 1978
666126 = 1919	856999 = 1949	987910 = 1979
673750 = 1920	860854 = 1950	993012 = 1980
680147 = 1921	863070 = 1951	998302 = 1981
687144 = 1922	866280 = 1952	1004456 = 1982
694999 = 1923	869300 = 1953	1010583 = 1983
702671 = 1924	872531 = 1954	1017131 = 1984
710165 = 1925	876067 = 1955	1024174 = 1985
718057 = 1926	879282 = 1956	1031358 = 1986
726330 = 1927	882949 = 1957	1039055 = 1987
734370 = 1928	887079 = 1958	

Geoffrey Godden in his Encyclopaedia of British Porcelain Manufacturers, gives the following guidelines to dating marks:

Royal arms appear in printed marks only after 1795, and most are post-1830. The central inescutcheon (a shield within a shield) was dropped in June 1837, but would have continued in use on marks until the maker had a new copper plate engraved. Marks with the simplified, quartered shield must have been introduced in or after June 1837.

Limited (or Ltd or Ld) must date after 1861.

Trade Mark only appears after the 1862 Trade Mark Act. Descriptions such as Registered Trade Mark or Registered Trade Name are of a 20th-century date.

Royal appears post-1850, and is most often found in 20th-century marks. Many (but not all) firms using such 'Royal' prefixes or trade names had little or no connection with royalty or with royal commissions.

England indicates a date after 1880, and usually after the 1891 United States Tariff Act. However, the absence of 'England' does not mean that the pot is pre-1880. The word was only included if the manufacturer thought the ware might be exported. For example, the Upchurch Pottery in Kent (1913–63) did not begin to mark its wares until after the Second World War, when in the drive for export dollars, it began to produce tablewares for export to the United States. Another example is Minton, who had added England to their other marks in 1891, but did not include it on their Secessionist Wares made 1902–14.

Made in England usually indicates a date post-1920, but some manufacturers (e.g. Wedgwood and Minton) adopted this c.1910.

Bone China or English Bone China appears on 20th-century bone china wares.

Copyright, © and ® usually indicate a date post-1950.

Plc only appears following the manufacturer's name post-1975.

Detergent-proof, dishwasher safe and similar claims have appeared only since 1950.

Hand-painted appears on 20th-century wares, many of which are painted within transfer-printed outlines.

Limited Edition is usually post-1970, when so-called limited edition collectors' items, especially plates, became very popular.

WHERE TO SEE POTS

The three largest collections of ceramics are at the British Museum, the Victoria & Albert Museum and the City Museum & Art Gallery, Hanley, Stoke-on-Trent. The latter is a must for anyone with a special interest in ceramics, as the displays include explanations of manufacturing methods. Do not neglect the smaller, local museums, which often have interesting collections. If you have a special interest it is worth sending an inquiry to your local museums, as they may have pots of interest in their reserve collections (not on public display). Reserve collections are sometimes open by appointment to serious researchers, and a number of the ceramic societies arrange group visits to the reserve collections for their members.

The Gladstone Pottery Museum, Longton, Stoke-on-Trent is a 'living and working' museum, where visitors can actually see some of the techniques described above carried out. There is also a collection of tiles, pottery exhibitions and displays of equipment used in pottery manufacture.

It is important to handle and examine pots closely, which is not possible in museum collections. Visits to antique fairs and shops can provide this opportunity. Do not neglect big fairs such as the International Ceramics Fair held in London every June. Although these feature rare pots, beyond the means of most collectors, it is only by looking at such pieces that one can learn to recognise quality. At auction house viewings, you will have the opportunity to examine pots carefully without feeling any obligation to buy.

Several factories still in operation have museums on the premises, which are valuable for those interested in that factory. The best known are Wedgwood at Barlaston, Minton and Spode at Stoke, Royal Doulton at Burslem, Royal Worcester at Worcester and the Royal Crown Derby Works Collection at Derby. The collector will find the tours or demonstrations available at these factories invaluable. Always call ahead before making a journey, as some of these are only available by prior arrangement.

WHERE TO BUY POTS

There are many places to buy ceramics: all have advantages and disadvantages. Specialist dealers have the great advantage of knowledge, which they will share with collectors. They will provide detailed invoices, and many belong to the British Antique Dealer's Association (BADA) and/or the London and Provincial Antique Dealers' Association (LAPADA). In the rare case of any dispute, these associations will adjudicate. General antique dealers may or may not be knowledgeable about ceramics. If the dealer's speciality is in silver or furniture, for example, he may not have recognised a desirable pot. At the upper end of the market, dealers will automatically provide detailed invoices, but at the lower end of the market you may have to ask for these specifically.

Antique fairs run the gamut from those such as the Wakefield Ceramics Fairs, where all items have been vetted by experts, to small fairs which are only one step above flea markets. On the one hand one has the advantage of the knowledge of the specialist dealers and experts, on the other the knowledgeable collector may come away with a bargain. Flea markets and boot fairs may also turn up gems, but unless you enjoy these, in the long run the costs in time and petrol may outweigh the benefit of the occasional prize.

The novice collector may be frightened at the thought of purchasing at auction, afraid that a simple action such as scratching one's nose will commit one to the purchase of a costly object. Although some dealers have small signals which the auctioneer recognises, the newcomer will not be recognised unless he makes a clear signal, such as raising an arm or waving his catalogue. It is wise to attend a sale or two without any intention of buying, so that you get the feel of things. If you are afraid you might be drawn into the bidding in the heat of the moment, attend a sale where there is nothing you could conceivably want to buy.

When you decide to take the plunge be sure to attend the viewing and examine the items very carefully. Carefully read the conditions of sale in the catalogue even if they look boring and are in small print. Ascertain whether you will have to pay a buyer's premium and/or VAT. You will always have to pay VAT on the premium. Check the terms of sale with the auction-room staff if you are uncertain. Be cautious of catalogue descriptions. If they are inaccurate you have legal recourse, but descriptions may be vague. A catalogue may say that a vase is damaged, but not how extensively. You may quickly spot an obvious chip, and decide that you still want the vase. If you later discover there is also a crack, which you did not see, you have no recourse. So examine the pots *carefully*.

When you have examined the pot carefully decide what you are willing to pay for it. Do not pay too much attention to the estimate printed in the catalogue. If the lot is estimated at £200–300, you are not likely to purchase it for £30. On the other hand a lot estimated at £40–60 may go for £200. Remember to calculate the cost of the buyer's premium and VAT. When bidding stick to your resolve. It may be galling to see something you really wanted go to another bidder for only £5 more than your last bid, but this does not mean that you could have purchased it for that amount. The other bidder might have gone on for another £50.

CERAMIC SOCIETIES

There are many societies dedicated to the study of ceramics. These societies are wonderful resources for the collector. Their programmes often include seminars, lectures, and visits to museums and private collections. Most have interesting regular publications, which also afford the collector an opportunity to make inquiries. Meeting other collectors at these meetings is fun and very educational. There are sometimes opportunities to sell or swap pots with fellow collectors. Societies dedicated to specific types of wares or factories are mentioned throughout the text. The two important general societies are:

English Ceramic Circle, Membership Secretary, Mrs Joan Bennett, 5 The Drive, Beckenham, Kent BR3 1EE (membership by election only).

Northern Ceramic Society, Membership Secretaries, Anthony and Hilary Thomas, Bramdean, Jacksons Lane, Hazel Grove, Cheshire SK7 5JW.

SEMINARS

Seminars offer an invaluable opportunity to learn more about ceramics. Lectures, and social opportunities to meet other collectors, are often combined with field trips to museums.

Geoffrey Godden's Porcelain Collectors' Weekend, held annually in July or August at Malvern, Worcestershire. Address for bookings: Mrs Jean Godden, 19a Crescent Road, Worthing, West Sussex, BN11 1RL.

Ceramics Summer School, Keele University, an intensive week-long seminar held annually in August in association with the Northern Ceramic Society. Bookings: Department of Adult and Continuing Education, Keele University, Keele, Staffordshire ST5 5BG.

Antique Collectors' Club, weekend porcelain seminar held every summer. Details: The Secretary, Antique Collectors' Club, 5 Church Street, Woodbridge, Suffolk IP12 1DS.

Coalport Conference, Ironbridge Gorge Museum. Details: Dr Michael Stratton, Ironbridge Gorge Museum, Ironbridge, Telford, Shropshire TF8 7AW.

International Ceramics Fair & Seminar, held every June in London. Details: J. Thomas, Secretary, 3B Burlington Gardens, Old Bond Street, London W1X 1LE.

Morley College Weekend Seminar, held in November in London annually. Details: The Secretary, Morley College Ceramic Circle, Morley College, 61 Westminster Bridge Road, London SE1.

REFERENCE WORKS

There are further reading suggestions throughout this book and a lengthy Bibliography at the end. Whenever possible, the latest works still in print are listed. In many cases, however, the standard works have long been out of print and are rare and costly. If your local public library does not have books which you require, they can usually borrow these from another library through the inter-library lending system. The National Art Library at the Victoria & Albert Museum is open to all researchers, although some very rare or fragile manuscripts require a reading ticket. The Horace Birks Reference Library at Hanley is an invaluable resource for all who are interested in ceramics. One of its greatest assets is a catalogue which includes many hundreds of articles from periodicals.

The backbone of all ceramic research today is the extensive work of Geoffrey Godden. Many of his books about specific potteries or types of wares are referred to in the further reading suggestions accompanying entries. However, anyone with a comprehensive interest in British ceramics will find his general works indispensable, together with the other volumes listed below.

Elizabeth Cameron. *Encyclopaedia of Pottery and Porcelain. The Nineteenth and Twentieth Centuries* (Faber & Faber, 1986).

John Cushion. *Handbook of Pottery & Porcelain Marks*, 4th edn (Faber & Faber, 1980)

Geoffrey Godden. *British Porcelain, an illustrated guide* (Barrie & Jenkins, 1974).

Geoffrey Godden. *British Pottery, an illustrated guide* (Barrie & Jenkins, 1974).

Geoffrey Godden. *An Illustrated Encyclopaedia of British Pottery and Porcelain*, 2nd edn (Barrie & Jenkins, 1980).

Geoffrey Godden. *Encyclopaedia of British Porcelain Manufacturers* (Barrie & Jenkins, 1988).

Geoffrey Godden. *The Concise Guide to British Pottery and Porcelain* (Barrie & Jenkins, 1990).

Geoffrey Godden. *Encyclopaedia of British Porcelain Manufacturers* (Barrie & Jenkins, 1992).

Llewellyn Jewitt. *The Ceramic Art of Great Britain*, 2 vols (Virtue & Co., 1878; 2nd edn 1883). The 1883 edition is preferable as it contains more material. Facsimile reprints are available (New Orchard Editions, Poole, 1985), as well as an updated version with new illustrations by Geoffrey Godden, *Jewitt's Ceramic Art of Great Britain 1800–1900* (Barrie & Jenkins, 1972).

WHAT IS IT WORTH?

I⊤ is perhaps an evasion to answer this question, 'What you are willing to pay for it.' However, this is the bottom line. If you do not admire something, it is not worth anything to you, unless you are planning to sell it. None the less, we all want to know how much we should pay for an antique, how much we might receive when selling one, what value to use for insurance purposes or just how much an object in our possession has appreciated in value.

In the course of preparing this book I have spoken to many dozens of collectors and dealers. Price guides are an emotive subject and I was given much advice and criticism. When deciding what prices to use I was presented with several options. The first was to use auction house estimates. As anyone who has attended an auction will tell you, these are only *estimates*. They often bear no relation to the price finally reached. The second problem with estimates is that the ranges are too wide. A typical value might be £40–60 or £200–300. This is fine for auction house purposes, but to most of us, whether dealers or collectors, there is a big difference between the upper and lower values in these ranges.

The second alternative was to make up prices based on the market experience of myself and my consultants. Apart from the subjectivity of such an approach, it would mean in some cases assigning a value to a pot which was much lower than what its owner was asking.

The approach I have chosen is to print the *actual ticket price* on the objects, which have been photographed by myself in shops all over Britain. Some dealers will give trade discounts, some will enjoy haggling and others will most certainly not. There seemed little benefit to printing '£38 but will probably take £34', so I have confined myself to the asking price.

This leads to the issue of how dealers price their objects. There are three key elements in retail pricing in the antiques trade. The first is the cost to the dealer. If a dealer has managed to pick up an item quite cheaply, he may price it accordingly, in the hope of a quick sale. On the other hand, a dealer might pay rather a lot for an item, and even with a considerably reduced price margin, need to charge a bit more than he would like. The second consideration is the general cost of the item on the market. If a dealer knows that every shop in town has a stock of late Victorian Willow pattern plates for sale at £10–12, it makes no sense to price his own at £16. The third consideration is the dealer's clientele. A dealer known for 18th-century porcelains might price a piece of 19th-century art pottery on the low side, hoping to sell it on to the trade, e.g. a dealer with collectors of art pottery among his customers.

One must not forget that the antique dealer, like any merchant, has overheads. These are higher in some areas of the country than others, and this is to a small degree reflected in prices. However, a London dealer has a much wider access to auction houses, fairs, markets and shops, which may result in a much wider range of stock at a reasonable cost.

One cannot discuss the prices of antiques without discussing the 'chain'. Most items pass through the hands of several dealers before finding a home. For example, Dealer A purchased a lovely pair of porcelain candlesticks for £80. As a general dealer he recognised only that these were old and very attractive. The next time he took a stall at an antiques fair he sold them for £200 to Dealer B. This dealer specialised in porcelains, and realised that the candlesticks were rare 18th-century examples by a major maker. Dealer B contacted Dealer C, who specialised in the wares of this factory and purchased them for £800. Dealer C contacted an important collector in the United States and sold them for £8,000.

So which is the 'correct' price for the candlesticks? Each transaction involved a good profit on investment for the dealer concerned, and doubtless the final purchaser was delighted as well. The price *you* pay for an item may well depend upon where in this chain you find it.

This leads to the inevitable question – was anybody, especially the final buyer, in this chain cheated? At first it may seem to have been a bonanza for Dealer C, and a disaster for the final purchaser. However, several things must be considered. Each dealer was relying on his knowledge of ceramics and the market to which he had access. Dealer C had invested twenty years in the study of a small group of ceramics and developing relationships with important collectors all over the world. The profit he made reflects long years of study and travel, a large investment of both time and money. He might only make such a sale a few times a year. The final buyer was paying not only for a very rare and valuable pair of candlesticks, but for the expertise and guarantee of authenticity of Dealer C, and the luxury of having a very desirable object delivered to his door.

This example, although true, is untypical only with regard to the large sums involved. On a smaller scale many collectors find that it is worth employing the skills of their own Dealer C. For example, I collect the wares of a small local pottery. Several dealers in my vicinity look for these wares on my behalf. They buy these at fairs and markets for small sums, and tack on a fair profit. Of course, if I purchased these items from the fairs and markets myself, they would cost me less, but nobody can attend every fair and market! I also save time and petrol. If you decide to collect a particular type of ware, it is well worth seeking out a dealer who specialises in the wares. If you are original and collect something which is generally unrecognised by other collectors, it may well be worth the time to educate a friendly dealer about your collection so that he will know what to look for.

I have referred to 'the market' for items several times. So what determines the market value of a pot? There are three key elements in this: the pot, its rarity and current fashion. One must first carefully examine the pot itself – its condition, quality and attractiveness. The importance of condition varies wildly according to the types of wares, their age and rarity. For example, delftware tiles are often chipped at the edges, having been removed from their original setting. On the other hand, a Spode dessert plate with several chips on the rim loses a great part of its value. Condition is discussed in detail in the next section of this chapter.

The quality of the pot is relative to the potter's intention. The quality of an 18th-century slipware charger is judged entirely differently from the quality of an early 19th-century bone china teapot. This is why potting techniques are so extensively discussed in the Introduction. Some types of decoration are laborious and involve considerable expense to the potter. The use of such techniques made the pot more costly to its first purchaser, and can increase its value today.

Attractiveness is, of course, relatively subjective. Again, it must be judged relative to the type of ware, but if you find something ugly, *don't buy it*, no matter how wonderful anyone else tells you it is!

Rarity is an enormously important factor to any collector. The only way to judge an item's rarity for yourself is to note carefully how often you see similar items for sale. The advice of reputable dealers can be very useful here, as in addition to their personal experience they often subscribe regularly to auction house catalogues, and will know how often, if ever, such items have appeared for sale at auction. Reference books will often give some guide to rarity, but these must be treated with caution. More than one author who has declared an item rare or unique has subsequently heard from numerous excited collectors who had identical objects in their collections. This is not the fault of the author, who must judge rarity on recorded examples. Unrecorded examples, those sitting happily on collectors' shelves (often unidentified), do not come to light unless the rarity of recorded examples is mentioned in print.

However, a few general guide lines to rarity can be given. First, any object which was very expensive when it was made is likely to be uncommon if not rare, as not many of them would have been made, or purchased. Secondly, useful wares of previous centuries tend to be quite rare, simply because they were used until broken. How many of us keep our baking dishes in a display cabinet in our dining-rooms? Only when such an item has survived in use long enough to be recognised as an antique, is it transferred from the kitchen cupboard to the dining-room sideboard.

The last and most volatile issue is fashion. Antiques, just like short skirts, come in and out of fashion as decades pass. A good and often repeated example is Art Deco. The prices of good examples of Art Deco ceramics, such as Clarice Cliff or Susie Cooper, have multiplied ten-fold or more in the past fifteen years, although the values have dropped somewhat recently. On the other hand, wares can go out of fashion, and considering their quality and rarity they will be undervalued. Basalt of all styles is an example of this at the present time.

Factories, as well as styles, go in and out of fashion. A new reference book about a factory will often awaken enthusiasm for a factory's wares, some of which may not have been previously identified. Certain factories, such as Wedgwood, Spode or Doulton, are the focus of specialist societies or collectors' clubs. These enthusiastic groups keep interest in the factory's wares alive and encourage further research and study. This tends to keep prices of these factory's wares (especially if marked) higher than for equivalent wares made by lesser-known or unpopular factories.

A pot with the signature or mark of a well-known artist is considerably more valuable than an unsigned pot. However, this is not the case with modern so-called 'limited editions' (generally made in such large numbers as to make the adjective 'limited' a joke), which may have lithographic transfers incorporating a signature.

CONDITION

Condition may be roughly divided into two categories, namely factory flaws and damage, or wear which has occurred since the pot left the factory. It is very important to examine a pot carefully before making a purchase. The degree to which flaws, damage or wear affect the value varies widely. Certain flaws occur in early English porcelains so frequently that they become characteristics and are not a problem if they are not disfiguring. For example, the Chelsea factory had difficulties with firing and small flaws frequently occurred on the surface of the wares. The factory often disguised these by painting them over with insects or flowers. This is considered charming and characteristic of the wares and does not affect the value at all. However, if the wares have a firing crack, which has been glazed over, they were clearly 'seconds' and the value is affected.

If you are purchasing 18th-century pottery, you must expect a certain amount of damage. Damage on pottery is much more acceptable than on porcelain. These wares may well have been in daily use for a century or more, before anyone thought to place them in the china cabinet as curios. The degree to which damage affects these wares depends on the degree to which the damage is disfiguring, and on the rarity of the individual item.

Wares may *craze* in the kiln if the body expands or contracts at a greater rate than the glaze. Another glaze fault which may be found is *crawling*, where a glaze has receded from the edge of the ware. It is not uncommon to find this inside footrims, but if it occurs, for instance, on the side of a vase it is a serious manufacturing flaw and greatly reduces the value of the pot.

Firing cracks occurring during firing or subsequent cooling can be distinguished from damage because they will have been glazed over. The degree to which they affect the value of the ware depends upon its rarity. For example a transfer-printed Spode plate would be significantly affected because there are so many of them about, even though they are avidly collected.

Spitting is the name for the small black specks which occur on the surface of the ware when impurities in the body explode during firing. This is generally associated with early porcelain manufacture, but in 1909 losses from spit-out cost manufacturers £15,000. The introduction of filter presses has largely eliminated this difficulty. The clay is mixed with water, and the resulting slip is forced through a series of filters to remove impurities. *Red staining* during manufacture is caused by iron in the body. This seems to be uniquely a problem with porcelains, and even in 1905 losses to manufacturers from red staining were £50,000. Today the iron is removed from the clay with electro-magnetic filters.

Opinions vary greatly about the degree to which *damage and wear* affect the value of ceramics. Damage includes chips, cracks, broken-off pieces, rubbing of gilding or glaze, crazing subsequent to manufacture, staining, scratching of glaze and even lifting or flaking of the glaze. Always ask the dealer for a receipt detailing all damages and restoration. If there is no damage or restoration the receipt should say so. Inspect the pot very carefully in good light. Run your fingers over the surface of the pot, as usually filling and spraying, not easily detectable to the naked eye, will have a different texture which you can feel.

Restoration considerably increases the cost of a pot, while reducing its value. Restoration is very expensive, and the dealer must add that cost to the price of the object. On the other hand, many experienced collectors prefer a damaged piece to one which has been restored. That way they know just what they are getting and how extensive the damage was. If they find the damage too disfiguring, they can always choose to have it restored themselves.

Also, the vast majority of repaired and restored pots are very inexpertly done. A badly restored piece is worth much less than an unrestored one, because the next restorer will have to devote a considerable amount of care and time, reversing the previous repair, before getting on with doing the job properly. I have avoided restored pieces where possible in the *Guide*, but when dealing with very rare and early pots it can be nearly impossible to find examples without restoration. The restored objects shown have been very well restored by the best professionals. The repairs are virtually undetectable to the naked eye, unless otherwise noted.

A detailed receipt describing any restoration, preferably with details of the materials used, should be made out by the dealer. Most repairs and restorations will break down over time, and it is of considerable assistance to the next person to work on the pot to know what glues etc. have been used.

It is necessary to mention rivets. Opinion has changed about these in recent years. Once considered horrid and unsightly objects to be removed, the holes filled and sprayed over, rivets are now generally considered to be a part of the pot's history. There is no question that they reduce the pot's value, but they are evidence that the pot was valued by its owner in times past, and in most cases it is advised that they be left intact.

FORGERIES, FAKES AND REPRODUCTIONS

Some people are nervous about collecting art and antiques of any description for fear of getting 'a wrong one', that is an item which is not what it is purported to be. The best way to avoid this pitfall is to purchase from a knowledgeable and reliable dealer, until such time as one develops confidence in one's own knowledge in the field. However, the novice collector may take comfort in the fact that the vast proportion of collectable ceramics for sale would cost more to reproduce than the originals fetch. For the purposes of this book the following definitions are used.

Forgeries and *fakes* are deliberate attempts to defraud the purchaser. These may be pots made with the intent of passing them off as antique, or genuine pieces whose faults or defects have been covered up for the purposes of deception to alter their value: for example, grinding down and painting over part of the plinth of a figure group where an additional figure might have been standing.

However, it is seldom possible to decide the potter's intent at a distance. The reproductions of Samson of Paris, who copied many 18th-century porcelains, were sold as modern reproductions in his Paris shop, but these found their way to the market as originals. These 19th-century reproductions are of such high quality that they are collectable in their own right today, although worth far less than the originals they copied. Most copies of 18th-century porcelains are hard-paste Continental porcelain, as opposed to soft-paste porcelain, and so may be fairly easily detected.

Earthenware frog loving cup with enamel decoration.

This cup is one of a group of loving cups with inscriptions which are now believed to have been made at William Kent's factory in Burslem during the early part of this century. Examples falsely dated 1802 have been recorded with inscribed names Peter Bates, John Mytton or William Smith. The quality of potting, the colour of the body and colour of the glaze all point to manufacture later than 1802, but the date has misled many collectors and these have found their way into a number of museum collections.

Reproduction porcelain Bacchus mug, painted enamels and modern gilding. 10 cm height.

Mugs in this shape have been made in stoneware, earthenware and porcelain since the late 18th century. Reproductions continued to be made well into the 20th century, and some examples, such as the one here, may be unmarked. The later examples are detected by the palette of the enamels, the brassy appearance of the liquid gilding and the quality of the body and moulding.

Marriages are perfectly all right, if they are sold as such. A marriage might be a pair of figures or vases which have not always been together, but have been 'married' at a more recent date. Many lidded items, such as teapots, have lost their lids or the lids are damaged. A dealer or collector may have substituted an identical or nearly identical lid. Sometimes one may find cups and saucers which at first glance appear to be identical in pattern, but on closer examination are shown to be different. Entire tea sets are sometimes made up in the same pattern, but on close examination of marks, body and decoration the items will turn out to have been made over a long period of time. This is particularly common when the pattern was used for many years by the same firm. For example, the Spode factory have used their underglaze Blue Italian transfer-print continually since its introduction before 1820. Without intent to defraud, broken items from a dinner service in this pattern might easily be replaced by succeeding generations.

The collector should always carefully examine pots with more than one part. As some manufacturers put the same pattern on more than one shape, check not only that the pattern is identical, but that the shapes of the different pieces are all the same. Marks should be nearly identical, although in the case of tea or dessert services many manufacturers only marked one piece in the service.

Replacement pieces are copies made by manufacturers. Factories such as Spode boasted that they could copy almost anything. The intent was not to defraud, and the pots are frequently marked. This was, rather, a service offered to those who could not replace a broken piece, because the original manufacturer was no longer available. A Spode replacement piece for a Chinese export porcelain service is shown below. It is interesting because the borders are transfer-printed but the centre is hand-painted. Replacements are much sought after by collectors, as they are usually unique. To reproduce such replacements was an example of the potter's skills, and so these pots usually hold particular pride of place in a collection.

Spode stone china vegetable dish with blue transfer-printed border and centre painted in blue.

c.1820. 24 cm square   AF
£65

Presumably Spode was asked to match a broken dish from a service of Chinese export porcelain. The grey-blue tint of the stone china body is closer to the colour of the Chinese hard-paste porcelain body. The outer border is normally found on Spode's 'Temple Landscape' pattern, and the inner border is usually found on Spode's 'Grasshopper' pattern.

Reproductions are deliberate reproductions of earlier pieces. Many of these are marked in such a way as to prevent confusion or fraud. However, they do find their way into the antiques market. In some cases the items were never marked, and as they may be some fifty or a hundred years old they have 'a bit of age'. Some reproduction Staffordshire figures are deliberately crazed to give them the appearance of age. This artificial crazing is easy to detect as it is very regular. Real crazing takes place over a period of years as the pot is exposed to changes of temperature, and is thus quite irregular, rather than evenly spaced over the figure. In other cases, modern marks may have been ground over, or even sprayed over. The collector's defence against this is knowledge of the methods of decoration and palettes used on the originals. The modern Portmeirion firm, for instance, reproduces various relief-moulded jugs. These are clearly marked, but even if they were not, the body is so different from the 19th-century versions that deception is not likely for the collector who has done even a minimal amount of study.

It should be pointed out that items made *continuously* by a firm for many decades or even a century or more are *not* reproductions, for example, Spode's Blue Italian, as mentioned above, or the green-glazed or jasper wares of Wedgwood. These wares are marked clearly with the firms' modern marks.

Reproduction bust of Shakespeare.

1930s. Chips to enamel. 21 cm height.

£50. The late Victorian reproductions c.1870–80, £150. Original c.1810, £450–500.

Here is a page from a retailer's catalogue of reproductions.

Copies and *imitations* are not meant to deceive the buyer so much as his friends and neighbours. This Crown Devon plaque made by Fieldings is an imitation of the Highland Cattle paintings by Harry Stinton at Royal Worcester. The plaque is clearly marked, so the buyer would not be deceived, but might purchase it in the hope that visitors would assume it to be a much more expensive Royal Worcester plaque.

Painted plaque in imitation of Harry Stinton.

c.1905. Printed mark with 'CROWN DEVON/FIELDINGS/ STOKE-ON-TRENT/ENGLAND'. 24 cm length   TV

£465

However, some copies and imitations can be altered by subsequent sellers, and may cause difficulties for the novice collector (and even on occasion some of the experts!). In the case of this plaque an unscrupulous dealer might grind off the mark and add a spurious signature. Such alterations can often be detected by touch rather than eye. It is always a good idea carefully to run your fingertips over a piece, as this can also detect restorations and faults which the eye might not see.

CONCLUSION

Unless you are putting together a documentary collection for study, do not buy a pot just because it was designed or manufactured by a popular name. It is wiser to purchase a good quality pot by an unknown manufacturer, than a poor quality pot whose maker is well known.

Having conducted the reader through the minefield of factors affecting the value of a pot, it is perhaps fitting to repeat that the pot is only worth what you are willing to pay for it. A purchase is not a bargain if you return home with an object which does not please you. Nor is it an extravagance if it brings you great pleasure. It is far better to buy a piece you really like at a higher price than may be quoted here, than to buy a poor example just because it happens to cost less than the price indicated in this *Guide*.

The prices in this guide are the actual ticket prices on items found for sale in late 1991 and early 1992 by the author. This does not mean that the same item can be found at the same place for that same price now. The prices given are from dealers in the middle and upper end of the chain, representing fair, average retail prices. In cases where prices were exceptionally low, I have also indicated the prices one would normally expect to pay.

These retail prices should not be confused with the price which the collector can expect to receive when selling a piece. The selling price could be considerably less, if the dealer approached expects the item to be difficult to sell. Sale by auction, an alternative, can also be costly. Expenses will include the auctioneer's commission (plus VAT) and insurance charges. The seller must also take into account the buyer's premium, where applicable. If a dealer thinks that a vase is worth £200 to him, he will not bid more than £180, as a 10% buyer's premium will make the cost to him £198.00. Thus the amount received by the seller is effectively reduced by the buyer's premium. The item may be tied up at the auction house for months, awaiting sale, and if it goes unsold the seller must still pay a commission on the highest bid, as well as any insurance costs. If an item is illustrated the photographic costs are also paid by the seller.

Insurance values should generally be about 25% over the retail price, to account for future possible increases. However, remember that one will have to pay the insurance premium on the inflated value.

1 SLIPWARE

SLIPWARE, decorated by a technique used since the Roman occupation, is still popular with collectors today for the charm and warmth of the naïve designs. Slipwares are earthenwares decorated with slip (clay mixed with water) made from a different colour clay, then glazed. Most often red-bodied pots were dipped in a white slip. Potters would use this technique for economic reasons if, for example, their own clay beds provided only red clay and they needed a white surface to show off the glaze. If a green glaze, for instance, were put on to a red clay body the glaze would appear to be a chocolate brown colour: for a green colour the glaze must be applied to a white body. In the sgraffito method of decoration, the slip coating is sometimes incised to expose the clay body underneath the slip. A thicker slip can be used to decorate pots in much the same way as one decorates a cake with icing: this is known as slip trailing. In impasto decoration whole areas of the slip are removed to expose the body beneath.

These techniques used separately or together were used at many places in the country from the 16th century. Although these wares were largely superseded by delftwares during the 17th and 18th centuries, in 1885 M. L. Solon noted: 'At the present time, indeed, at Buckley, a few miles from Chester, they have not discontinued the practice of the oldest style, and are turning out slip pieces which, with a little scratching and chipping, might be mistaken for the work of 200 years ago.'

Early slipwares were made by many small potteries scattered throughout Britain. A few of these potters inscribed their names on the pots, and so they are known to us today. Pots from Wrotham in Kent have been recorded with dates from 1612 to 1721. In the early 20th century Reginald Wells made slipwares inspired by these early Wrotham pots at Coldrum in Kent. Other centres of slipware production in the 17th and 18th centuries were Bideford, Fremington and Barnstaple in Devon; Rye and Chailey in Sussex; Tickenhall and Bolsover in Derbyshire; Buckinghamshire; Cambridgeshire; Fareham and Fordingbridge in Hampshire; High Halden in Kent; Nottingham; Donyatt and Pill near Bristol; Polesworth in Warwickshire; near Salisbury in Wiltshire; Midhope, Burton-in-Lonsdale, Halifax and near Wakefield in Yorkshire; Bridgend and Ewenny in Glamorganshire. During the 19th century slipwares were also made at Gestingthorpe and Castle Hedingham in Essex.

Some of the finest slipwares were made c.1670–1710 in Staffordshire. The potters whose names are known to us today include Thomas Toft (senior and junior), Ralph Toft, James Toft, John and William Wright, George Taylor, William Talor and Ralph Simpson.

During the late 19th century there was a resurgence of interest in sgraffito, slip-trailed and impasto wares. Traditional wares were reproduced by potteries especially in Barnstaple and in Wales. Some of these wares are shown in chapter 13. Slip-trailed baking dishes in the traditional style were still being made in Wales in the 1930s, and some studio potters have excelled in using the old techniques (see chapter 26).

Reproduction slipwares were made in potteries such as the Buckley Pottery near Chester in the present century. In 1915, I & W. Powell at the Ewloe Pottery at Buckley advertised 'Reproductions of the 17th Century Slip Decorated Ware.' Reproductions of these types were also made at the Ewenny Pottery in the late 19th and early 20th century. These are very collectable, although their value is considerably less than the originals.

17th and 18th-century examples are rare and costly but 19th and early 20th-century wares are more plentiful and affordable. Some delightful slipwares are being made by modern studio and craft potters. For a modest outlay you can purchase wares to grace your kitchen dresser, and make an investment for the future. These later wares are more affordable. However, it must be stressed that some of the later potters continued to use traditional patterns and techniques of decoration. Baking dishes in particular might date from the 1930s, and having been used for forty or fifty years take on a patina of age.

Dorothy Hartley described some Buckley pottery made in the 1930s: 'The ware is a deep reddish colour, fairly thick in substance; when glazed, it takes every shade of wallflower colouring, a fine golden brown, rimmed or lined with a "slip" of primrose yellow. Sometimes this last colour is used for a very simple decoration of swiftly-drawn curves and lines, sometimes for labelling of the dishes. The dripping dishes, for instance, will have "Beef" or "Mutton" or "Pork" writ plainly across them . . .' A bargain piece of slipware is likely to be one of these later pots.

The best collection of early Staffordshire slipwares can be seen at the City Museum and Art Gallery at Hanley. The Museum at the University of Wales at Aberystwyth has an interesting collection of Buckley slipwares. The Welsh Folk Museum at St Fagans, Cardiff, has a good display of Ewenny slipwares. Fine slipwares may also be seen at the Fitzwilliam Museum, Cambridge and the British Museum, London.

Further Reading

R. G. Cooper. *English Slipware Dishes* (Alec Tiranti, 1968).

Peter Davey, *Buckley Pottery* (Buckley Clay Industries Research Committee, Chester, 1975).

Dorothy Hartley, *Made in England* (Century, 1939, reprinted 1987).

Jonathan Horne, *A Collection of Early English Pottery*, Parts I–XII (Jonathan Horne, 1982–92).

J. M. Lewis, *The Ewenny Potteries* (National Museum of Wales, Cardiff, 1982).

Mostyn Art Gallery, *Buckley Pottery* (Gwynned, 1983).

Bernard Rackham and Herbert Read. *English Pottery: its Development from Early Times to the end of the Eighteenth Century* (London, 1924; reprinted E. P. Publishers, Wakefield 1973).

M. L. Solon, *Art of the Old English Potter*, 2nd edn (1885).

Ross E. Taggart. *The Frank P. and Harriet C. Burnap Collection of English Pottery in the William Rockhill Nelson Gallery*, revised edn (Nelson Gallery/Atkins Museum, Kansas City, Missouri, 1967).

Mary Wondrausch. *Mary Wondrausch on Slipware* (A. & C. Black, 1986).

Slipware dish with pie crust rim.

c.1775. Crack. 28.5 cm diameter   AS

£8,000

Birds of various types are often found on slipware dishes.

Slipware dish with pie crust rim.

Dated 1780. 29.5 cm diameter   AS

£8,800

Small slipware dish with pie crust rim.

c.1800. Repaired. 17.5 cm diameter   JH

£385

Large slipware charger with pie crust rim.

Late 18th century. 33.5 cm diameter   JH

£1,650

Slipware dish with unusual three-colour slip decoration and pie crust rim.

Late 18th century. 22 cm diameter   JH

£2,500

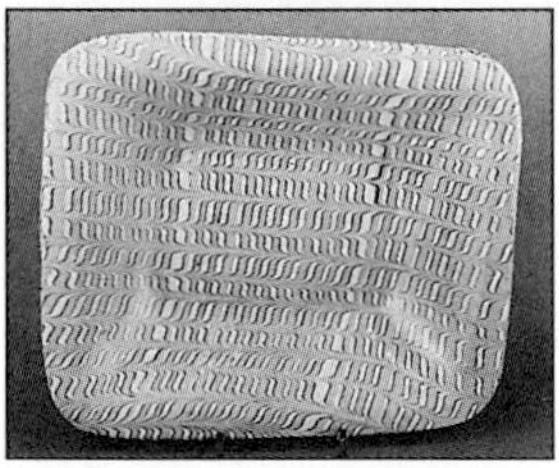

Staffordshire slipware dish with combed decoration.

Mid 19th century. 28.5 cm length   HBW

£125

Staffordshire slipware dish.

Dated 1859. 33.5 cm length   AS

£2,950

Staffordshire slipware one-handled bowl found in Stoke.

c.1700. Restored. 8 cm height   JH

£780

Slipware 'honey pot'.

c.1700. Chip and crack. 14.5 cm height   JH

£2,800

Marbled slipware 'honey pot'.

c.1690. Rim chips. 14 cm height   JH

£2,800

Slipware mug with 'diced' sgraffito pattern.

c.1730. 12.8 cm height   AS

£1,700

37

2 DELFTWARE

DELFTWARE is a term commonly used to describe tin-glazed earthenware. In Italy it is called maiolica or faenza and in France faience. The first tin-glazed wares in England were made by Jasper Andries and Jacob Jansen, Huguenot refugees from Antwerp who set up business in Norwich in 1567. In 1571 they moved to London and joined other Flemish potters who were working in the city at Aldgate. From the early 17th century and into the 18th century, delftware potteries sprang up on the south bank of the Thames, firstly in Southwark and then spreading to Lambeth. The products of this group of some twenty factories are generically known as London delftwares. Fine wares continued to be made up to the end of the 18th century. Production continued well into the 19th century, but these late products are simple objects such as blacking bottles, ointment pots etc.

About 1645 a potter from London set up in Bristol. Thus the early Bristol wares are very like the London wares. However, during the 18th century Bristol developed a distinctive style of its own. The best known decorations used at Bristol were monochrome blue figures in landscape, sometimes known as 'Bowen' type after a Bristol decorator, and *bianco sopra bianco*, white decoration on a pale blue or grey ground. Both types were also made elsewhere.

The third major centre of delftware production was Liverpool, which was set up in the early 18th century by London potters. Fine quality wares were made here from the beginning. Liverpool is well known for its ship bowls, which were usually made for an occasion such as the launching of a ship or hiring of a new captain. During the second half of the 18th century they produced an impressive range of wall tiles, which included printed examples, the first transfer-printing on ceramics (see chapter 25).

Delftwares were also made in Dublin from 1745 (see p. 15), and in Glasgow from 1748 when the Delftfield Pottery was established, from which large quantities were exported to the American colonies.

Delftware has a soft earthenware body to which the tin glaze did not closely fit. Thus, chipping and crazing are the norm in the examples which have survived. During the late 18th century delftware rapidly went out of production after the introduction of more durable wares such as creamware, pearlware, etc.

The ware was twice-fired: the body was fired to a biscuit state, then dipped in the tin glaze, and decorated before the second firing. The decoration was created with a slurry from coloured oxides mixed with a bit of powdered glaze. This was a difficult process, as once the brush was touched to the tin glazed surface, it could not be wiped away.

The date and provenance of British delftwares can sometimes be difficult to determine. Pattern or styles of decoration persisted for decades. As the industries outside London were founded by or employed London potters, the early provincial pots closely resemble their London counterparts. Furthermore, some decorators apparently worked on a freelance basis, further confusing attribution. Therefore further reading and study of actual examples is recommended.

For further information on delftware tiles see chapter 25.

Further Reading

Michael Archer and Brian Morgan. *Fair as China Dishes, English Delftware* (International Exhibitions Foundation, 1977).

Bristol Fine Wares 1670–1970 (City of Bristol Museum & Art Gallery, 1979).

Frank Britton. *English Delftware in the Bristol Collection* (Sotheby Publications, 1982).

Frank Britton. *London Delftware* (Jonathan Horne, 1987).

Jonathan Horne. *A Collection of Early English Pottery*, Parts I–XII (Jonathan Horne, 1982–92).

Jonathan Horne. *English Tin-glazed Tiles* (Jonathan Horne, 1989).

Louis Lipski, ed. and augmented by Michael Archer. *Dated English Delftware Tin Glazed Earthenware 1600–1800* [Sotheby Publications, 1984).

Ross E. Taggart. *The Frank P. and Harriet C. Burnap Collection of English Pottery in the William Rockhill Nelson Gallery*, revised and enlarged edition (Nelson Gallery/Atkins Museum, Kansas City, Missouri, 1967).

LONDON

London delftware sack bottle.

Dated 1659. 16 cm height   JH

£4,500

London (Lambeth) delftware charger painted in blue with chinoiserie centre and floral swag border and brushed edge.

c.1785. Some crazing, chipping and flaking. 35 cm diameter
                                        SHA

£250

This type of floral border and brushed edge are typical of late London delftware plates. It is also found with balloon scenes which cannot be before 1784 when Vincent Lunardi made the first balloon ascent in England.

London (Lambeth) delftware plate painted in blue with chinoiserie centre and diaper border with floral reserves.

c.1775. Some crazing, chipping and flaking. 22.5 cm diameter   SHA

£60

This plate is a direct copy of a Chinese plate. The strong colours and the bluish background are typical of Lambeth.

39

London (Lambeth) polychrome painted chinoiserie floral delftware plate.

c.1750. Crazing and rim chips. 22.5 cm diameter   JH

£215

Plates in this pattern are illustrated in Britton 1982 and 1987. A shard in this pattern has been excavated in Lambeth High Street.

BRISTOL

Bristol delftware blue-dash charger portraying Adam and Eve with polychrome decoration.

c.1690. 34.5 cm diameter   JH

£5,500

One of a pair of Bristol *bianco sopra bianco* delftware plates with chinoiserie centre scenes painted in cobalt, yellow and manganese.

c.1760. Prominent straight stilt marks, unglazed foot rims. 23 cm diameter   AS

£1,800 the pair

The very attractive *bianco sopra bianco* decoration is uncommon and much sought after by collectors. It is thought that the decoration was an attempt to imitate Chinese porcelain patterns achieved by carving the leather-hard pot before glazing. The technique was brought to England from the Rörstrand factory in Sweden. Bristol *bianco sopra bianco* is characterised by a grey-blue background with a strong white decoration. A very similar plate is in the collection of the Bristol Art Gallery (illustrated in Britton 1982).

Stilt marks are made by the 'stilts' which hold the plates apart in the kiln during firing to prevent them from sticking together. After firing, the stilts are knocked off and the marks sometimes filed down. In some cases where stilt marks remain, they can be a clue to the manufacturer, as different types of stilts leave differently shaped blemishes.

Bristol delftware plate with peacock pattern painted and sponged in manganese, red, blues and yellow.

c.1730. Some chipping. 20 cm diameter   AS

£2,100

This example is one of half a dozen bird designs recorded, collectively known as 'Farmyard' patterns. A very similar plate is in the collection of the Bristol Art Gallery (illustrated in Britton 1982).

Bristol delftware plate with rim-to-rim hunting scene, possibly painted by Joseph Flower, painted and sponged in cobalt blue, with red rim.

c.1700s. Slight chipping and flaking. 22 cm diameter   AS

£1,800

Most delftware painting appears rather stiff and stilted, but the wonderful motion in this hunting scene makes it very desirable. Flower is one of the few delftware painters whose name is known, with several signed pieces surviving.

Bristol delftware blue-dash charger painted with a floral design in polychrome enamels.

c.1700. Rim crack and some wearing of glaze. Glaze lifted from reverse. 35 cm diameter   JH

£4,500

This is a very unusual, unrecorded design.

Delftware pierced brick with blue chinoiserie floral pattern, possibly Bristol.

c.1740. Some chipping and flaking. 12.5 cm length   SHA

£300

These bricks are a puzzle yet to be solved by the delftware scholars. Arguments put forward that they were flower holders, inkwells, or quill holders have all been persuasively disputed (see Britton 1982 and Archer & Morgan). They may have been used for pot-pourri, but would have been difficult to fill.

Delftware plate with chinoiserie pattern painted in blue and manganese, 'cracked ice' border, probably Bristol.

c.1760. Rim chips, one large. 23.2 cm diameter   JH

£195

'Cracked ice' is a Chinese symbol of spring. It was later used as a sheet transfer-print (see p. 116).

Delftware tulip blue-dash charger, with yellow, blue and green decoration, possibly Bristol.

c.1700. Cracked and repaired, rubbed. 30 cm diameter AS

£2,200

These chargers are named for their typical blue-dash borders and were meant for display on a dresser or hung on the wall, although they could on occasion have served as dishes. Tulips were a popular motif at the time. The flower had been introduced to Europe in the 16th century, and during the 17th century became the passion of connoisseurs in England and Holland, who paid fabulous prices for new hybrids. The actual patterns were inspired by Isnik pottery, in which the tulip and carnation (also a motif frequently found on delftware) were prominent. A number of blue-dash chargers with tulip motifs are illustrated in Taggart. An example in good condition would cost £3–4,000.

Delftware posset pot painted in blue, possibly Bristol.

c.1720. Chips and glaze rubbed at rim and handles. 18.5 cm height   JH

£2,650

A posset pot is a two-handled cup with a cover used for serving posset, a hot beverage made of milk curdled with ale or wine and flavoured with spices. Most examples have spouts. In the 17th century, the posset pot became an important item in terms of household status, although this example is simply decorated compared to some of the very elaborately modelled and decorated delftware and slipware examples.

All posset pots are rare, especially with their covers. Some of these covers may have cups for spices instead of knops.

LIVERPOOL

One of a pair of delftware plates with rim-to-rim chinoiserie decoration painted in blue with very bluish white tin glaze, possibly Liverpool.

Mid 18th century. Small rim chips, 25.5 cm diameter   AD

£420 the pair.

These chinoiserie designs were inspired by Chinese export porcelain.

Delftware armorial plate painted in blue, arms inscribed with motto 'Famae venientis amore', probably Liverpool.

c.1760. 22.5 cm diameter   SHA

£460

Armorial delftwares are quite rare, but a lot of the examples extant seem to have been made in Liverpool. Armorial porcelain dinner services were one of the products of the Chinese export trade, but delftware services were also produced.

Very rare delftware sauceboat with modelled fox handles and two spouts, blue painted with pastoral scene in centre, probably Liverpool.

c.1750. Chips. 21.5 cm length   JH

£2,200

This is a European silver shape, which was copied by the Chinese. Examples in Chinese export porcelain were found in the Nankin Cargo, a cargo of porcelains sunk c.1750 and recently recovered. A sauceboat with a related pastoral scene is in the Ashmolean Museum. (See Horne VIII.)

SURGEONS' & APOTHECARIES' WARES

Dry drug jars were used by pharmacists for powders, ointments and confections. The small sizes are known as pill pots. The top would usually have been covered with waxed parchment, or occasionally a tin or brass lid. Syrup or wet drug jars have spouts.

Standard dry drug jar with bluish tin glaze and blue painting, probably London.

c.1720. One bare patch. 18 cm height   AD

£450

The face motif beneath the label is similar to one which appears on a wet drug jar illustrated in Britton 1987.

London dry drug jar painted in blue and very dark manganese with songbirds and a basket of fruit above the label and an angel's head with swags and a tassel below.

Early 18th century. Inscribed 'C: RUTÆ' (rue). 19.5 cm height
                                                          JH

£660

Other dry drug jars with songbirds and a basket of fruit above the label and a face with swags and a tassel below are illustrated in Britton 1982 and 1987.

London pill jar painted in blue with songbirds and a basket of fruit above the label and an angel's head with swags and two tassels below.

c.1730. Inscribed 'P: D: STYRACE' (storax gum, for incense). 9.5 cm height   JH

£685

English delftware syrup jar, probably London.

18th century. Inscribed 'OXYM: SYRUP' (oxymel, vinegar and honey). Chips and rubbing to rim and base. 16.5 cm height   JH

£550

Very rare English delftware barber's bowl painted in blue with the barber's instruments.

c.1720. Glaze rubbed from rim, cracked and broken, one corner restored. 25 cm across   JH

£3,950

Barbers used to act as surgeons, a fact that is proven by the painting *The Foot Operation* by Isaack Koedijck, c.1645–50. In the foreground is the surgeon performing the operation, on the wall a barber's bowl hangs with various surgical implements below shelves lined with drug jars.

The indentation on the rim of the bowl is for a ball of soap. The cut out in the rim is to fit around the client's neck beneath his chin. The implements illustrated on this include surgical instruments as well as combs, brushes and scissors; the face in the middle represents a mirror.

3 CREAMWARE

THE development of cream-coloured earthenware by English potters in the 1740s created a ceramic revolution. This lead-glazed ware was more durable than the tin-glazed earthenwares commonly known as delftware, maiolica and faience. Although the lead in the glaze was deadly to work with over a period, the noxious fumes created by salt-glazing were avoided, and the lower firing temperature required for earthenwares saved fuel.

The finely and sometimes elaborately moulded shapes of these creamwares were made possible by the introduction of plaster of Paris moulds, c.1740. Wares at this time were usually press-moulded, the plastic clay being pressed into the mould. Slip-casting (pouring liquid clay into the mould and leaving it until most of the moisture had been absorbed by the porous plaster mould) was a technique often used with stoneware, but rarely used in the 18th century on earthenware unless the shape required was too elaborate and could not be produced in any other way.

The body was finely grained, and could be thinly potted and crisply moulded. Indeed, when one picks up a piece of 18th-century creamware, one's first impression is how light it is. The present day reproductions are very heavy in comparison, as they are machine-made. However, the reproductions made by James W. Senior in Yorkshire during the late 19th and early 20th century are quite light, and can deceive those who do not examine them carefully. Some of these were marked in an attempt to deceive.

Continental potters were not able to duplicate the ware until c.1800, and so the English had a virtual monopoly on the enormous export trade to Europe and the Western hemisphere. This created a boom in the English pottery industry and encouraged a flurry of new developments which made England the premier producer of pottery and porcelain in the world.

The earliest documented piece of creamware is a bowl initialled E B and dated 1743. The bowl has been attributed to Enoch Booth who, according to Simeon Shaw's *History of the Staffordshire Potteries*, was the Staffordshire potter responsible for this type of ware. Soon potters were making creamwares in all the principal potting centres of England: Staffordshire, Yorkshire, Derbyshire, Liverpool, Swansea etc. The pioneering work of Donald Towner, which inspired much of the research achieved since, has been largely overturned by new evidence, most notably the excavation of William Greatbatch's waste tip at Fenton Vivian in Staffordshire.

Creamware was created by the addition of calcined flint which improved the ware's resistance to thermal shock. This was fired at a temperature of 1100–1200 °C. The whitish body was then covered with a clear lead oxide glaze, which also contained a small amount of calcined flint. The flint in the glaze ensured that it fitted the body closely, preventing crazing. The relaxation of Richard Champions' monopoly on the use of Cornish stone (also known as China stone or kaolin) in non-translucent bodies resulted in the addition of this to the creamware body in the third quarter of the 18th century.

The smooth surface of the creamware made it ideal for the use of on-glaze transfer-prints and enamels. However, many pieces relied on pierced, sprigged or moulded decoration which also used the fine surface of the earthenware to advantage.

Creamware identification is complicated by the fact that wares were sometimes decorated outside the factories: Sadler & Green in Liverpool, for example, were used by Wedgwood and other manufacturers. Furthermore, manufacturers sometimes had difficulties in filling large orders. Contemporary correspondence shows that Wedgwood and others not infrequently took blanks from other potters for decorating. As most creamware is unmarked the collector must be a detective if he wishes to identify the manufacturer of a pot. This can sometimes be done by identifying shapes: Wedgwood creamware shapes are reproduced in Mankowitz (see Wedgwood below), the Spode shape book (1820) has been reproduced in Whiter and the 1807 Don Pottery and 1796 Castleford Pottery shape books have also been reproduced (see below). When identifying by shape, always remember that nearly is not all! Examine details such as knops, spouts, terminals (ends of handles) and handles as well as the overall shape of the pot.

Further Reading

David Barker. *William Greatbatch a Staffordshire Potter* (Jonathan Horne, 1991).
David Barker and Pat Halfpenny. *Unearthing Staffordshire* (Stoke-on-Trent City Museum & Art Gallery, 1990).
Don Pottery Pattern Book (Doncaster Library Service, 1983).
David Drakard. *The Castleford Pottery Pattern Book 1796* (EP Publishing, Wakefield, 1973).
Jonathan Horne. *A Collection of Early English Pottery*, Parts I–XII (Jonathan Horne, 1982–92).
Jana Kybalová. *European Creamware* (Hamlyn, 1989).
T. A. Lockett and P. A. Halfpenny, eds. *Creamware & Pearlware* (Stoke-on-Trent City Museum & Art Gallery, 1986).
Ross E. Taggart. *The Frank P. and Harriet C. Burnap Collection of English Pottery in the William Rockhill Nelson Gallery*, revised edn (Nelson Gallery/Atkins Museum, Kansas City, Missouri, 1967).
Donald Towner, *Creamware* (Faber & Faber, 1978). Note: this work has been largely superseded by recent scholarship.
Peter Walton. *Creamware and other English Pottery at Temple Newsam House Leeds* (Manningham Press, 1976).
Leonard Whiter. *Spode*, reprinted with new colour illustrations (Barrie & Jenkins, 1989).
Cyril Williams-Wood. *English Transfer-Printed Pottery & Porcelain* (Faber & Faber, 1981).

WILLIAM GREATBATCH
(1762–82)

The excavation of William Greatbatch's factory in Fenton has revealed the wide range of wares made there. Many wares which had been previously unattributed or attributed to other potters, have now been firmly attributed to Greatbatch. Such industrial archaeology is a relatively new field. Even in the 19th century, collectors and researchers had dug up shards from old pot banks, but only more recently have trained archaeologists begun to apply their painstaking methods to industrial sites. These methods, carefully revealing the past layer by layer, enable us to date wares as well as attribute them.

Greatbatch was probably an apprentice at Thomas Whieldon's pottery, although we have only second-hand accounts to confirm this. Greatbatch had set up his own pottery in 1762, supplying block moulds, finished ware and biscuit ware for glazing and decorating to Josiah Wedgwood and others. Correspondence from Greatbatch to Wedgwood (1762–5) confirms that they had a business relationship, but implies that Wedgwood was not Greatbatch's only customer.

After 1765, there is no written documentation of Greatbatch's pottery until a notice of bankruptcy in 1782. He then worked for Josiah Wedgwood c.1786–1807. This is only a brief summary, and the reader should consult Barker, who overturns many earlier presumptions about Greatbatch's career.

Further Reading

David Barker. *William Greatbatch a Staffordshire Potter* (Jonathan Horne, 1991).

Greatbatch creamware teapot with black on-glaze transfer-prints 'The Prodigal Son in Excess' and 'The Prodigal Son in Misery', overpainted in polychrome enamels.

c.1770–82. New knop. 13.5 cm height   AS

£950

There were six different Prodigal Son prints, which are illustrated in Barker. The prints were used on a number of different shapes of teapot. The subject can be found on wares made by another potter as well, but these are quite different in style.

Reverse.

Greatbatch creamware teapot with black on-glaze transfer-prints overpainted in polychrome enamels. *'Fortune Teller'* on obverse and *'The XII Houses of Heaven'* on reverse.

c.1778–82. Star crack on side, lifting of glaze on base. 15 cm height   BG

£985

The fortune teller subject was a popular one, and very similar prints were used by other potters. The Greatbatch version is always found with *'The XII Houses of Heaven'* print on the reverse. This second print includes: 'Published as the Act Directs Jany. 4, 1778 by W. Greatbatch Lane Delft Staffordshire'. It should be emphasised that Greatbatch *published* the print, but not (as some earlier writers had thought) engraved it.

Reverse.

NEALE
(1778–91)

The Church Works of Humphrey Palmer, earthenware manufacturer at Hanley, were taken over by James Neale in 1778. There followed a succession of partnerships which is confusing, as Neale was a London retailer, some of whose partnerships may not have involved the pottery itself. In 1791 the pottery was taken over by Robert Wilson, previously Neale's pottery manager. Robert Wilson was succeeded by his son David in 1798, continuing until 1820.

The firm made fine creamwares, pearlwares, black basalt. and other pottery wares typical of the period. They also produced porcelain 1783–90 (production possibly continued by the Wilsons to c.1800).

Further Reading

Diana Edwards. *Neale Pottery and Porcelain* (Barrie & Jenkins, 1987).

Rare Neale creamware footed basket-weave dish painted in brown enamels.

c.1788–91. Repaired crack. Printed red mark 'NEALE & BAILEY'. 17 cm length   G

£160

Thomas Bailey was one of James Neale's partners in London in 1783. The Neale & Bailey partnership began in 1788. The mark here is thus a retailer's mark. Although the Neale & Bailey partnership continued until 1808 or 1809, it is believed that these rare marked creamwares derive from the period 1788–91, when Robert Wilson took over the Church Works.

Creamware tureen with pierced ladle, attributed to Neale, painted in turquoise, lavender, green and brown enamels.

Late 18th century. 20.2 cm length   JH

£2,000

This is an exceptional piece in very fine condition. Very rarely do such tureens survive intact with the extremely delicate pierced spoons.

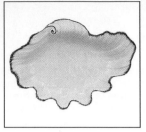

Neale creamware shell-shaped dish with green enamel-decoration.

c.1785+. Impressed mark 'Neale &Co/2'. 31 cm length G

£220

This rococo shell shape with feather border is typical of the period. Two similar Neale & Co. dishes, one with overglaze blue enamel floral painting, are illustrated in Lockett & Halfpenny. A Wedgwood version is illustrated in Kybalová.

WEDGWOOD
(1759 to the present day)

Josiah Wedgwood left Thomas Whieldon's pottery to establish his own pottery at Burslem in 1759. In 1769 he entered a partnership with Thomas Bentley and opened a new factory named Etruria. Wedgwood made a wide variety of wares typical of Staffordshire potters of the period, but through tireless experimentation he improved upon the existing formulas and decorating techniques. None the less, his name would not have reached pre-eminence in the pottery world, and even in the world at large, were it not for his brilliance in marketing his wares.

Josiah Wedgwood's fine creamware and clever marketing brought him great success. Wedgwood provided a green-glazed service, along with a gift of two creamware vases, to Queen Charlotte, and since 1767 Wedgwood's creamware has been sold under the trade name Queen's Ware. The most famous creamware service is that ordered by the Empress Catherine of Russia, comprising some 1,200 dishes, each hand-painted with a different English scene. The service is now at the Hermitage Museum in Russia, but occasionally sample pieces do turn up for sale elsewhere. The service is known as the Frog Service, because the Empress's arms incorporated a frog.

In the early 20th century Alfred and Louise Powell reintroduced the hand-painting of creamware at Wedgwood, often in patterns revived from the 18th-century pattern books. These wares are much more heavily potted than the early wares, and have modern marks. They are certainly undervalued at present and offer an attractive alternative to the collector of limited means.

Today Wedgwood still sells a number of Queen's Ware patterns, based on historical patterns. Some of these, such as 'Pot Pourri', are primarily manufactured for export to the United States where 'Colonial' furnishings are popular.

The Wedgwood Museum at the Wedgwood factory at Barlaston has many fine pieces of creamware, as does the Stoke-on-Trent City Museum & Art Gallery. The Wedgwood Society meets regularly in London, and publishes *Proceedings of the Wedgwood Society*. The membership secretary is Mrs Kathy Niblett, Department of Ceramics, City Museum & Art Gallery, Stoke-on-Trent, Staffordshire ST1 3DW.

Further Reading

Alison Kelly. *Wedgwood Ware* (Ward Lock, 1970).
Wolf Mankowitz. *Wedgwood* (Spring Books, 1966).

Robin Reilly. *Wedgwood*, 2 vols (Macmillan, 1989).
Robin Reilly and George Savage. *The Dictionary of Wedgwood* (Antique Collectors' Club, Woodbridge, 1980).
Geoffrey Wills. *Wedgwood* (Country Life Books, 1980).

Wedgwood creamware plate with transfer-printed 'Shells and Seaweeds' pattern filled in with green enamel and feather edge border, also enamelled.

c.1776. Small chips to rim, 22 cm diameter   V

£155

In a letter to his partner Thomas Bentley about this pattern in 1776, Josiah Wedgwood was concerned that the green was 'coloured too high', but consoled himself: 'But this pattern was intended chiefly for abroad, and foreigners in general will bear higher colouring and more forcible contrasts than we English' (quoted in Mankowitz). A dish in this pattern is illustrated in Wills.

Wedgwood creamware jug with floral painting in purples, yellow and green, possibly painted by W. Bourne at the Chelsea Decorating Studio.

c.1780. Painted mark in purple 'WB'; 'WEDGWOOD' impressed. 17.5 cm height   AS

£1,300

W. Bourne was a creamware decorator who was employed at Wedgwood's Chelsea Decorating Studio from 1770. The undecorated ware was sent from Etruria to the Studio, where it was enamelled and fired. The fine painting which fits the graceful form of the jug make this an exceptional piece.

These supper set sections fitted together in a ring inside a wooden tray; in the centre would be a tureen or a stand for condiments. The sections may have inner rims on which the covers rest, or they may have been designed without covers. A section missing its cover is worth considerably less than one with the cover. A complete supper set, especially with a contemporary wooden tray, can fetch upwards of £2,000.

A pair of Wedgwood creamware supper set sections with 'Barley-ear' border in brown.

c.1780. Very slight chips to rims. 15 cm width   G

£120

The 'Barley-ear' border appears in Wedgwood's first pattern book. A gravy tureen In this pattern is illustrated in Mankowitz.

Wedgwood creamware supper set section with lid, decorated with 'Strawberry Leaf' border in brown.

c.1780. Hairline to base. Impressed mark 'WEDGWOOD'. Painted mark 87. 28 cm length   AF

£175

'Strawberry Leaf' is pattern 31 in the first Wedgwood pattern book (illustrated in Mankowitz).

One of a pair of Wedgwood crested creamware dishes. Motto 'Ein Doe and Spare Not Striogal mo Derahn'.

c.1790. Impressed mark 'WEDGWOOD'   V

£198 the pair.

Josiah Wedgwood was not anxious to produce armorial wares. Reilly & Savage quote a 1766 letter to his partner Bentley complaining that crested ware seconds were unsaleable. By 1776, Wedgwood was making armorials hand-painted with enamels. After 1780 the decoration was transfer-printed and filled in with enamel.

The crest is an arm, in armour, embowed, in hand a scimitar. This crest and the mottos 'E'en do and spair not' and 'S'Rioghal mo Dhream' belonged to Robert-Hyde Greg Esq. of Norliffe Hall, Chester and Cole's Park, Herts.

Wedgwood creamware dish decorated with a viola border in green, yellow and purple enamels.

c.1810. Part of a dessert service consisting of a comport, six plates and four dishes (one restored). Impressed 'WEDG-WOOD'. 22 cm length   VH

£1,250 the service.

Wedgwood creamware plate decorated with a Japan-type pattern in red and blue enamels and gilding.

c.1810. 20 cm diameter   WG

£42

One of a pair of Wedgwood creamware footed drainers pierced and decorated with ribbon and dart border in brown and red enamels.

c.1820. One foot restored   VH

£275 the pair.

This shape (1046) was included in the 1817 Wedgwood shape book (illustrated in Mankowitz). The drainers should have matching diamond-shaped dishes. An identical drainer dish, but with the border in pink and black, is illustrated in Kelly.

OTHER MANUFACTURERS

Creamware teapot 'Let not Liberty be sold for Silver nor Gold/Your Votes Freely given to the Brave & the Bold', painted in red and black enamel with coloured glazes on flowers and leaves, rouletted decoration.

c.1765–70. Spout repaired. 14 cm height   BG

£1,850

Reverse.

Creamware coffee pot, painted with sailing ships pattern on obverse and lady reading on reverse in red, blue, brown and green enamels.

c.1770. Replacement knop. 24.5 cm height   AS

£2,250

The decoration on this coffee pot is reminiscent of that used on white salt-glazed stoneware. Coffee pots are rarer than teapots.

Reverse

Creamware coffee pot with iron red and black painting, possibly Leeds.

c.1770. Repairs to a crack near spout and rim chip. 22 cm height   AS

£2,950

A teapot similar to this coffee pot is illustrated in Walton no. 634. The knop is 'firmly linked with the earlier products of the Leeds Pottery'

Creamware bowl with red, green and black painting.

Dated 1795. Repaired chips to foot rim. Painted 'WMP Success to Lead Mines 1795'. 9 cm diameter   AS

£1,400

Creamware teapot, manganese oxide sponged panels with red, green, black and blue painting.

c.1775. Repaired tip of spout and lid. 13 cm height with lid
AS

£2,400

Creamware teapot with turned decoration and red, green, yellow and black painting.

c.1780. 13 cm height with lid   AS

£950

Staffordshire or Yorkshire creamware centre-piece with very green tinge to glaze.

c.1775. 19.5 cm height   AS

£1,100

Creamware dessert service dish with botanical painting in polychrome enamels with gold borders.

c.1790. Painted mark 'Hony Sulle' (honeysuckle) in red script. 31 cm length   AS

£860

Creamware bough pot with green edges.

c.1780. Chip inside rim. 20.5 cm length   AS

£1,950

The development of creamware in England, and its prolific import into the Netherlands from the 1760s, was one of the factors leading to the destruction of the Dutch delftware industry. Delftware decorators found occupation in painting imported English wares, until local production of creamware began at the beginning of the 19th century. The Dutch-decorated wares can be easily identified by the style of painting, and the frequent use of Dutch inscriptions.

The Dutch-manufactured creamwares made by Petrus Regout at Maastricht can be easily distinguished from English manufactures as they bear an impressed mark MAAS-TRICHT. However, the shapes used by Regout were so similar to those of Wedgwood that Regout was tried for forgery.

Creamware jug with Dutch decoration painted in polychrome enamels, probably Leeds.

c.1780s. Repaired lip. 14 cm height   AD

£350

This jug is tentatively attributed on the basis of the terminals as similar types occur in the Leeds Original Drawing Book No. 1 at the Victoria & Albert Museum (see Walton p. 275).

Creamware tea canister with Dutch decoration painted in polychrome enamels.

c.1780s. 13 cm height   AD

£175

Creamware plate with rare transfer-print of 'Bee Shooting' overglaze and decorated with polychrome enamels, caption reading 'Damme where a blow at them better small birds than one'.

c.1820. 24.5 cm diameter AD

£250

Creamware plate with peasant style polychrome enamelled decoration.

c.1810. 25 cm diameter AD

£260

Pair of creamware syrup jars with spouts for pouring.

Late 18th century. 17 cm height G

£360

A series of creamware syrup jars in this shape are illustrated in John Austen's *Historical Notes on Old Sheffield Druggists* (J. W. Northend, Sheffield, 1961). Creamware drug jars such as these replaced the less durable delftware ones during the third quarter of the 18th century. The jars were usually supplied plain, the druggists affixing their own labels.

One of a pair of creamware plates with 'Forestry' pattern transfer-printed and painted in polychrome enamels, inscribed 'MARCULA FUNDUS ARGUS'; also in capitals the verse 'Hail forestry try thy lovely charm/Does stamp a beauty on the mind/A noble scene that tends no harm/ Friendly theme to all mankind'.

One with hairline crack. 22 cm diameter LM

£550 the pair.

Creamware custard cup with square French shape handle with brown vine border.

c.1800–10. 10 cm height   TA

£28

Creamware plate with black overglaze transfer-print of ship under sail painted with enamels, and six prints of exotic birds on the border.

Some rubbing. 25 cm diameter   V

£140

Ship prints similar (but certainly different) to this were made by Neale & Co. (illustrated in Edwards, see above), Ralph Wedgwood at Ferrybridge in Yorkshire (illustrated in Locket & Halfpenny), Herculaneum at Liverpool (illustrated in Locket & Halfpenny), Newcastle Pottery (illustrated in Lockett & Halfpenny), Josiah Wedgwood, printed in Liverpool by Sadler & Green (illustrated in Williams-Wood), Thomas Wolfe (attributed, illustrated in Kybalová), Swansea (illustrated in Williams-Wood) and doubtless others.
Similar exotic birds appear on the borders of the 'Liverpool Birds' (Peafowl) pattern made by Josiah Wedgwood and Leeds Pottery (both illustrated in Williams-Wood). It also appears on a plate formerly attributed to 'Melbourne Pottery', whose very existence now seems doubtful.

Creamware Freemason's mug.

c.1800. 14.5 cm height   V

£190

Sunderland creamware frog tankard with on-glaze print of a ship and 'Success to the COAL TRADE/Here's May Colliers Flourish, our Trade increase/And Victory bring us a lasting Peace.'

c.1813–19. Small chip. Print signed 'SUNDERLAND POTTERY'. 12.5 cm height   JH

£550

This mug but with polychrome enamel over the print is illustrated in John C. Baker's *Sunderland Pottery*, revised edn (Tyne and Wear County Council Museum, 1983). That example has a printed mark 'DIXON & CO., SUNDERLAND POTTERY.'

Frog mugs are very collectable, but beware as unscrupulous dealers have been known to add frogs to ordinary mugs to increase their value. I know of one case where the spurious frog was actually plastic! The frog should have been attached before glazing and enamel decoration would be added afterwards. There should be evidence of the glaze running continuously from the frog's feet on to the surface of the interior of the mug, as seen on the frog's forefeet in the photo below

Frog tankard interior,

Sunderland Pottery creamware jug with on-glaze print of the Farmers Arms inscribed 'GOD SPEED THE PLOUGH'; 'DIXON AUSTIN & Co/SUNDERLAND' and signed 'Downing Sct.'

c.1820–6. Chipped. 13 cm height   JH

£365

The Farmers Arms was a popular subject, used by many manufacturers well into the 20th century. See p. 120 for a later underglaze transfer-printed example.

Unusual small creamware supper set section with brown painted grape and vine border.

c.1780. Crazed and slightly stained, two very small rim chips. 15.2 cm length   AF

£0.10

Even in this condition, this piece is a rarity and would ordinarily cost about £30.

Creamware toy plate with green glaze decoration.

c.1770. Many tiny rim chips. 9 cm length   AS

£560

TORTOISESHELL WARES

Tortoiseshell wares have the same body as creamware, but are decorated underglaze with metallic oxides. These were in a liquid form which was sponged or painted on the biscuit ware, then covered with a clear lead glaze. When the ware was fired the colours flowed to produce a streaky or mottled effect.

These wares are often incorrectly referred to as Whieldon or Whieldon-type wares. As Whieldon was only one of many tortoiseshell manufacturers in Staffordshire, the term should be avoided as a generic name for the wares. The excavation of Whieldon's factory at Fenton Vivian has made it possible to attribute only a few wares to him with certainty.

Staffordshire tortoiseshell plate.

c.1770. One chip. 27.8 cm diameter   JH

£1,650

Staffordshire tortoiseshell earthenware teapot with crab-stock spout and handle and sprigged vine decoration, possibly by Thomas Whieldon.

c.1765. 11 cm height   JH

£3,500

Shards with similar sprigged decoration have been recovered from the Whieldon site at Fenton Vivian.

Staffordshire tortoiseshell plate.

c.1770. One chip. 21.3 cm diameter   JH

£1,350

Staffordshire tortoiseshell press-moulded trellis diaper bordered dish.

c.1765. 25.5 cm diameter   JH

£2,500

This is a shape commonly found in white salt-glazed stoneware.

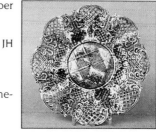

Tortoiseshell mug with sponged manganese, and yellow and green strips of decoration.

Late 18th century. Greenish cast to glaze. Star crack. 16.5 cm height   AS

£1,950

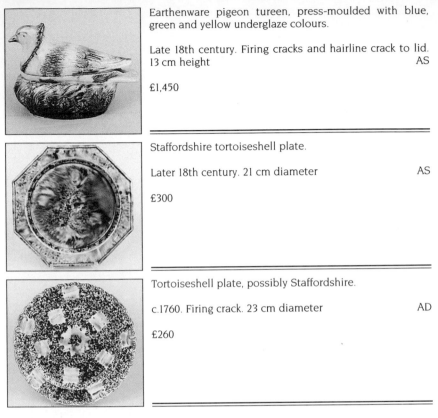

Earthenware pigeon tureen, press-moulded with blue, green and yellow underglaze colours.

Late 18th century. Firing cracks and hairline crack to lid. 13 cm height   AS

£1,450

Staffordshire tortoiseshell plate.

Later 18th century. 21 cm diameter   AS

£300

Tortoiseshell plate, possibly Staffordshire.

c.1760. Firing crack. 23 cm diameter   AD

£260

CREAMWARE WITH COLOURED GLAZES

Thomas Whieldon mentions his experiments to perfect a green glaze in his notebooks of 1759. This was also a special project of Josiah Wedgwood, and as a result the wares have often been called Whieldon-Wedgwood. However, as with the tortoiseshell wares, many of their contemporaries were producing these popular wares in the 1760s and 1770s.

Creamware teapot with yellow glaze painted in red and green enamels.

c.1765. Lid restored. 13.8 cm height   JH

£950

Rare creamware plaque decorated in green and blue glazes, with sprigged decoration of Peace and Plenty.

c.1785–90. 16.5 cm length; 12.7 cm width   LR

£800

Staffordshire creamware relief-moulded teapot painted in coloured glazes.

c.1765. Tip of spout restored. 14 cm height   JH

£5,500

This was obviously a popular pattern in the 1760s. Pine-apples were a great luxury, available only to those with greenhouses (also a great luxury given the large tax on glass). Horne (Part X) illustrates this teapot and a bowl by a different maker with a very similar pattern. Shards of this pattern (with slight differences) have been excavated at the William Greatbatch excavation. A very similar teapot is illustrated in Taggart.

Melon ware creamware teapot painted in yellow and green glazes.

c.1765. 10.5 cm height   JH

£4,000

Melon ware is the term generally used for wares decorated with bands of yellow and green glazes, presumably derived from the green rind and yellow flesh of melons, which were a delicacy in the 18th century.

4 PEARLWARE

JOSIAH Wedgwood introduced his Pearl White or pearlware in the 1770s, although he may not have been the first manufacturer to use a cobalt-tinted transparent glaze on creamware bodies. This glaze made the wares appear whiter, more like porcelain, and many factories were producing it by the 1780s. The glaze often pools inside the footrims of plates, jugs, etc. and will appear distinctly blue, as opposed to the yellow or greenish cast of the creamware glazes. Underglaze blue transfer-prints were set off well by the pearlware glazes (see chapter 7). Most post-1790 blue transfer-printed earthenwares were pearlwares.

Pearlware decorated with high-temperature underglaze colours, most often blue, yellow, green and brown, is known as Prattware (see below).

During the 1840s a number of manufacturers, including Wedgwood and Thomas Dimmock, produced an earthenware body which they called 'pearlware', which may be impressed on the wares. This is different from the pearlwares discussed here.

For pearlware figures see chapter 9.

Further Reading

Miranda Goodby. *Oriental Expressions: The Influence of the Orient on British Ceramics* (Northern Ceramic Society, 1989).

Jonathan Horne. *A Collection of Early English Pottery*, Parts I–XII (Jonathan Horne, 1982–92).

T. A. Lockett and P. A. Halfpenny, eds. *Creamware & Pearlware* (Stoke-on-Trent City Museum & Art Gallery, 1986).

Peter Walton. *Creamware and other English Pottery at Temple Newsam House Leeds* (Manningham Press, 1976).

UNDERGLAZE PAINTED OR ENAMELLED

NEALE (1778–91)

The Church works at Hanley of Humphrey Palmer, earthenware manufacturer, were taken over by James Neale in 1778. There followed a succession of partnerships which is confusing, as Neale was a London retailer, some of whose partnerships may not have involved the pottery itself. In 1791 the pottery was taken over by Robert Wilson, previously Neale's pottery manager. Robert Wilson was succeeded by his son David in 1798, continuing until 1820.

The firm made fine creamwares, pearlwares, black basalt and other pottery wares typical of the period. They also produced porcelain 1783–90 (production possibly continued by the Wilsons to c.1800).

Further Reading

Diana Edwards. *Neale Pottery and Porcelain* (Barrie & Jenkins, 1987).

Rare Neale pearlware relief-moulded jug with scene of a parson, clerk and sexton smoking and drinking, highlighted with polychrome enamels.

c.1790. Small crack to spout. Impressed mark NEALE & CO. 20.3 cm height   G

£480

This jug and a similar Prattware jug, possibly Scottish, are illustrated in Lockett & Halfpenny. Fragments of a similar jug were recovered from the site of the Delftfield Pottery, Glasgow.

Rare Neale pearlware basket painted in green enamel.

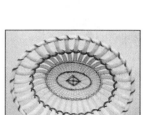

c.1785. Impressed mark 'NEALE & CO.' 24 cm length   G

£285

Neale pearlware baskets and stands are illustrated in Edwards.

SPODE (1770–1833)

Pearlwares, many of them underglaze blue transfer-printed, were one of the principal specialities of the Spode factory during its early years, although as few of these were marked, few have been identified. Pattern numbers were only used after 1800 on wares which have some on-glaze decoration. A list of Spode pattern numbers with dates of introduction is given on p.375.

Spode collectors will want to join the Spode Society, which has regular meetings and outings, also publishing a very fine Review. The membership secretary is Mrs Rosalind Pulver, PO Box 1812, London NW4 4NW. The Spode factory (Church Street, Stoke-on-Trent ST4 1BX) has a fine museum and factory tours are also available by prior arrangement.

Further Reading

David Drakard and Paul Holdway. *Spode Printed Ware* (Longman, 1983).
Leonard Whiter. *Spode*, reprinted with new colour illustrations (Barrie & Jenkins, 1989).
The Spode Society, *Recorder & Review* (1986 to the present day). Referred to as SSR in the text.

Very rare Spode pearlware plate with moulded feather border and pleated design to the well, painted in underglaze blue with flower sprays and leaf swags to the rim. Gilded.

c.1780–1800. Impressed mark SPODE. One chip, some fine crazing and staining. 20 cm diameter   WG

£90

Early marked pearlwares are extremely rare, making this plate, despite its condition, relatively valuable. It is an exact copy of a Caughley porcelain pattern. A similar plate with an impressed mark IH (possible for Joshua Heath) is illustrated in Lockett & Halfpenny.

Spode pearlware plate, transfer-printed and painted in polychrome enamels.

c.1820. Impressed mark 'SPODE/3'; blue printed mark 'Spode'; red painted pattern number 2963. 16 cm diameter
WG

£40

This popular pattern, named 'Chinese Flowers' by Whiter, was produced from c.1815, as an unadorned transfer-print (see Drakard & Holdway) and painted in several different combinations of coloured enamels (each of which had a different pattern number).

A part service is pattern 2963 is illustrated in SSR, vol. 1, p. 99.

OTHER MANUFACTURERS

Octagonal pearlware plate with moulded rim, Chinese landscape painted in underglaze blue.

c.1780. Impressed triangle mark. 23 cm diameter   T

£175

These underglaze blue painted Chinese landscape scenes are frequently found on pearlwares of the 1780s. A plate, attributed to William Greatbatch, with a very similar scene but an entirely different shape, is illustrated in Lockett & Halfpenny.

Pearlware plate with underglaze blue painted decoration and feather moulded border.

Late 18th century. A few small chips to border. 23 cm diameter   AF

£5

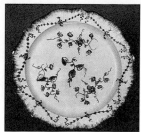

This is another popular pattern, made by many manufacturers. A Spode example is illustrated in Lockett & Halfpenny. The normal retail price for this plate would be £80–100.

Unusual pearlware octagonal shape teapot with sprigged figures of dancers, painted in polychrome enamels.

c.1810. 13.3 cm height   LR

£480

Pearlware obelisk painted in polychrome enamels and gilded.

c.1800. 23 cm height   AD

£885

Obelisks were popular neo-classical ornaments.

Pearlware jug with painted polychrome enamel and lustre decoration.

c.1810. 13 cm height   JJB

£185

67

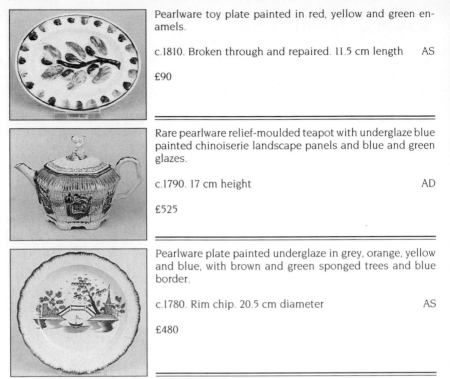

Pearlware toy plate painted in red, yellow and green enamels.

c.1810. Broken through and repaired. 11.5 cm length   AS

£90

Rare pearlware relief-moulded teapot with underglaze blue painted chinoiserie landscape panels and blue and green glazes.

c.1790. 17 cm height   AD

£525

Pearlware plate painted underglaze in grey, orange, yellow and blue, with brown and green sponged trees and blue border.

c.1780. Rim chip. 20.5 cm diameter   AS

£480

PRATTWARE
(c.1790–1840)

'Prattware' is a term commonly used to describe pearlware painted, sponged, or stippled with underglaze high-temperature colours c.1790–1840. The colours (orange, yellow, green, blue, black, brown and occasionally a dark raspberry) were often used to highlight relief-moulding. They were produced from oxides which could withstand the high temperature necessary to fuse the glaze. The body is a cream-coloured earthenware, and the lead glaze often has the blue tinge associated with pearlware. A great many commemoratives were made, also Toby jugs, cow creamers and figures.

The name 'Prattware' comes from the firm of F. & R. Pratt, whose name is impressed on a very few examples from the early 19th century, although many other firms manufactured the ware at Bovey Tracey (Devon), Liverpool, Scotland, Shropshire, Staffordshire, Sunderland, Tyneside, and Yorkshire. William Pratt (d.1799) worked at Lane Delph and his sons carried on there and at Fenton. In the middle of the 19th century F. & R. Pratt manufactured multicoloured transfer-print pot lids and dinner services and also terracottas with transfer-prints which are both also referred to as Prattware (see pp. 124 and 150).

As with all relief-moulded wares the crispness of the moulding is very important. A number of marked pots have been recorded. Any marked piece is of considerable interest to scholarly collectors. Be warned that some jugs and tea caddies were reproduced by J. W. Senior and his sons George and James who worked at Hunslett near Leeds from c.1888. These wares were impressed LEEDS POTTERY, and the business continued until 1957.

Their reproductions are usually painted in enamel colours *over* the glaze and so should be easily distinguishable from the originals, whose colours are underglaze.

Further Reading

John and Griselda Lewis. *Pratt Ware: English and Scottish Relief Decorated and Underglaze Earthenware* 1780–1840. (Antique Collectors' Club, Woodbridge, 1984).

Prattware type plaque.

c.1800. 17.8 cm length   LR

£800

Prattware type plaque with Venus, Cupid and Bacchus.

c.1801. Impressed mark 'EC 1801'. 20 cm length   LR

£700.

Other classical subjects are known including the Judgement of Paris.

Prattware type plaque of a horse.

c.1800. Restored. 17 cm length   LR

£500; £800 if perfect

Staffordshire Prattware type toy plate with green trim painted in yellow, orange and brown enamels.

Late 18th century. Repaired rim piece. 13 cm length   AS

£480

Prattware type tea canister decorated with blue, green, yellow and brown underglaze colours.

c.1790. 16 cm height   BG

£375

Staffordshire Prattware type teapot.

c.1800. Restored. 12 cm height   JH

£680

Prattware type gothic cottage.

c.1790–1800. 15.2 cm height   LR

£550

Swansea Prattware type plate.

c.1800. Small rim chip restored. Impressed mark 'SWAN-SEA'. 16.2 cm diameter   JH

£285

5 STONEWARES

STONEWARE is fired at a very high temperature which vitrifies the silica in the body, giving it great strength. Some very fine stonewares are slightly translucent, the only exception to the rule that pottery is always opaque. Coarse brown stoneware is usually salt-glazed, but finer stonewares were smear-glazed or fully glazed. Dry-bodied wares are unglazed stonewares including basalt, cane ware and jasper wares. Ironstone or stone china is a feldspathic stoneware, which was glazed and decorated in the manner of ordinary earthenware (see chapter 10).

Although there has been a good deal of dispute about the earliest potter to manufacture stoneware in Britain, it is certain that John Dwight was making salt-glazed stonewares at Fulham in 1672. The earliest wares were imitations of German tavern wine bottles, imported into this country. These are known as Greybeards after the bearded faces with which they are frequently decorated or Bellarmines after Cardinal Bellarmine (1541–1621). The faces are believed to have been caricatures of the Cardinal, who was despised by Flemish Protestants.

During the 18th century a number of finer stonewares were developed. White salt-glazed stoneware is light and easily moulded and was suitable for tablewares. Dry-bodied stonewares such as basalt and jasper were mostly used for ornamental wares, and continue in production at Wedgwood today. White feldspathic stonewares developed in the 1780s are often very translucent and were used for tablewares and ornamental wares.

In the middle of the 19th century developments in slip-casting techniques led to the production of highly decorative smear-glazed relief-moulded stonewares, especially jugs (see chapter 23). From the 1870s Doulton and the Martin Brothers adapted stoneware to make huge original art pottery, extending the palette of the glazes which could withstand the high firing temperature (see chapter 13).

In the present century stoneware has been the preferred medium for many studio potters. Industrial potters have used stoneware for oven-to-tableware ranges which have been very successful during the past three decades.

BROWN STONEWARE

Brown stoneware is a buff-bodied stoneware, which until the 1830s was always salt-glazed. The discovery of an impermeable glaze in which pots could be dipped by William Powell at Bristol c.1835 led to a change in techniques over the following decades. However, many brown stoneware items continued to be salt-glazed.

The largest part of brown stoneware production was always devoted to utilitarian wares – bottles, baking dishes, foot warmers, fountains for barnyard fowl, water filters and from the late 1840s sewer pipes. Jugs and mugs for pubs were another large part of production. Teapots, coffee pots and other table wares for domestic use were also made. Utilitarian wares have little or no decoration, but other wares may have elaborate sprigging and/or incised decoration.

John Dwight first produced brown salt-glazed stoneware at Fulham, later developing fine white salt-glazed stoneware. The factory had nearly fallen into ruin by the middle of the 19th century, but its fortunes were revived by C. J. C. Bailey, who made architectural stonewares, working with prominent architects such as J. P. Seddon, and followed Doulton into art pottery production. In 1888 the firm passed to new ownership and has remained a centre of salt-glazed stoneware production well into the 20th century.

Lambeth came to the fore as the largest centre of brown salt-glazed stoneware production in the 19th century. There were many firms operating in the area in the middle of the century, but by 1900 most of these had been swallowed by Doulton (see below).

Brown salt-glazed stonewares were made at Nottingham throughout the 18th century. Today they are associated particularly with bear jugs, although these were also made elsewhere in the country. The industry declined at the end of the 18th century, losing out to the competition from Staffordshire and Derbyshire potters.

Derbyshire became a centre for the production of brown salt-glazed stonewares at the beginning of the 18th century and remained an important producer until the Second World War. Perhaps the best known firm is Joseph Bourne's Denby pottery. The Denby Pottery was established in 1809 and taken over by Joseph Bourne in 1812. The firm operated under the Bourne family ownership until 1961, and today continues as Denby Tableware Ltd.

In Scotland the wares were made at Prestonpans, Portobello and Port Dundas. Bristol was also an important centre in the 18th and 19th centuries, particularly after William Powell's invention of a new impervious glaze c.1835. Staffordshire produced similar wares along with many others during the 18th and 19th centuries. However, potteries in many other parts of Britain produced brown stoneware, mostly confined to utilitarian wares to meet local demand.

Further Reading

Graeme Cruickshank. *Scottish Saltglaze* (Scottish Pottery Studies, no. 2, Edinburgh, 1982).

Rhoda Edwards. *Lambeth Stoneware: The Woolley Collection including Doulton Ware and Products of Other British Potteries* (London Borough of Lambeth, 1973).

Dennis Haselgrove and John Murray. *John Dwight's Fulham Pottery, 1672–1978. A Collection of Documentary Sources* (Journal of Ceramic History, no. 11, Stoke-on-Trent City Museums, 1979).

Robin Hildyard, *Browne Muggs* (Victoria & Albert Museum, 1985).

Jonathan Horne. *A Catalogue of English Brown Stoneware from the 17th and 18th Centuries* (Jonathan Horne, 1985).

Jonathan Horne. *A Collection of Early English Pottery, Parts I–XII* (Jonathan Horne, 1982–92).

Adrian Oswald, R. J. C. Hildyard and R. G. Hughes. *English Brown Stoneware 1670–1900* (Faber & Faber, 1982)

18TH-CENTURY

London brown salt-glazed tankard with silver hallmarked mounts.

c.1711. 13 cm height   JH

£850

Brown salt-glazed stoneware tankard with silver mounts and sprigged decoration.

c.1750. 21.2 cm height   JH

£1,350

Staffordshire brown salt-glazed stoneware bear.

c.1770. 26 cm height   JH

£1,850

This bear is very unusual as salt-glazed bear-baiting jugs are usually white. The 'fur' was made by forcing small pieces of clay through a sieve. White or brown salt-glazed stoneware bears were made in Staffordshire, Chesterfield and Nottingham during the 18th century. An earthenware bear jug is illustrated on p. 132.

19TH-CENTURY

Brown salt-glazed stoneware coffee pot with sprigged decoration possibly Derbyshire.

c.1830–40. Lid chipped. 24 cm height with lid.   AD

£185

These pots were also made at Eccleshill in Yorkshire, but with differing sprigs and shape.

Brown salt-glazed stoneware sprigged jug.

c.1830. 10 cm height   HBW

£48

73

Uncommon Stephen Green brown salt-glazed stoneware relief-moulded jug.

c.1840. Moulded mark 'Stephen Green Lambeth' in wreath. 19 cm height   G

£285

Stephen Green potted at Lambeth c.1833–60, making fine quality brown salt-glazed stonewares. Several shapes of relief-moulded stoneware jugs have been noted (see p. 534 for a very fine commemorative of the wedding of Queen Victoria and Prince Albert).

DOULTON (LAMBETH) (1858–1956)

Having apprenticed at the Fulham Pottery, where he became a noted big ware thrower, John Doulton purchased the Vauxhall pottery in 1815. After John Watts, foreman and manager of the pottery, became Doulton's partner, they traded as Doulton & Watts (1820–58). In 1828 they moved their pottery to High Street, Lambeth.

After Watts's death, John Doulton carried on the business in partnership with his sons, John and Henry, under the style Doulton & Co. Henry Doulton (1820–97) was an inventive and innovative businessman. In 1846 he introduced the manufacture of stoneware pipes, which were soon in great demand for the thousands of miles of drains and sewers which were being laid all over Britain.

Today Doulton Lambeth is best remembered for the enormous range of art pottery, much of which was salt-glazed stoneware, which they produced from the late 1860s (see chapter 13). However, the pottery's utilitarian salt-glazed stonewares were always the more important part of their production.

Further Reading

Paul Atterbury and Louise Irvine, *The Doulton Story* (Royal Doulton Tablewares, Stoke-on-Trent, 1979).

Richard Dennis, *Doulton Stoneware Pottery 1870–1925* (Richard Dennis, 1971).

Rhoda Edwards, *Lambeth Stoneware. The Woolley Collection Including Doulton Ware and the Products of Other British Potters* (Borough of Lambeth, 1973).

Desmond Eyles. *The Doulton Lambeth Wares* (Hutchinson, 1975).

Edmund Gosse. *Sir Henry Doulton* (Hutchinson, 1970).

Doulton brown salt-glazed stoneware jug with sprigged decoration and slip-trailed inscription.

c.1902–14. Impressed lion, crown and seal mark; '2846'; 'No. 536'. 20 cm height   V

£55

Doulton brown salt-glazed stoneware three-handled tyg with greyhound handles.

c.1869–72. Oval mark 'DOULTON LAMBETH'. 10.8 cm height   G

£65

Unusual Doulton salt-glazed stoneware wall pocket with sgraffito decoration under brown and blue glazes.

c.1891–1910. Impressed 'DOULTON/LAMBETH/ENGLAND; '15SQ'. 10.5 cm height   WG

£40

Doulton brown salt-glazed stoneware jug with white sprigging. Impressed mark 'DOULTON/LAMBETH/ENGLAND'. 4.8 cm height   TA

£18

Doulton brown salt-glazed stoneware mug.

c.1905. Impressed mark 'DOULTONS/LIMITED/LAMBETH'. 13.5 cm height   TA

£12

Brown salt-glazed stoneware tankard with sprigged moulding, possibly Doulton.

Late 19th-century. 11 cm height   JM

£38

These sprigged patterns were also copied by the Port Dundas Pottery in Glasgow in the late 19th century and probably elsewhere.

WHITE SALT-GLAZED STONEWARES

Pure white salt-glazed stonewares first appeared in Staffordshire in the 1720s, and remained popular for eighty years, eventually being supplanted by cream-coloured earthenwares. The wares were fired to a high temperature which partly vitrified the body. When the kiln was at maximum temperature, salt was thrown into it. This vaporised and sealed the body with a thin, clear glaze, which did not obscure relief-moulded detail. Enamels, which began to be used in the late 1740s, required one or more additional firings at a lower temperature in a muffle kiln. Gilding, which required another firing, was also sometimes applied, but has frequently worn off over the years. Transfer-prints were also used for decoration.

These salt-glazed stonewares are some of the finest wares ever to be produced in Britain, and often have wonderfully intricate relief-moulding, which would be obscured by thicker lead glazes. A few items were slip-cast in moulds (from just before 1750), and modelled figures and groups were also produced, the most famous being the charming Pew Groups.

White salt-glazed stonewares are not marked, and attributions can only be made on the basis of archaeological evidence. The recent excavation at Fenton revealed that the white salt-glazed stonewares made by William Greatbatch were of the same sort known to have been made by many of his contemporaries. The wares were made not only in Staffordshire, but at Swansea, Bovey Tracey in Devon, Yorkshire and Liverpool.

Further Reading

David Barker. *William Greatbatch a Staffordshire Potter* (Jonathan Horne, 1991).

David Barker and Pat Halfpenny. *Unearthing Staffordshire* (Stoke-on-Trent City Museum & Art Gallery, 1990).

Jonathan Horne, *A Collection of Early English Pottery*, Parts I–XII (Jonathan Horne, 1982–92).

T. A. Lockett and P. A. Halfpenny, eds. *Stonewares & Stone Chinas of Northern England to 1851* (Stoke-on-Trent City Museum & Art Gallery, 1982).

Arnold R. Mountford. *The Illustrated Guide to Staffordshire Salt-glazed Stoneware* (Barrie & Jenkins, 1971).

Ross E. Taggart. *The Frank P. and Harriet C. Burnap Collection of English Pottery in the William Rockhill Nelson Gallery*, revised and enlarged edition (Nelson Gallery/Atkins Museum, Kansas City, Missouri, 1967).

Peter Walton. *Creamware and Other English Pottery at Temple Newsam House Leeds* (Manningham Press, 1976).

Staffordshire press-moulded white salt-glazed stoneware plate.

c.1760. 20 cm diameter   V

£170

Staffordshire press-moulded white salt-glazed stoneware dish.

c.1750–70. Firing crack and grey kiln damage. 30 cm diameter   V

£350

Barker & Halfpenny illustrate a plate identical to this one, alongside a cream-coloured earthenware example with a tortoiseshell glaze. The shape is also known in porcelain.

One of a pair of rare white salt-glazed stoneware drainers.

c.1750. 27 cm length   AS

£1,800 the pair.

Drainers are uncommon, compared to dishes and plates. These would originally have had stands to catch the fluids (an example with stand is illustrated in Lockett & Halfpenny). This is an uncommon shape and the fact that the pair have been kept together over the years makes them particularly desirable. The flower-shaped feet are an attractive finishing touch.

Reverse.

Very rare slip-cast white salt-glazed stoneware coffee cup.

c.1750. 7 cm height   AS

£950

There are other examples of slip-cast white salt-glazed stoneware cups in the collection at Temple Newsam House, Leeds.

White slip-cast salt-glazed stoneware sauceboat.

c.1760. Bleached cracks. 17 cm length   AS

£850

White slip-cast salt-glazed stoneware sauceboat.

c.1760. Repaired rim chip. 22 cm length   AS

£1,100

Note the indentations visible on the interior of the back side. These are typical of slip-cast, as opposed to press-moulded pots. The feet are imitative of rococo silver of a slightly earlier period.

White slip-cast salt-glazed stoneware coffee pot with notched animal head spout and pecten pattern.

c.1750. Crack in lid and chips to base. 23 cm height   JH

£5,500

The pecten, or scallop shell, was a popular element of rococo design, found frequently on Staffordshire white salt-glazed stonewares of the period (many examples are illustrated in Mountford). The simple strap handle with a pinched terminal is a charming contrast to the more sophisticated rococo relief-moulding. It was very difficult to slip-cast handles.

White salt-glazed stoneware thrown teapot with moulded spout and handle and bands of shredded clay.

c.1750. 13 cm height   JH

£3,850

An identical teapot with unfired enamel colours and the remains of gilding is illustrated in Robin Emmerson's *British Teapots & Tea Drinking* (HMSO, 1992). The teapot shown here may have been gilded originally, but no traces of this now remain.

White salt-glazed stoneware leaf dish with three feet.

c.1765. Small firing crack. 15.5 cm length JH

£1,350

White salt-glazed stoneware bottle with sprigged decoration.

c.1750. 23 cm height AS

£1,100

White salt-glazed stoneware sauceboat painted in polychrome enamels.

c.1765. 20 cm length AS

£1,600

White salt-glazed stoneware vase (bottle?) inscribed 'IHS' (the Greek letters symbolising the name of Jesus) painted in polychrome enamels and gilded.

c.1765. Repaired chip and crack. 18.5 cm height AS

£5,000

Staffordshire white salt-glazed stoneware jug with chinoiserie pattern painted in polychrome enamels.

c.1760. Minor repair to spout. 13.5 cm height   AS

£1,400

A teapot with this pattern is illustrated in Mountford.

Staffordshire white salt-glazed stoneware teapot with 'Peony' pattern in polychrome enamels of red, green, and yellow on blue enamel background, crabstock handle and spout.

c.1760. Finial restored. 10.8 cm height   LR

£1,000.

Similar teapots with peonies painted on a blue enamel ground are illustrated in Mountford, Taggart and Walton, an example with a green ground is illustrated in Horne XII.

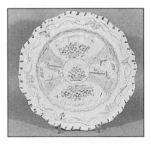

White salt-glazed stoneware plate with chinoiserie panels of fishermen and baskets of flowers painted in red and green enamels, possibly Dutch decorated.

c.1770. 23.5 cm diameter   BG

£795

White salt-glazed teapot with European style pattern and a chinoiserie landscape painted in red enamels and replacement silver spout.

c.1760. 12.3 cm height   JH

£1,250

The replacement silver spout is a part of the history of the piece and illustrates how highly their owners valued these wares. This style of painting is usually found on creamware.

Reverse.

Staffordshire white salt-glazed stoneware plate with orange on-glaze transfer-print from Aesop's Fables.

c.1760. Small rim chip. 21.5 cm diameter   AS

£2,600

Although the finely pitted surface of salt-glazed stoneware is not ideal for transfer-printing, it seems that some of the earliest on-glaze transfer-prints were used on this body. Mountford suggests that these prints may pre-date those of Sadler & Green, who are generally credited as the inventors of ceramic printing in 1756. One John Brooks, an Irish engraver residing in Birmingham, applied for a patent for printing on 'stone and earthenware' in 1754.

Sadler & Green printed a large series (forty-five subjects recorded) of Aesop's Fables tin-glazed tiles, and examples printed on Wedgwood creamware are also known. In the 19th century, Spode also printed an Aesop's Fables series in underglaze blue.

White salt-glazed stoneware figure, hollow press-moulded.

c.1750. Neck repaired. 10 cm height   JH

£1,450

All white salt-glazed stoneware figures are rare, but this figure is exceptional for the clarity of detail.

81

Scratch blue is incised decoration highlighted with powdered cobalt oxide.

Staffordshire scratch blue salt-glazed stoneware tankard.

c.1765. Crack repaired. 16 cm height   JH

£1,650

Staffordshire scratch blue salt-glazed stoneware puzzle jug.

c.1760. Crack in base and repair to spout. 17.3 cm height
JH

£2,200

WHITE FELDSPATHIC STONEWARE

White feldspathic stoneware is a fine-grained white stoneware developed c.1780. Although these wares are often referred to as Castleford stonewares, the firm of David Dunderdale at Castleford, Yorkshire (c.1790–1820) was only one of many manufacturers who made them. The wares are usually slip-cast as the body allowed very crisp moulding.

These stonewares are an exception to the rule that pottery is opaque and porcelain translucent, as some of them are more translucent than bone china. Indeed, Geoffrey Godden has suggested 'There seems to be a good case for calling such wares porcelain or china, and some glazed examples can be mistaken for standard porcelains.' Some are smear-glazed and some are unglazed. The feldspar in the body contributed to the whiteness and transparency of the body. The wares are sometimes enamelled, but usually this is confined to a few simple lines which would not detract from the moulded design.

Further Reading

Geoffrey Godden. *Encyclopaedia of British Porcelain Manufacturers* (Barrie & Jenkins, 1988).
Griselda Lewis. A *Collector's History of English Pottery*, 3rd edn revised (Antique Collectors' Club, Woodbridge, 1985).
T. A. Lockett and P. A. Halfpenny, eds. *Stonewares and Stone chinas of Northern England to 1851* (Stoke-on-Trent City Museum & Art Gallery, 1982).
Diana Roussel. *The Castleford Pottery 1790–1821* (Wakefield Historical Publications, 1982).

Castleford type smear-glazed stoneware jug painted in polychrome enamels.

c.1800. Star crack. 18 cm height at spout   AD

£250

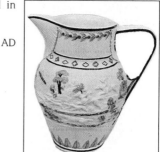

Feldspathic smear-glazed stoneware jug with blue sprigged decoration and blue enamelling.

c.1800. Star crack to base. Painted mark on base 'P*B'. 14.5 cm height   WG

£120 (£180 if perfect)

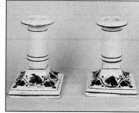

Pair of Castleford type stoneware candlesticks painted in mauve enamels.

c.1800. 11 cm height   D

£300

Castleford type stoneware candlesticks painted in polychrome enamels.

c.1800. 19 cm height   AD

£520

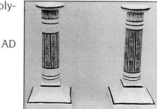

TURNER'S BODY

The Turner family potted at Lane End, Longton for many years. Their products were fine quality earthenwares, stonewares and some porcelains. Turner's body is a semi-porcelain which was relief-decorated, and sometimes mounted in silver. The pots illustrated below are Turner products, but other firms made similar wares. The names and styles under which they operated are as follows:

John Turner c.1762–87
William & John Turner c.1787–1803

Turner, Glover & Simpson c.1804–6
William Turner (& Co.) c.1807–30 (also at Fenton)

Further Reading

Bevis Hillier, *Master Potters of the Industrial Revolution. The Turners of Lane End* (Cory, Adams & Mackay, 1965).

Turner feldspathic stoneware tankard with brown-glazed rim and handle, engine-turned foot and rim.

c.1800. Slight repair. Impressed mark 'TURNER'. 17.7 cm height   HBW

£225

This tankard has an unusual relief-moulded scene of a fox-hunter holding the fox aloft, surrounded by the hounds.

Feldspathic stoneware mug with sprigged decoration of a Bacchanalian scene, possibly Turner.

c.1800. 8.5 cm height   HBW

£90

A jug with this sprigging impressed Turner is illustrated in Lockett & Halfpenny. However, it is not possible to make attributions on the basis of sprigs alone.

DRY-BODIED STONEWARES

Dry-bodied or unglazed stonewares include red stonewares, basalt, cane ware and jasper. The wares were most often decorated with relief-moulding, engine turning or applied moulded reliefs (sprigging).

Further Reading

David Barker. *William Greatbatch, a Staffordshire Potter* (Jonathan Horne, 1991).
David Barker and Pat Halfpenny. *Unearthing Staffordshire* (Stoke-on-Trent City Museum and Art Gallery, 1990).
T. A. Lockett and P. A. Halfpenny. *Stonewares and stone chinas of Northern England to 1851* (City Museum and Art Gallery, Stoke-on-Trent, 1982).
Philip Miller and Michael Berthoud. *An Anthology of British Teapots* (Micawber Publications, Broseley, 1985).

RED STONEWARES

Red stonewares from Yi-hsing, China were exported to Europe in the 17th century. In the 1670s, two Dutch silversmiths, the brothers Elers, began to make imitations of these wares in Staffordshire, slip-cast in plaster moulds and turned upon a lathe. The extreme delicacy of these wares reflects the Elers' experience as silversmiths.

After this period red stoneware was not made in England until the 1760s when the Staffordshire potters produced mostly tea and coffee wares, often with elaborate relief-moulding and/or sprigged decoration. Some of these have impressed pseudo-Chinese seal marks. The 1760s also saw the advent of neo-classical designs which were well suited to red stonewares, and Josiah Wedgwood introduced a red stoneware marketed as Rosso Antico (referring to Roman redwares, sometimes known as Samian ware). Black sprigging was often used on these later pots.

Red stoneware teapot with sprigged decoration of birds and oriental figures.

c.1765. Some damage to sprigging. 15 cm height   BG

£475

A punch pot with a similar central sprig is illustrated in Lockett & Halfpenny.

Reverse.

A number of red stonewares are now attributed to Thomas Barker on the basis of excavations at the Foley Pottery, Fenton.

Thomas Barker, Foley Pottery, Staffordshire red stoneware teapot.

c.1765. Spout and chip restored. 11 cm height   JH

£685

This teapot can be dated by the appearance of George III among the sprigged figures.

Reverse.

85

Thomas Barker, Foley Pottery, Staffordshire red stoneware coffee pot.

c.1770, 18.5 cm height   JH

£660

A very similar coffee pot is illustrated in Barker & Halfpenny.

BASALT

Basalt, which takes its name from the mineral basalt, is a black vitreous stoneware first refined by Josiah Wedgwood during the 1760s. 'Egyptian black' was originally the cruder ware which had been made in Staffordshire previously but the term continued in use for the finer body. The biscuit body is stained with iron oxide and manganese oxide, and is left unglazed (except for interiors of vessels).

Basalt was an ideal medium for neo-classical designs. The shapes are often simple, with applied moulded or sprigged decoration. Many other potters made basalt in the late 18th century, but as they did not often mark their wares, they are difficult to attribute.

During the Victorian era, Egyptian black was used for relief-moulded useful wares, especially teapots. It was said that the black body was ideal for showing off the lily whiteness of the hostess's hands!

Further Reading

M. H. Grant. *Makers of Black Basalt* (W. Blackwood & Sons, 1910, new edition Holland Press, 1967). The only book devoted entirely to basalt is rare and expensive. Lockett & Halfpenny give a good general synopsis and illustrate a number of fine examples, as do several of the general works on English pottery.

Wedgwood (1759 to the present day)

Josiah Wedgwood left Thomas Whieldon's pottery to establish his own pottery at Burslem in 1759. In 1769 he entered a partnership with Thomas Bentley and opened a new factory named Etruria. Wedgwood made a wide variety of wares typical of Staffordshire potters of the period, but through tireless experimentation, he improved upon the existing formulas and decorating techniques. None the less, his name would not have reached pre-eminence in the pottery world, and even in the world at large, were it not for his brilliance in marketing his wares.

Initially Josiah Wedgwood called his basalt Etruscan Ware, and it was first called 'Black Basalte' in the Wedgwood Ornamental Pattern Book of 1773. Wedgwood still makes basalt wares today, as the body lends itself to the sleek lines of modern design.

The Wedgwood Museum at the Wedgwood factory at Barlaston has many fine pieces of basalt, as does the Stoke-on-Trent City Museum & Art Gallery. The Wedgwood Society meets regularly in London, and publishes *Proceedings of the Wedgwood Society*. The membership secretary is Mrs Kathy Niblett, c/o Department of Ceramics, City Museum & Art Gallery, Stoke-on-Trent, Staffordshire ST1 3DW.

Further Reading

Wolf Mankowitz. *Wedgwood* (Spring Books, 1966).
Robin Reilly. *Wedgwood*, 2 vols (Macmillan, 1989).
Robin Reilly and George Savage. *The Dictionary of Wedgwood* (Antique Collectors' Club, Woodbridge, 1980).

Wedgwood basalt kettle with overhead handle, sibyl finial and stand.

c.1770–80. Impressed mark 'Wedgwood'; 'M'; '5'. 28 cm height with stand including handle.   AD

£850

These kettles may have been intended for punch as well as tea. A smaller basalt tea kettle in a similar shape with the same handle and sibyl finial, but with sprigged decoration is illustrated in Lockett & Halfpenny. Another impressed 'Wedgwood and Bentley' is illustrated in Miller and Mankowitz.

Wedgwood basalt cache-pot with engine-turned decoration.

c.19th century. Impressed mark 'WEDGWOOD'. 10 cm height   AD

£85

Wedgwood basalt cream jug with engine-turned vertical bands and glazed interior.

c.1810. Impressed mark 'WEDGWOOD'. Foot rim chip. 9 cm height at spout.   AD

£85

Wedgwood basalt bowl with sprigged decoration.

c.19th century. Impressed mark 'WEDGWOOD/36'. 11 cm diameter   HBW

£45

Other Manufacturers

Oblong moulded basalt sucrier, possibly Leeds.

c.1820. 14.5 cm height   HBW

£90

Miller & Berthoud illustrate two basalt teapots in this shape, one of which is impressed 'HARTLEY GREENS & CO.' Another is illustrated in Joseph R. and Frank Kidson's *Historical Notes of the Leeds Old Pottery* (W. R. Publishers and The Connoisseur, 1970, first published by J. R. Kidson, Leeds, 1892).

CANE WARE

Cane or bamboo ware is an unglazed buff-coloured stoneware. it had been generally accepted that the ware was introduced first by Wedgwood. However, wasters from the excavation at Fenton Vivian have shown that William Greatbatch (see p. 47) was producing cane ware before his bankruptcy in 1782. Wedgwood had been experimenting with cane ware or *Fawn colour* from 1771, but the ware, which was porous and stained easily, was not perfected until the mid 1780s. Many manufacturers were soon producing a wide variety of ornamental and useful wares in the cane body, and some cane ware continued to be produced throughout the 19th century.

Cane ware is usually relief-moulded, often simulating canes of bamboo from which it takes its name, and sometimes embellished with coloured enamels. During the flour shortage of the Napoleonic Wars, a coarser caneware simulating crust was used for game pie dishes and pastry ware.

Very rare Neale & Co. cane ware relief-moulded sucrier highlighted with green enamel.

c.1790. Impressed marks on base; 'NEALE & CO.'; '31'; and inside lid incised 'N'. 13 cm length excluding handles   G

£220

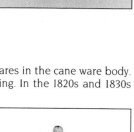

Neale & Co. (1778–91) made ornamental cane wares as well as tablewares.

Wedgwood made a wide variety of ornamental and useful wares in the cane ware body. The wares were sometimes decorated with coloured sprigging. In the 1820s and 1830s smear glazed caneware was produced.

Wedgwood cane ware *Roman Covered Jug* and saucer with grey-blue sprigged acanthus leaf decoration.

c.1810. Impressed mark 'WEDGWOOD'. 19 cm height excluding knop.   D

£950

A milk jug with identical sprigging, but in brown, is illustrated in Mankowitz. The shape (number 650) remained in production for many years and appears in *The Wedgwood 1880 Illustrated Catalogue of Shapes* (reprinted by the Wedgwood Society, 1971).

Wedgwood cane ware honey pot with smear glaze.

c.1820s–30s. Impressed mark 'WEDGWOOD'. 11 cm height   D

£175

The shape (number 340) appears in the Wedgwood shape book for 1817 (reproduced by Mankowitz).

JASPER

Jasper is a fine unglazed stoneware invented by Josiah Wedgwood in 1774. The body is stained, most often blue, but sometimes green, black, pink, and more rarely lavender, yellow or red. The jaspers produced by manufacturers other than Wedgwood were usually blue, as colours produced by metallic oxides other than cobalt were difficult at the high temperatures needed to fire stoneware and required a good deal of experimentation. Originally the body was blue-stained throughout, but when the cost of cobalt rose, white jasper wares were dipped in stained jasper slip. In later years there was a return to the solid jasper.

Jasper is usually decorated with white jasper sprigging, but a number of contrasting colours may be used. The best sprigging was carefully undercut, creating areas so thin that they are translucent. Later jasper wares have little or none of this hand-finishing, which requires immense skill.

Although the ware is most closely associated with Wedgwood, who have produced the ware continuously to the present day, many other potters have produced it.

Wedgwood (1759 to the present day)

Josiah Wedgwood was experimenting with his 'porcelain bisket' as early as 1771. The ware was in limited production by early 1775 and was christened Jasper in November of that year. Jasper dip was introduced in 1778 and the solid blue body was not reintroduced until 1854. The jasper sprigged decoration on jasper is made in shallow moulds. Some of the classical subjects remain popular today, but modern sprigging has less hand-finishing, appearing thick and solid.

The first jasper wares were medallions and plaques in the style of cameos, as sprigged decoration on rounded surfaces tended to crack when fired. These were made in great quantities, for use in jewellery and furnishings. Most jasper wares have always been ornamental wares, but small tea and coffee wares were made. After the introduction of *pâte-sur-pâte*, some jasper sprigged decoration was augmented with slip-painting.

Jasper has been produced continuously at Wedgwood since its introduction. It has always been expensive to produce and its market has waxed and waned with economic booms and declines. During the late 19th and early 20th century biscuit barrels, often with silver mounts, were popular. During the second half of the 20th century a wide range of trinket boxes, small vases, ashtrays, miniatures and other small items have been very popular, especially in the United States. Some of these have been in contemporary styles, but the classical shapes and sprigging have remained popular. These later wares have a dry chalky feel and the sprigging is quite thick compared with earlier examples. A few very expensive but more finely finished limited editions have also been produced in recent years.

Although we usually associate jasper with blue, many other colours have been produced by Wedgwood over the years. There may be variations in the colours listed below, created by mixing varying amounts of the metallic oxides with the white body and by accidental variations in temperature or atmospheric conditions in the kiln.

Black dip 1778–1854.
Black solid was also made, most notably for a chess set modelled by Arnold Machin in 1939 (also produced in blue or white jasper, and other bodies). It was usually only used for decoration.

Blue solid 1775–7; 1854 to the present day.
Blue dip from c.1778.
Dark blue discontinued 1939.
Pale blue solid and *dip* discontinued late 18th century; reintroduced in 1949.
Royal blue solid introduced for the coronation of Queen Elizabeth II, 1953.
Portland blue solid introduced 1972.
Turquoise dip 1875–c.1885 is not of very high quality, but has rarity value.

Brown dip trial pieces c.1778 and some medallions in the early 19th century.
Brown solid for decoration late 18th and early 19th century.

Crimson dip 1910; 1925–32. Due to the limited period of production, these wares are quite rare and very collectable. The crimson colour tended to bleed into the white sprigging, and production was discontinued.

Terracotta solid for decoration from c.1775. and with black or white reliefs 1957–9.
Pink solid produced in the 1980s.

Sage green solid 1775–8; reintroduced 1957.
Sage green dip 1778–1854.
Dysart green dip was specially developed for plaques used in the architect Halsey Ricardo's redecoration of Lord Dysart's house at Buckminster Park, c.1882.
Dark olive green dip 1910–29, typical of the 'tasteful' colours popular during the Edwardian era. The colour tended to stain the white sprigging. Wedgwood discontinued this colour with the advent of the Jazz Age when bright, clear colours became fashionable.

Grey dip 1778–1854, rare.
Grey solid occasionally used for decoration after c.1785. Trials made in 1960, but not put into production.

Lilac dip 1778–1854, rare.
Lilac solid for decoration 1778–1854, rare. In full production 1960–2 and in the early 1980s, since discontinued.
Primrose solid introduced 1976 with white or terracotta reliefs.
Yellow/buff solid with black ornament 1929–33, attractive and rare.
Yellow/buff dip used rarely from 1778; for portraits c.1878–90.

White solid is the body most often used for sprigged decoration. It is also used as a base for the coloured dips. As a body it was used from 1775; from 1785 to c.1845 with as many as three different coloured reliefs. This style of decoration was reintroduced in 1885. Trials of white jasper with white reliefs were made in 1961.

Wedgwood jasper is usually impressed 'WEDGWOOD'. For some reason the three-letter date code used 1860–1929 is not often found on jasper pieces of that period. Modern pieces will be impressed 'MADE IN ENGLAND', and the last two numbers of the year (e.g. 83 for 1983) usually appear.

The Wedgwood Museum at the Wedgwood factory at Barlaston has many fine pieces of Jasper as does the Stoke-on-Trent City Museum & Art Gallery. The Wedgwood Society meets regularly in London, and publishes *Proceedings of the Wedgwood Society*. The membership secretary is Mrs Kathy Niblett, c/o Department of Ceramics, City Museum and Art Gallery, Stoke-on-Trent, Staffordshire ST1 3DW.

Further Reading

David Bindman, ed. *John Flaxman* (Thames & Hudson, 1979).
The Book of Wedgwood Bas-reliefs (Josiah Wedgwood & Sons Ltd, Barlaston, 1982).
Wolf Mankowitz. *Wedgwood* (Spring Books, 1966).
Robin Reilly. *Wedgwood*, 2 vols (Macmillan, 1989).
Robin Reilly and George Savage. *The Dictionary of Wedgwood* (Antique Collectors' Club, Woodbridge, 1980).
The Wedgwood Illustrated Catalogue of Ornamental Shapes 1878 (reprinted by the Wedgwood Society, 1984).

Wedgwood solid white jasper vase decorated with black jasper sprigged 'Greek Key' border and acanthus leaves, with flower holder insert.

c.1815. 'WEDGWOOD' impressed. 10 cm height   AD

£250

Wedgwood sage green dip jasper mug decorated with white jasper sprigging.

c.1815. Impressed 'WEDGWOOD'. 8 cm height   HBW

£300

Wedgwood dark blue dip jasper vase decorated with white jasper sprigging of a Sacrifice scene.

c.1850. Lid missing. 17 cm height   AD

£175

Wedgwood blue dip jasper garden pot decorated with white jasper sprigging of the Muses.

c.1878. Impressed 'WEDGWOOD'. Very slightly damage to sprigging. 17 cm height   JJB

£135

This garden pot appears in the Wedgwood shape book of 1878. The figure on the left is Euterpe and that on the right is Thalia, from the series of Muses originally modelled by John Flaxman c.1775.

Pair of Wedgwood dark blue jasper *Octagon* candlesticks decorated with white jasper sprigging.

c.1878. Impressed mark 'WEDGWOOD/ENGLAND'. 17.7 cm height   TA

£65

One of these candlesticks appears in the Wedgwood shape book of 1878.

Black dip jasper biscuit barrel decorated with white jasper sprigging.

c.1885. Worn silver plated rim, handle and lid. Impressed 'WEDGWOOD'. 13.2 cm height excluding knop.   G

£95

Wedgwood solid pale blue jasper vase with flower holder decorated with a sacrifice scene in white jasper sprigging.

c.1920. Impressed marks 'MADE IN ENGLAND WEDG-WOOD'; 'X 65 HR'. 16.5 cm height   G

£68

Other Manufacturers

Superb Turner style blue dip (over a dark coloured body) jasper teapot.

c.1800. Minute chips to base. 10 cm height excluding knop.   G

£450

John Turner invented his jasper independently of Wedgwood. The colour is a slate blue and the body appears more vitreous (glassy) than that of Turner's contemporaries. Later a bright peacock blue was most often employed. No examples of Turner jaspers in colours other than blue are recorded. The classical reliefs were copied from Wedgwood designs. See Bevis Hillier, *Master Potters of the Industrial Revolution. The Turners of Lane End* (Cory, Adams & Mackay, 1965).

One of a pair of Spode violet baskets with dry white body, covered with blue dip, blue and white sprigged decoration.

c.1810–20. 10.5 cm diameter   D

£250 the pair

Spode's jasper are nearly always blue dip. Solid blue has been recorded, but is extremely rare.

Spode blue jasper dip jug with white sprigging with straining holes inside spout.

c.1815–25. Some minor damage to sprigging. Impressed mark 'SPODE'. 14 cm height   JM

£145

Two William Adams vases and a covered bowl in blue dip jasper with sprigged white jasper decoration, including a crest of Worthing.

c.1900. Impressed marks 'ADAMS/ESTBD 1657/TUNSTALL/ ENGLAND. Left to right: vase 15 cm height, £25; vase 10 cm height, £25; bowl 8.5 cm height, £35   GCC

This mark was used on Adams jasper from 1896.

OTHER STONEWARES

Dudson brown stoneware jug with rope handle, sprigged 'Ribbon and Daisy' border and classical figures.

c.1870. Incised mark 1302; impressed mark 12 (size). 19 cm height   G

£48

Dudson called both their dry-bodied and glazed fine-grained stonewares Jasper Ware, although the term usually refers to dry-bodied wares. The glaze on these wares was brushed on, and brush marks can often be seen in the glaze. Incised numbers usually appear on Jasper Wares from the mid 1840s to 1882. Dudson continued production of these wares well into the 20th century. For more about Dudson see p. 502.

Low 'Round Egyptian' shape stoneware cream jug with sprigged decoration.

c.1820. Impressed mark 'STONE 5'. 3 cm height excluding handle   V

£95

A Wedgwood stoneware teapot in this shape is illustrated in Miller & Berthoud, *An Anthology of British Teapots*. Spode also made this shape, but the handles on recorded and illustrated examples are slightly different.

Wedgwood stoneware mug with sprigged decoration.

c.19th century. Impressed mark 'WEDGWOOD'. 8.5 cm height   HBW

£95

Stoneware mug with blue enamelled ground, sprigged decoration and engine-turned base.

c.1810. 11 cm height   RS

£48

These hunting scenes are very common.

Rare Herculaneum stoneware mug, with sprigged decoration and gilded rim.

c.1805. Tiny crack. Impressed mark 'HERCULANEUM 14'. 13 cm height   D

£375

Rare Neale jug in buff stoneware with sprigged decoration and brown neck and handle.

c.1790. Silver lid. Impressed mark 'NEALE & Co.'. 18 cm height   G

£320

Sprigged stoneware jug with chocolate brown enamel ground.

c.1801–7. 9.6 cm height   JM

£60

A jug with identical sprigging impressed 'WILSON' is illustrated in Lockett & Halfpenny but attribution cannot be made on sprigging alone. David Wilson potted at Hanley 1801–7.

Brown tinted smear-glazed stoneware jug with white sprigging probably by William Ridgway.

c.1830s. 10 cm height   JM

£68

This design is William Ridgway's number 36. The jug usually has an applied pad with the number on the base.

6 GREEN-GLAZED EARTHENWARE

G REEN glazes were used in Britain on the simple pottery of the Tudor era, and later on salt-glazed stonewares. These are extremely rare and are only likely to be found through specialist dealers. It was the Staffordshire potters of the mid 18th century who first successfully developed a lead glaze coloured with copper oxides for their lightweight but sturdy creamware bodies. In some cases the green glaze was used in combination with other colours, resulting in cauliflower ware, pineapple ware and melon ware (see p. 63).

In the later 18th and early 19th century, green-glazed wares, especially dessert wares, continued to be popular. Most Staffordshire earthenware manufacturers included green glaze in their repertoire. Similar wares were also made in Wales, particularly by Baker, Bevans & Irwin, in Yorkshire and in Scotland.

There seems to have been something of a lull in production between about 1820 and 1840, but thereafter, for the first fifty years of Queen Victoria's reign, the wares became immensely popular. Nearly every major Staffordshire manufacturer produced them, and they were a staple of many smaller firms.

Among the many unmarked Victorian dessert wares are several patterns which are very plentiful. The 'Leaf and Tendril' pattern is the most commonly found, but no marked example has ever been recorded.

Green-glazed relief-moulded earthenware 'Leaf and Tendril' pattern dessert plate.

c.1860. Chips to rim. 22 cm diameter   AF

£8

Plates in this pattern are seldom as crisply moulded as this one. An excellent example in perfect condition would cost about £12–15.

Also very commonly found is the 'Strawberry' pattern. Wedgwood made it with majolica glazes, but no green-glazed Wedgwood examples have been recorded.

Thomas Till & Sons green-glazed relief-moulded earthenware 'Strawberry' pattern dessert service dish.

c.1865. Rubbing to raised surfaces. Impressed oval mark 'TILL & SONS/BURSLEM'. 24 cm length   AF

£15

The Thomas Till examples are always very crisply moulded, whereas most examples will be poorly moulded and blurred in appearance. Unmarked dessert plates are more usually priced at £10–12.

The 'Leafage' pattern is also very common, with some examples finely potted and some crudely potted. The only marked examples recorded were made by Copeland or at Clairfontaines in France. The pattern was also made by several other British manufacturers, but these are always heavy, poorly modelled and blurred in appearance. I have illustrated a French example here, as they are often mistakenly attributed to English factories.

Clairfontaines green-glazed relief-moulded earthenware 'Leafage' pattern dessert plate.

c.1870. Impressed anchor with RS. 19.5 cm diameter   AF

£12

Green-glazed wares by Rigal & Sanejonaud, at Clairfontaines, Haute-Saône, France must have been imported abundantly into Britain, for they are very common. They may sometimes be found with the addition of 'Medaille d'or 1878' impressed around the anchor mark. This is the most common pattern, but several others have been recorded.

The vast majority of green-glazed wares are unmarked. Even the large manufacturers sometimes only marked one piece in a dessert service. Marked pieces are always more desirable. For the beginner, the first thing to look for is quality. Early pieces are light in weight and the relief-moulding will be very crisp and clear.

The glazes vary greatly in colour from dark olive to emerald to blue-green. A good quality glaze will be thick and glossy, pooling in the recesses of the moulding, without obscuring detail. Genuine 18th and 19th-century glazes have an iridescence which does not occur on 20th-century copies.

It should be pointed out that wares made by Wedgwood today are not copies or reproductions, as they have been made continuously for more than 200 years. Reproductions of Victorian patterns *are* being made in Portugal. In one case the plate by Ridgway & Abington (see Other Manufacturers below) has been closely copied, possibly from an original mould. The difference between these reproductions and the originals is obvious to the more experienced collector. It would be wise for the novice to seek out some reproductions in a large department store or china shop and examine them closely. Bring along an older plate for comparison. Note the differences in weight, colour, texture of glaze and crispness of moulding.

Dessert plates are by far the most common green-glazed wares, followed by dessert service dishes (usually with one or two handles) and comports. A document in the Minton Archives c.1854 listed the pieces of a twenty-seven piece earthenware dessert service as including a dessert centre, a pair of high comports, a pair of low comports, a cream bowl and stand, a basket and stand and eighteen dessert plates. However, this would have been the most expensive service, and items such as baskets or sauce tureens were not included in smaller, cheaper dessert services.

DAVENPORT
(1794–1887)

The recorded Davenport green-glazed wares date from the 1830–50 period. They probably made these wares in their early years, but as they were not marked, few early Davenport earthenwares have been identified. It has been conjectured that the '56' which appears on the reverse of the two Davenport examples shown below is a date code, but the frequency with which certain numbers appear has thrown doubt on this theory.

Further Reading

Terence A. Lockett. *Davenport Pottery and Porcelain, 1794–1887* (David & Charles, Newton Abbot, 1972).

Terence A. Lockett and Geoffrey A. Godden. *Davenport China, Earthenware, Glass* (Barrie & Jenkins, 1989).

Davenport green-glazed relief-moulded earthenware nasturtium pattern dessert service dish.

c.1845. Impressed anchor mark 'Davenport' with '56'. 29 cm length   AF

£35

Davenport made several patterns of green-glazed dessert wares. The nasturtium design is uncommon, although an unmarked version by another manufacturer may be found more frequently. Lockett & Godden illustrate two other Davenport green-glazed patterns.

Davenport green-glazed relief-moulded earthenware dessert service dish.

c.1860. Impressed anchor mark 'Davenport' with '56'. 29.3 cm length   AF

£35

This pattern is common, although dessert plates are more frequently found than dessert service dishes.

MINTON
(c.1796 to the present day)

Green-glazed wares are included in Minton stock accounts 1810–13, but these wares were unmarked and no patterns have been firmly attributed.

Minton made a great deal of green-glazed dessert ware during the Victorian period, but only the two patterns shown here are commonly found. A few other patterns have been recorded, but are rare.

Minton used a wide range of green glazes. Some are very blue, some very yellow and some a pure emerald. In the Minton Archive there are a number of different recipes for 'green glaze for dessert ware'.

Further Reading

Paul Atterbury and Maureen Batkin. *The Dictionary of Minton* (Antique Collectors' Club, Woodbridge, 1990).

Minton green-glazed relief-moulded earthenware *Leafage Embossed* pattern dessert service dish.

c.1848. Impressed date cypher for 1848. 24 cm length   AF

£18

This is one of the two common Minton shapes used for green-glazed ware.

Minton green-glazed relief-moulded earthenware *Wicker* pattern dessert comport.

c.1866. Impressed marks 'MINTON/BB'; date cypher for 1866. 11.5 cm height   AF

£35

The *Wicker* pattern was registered in 1860. It was produced in other bodies, and with a variety of different decorations. The mark BB stands for Best Body.

WEDGWOOD
(1759 to the present day)

Josiah Wedgwood devoted much effort to developing his famous green glaze, and green-glazed wares were among the first to be produced at Wedgwood's Etruria factory in 1759. They proved so successful that he was soon shipping them all over the world. The Wedgwood factory has produced green-glazed wares continuously to the present day. Although some shapes have remained more or less consistent for nearly two centuries, there is no excuse for confusing the early wares from the late. Most Wedgwood is well marked, and since 1860 impressed date codes have been employed. The earliest pieces are lighter in weight, and often more crisply moulded than the Victorian wares. During the 20th century the reduction of lead in the glazes has resulted in a glaze which appears weak and watery in comparison to earlier examples.

19th century Wedgwood green-glazed relief-moulded dessert patterns are nearly all plentiful. Nevertheless, they are the most expensive Victorian green-glazed wares, because Wedgwood of all descriptions is so popular with collectors. Wedgwood marked nearly all their wares, so only pieces marked Wedgwood should be assumed to be so.

Further Reading

Maureen Batkin. *Wedgwood Ceramics, 1846–1959* (Richard Dennis, 1982).
The *Wedgwood Illustrated Catalogue of Ornamental Shapes* 1878 (reprinted by the Wedgwood Society, 1984).
The *Wedgwood 1880 Illustrated Catalogue of Shapes* (reprinted by the Wedgwood Society, 1971).

Rare Wedgwood green-glazed earthenware bird feeder.

c.1800. Impressed marks 'WEDGWOOD'; 'OH'. 7.5 cm height   HBW

£68

Wedgwood pale green-glazed relief-moulded earthenware dessert service dish.

c.1805–10. Deep (1 cm) applied foot rim. 24.5 cm length
                                                    AF
£8

One should normally expect to pay at least £50–60 for one of these early 19th-century Wedgwood dishes.

Wedgwood green-glazed relief-moulded earthenware dessert plate.

c.1850. Impressed mark 'WEDGWOOD'. 22.7 cm diameter
                                                    AF

£28

This pattern still appeared in a Wedgwood catalogue of 1947. Other shapes in the dessert service are illustrated in Batkin.

Wedgwood green-glazed relief-moulded earthenware *Leafage* pattern dessert service dish.

c.1883. Impressed marks 'WEDGWOOD'; 'XYL' (date code for July 1883). 24 cm length   AF

£35

Batkin illustrates a *Leafage* dish decorated with majolica glazes, c.1873. This dish is quite common, but no associated plates or comports have been recorded.

Wedgwood green-glazed relief-moulded earthenware 'Sunflower' pattern dessert plate.

c.1840–60. Impressed mark 'WEDGWOOD/F' (F is the shape). 22 cm diameter   AF

£20

This is a very common pattern, which was copied by other manufacturers. If it is not marked 'WEDGWOOD', your plate was probably made by one of these. Although the copies seem identical at first glance, the number of petals will differ. The shape is in the reprinted 1878 and 1880 shape books, and also appears in an 1840 shape book in the Wedgwood Archive. A majolica example is illustrated in Batkin.

Wedgwood green-glazed relief-moulded earthenware hexagonal dessert service dish.

c.1869. Impressed mark 'WEDGWOOD'; 'ASX' (date code for April 1869); '4' (shape number). 21 cm diameter   AF

£30

Comports with tops in this shape appear in the 1880 shape book. Other shapes in the service are illustrated in Batkin.

YORKSHIRE POTTERIES

The Yorkshire factories made particularly fine wares. Brameld, Don Pottery, Ferrybridge Pottery, Leeds, Rotherham, Swinton, and Twigg, among others, made crisply moulded wares with wonderful glossy green glazes during the first thirty years of the 19th century.

Further Reading

Alwyn Cox and Angela Cox. Rockingham Pottery & Porcelain 1745–1842 (Faber & Faber, 1983).
Arthur A. Eaglestone and Terence A. Lockett. The Rockingham Pottery, revised edition (David & Charles, Newton Abbot, 1973).
Heather Lawrence. Yorkshire Pots and Potteries (David & Charles, Newton Abbot, 1974).
D. G. Rice. The Illustrated Guide to Rockingham Pottery & Porcelain (Barrie & Jenkins, 1971).

Yorkshire, possibly Don Pottery, green-glazed relief-moulded earthenware 'Thistle' pattern dessert service dish.

c.1820. Two chips. 27.7 cm length   AF

£11

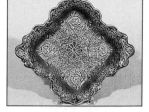

The Don Pottery at Swinton, South Yorkshire operated under various ownerships 1801–93. During the early years they produced green-glazed wares in large quantities, but examples are now rare. This 'Thistle' pattern is the commonest of these. The moulds are thought to have been purchased by the Twiggs in 1835, and examples with an impressed mark 'TWIGG' have been recorded. A perfect example would cost £60–70.

Brameld green-glazed relief-moulded earthenware dessert service dish. Distinctive turned, ribbed decoration on reverse.

c.1820. Impressed mark 'BRAMELD +4'. 24 cm length   AF

£60

The Brameld family owned the pottery at Swinton (known as the Rockingham works from 1826) between 1805 and 1842. They are best remembered for their fine quality porcelains, although they only produced these c.1826–42. The majority of the factory's production was good quality earthenwares. For more about Rockingham porcelain see chapter 16.

Brameld's green-glazed wares are light, crisply moulded and the consistency of the glaze is thin, although it is rich in colour and covers the pot well. Brameld also made green-glazed ornamental wares and jugs. A dessert plate and tureen in the same pattern as this dish are illustrated in Cox & Cox.

Brameld earthenwares appear with marks as above with numbers up to 16. The significance of the numbers is not known.

OTHER MANUFACTURERS

Green-glazed relief-moulded earthenware water-lily pattern dessert comport, attributed to John Adams & Co. or their successors Adams & Bromley.

c.1860–86. 10.2 cm height   AF

£40

A plate in this pattern marked 'ADAMS & BROMLEY' is in the Victoria & Albert Museum. However, this firm continued many of the wares including green-glazed made by their predecessors at the Victoria Works, Hanley, John Adams & Co., who could have made this comport.

W. T. Copeland green-glazed relief-moulded earthenware *Leafage* pattern dessert service dish.

c.1847–67. Impressed mark 'COPELAND'. 26 cm length AF

£15

Spode made quite a wide range of green-glazed wares. Recorded pots include garden seats, pineapple stands, baskets, plates and vases. Only a few of these wares seem to have been made during the Copeland & Garrett period (1833–47).

The *Leafage* pattern dessert service is the only recorded W. T. Copeland green-glazed pattern. The shape was very popular and green-glazed examples are very common. The shape was also used by Copeland for ivory and coloured majolica glazes, and by Copeland & Garrett, although no Copeland & Garrett green-glazed examples have been recorded.

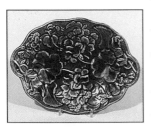

Hope & Carter green-glazed relief-moulded earthenware geranium pattern dessert service dish.

c.1862–80. Impressed mark 'HOPE & CARTER/BURSLEM'. 30 cm length   AF

£15

This is a very common pattern used by several Staffordshire manufacturers. Hope & Carter (1862–80) produced medium quality earthenwares, mostly tablewares.

Rare early Ridgway green-glazed relief-moulded earthenware dessert plate.

c.1805. Impressed mark 'Ridgway'. Slight chips. 21 cm diameter   G

£35

Ridgway made some green-glazed wares during this period, which are now exceptionally rare. This pattern was also made by Baker, Bevans & Irwin at Swansea (see illustration in Griselda Lewis, A Collector's History of English Pottery, 2nd edn, Antique Collectors' Club, Woodbridge, 1985), and by an unidentified maker (see next section, last item).

Ridgway & Abington green-glazed relief-moulded earthenware dessert plate.

c.1865. 22 cm diameter   AF

£15

A marked example of this plate is illustrated in Geoffrey Bemrose's 19th Century English Pottery and Porcelain (Faber & Faber, 1952). The design was by Leonard Abington. This shape is now being manufactured in Portugal, but the weight of the plates and the lack of iridescence in the glaze, which seems flat, should prevent any confusion.

Green-glazed relief-moulded earthenware dessert service dish.

c.1798–1815. Marked W(***). 26 cm length   AS

£250

The mark W(***) has been the cause of great controversy among scholars. The firm seemed to have made quite a few of these green-glazed wares, as well as creamwares, black basalt, printed earthenwares and hybrid hard-paste porcelains. Although cases have been put forward for attributing these wares to James Whitehead (& Co.), Thomas Wolfe and the Warburtons, none of these arguments is conclusive.

UNATTRIBUTED WARES

Green-glazed earthenware child's mug with turned decoration, possibly of Yorkshire origin.

c.1810–20. 6.5 cm height   D

£58

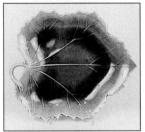

One of a pair of green-glazed relief-moulded earthenware leaf dishes.

c.1800. Impressed mark 2. 23 cm length   D

£145 the pair

Green-glazed relief-moulded earthenware leaf dish.

c.1820. Impressed mark 1. 25 cm length   D

£75

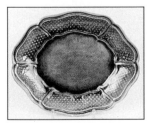

One of a pair of green-glazed relief-moulded earthenware dessert tureen stands with moulded barleycorn edges.

c.1800. 24 cm length   D

£145 the pair

Moulded barleycorn edges were made by many Staffordshire potters in the late 18th century. These particular stands are very heavy for the period, possibly to stand the weight of a full tureen.

Green-glazed relief-moulded earthenware dessert service dish.

c.1830. 26 cm length   AD

£34

Green-glazed relief-moulded earthenware dessert plate.

c.1810. Unrecorded impressed mark with eight-petalled flower. 20.5 cm diameter   VH

£38

This plate is very similar to the Ridgway plate in the previous section.

7 UNDERGLAZE TRANSFER-PRINTED POTTERY

INITIALLY blue transfer-prints were introduced as a cheaper method of reproducing hand-painted patterns found on Chinese export porcelains. Soon the potters realised the potential of this method of decoration and the patterns became extremely complex, exploiting the medium's ability to delineate light and shadow. The landscape patterns mostly introduced 1815–40 had exquisite depths of perspective and marvellously detailed foregrounds. These patterns were nearly all taken from printed sources, and the hunt for these has become a popular pastime among collectors of printed wares.

Underglaze transfer-prints do not rub or wear off as do the overglaze prints. Cobalt was first used for underglaze prints as the pigment was more stable than that used for other colours. It has, to the present day, remained the most popular colour for this method of decoration.

By far the most popular blue transfer-printed pattern is *Willow*. Indeed the name is sometimes erroneously applied to all of the dozens of chinoiserie patterns. A true *Willow* pattern has the distinctive temple on the right, a willow tree, a bridge with three figures, a boat, an island and two birds flying overhead, although many variants can be found. A marketing survey taken as late as the 1950s still showed *Willow* as the most popular pattern for crockery! 20th-century transfer-printed wares are usually clearly marked with 'England' or 'Made in England'.

Pearlware indented shape plate with *Willow* blue transfer-print.

c.1810. Transfer-printed blue workman's mark X. 25 cm diameter   AF

£25

This is the standard *Willow* pattern, often also known as 'Three Man Willow' because of the three figures on the bridge.

Earthenware indented shape plate with 'Two Man Willow' blue transfer-print.

c.1810. 25 cm diameter   AF

£25

This *Willow* pattern has only two figures on the bridge, a fairly common variant. There are no birds flying overhead. It was made by many manufacturers.

Pearlware indented shape soup plate with 'Long Bridge' blue transfer-print.

c.1800. One very small chip to rim. 24 cm diameter   AF

£25

Often mistakenly called a *Willow* pattern, although it does not even have a willow! It always has a bridge with three arches upon which there are two figures. There are no birds flying overhead. The pattern was made by many manufacturers.

Another popular pattern which is still in production at several factories is *Asiatic Pheasants*. This is a later pattern, printed in pale blue, which was introduced by Podmore, Walker & Co. at Tunstall, probably in the 1850s. They were succeeded by Wedgwood & Co., who claimed to be the original manufacturers (not to be confused with the famous Josiah Wedgwood & Sons at Etruria and later at Barlaston). Dozens of firms made this pattern in the second half of the 19th century.

Large Wedgwood & Co. earthenware meat plate with *Asiatic Pheasants* pale blue transfer-print.

c.1860–90. Impressed mark 'WEDGWOOD & CO'; transfer-printed mark 'THE ORIGINAL MANUFACTURER/Asiatic Pheasants/WEDGWOOD CO.' 54.5 cm length   AF

£110

Also very commonly found is the *Wild Rose* pattern, which was made right through the 19th century. The scene is now known to have been taken from a print of Nuneham Courtenay, Bridge and Cottage. Nuneham Courtenay was a famous 18th-century house and landscape garden in Oxfordshire.

Pearlware indented shape plate with *Wild Rose* blue transfer-print.

c.1820. Blue transfer-printed workman's mark +. 21.5 cm diameter   AF

£35

This is an unusually fine example, well potted and well printed. Later Victorian examples are more heavily potted and sometimes poorly printed, fetching more like £15–20 depending on the quality of the plate.

Many 19th-century transfer-printed wares have transfer-printed marks. After c.1820 these often include the name of the pattern. As transferers were paid on a piece-rate, workmen's marks are often found as well. In the case of a few well-documented firms, such as Spode, these can sometimes serve as a means of identification.

Blue transfer-printed wares are among the most collected of British ceramics. The Friends of Blue hold meetings and publish regular Bulletins reporting the latest developments in the never-ending search for new transfer-printed patterns and attributions. The membership secretary is Mr Ron Govier, 10 Sea View Road, Herne Bay, Kent CT6 7JQ.

Further Reading

Robert Copeland. *Spode's Willow Pattern and Other Designs after the Chinese* (Studio Vista, 1980).
Robert Copeland. *Blue and White Transfer-Printed Pottery* (Shire Publications, Aylesbury, 1982).
A. W. Coysh. *Blue Printed Earthenware 1800–1850* (David & Charles, Newton Abbot, 1972).
A. W. Coysh. *Blue and White Transfer Ware 1780–1840*, 2nd edn (David & Charles, Newton Abbot, 1974).
A. W. Coysh and R. K. Henrywood. *Dictionary of Blue and White Printed Pottery 1780–1880*, vol. I (Antique Collectors' Club, Woodbridge, 1982).
A. W. Coysh and R. K. Henrywood. *Dictionary of Blue and White Printed Pottery 1780–1880*, vol. II (Antique Collectors' Club, Woodbridge, 1989).
Friends of Blue (FOB). *Bulletin* (1973 to the present day).
W. L. Little. *Staffordshire Blue* (Batsford, 1969, reprinted 1987).

DAVENPORT
(1794–1887)

Underglaze blue transfer-printed wares were probably among the first wares produced at the Davenport factory. However, as the earliest marked examples seem to date from c.1810, we know little about the earlier patterns.

Further Reading

Terence A. Lockett and Geoffrey A. Godden. *Davenport China, Earthenware, Glass* (Barrie & Jenkins, 1989).
Terence A. Lockett. *Davenport Pottery & Porcelain, 1794–1887* (David & Charles, Newton Abbot, 1972).

Davenport pearlware meat plate with draining well with 'Chinoiserie Bridgeless' blue transfer-print.

c.1810–15. 47 cm length   WG

£195

The name for this pattern alludes to the fact that it is a willow-type pattern, but it does not have the bridge, the willow tree or the pair of birds. This pattern was made by many firms. Davenport introduced it c.1795–1805, and it had a long life.

Davenport stone china soup plate with 'Bamboo and Peony' blue transfer-print.

After c.1825. Blue transfer-printed mark. 24 cm diameter
JJB

£65

This pattern also occurs on earthenware. Its introduction has been dated to c.1825–30, but it had a very long life (an example dated 1878 has been recorded).

Mark on reverse.

Davenport earthenware jug with unrecorded blue transfer-print.

c.1850. Impressed mark '22/DAVENPORT', with anchor; blue transfer-printed mark 'DAVENPORT'. 23 cm height
AF

£75

It has been suggested that the numbers e.g. '22' appearing on the Davenport impressed marks are dates. However, the frequency with which certain numbers occur, namely 22, 38, 44 and 56, has cast some doubt on this theory.

MASON
(c.1813–53)

Miles Mason started as a Chinaman, a dealer in pottery and porcelain, principally dealing in the Chinese export wares which were flooding Britain in the 18th century. In the 1790s when these imports ceased, Mason decided to manufacture porcelain himself (see chapter 16). In 1813 Miles's sons succeeded him under the style George & Charles Mason, producing earthenwares and porcelain. They introduced Mason's Patent Ironstone, which was to become the mainstay of the firm, in that same year. George Mason retired in 1830, and the firm was continued under the style C. J. Mason & Co. by Charles Mason c.1830–48 and c.1849–53. The moulds, pattern books, etc. were purchased by Francis Morley & Co., and subsequently passed on to G. L. Ashworth & Bros (see chapter 10).

Most of the Mason's ironstone wares show a very strong oriental influence, particularly the many Japan-type patterns, using an Imari palette of iron red and cobalt blue. However, many were decorated with blue transfer-prints. Porcelain manufacture was eventually phased out in favour of Mason's successful ironstone.

Further Reading

Geoffrey Godden. *Mason's China and the Ironstone Wares*, 3rd edn (Antique Collectors' Club, Woodbridge, 1991).
Reginald Haggar and Elizabeth Adams. *Mason Porcelain & Ironstone, 1796–1853* (Faber & Faber, 1977).

Examples of the common 'Blue Pheasants' pattern are illustrated in Godden, Coysh 1974 and Little.

One of a pair of moulded Mason's Ironstone China dishes with 'Blue Pheasants' transfer-print.

c.1820–5. 26 cm length   G

£130 the pair

Very unusual shaped Mason's Ironstone porringer and lid with 'Blue Pheasants' transfer-print.

c.1820. 17.5 cm diameter   VH

£165

The rare shape of this item is reflected in the high price.

Large Mason's pearlware tray with 'Broseley' blue transfer-print.

c.1807–13. Blue transfer-printed mock Chinese seal mark. 39 cm length   VH

£190

Mason also used the 'Broseley' pattern (sometimes known as 'Pagoda') on their porcelains. The pattern is very common, but the size and unusual shape of this tray are reflected in the high price.

RIDGWAY
(1802–54)

The brothers Job and George Ridgway ran the Bell Works at Shelton from 1792 until Job left to found the Cauldon Place factory in 1802. Little is known of the wares made by the Ridgway brothers at Bell Works, although in 1797 they were in a partnership with William Smith. Job's sons joined his firm and then c.1830 split up, with William Ridgway moving to the Bell Works and John Ridgway continuing at Cauldon Place. The Ridgway firms of the 19th century are as follows:

Job Ridgway, c.1802–8
Job Ridgway & Sons, c.1808–14
John & William Ridgway, John Ridgway & Co. or J. & W. Ridgway & Co., c.1814–30
John Ridgway (& Co.), c.1830–54
William Ridgway & Co. or W. Ridgway, Son & Co., c.1830–45.

The Ridgways made a good deal of blue transfer-printed wares, but most early examples were unmarked, and relatively few patterns made before c.1820 have been recorded.

Further Reading

Geoffrey A. Godden. *Ridgway Porcelains*, 2nd edn (Antique Collectors' Club, Woodbridge, 1985).

Early Job Ridgway pearlware soup plate with 'Curling Palm' blue transfer-print.

c.1802–8. Impressed worker's mark x in circle. 24 cm diameter   G

£60

This pattern is usually unmarked, but examples with the mark 'J. Ridgway' impressed in a curve over a beehive have been recorded. See Coysh & Henrywood 1982.

Ridgway earthenware soup plate with 'Eastern Port' blue transfer-print.

c.1814–30. 24 cm height   JM

£48

Illustrated in Coysh & Henrywood 1989. One example has been recorded bearing the rare impressed lower-case 'Ridgway' mark, which is believed to have been used by John & William Ridgway c.1814–30.

John Ridgway stoneware plate with *Giraffe* brown transfer-print.

c.1836. Brown transfer-printed crown and garter mark with 'Published Aug. 30th 1836 according to the Act/Giraffe/Stone Ware/J-R'. 25.4 cm diameter   G

£85

The scene is taken from part of a coloured lithograph by G. Scharf dated 1836, which shows four giraffes captured in the Sudan for the London Zoo. The print is also known in blue.

SPODE
(c.1784–1833)
COPELAND & GARRETT
(1833–47)
W. T. COPELAND (& SONS LTD)
(1847–1970)
SPODE
(1970 to the present day)

As Josiah Spode I had been an engraver for John Turner at the Caughley porcelain factory, it is not surprising that his first wares at the Spode factory in Stoke were blue transfer-printed. The early wares were seldom marked and few have been identified. However, Spode became a leading manufacturer of blue transfer-printed wares. Two of their patterns, *Blue Italian* and *Tower*, are still in production today.

After the death of Josiah Spode III, the firm was purchased by William Taylor Copeland (who had been a partner in Spode's London retail business) and Thomas Garrett, operating under the style Copeland & Garrett, and continued to produce many of Spode's blue transfer-printed patterns, often printed in other colours. In 1847 W. T. Copeland took over the firm, which remained in the family until 1970.

Spode marked many blue transfer-printed wares after c.1800 with 'SPODE' impressed or transfer-printed. Copeland & Garrett used a variety of elaborate transfer-printed marks. Copeland used a series of impressed and printed marks. They also introduced a system of impressed date codes in 1870. The last two digits of the year are surmounted by a letter for the month. The system was used on earthenwares until 1957.

Spode collectors will want to join the Spode Society, which has regular meetings and outings, also publishing a very fine *Review*. The membership secretary is Mrs Rosalind Pulver, PO Box 1812, London NW4 4NW. The Spode factory (Church Street, Stoke-on-Trent ST4 1BX) has a fine museum and factory tours are also available by prior arrangement.

Further Reading

Robert Copeland. *Spode's Willow Pattern & other designs after the Chinese* (Studio Vista, 1980).
David Drakard and Paul Holdway. *Spode Printed Ware* (Longman, 1983).
The Spode Society. *Recorder & Review* (1986 to the present day).
Lynne Sussmann. *Spode/Copeland Transfer-Printed Patterns* (Parks Canada, Ontario, 1979).
Leonard Whiter. *Spode* (Barrie & Jenkins, 1970, reprinted with new colour illustrations 1989).
Sydney B. Williams. *Antique Blue and White Spode*, 3rd edn (Batsford, 1949, reprinted 1987).

Spode pearlware plate with 'Buffalo' blue transfer-print.

c.1805. Workman's mark X in blue. 25 cm diameter   TV

£50

The 'Buffalo' pattern was one of the earliest blue transfer-printed patterns. It was a popular pattern used on Chinese export porcelain. A number of Chinese painted porcelain examples and British transfer-printed earthenware examples by various makers are illustrated in Copeland. The pattern was probably introduced at Spode before 1800, and continued in production for a long time.

Earthenware jug with 'Gothic Castle' blue transfer-print attributed to Spode.

c.1820. Blue transfer-printed workman's mark. 11 cm height
JM

£68

This interesting print combines Chinese and European design elements. It was introduced c.1811–12.

Spode earthenware soup plate with blue transfer-print 'Flower Cross' pattern.

c.1820. 25 cm diameter   JJB

£85

Drakard & Holdway illustrate this rare pattern, and state that it is often unmarked. It is also illustrated in Whiter.

Spode earthenware dish with blue transfer-print 'Bowpot' painted with orange enamel and gilded.

c.1818. Impressed mark 'SPODE/56'. Painted pattern number 2954. 23 cm length   JJB

£95

This pattern is usually found painted with enamels. The first enamelled version was introduced in 1812. The impressed number '56' is a workman's mark.

Earthenware plate with *Rome* blue transfer-print attributed to Spode.

Pattern introduced in 1811. 15.5 cm diameter   T

£78

The view is based on two aquatints by J. Merigot and R. Edwards published in *Views and Ruins of Rome and its Vicinity* (1798). Spode called their version of this pattern *Rome*, but *Tiber* versions by Joseph Stubbs of Longport (identical to the Spode version) and Thomas Lakin have been recorded. Don Pottery's version, the *Castello St. Angelo* pattern in their Landscape Series, is illustrated in Coysh & Henrywood 1982. This pattern is quite commonly found, but it is a favourite with collectors, which is reflected in the price.

Spode earthenware plate with 'Tumbledown Dick' brown and blue transfer-prints painted in polychrome enamels.

c.1833. Impressed mark 'SPODE' and transfer-printed 'Copeland & Garrett Late Spode' mark. Painted pattern number 3718 in brown. 22 cm diameter   WG

£65

The 'Tumbledown Dick' pattern was introduced in 1822, and was usually printed in two colours using the Ackey method and painted in polychrome enamels and sometimes gilded. The sheet pattern on the ground is known as the 'Cracked Ice' pattern, of Chinese origin, symbolising spring. (For delftware example see chapter 2.)

The popularity of the 'Tumbledown Dick' pattern is evidenced by the fact that there were twelve versions on earthenware alone. Whiter illustrates versions with pattern numbers 3716 and 3967 (a rare gold-printed version).

This particular plate can be dated quite precisely because it bears the marks of both Spode and Copeland & Garrett, who succeeded Spode in 1833. The Spode mark was impressed before the biscuit firing. The Copeland & Garrett mark was transfer-printed when the plate was decorated.

Spode earthenware dessert dish with 'Filigree' grey transfer-print painted in yellow enamel.

c.1830. Impressed mark 'SPODE/56'. 24 cm length   TA

£45

Most often found in blue, 'Filigree' is thought to have been introduced in 1823. It was one of Spode's most successful floral designs, continued by Copeland & Garrett. This grey and yellow example is particularly attractive.

Copeland & Garrett earthenware meat plate with *Camilla* brown transfer-print.

c.1833–47. Brown transfer-printed Copeland & Garrett mark. 37 cm length   WG

£55

Camilla was a pattern introduced by Copeland & Garrett, and still in production. It has been produced in several different colours.

Copeland & Garrett earthenware dessert dish with *Italian Garden* green transfer-print.

c.1833–47. Green transfer-printed mark COPELAND/AND/ GARRETT/STOKE   UPON   TRENT/&/LONDON/CHINA GLAZE/ITALIAN GARDEN'. 27 cm length   JJB

£55

This print is from the *Seasons* series, for which this special print mark was used. Versions of *Italian Garden* were used for the months of June and August. The cherubs in the vignettes on the border each represent a different season. The series was introduced c.1833, and reissued by W. T. Copeland at the end of the 19th century. The title *Seasons* is only found on these later Copeland examples.

Mark on reverse.

Copeland earthenware soup plate with *Continental Views* purple transfer-print and *Louis Quatorze* border.

c.1847. Purple transfer-printed mark 'COPELAND LATE SPODE'; impressed mark 'COPELAND'. Diamond registration mark for 21 October 1845. 22.5 cm diameter WG

£41

The *Continental Views* series was registered by Copeland & Garrett in 1845, the *Louis Quatorze* border having been registered in 1844. W. T. Copeland carried on production of the pattern, and it was still in the firm's catalogue as late as 1882.

Copeland earthenware soup plate with geometric floral blue transfer-print.

c.1889. Impressed mark 'COPELAND'; impressed date code 'J/89', for January 1889. 26 cm diameter WG

£35

This is a typical example of the transfer-prints popular in the late 19th century.

Unusual Copeland earthenware two-handled vase with *Blue Italian* transfer-print.

c.1960. Blue transfer-printed mark 'SPODE' in seal; 'C/L' printed in black above (date code for July 1960). 27 cm height   G

£140

Spode's immensely popular *Italian* pattern, today known as *Blue Italian*, was copied by many other potters. The pattern has continued in production to the present day.

TURNER FAMILY
(1759–1829)

John Turner was an earthenware manufacturer at Lane End, Longton (not to be confused with Thomas Turner of Caughley, the porcelain manufacturer). His family operated the Lane End pottery under various styles and partnerships. A rare impressed mark incorporating 'TURNER' with the Prince of Wales's feathers was used from 1784, when John Turner was appointed potter to the Prince of Wales. Other wares will be impressed 'TURNER' or 'TURNER & CO.' (1803–6).

Further Reading

Bevis Hillier. *Master Potters of the Industrial Revolution. The Turners of Lane End* (Cory, Adams & Mackay, 1965).

Rare early Turner pearlware meat plate with 'Stag' blue transfer-print.

c.1785–90. Four rim chips. Impressed mark 'TURNER' with the Prince of Wales's feathers. 57.4 cm length   WG

£480

A dish and a plate in this pattern, both also marked Turner, are illustrated in Coysh 1974.

Turner pearlware meat plate with 'Elephant' blue transfer-print.

c.1790–1800. Impressed mark 'TURNER' with Prince of Wales's feathers. 36.5 cm length   HBW

£145

A plate in this pattern impressed 'TURNER' is illustrated in Coysh & Henrywood 1982.

OTHER MANUFACTURERS

Rare W. Adams & Sons earthenware barber's bowl with *Spanish Festivities* pink transfer-print.

c.1853. Pink transfer-printed diamond registration mark for 30 November 1850, parcel 5; 'SPANISH FESTIVITIES'. Impressed mark 'W. ADAMS & SONS/No. 93483' (patent number). 25.8 cm width   HBW

£250

These are also known as bleeding bowls, as barbers used to act as surgeons. The well on the rim is for a ball of soap. The cut out in the rim is to fit around the client's neck beneath his chin. The holes on the rim are for threading with a string to hang the bowl on the wall. A delftware example is illustrated on p. 45. Transfer-printed barber's bowls are very rare.

Burgess & Leigh earthenware mug with *Farmers Arms* black transfer-print.

c.1880. Inscribed 'GOD SPEED THE PLOUGH'. Black transfer-printed mark 'FARMERS ARMS/B & L'. 11 cm height   V

£88

Burgess & Leigh (1862 to the present day) have always specialised in useful earthenwares. Today they make a number of reproductions of 19th-century transfer-prints.

Thomas Dimmock stone china meat plate with *Morea* blue transfer-print.

c.1840. Blue transfer-printed mark with 'MOREA/STONE CHINA'. Impressed monogram of Thomas Dimmock. 43 cm length   JJB

£125

J. Goodwin of Seacombe Pottery also made a *Morea* pattern, which is an entirely different scene. Morea is the peninsula forming the southern part of Greece.

Elkin, Knight & Bridgwood earthenware plate with *Chinese Pagoda* magenta transfer-print.

c.1827–40. Magenta transfer-printed mark 'CHINESE PAGODA/ E K B'. Some staining. 25.5 cm diameter   JJB

£68

Mark on reverse.

Thomas and Benjamin Godwin earthenware soup plate with pale blue *Surseya Ghaut, Khanpore* transfer-print.

c.1830. Blue transfer-printed mark 'SURSEYA GHAUT/ KHANPORE/T&BG'. 25.5 cm diameter   WG

£32

This scene is part of the Godwins' *Indian Scenery* series. The same scene was used by several other manufacturers including Edge, Malkin & Co. (illustrated in Coysh & Henrywood 1982) and John Hall & Sons.

Robert Hamilton earthenware pickle dish with blue transfer-print of Hotun on the Canton River.

c.1820. 14.5 cm length   JM

£78

This pattern Is after an engraving in Thomas and William Daniell's *Picturesque Voyage to India by way of China* published in 1810: see FOB, 74. Robert Hamilton made blue-printed wares at Stoke c.1811–26.

Octagonal pearlware plate with Joshua Heath's version of Caughley *Willow* pattern transfer-printed in inky dark blue.

c.1780. Impressed mark I●H. 24 cm diameter   CE

£60

Joshua Heath was one of the pioneers of blue transfer-printing on earthenware.

Herculaneum earthenware dessert dish with one of the *French Scenery* brown transfer-prints.

c.1830–40. Two chips to foot rim. Impressed mark 'HERCU-LANEUM'; brown transfer-printed mark 'French Scenery'. 23 cm length   G

£75

This series was also printed in blue. Sepia versions were sometimes enamelled. Another of the series prints is illustrated in Alan Smith's *Liverpool Herculaneum Pottery* (Barrie & Jenkins, 1970).

Lockett & Hulme earthenware jug with a caravan scene blue transfer-print filled in with enamels.

c.1822–6. Minor chips. Blue transfer-printed mark in dontil edge oval frame 'Opaque China/L&H'. 11 cm height   AD

£85

A Lockett & Hulme jug in this shape with another blue transfer-print also filled in with enamels is illustrated in colour in Coysh & Henrywood 1982. Little illustrates the mark.

Semi-China meatplate with 'Bamboo' blue transfer-print, probably Minton.

c.1820–50. Blue transfer-printed octagonal mark 'Semi-China' with border with mock Chinese characters. 47.5 cm length   AF

£175

Although it is known that Minton made a great quantity of blue transfer-printed wares, they have been difficult to identify.

Royal Crown Derby Crown Earthenware Imari-style dish painted in polychrome enamels and gilded over a red transfer-print.

c.1880. Transfer-printed blue mark with crown and monogram; impressed crown with 'DERBY'. 26.5 cm diameter   HBW

£90

Royal Crown Derby's Crown Earthenware can be identified by the impressed crown mark on the reverse. It was used 1875–1914, mainly for dinner wares. It was often transfer-printed. An oval dish in this pattern is illustrated in Twitchett & Bailey, *Royal Crown Derby* (Antique Collectors' Club, Woodbridge, 1988).

Earthenware plate with 'Lovick' blue transfer-print attributed to Ralph Stevenson & Son.

c.1830–40. 22 cm diameter   JM

£54

This pattern, which was made by several manufacturers, is often called 'Lovick' because a marked plate by Ralph Stevenson & Son bears the mark 'LOVICK's/China and Glass/Emporium/NORWICH'. The author has also had an unmarked example printed in black.

Earthenware plate with 'Ornate Pagodas' blue transfer-print attributed to Richard Woolley.

c.1809–14. 24 cm diameter   WG

£54

An example of this pattern impressed 'WOOLLEY' has been recorded (see Coysh & Henrywood 1982).

F. & R. Pratt earthenware pot lid with 'The Shrimpers' multi-colour transfer-print.

c.1850-70. 11 cm diameter   WG

£85

The multicoloured printing technique brought to perfection by Jesse Austin of F. & R. Pratt was used on a variety of wares. The best known are the pot lids, which were used on jars of products ranging from fishpaste to bear's grease hairdressing. The colours were laid on individually, with the final transfer being a sepia outline. Obviously the greatest difficulty in such a technique was to assure that the individual colour prints were positioned accurately.

F. & R. Pratt showed these wares (not to be confused with the Prattwares discussed in chapter 4) at the Great Exhibition in 1851. They continued their manufacture into the early 20th century. See A. Ball, *The Price Guide to Pot Lids* (Antique Collectors' Club, Woodbridge, 1980).

UNATTRIBUTED WARES

Pearlware plate with 'Lady with Parasol' blue transfer-print.

c.1790–1800. Marked in blue with a dot surrounded by a circle. 19 cm diameter   T

£80

A slightly different version of this print is illustrated in Coysh & Henrywood 1982. The pattern is as yet unattributed.

Pearlware mug with blue chinoiserie transfer-print.

c.1810–15. Hairline crack. 13 cm height   AD

£160

Pearlware leaf-shaped pickle dish with elements of the *Willow* pattern blue transfer-printed.

Early 19th century. 13.5 cm length   JM

£46

Leaf-shaped pickle dishes were made by many manufacturers. They are very seldom marked and as they usually only bear a small portion of a larger chinoiserie print, they are very hard to attribute. Marked examples are considerably more valuable. Many of them have a very attractive moulding of veins on the reverse.

Earthenware pickle dish with 'Palladian Porch' blue transfer-print.

c.1820. 15.5 cm length   JM

£78

No marked example of the 'Palladian Porch' pattern has been recorded. The print of an 'Ancient Sepulchre near Macri' was taken from Luigi Mayer's *Views in the Ottoman Empire* (1803), the source of Spode's *Caramanian* series.

Pearlware cream jug with unrecorded chinoiserie pattern portraying fishermen on barrels.

c.1810. 7 cm height   JM

£85

125

Pearlware mug with chinoiserie blue transfer-print filled with polychrome enamels and lustre rim.

c.1825–30. 12.5 cm height   JM

£130

Several manufacturers made wares of this type including Mayer & Newbold, Lockett & Hulme, Baggaley & Ball and Pountney.

Stone china jug with reverse 'Broseley' blue transfer-print.

c.1820. Blue transfer-printed 'STONE CHINA' seal mark. 12 cm height   JM

£85

This pattern most often appears on wavy-edged porcelain tea wares.

Earthenware plate with chinoiserie oriental vase blue transfer-print.

c.1820. 21 cm diameter   JM

£42

This is a common pattern, whose maker or makers are unknown.

Earthenware plate with blue transfer-print of two men in turbans pulling in a fishing net.

c.1810–15. 24 cm diameter   JM

£48

Earthenware teapot with unrecorded rural blue transfer-print.

c.1820. Restored chip to knop. 15 cm height   JM

£138

The patterns used on tea wares are usually different from those found on the dinner services. Since most tea wares are unmarked many patterns like this one are unrecorded in existing literature.

Pearlware jug with chinoiserie blue transfer-print and engine-turned bands.

c.1800. Slight crack and tiny rim chip. 15 cm height   JM

£80

These early chinoiserie patterns can rarely be attributed with any safety.

Gadroon-edged earthenware jug with pale blue chinoiserie transfer-print.

c.1840. 26 cm height   JM

£128

Chinoiserie scenes of this type, usually printed in paler blue, were quite common in the 1830–45 period. The pattern is similar to designs called 'Chinese Fountains' by Elkin, Knight & Bridgwood and 'Chinese Porcelain' by John Rogers & Son, both of which were produced on wares with gadrooned edges.

Pearlware plate with dragon blue transfer-print filled with green and red enamels.

c.1810. Reverse with pseudo-Chinese marks. 22 cm diameter.   TV

£95

Reverse.

Pearlware arcaded plate with blue transfer-print of cows grazing before Gothic ruins.

c.1820. 18.5 cm diameter   VH

£85

Very large earthenware meat plate with brown transfer-printed scene with pink transfer-printed ground.

c.1840. 56 cm length   AD

£340

Although brown transfer-prints are not as popular as blue, the exceptional quality of this print and the unusually large size of the plate make it a highly desirable and quite costly item.

Pearlware tea cup with square handle and saucer with brown transfer-print.

c.1810. Cup 4.7 cm height; saucer 13.2 cm diameter   JJB

£85

One of a pair of earthenware cake plates with blue transfer-print, painted in green enamel with liquid lustre glaze, possibly F. & R. Pratt.

c.1850–60. Blue transfer-printed mark 'ETRUSCAN' with picture of a figure holding a vase. 27.5 cm length   TA

£95 the pair

8 OTHER EARTHENWARE BEFORE 1900

EARLY BRITISH EARTHENWARES

IT is impossible to show a representative selection of British pottery before 1700 in the present context. The pieces which have survived seldom come on the market for sale. However, many museums, including small local ones, will have examples. Pots or parts of pots (shards) are frequently found in the course of archaeological digs and over the years a fair number of Roman or medieval pots have been discovered by farmers, builders or gardeners. In the past these were judged curiosities and often donated to the local museum.

Further Reading

K. J. Barton. *Pottery in England from 3500BC–AD1730* (David & Charles, Newton Abbot, 1975).

Jeremy Haslam. *Medieval Pottery* (Shire Publications, Aylesbury, 1984).

Jonathan Horne. *A Collection of Early English Pottery*, Parts I–XII (Jonathan Horne, 1982–92).

Griselda Lewis. *A Collector's History of English Pottery*, 3rd edn (Antique Collectors' Club, Woodbridge, 1985).

J. N. L. Myers. *Anglo-Saxon Pottery and the Settlement of England* (Clarendon Press, Oxford, 1969).

Ross E. Taggart. *The Frank P. and Harriet C. Burnap Collection of English Pottery in the William Rockhill Nelson Gallery*, revised edn (Nelson Gallery/Atkins Museum, Kansas City, Missouri, 1967).

Anglo-Saxon low-fired earthenware cremation urn with incised decoration and impressed rosettes.

c.5th–6th century. 16 cm height   JH

£5,500

A pot such as this one would have been made in a small community for local use. There are certain characteristics which enable us to relate such pots to specific areas, and this one is believed to have been made in East Anglia or the East Coast. This is a superb example in very fine condition. Items like this are seldom found outside museums. This and another pot of the period are illustrated in Horne XI.

Buff earthenware jug decorated with splashes of yellow and green lead glazes.

c.13th–14th century. Chips. 20 cm height   JH

£880

Buff earthenware bottle with two lugs with green and yellow glazes.

c.16th century. Chips. 14 cm height   JH

£435

A bottle of this type would probably have been attached to the waist with a leather thong to serve as a flask.

Tudor green ware buff earthenware jug decorated with green lead glaze.

c.16th/17th century. 18.5 cm height   JH

£660

Tudor green wares were made at Farnborough Hill in Surrey from the late 15th century. These wares represented a technical development, as for the first time in English pottery a biscuit firing and a glost firing were necessary. This technique may have been imported from France.

18TH-CENTURY EARTHENWARES

To the extent possible 18th-century earthenwares have been grouped by types in this book. However, there are many earthenwares which do not fit neatly into a category, and these are dealt with in this section.

Further Reading

Patricia A. Halfpenny and Stella Beddoe. *Circus & Sport, English Earthenware Figures 1780–1840* (The JBSpeed Art Museum, Louisville, Kentucky, 1990).

Jonathan Horne, *A Collection of Early English Pottery*, Parts I–XII (Jonathan Horne, 1982–92).

Griselda Lewis. *A Collector's History of English Pottery*, 3rd edn (Antique Collectors' Club, Woodbridge, 1985).

Ross E. Taggart. *The Frank P. and Harriet C. Burnap Collection of English Pottery in the William Rockhill Nelson Gallery*, revised edn (Nelson Gallery/Atkins Museum, Kansas City, Missouri, 1967).

Peter Walton. *Creamware and Other English Pottery at Temple Newsam House Leeds* (Manningham Press, 1976).

One of a pair of Staffordshire earthenware duck sauceboats painted in polychrome enamels, with splashed pink lustre interiors.

c.1790. 18 cm length   AS

£3,750 the pair

These very colourful and attractive sauceboats are rare, especially in pairs.

Earthenware bear jug and cover, decorated with honey and brown glazes and very unusual blue-painted handle.

c.1780. 8 cm height   LR

£3,500

Although this bear has an appealing expression, he is actually trying to kill the dog which has been set upon him. Bear-baiting was a popular sport from medieval times and was a favourite of Queen Elizabeth I. The Bear Gardens once adjoined Shakespeare's Globe Theatre in London. The Puritans banned the sport, but it was reinstated by Charles II. The practice finally died out as bears became scarce.

The bear's head is a removable lid, which could be used as a cup; the dog forms the spout. These bear jugs are usually found in white salt-glazed stoneware. An unusual brown salt-glazed stoneware bear figure is shown on p. 73. Bear-baiting is the subject of figure groups as well as jugs.

Staffordshire fox and swan earthenware sauceboat decorated with brown, blue, green and yellow glazes.

Late 18th century. Crack in swan's neck. 19 cm length   AS

£1,650

This sauceboat presents an amusing image of a fox forever frozen in time with his prey tantalisingly at his back.

Rare Portobello earthenware flask painted in green, pink and blue enamels.

One handle repaired. 22 cm height   BG

£490

Portobello Pottery, one of the Scottish East Coast potteries, was established in 1767, and making creamwares by the 1790s. These wares had a yellowish glaze, and in the early 19th century bright low-temperature colours and pink lustre were employed for decoration.

AGATE WARES

Agate wares are made by mixing slices of two or more stained clays to form a pattern. The wares were then turned on a lathe to make the walls thinner, to add turned decorations and to remove any smear of clay from the potter's hands which might obscure the pattern. The fired pot was sealed with a clear lead glaze. The technique became popular in Staffordshire c.1730; press-moulded agate wares appeared c.1745. Agate ware is also known as onyx ware, pebble ware or in the United States as scroddled ware or lava ware.

Since the patterns of agate ware are created by the clay itself, the pattern will run consistently throughout the pot and will be visible on the base and inside the pot. Agate-like effects created with oxides, slips, glazes, transfer-prints or enamels will be on the surface of the pot, usually only on the parts which are easily visible.

Agate wares continued in production into the 19th century, but the later wares are usually heavier, fewer colours were employed and the patterns are not so intricate (see Wedgwood example below). The technique was also used by the Vallauris Pottery in France in the 20th century, but these will have impressed factory marks, and some very brightly coloured clays were used.

Agate ware teapot stand.

c.1755. 16 cm height   JH

£3,850

Very rare Staffordshire Pecten shape press-moulded agate ware teapot with lion knop and dolphin handle.

c.1755. 14 cm height   JH

£7,800

This teapot is an exceptional example of press-moulded agate ware. The handles were difficult to mould, and the clays are typically smudged. A similar example is illustrated in Taggart.

Agate ware tankard.

c.1800. 15 cm height   JH

£550

The pattern of this tankard is less intricate than that of the two earlier examples shown above.

Wedgwood agate ware potpourri base.

c.1864. Impressed mark 'WEDGWOOD'; date code for 1864 'AAS'; incised shape number 496. 9.8 cm height   HBW

£90

This is more heavily potted than 18th-century agate ware. The number of different coloured clays is reduced and the resulting pattern is less interesting. The low shape number indicates that this was a shape revived from the Wedgwood archives, a common practice at the factory.

ROCKINGHAM-GLAZED WARES

Rockingham glazes are dark brown lead glazes containing iron oxide and manganese oxide. They are believed to have originated at the Rockingham Pottery In Yorkshire c.1790, but were used extensively throughout Britain during the 19th century. Generally the glaze was used for sturdy tablewares, but some commemoratives (see chapter 24) and decorative items were made.

Cadogan teapots were a novelty introduced in the late 18th century. There is no immediately apparent means of filling the pots, for they are filled by means of a spiral tube from a hole in the base. Once the pot is turned upright, the fluid can only escape through the spout. These pots are usually found with a Rockingham glaze, but Spode green-glazed examples are also known. The pots were first made by Thomas Bingley at Swinton (later Brameld's Rockingham Works) after an Indian peach-shaped wine pot given to the Bramelds by the Hon Mrs Cadogan, and also by John Turner of Lane End and Spode.

Further Reading

Alwyn and Angela Cox. *Rockingham Pottery & Porcelain 1745–1842* (Faber & Faber, 1983).
Heather Lawrence. *Yorkshire Pots and Potteries* (David & Charles, Newton Abbot, 1974).

Brameld earthenware Cadogan teapot with Rockingham glaze.

c.1820–40. Impressed mark 'BRAMELD'. 17 cm height   JJB

£425

Late Rockingham-glazed earthenware Cadogan teapot.

c.1840. Impressed mark 'ROCKINGHAM'. 15.5 cm height excluding handle   V

£112

The 'ROCKINGHAM' marks on these teapots refer to the glaze rather than to the Rockingham works of Brameld. Makers known to have used this mark include Spode, Copeland & Garrett and Wedgwood. Marked Brameld and Spode examples are the most valuable.

MOCHA WARE

Mocha ware is named after the Mocha stone which has dark markings similar to the branches of trees. As the ware was largely utilitarian, there were few references to it in contemporary writings. Early wares are rare for the same reason, that is, they were used until broken. Many bodies were decorated with the mocha technique: creamware, pearlware, granite ware, chalkware and white ware.

The most abundant wares were mugs for pubs, which were made until the Second World War. From Victorian times many of these will have sprigged marks indicating that they had been passed by the Standards Office. Mugs, jugs and tankards are the most commonly found, but many other simple shapes do turn up. Extra thick bottoms were made for false measures, but these will not bear the standards mark.

The pots were decorated with a band of coloured slip, often blue, greenish grey or tan. While the slip was damp, the potter applied 'tea', a mixture of tobacco juice, urine and manganese, which fanned out to created the design. Bands of black were then used to finish off the decoration.

Mocha ware earthenware jug.

Late 19th century. Cracked. 15.5 cm height   VH

£80

One of pair of mocha ware mugs.

Late 19th century. Crack in one handle. 13 cm height   VH

£130 the pair.

Mocha ware mug with pint mark 'Pint G R 790 P'.

c.1910–39. 12 cm height   RS

£45

This example illustrates the continuity of mocha ware design well into the 20th century.

CRADLES

Pottery cradles have long been popular collectors' items. They are also known in slipware and stoneware. It is sometimes said that these were given as christening presents, and some are known with dated inscriptions. However, they may also have been toys.

Staffordshire earthenware cradle with baby, decorated with yellow and blue underglaze colours.

c.1800. 9 cm length   BG

£295

Staffordshire earthenware cradle with yellowish glaze.

c.1800. 13 cm length   V

£165

Yorkshire earthenware cradle with baby, sponged in red and black underglaze colours and painted in red and green enamels.

c.1815. 12.5 cm length   BG

£795

Earthenware cradle with tan glaze and spattered brown and white decoration.

c.1825. Chip. 12 cm length   AD

£95

BRISTOL POTTERY

The Bristol pottery started to manufacture creamware soon after being taken over by Joseph Ring in 1784, and following various partnerships, including Ring, Taylor & Carter, Ring & Carter, and Henry Carter & Co., the famous Pountney name first appeared as Carter & Pountney in 1813. The main partnerships were Pountney & Allies (from 1816), Pountney & Goldney (from 1836), J. D. Pountney (from 1850), and finally Pountney & Co. (from 1858). Throughout the 19th century the pottery concentrated on useful earthenwares, particularly blue-printed wares, but some of the earlier products were more decorative, particularly the polychrome enamelled creamwares, mainly associated with the painter William

Fitfield, made until the 1840s. The firm continued the production of utilitarian earthen-wares at a new pottery built in 1905, and survived at Bristol until 1969.

Further Reading

Ceramics in Bristol: The Fine Wares (City of Bristol Museum & Art Gallery, 1979).
R. K. Henrywood. *Bristol Potters 1775–1906* (Redcliffe, Bristol, 1992).
Sarah Levitt. *Pountneys, The Bristol Pottery at Fishponds 1905–1969* (Redcliffe, Bristol, 1990).
J. D. Pountney. *Old Bristol Potteries, being an Account of the Old Potters and Potteries of Bristol and Brislington, between 1650 and 1850* (J. W. Arrowsmith, Bristol, 1920; reprinted by E. P. Publishing, Wakefield, 1972).

Bristol earthenware barrels painted in polychrome enamels.

c.1835. Left, 10 cm height; right 11.5 cm height   AD

£350 each

A spirit barrel dated 1801 with enamelled flowers is listed in the *Ceramics in Bristol* catalogue.

Two Bristol earthenware barrels.

c.1820. Small barrel with initials and date 1821, 11 cm height; large barrel has small chip, 13.5 cm height   HBW

Small barrel £375; large barrel £275

This is an example of how much even minor damage can sometimes affect the value of a pot.

Bristol earthenware puzzle jug painted in polychrome enamels.

c.1830. 13 cm height   AD

£575

Bristol earthenware cup and lid painted in polychrome enamels.

c.1830. 13 cm height   AD

£185

MINTON
(c.1796 to the present day)

From the time that Thomas Minton founded this firm c.1796 until 1884, the firm went under a number of styles, passing through various Minton partnerships. Thomas Minton had worked as an engraver for the Caughley factory, and blue transfer-printed earthenwares were among his earliest productions. Minton continued to produce a wide variety of fine quality earthenwares throughout the 19th century. The best known of these were their majolica wares (see chapter 11).

Further Reading

Elizabeth Aslin and Paul Atterbury. Minton 1798–1910 (Victoria & Albert Museum, 1976).
Paul Atterbury and Maureen Batkin. The Dictionary of Minton (Antique Collectors' Club, Woodbridge, 1990).
Geoffrey Godden. Minton Pottery & Porcelain of the First Period, 1793–1850 (Barrie & Jenkins, 1968).

Large Minton earthenware plaque painted in grey and blue enamels in the style of Émile Lessore, inscribed 'After Bassano' on reverse.

c.1877. Impressed marks 'MINTONS'; impressed date cipher for 1877. Signed 'AH' with a picture of an axe. 30 cm diameter   MB

£32

Minton earthenware vase with pierced neck and applied modelled flowers.

c.1872. Painted pattern number E826. Impressed mark 'MINTON'; date cipher for 1872; shape number 2229. 24.8 cm height   TA

£70

SPODE
(1770–1833)
COPELAND & GARRETT
(1833–47)
W. T. COPELAND & SONS
(1847–1970)

Before the introduction of bone china in the 1790s, Spode was exclusively a pottery manufacturer, specialising in blue transfer-printed wares (see chapter 7). Although the firm later became known for fine bone chinas, earthenware has always been a large part of their output. They also made fine stone china and other stonewares (see chapters 5 and 10). The early wares were seldom marked, and difficult to attribute.

After the death of Josiah Spode III, the firm was purchased by William Taylor Copeland, (who had been a partner in the Spode's London retail business) and Thomas Garrett, under the style Copeland & Garrett. W. T. Copeland, assuming control of the firm in 1847, continued to use many of the shapes and patterns introduced by the previous firms.

After 1800 Spode marked many of its earthenwares, most often with 'SPODE' impressed, although other marks can be found. However, like many other manufacturers of the period, they sometimes only marked a few pieces in a service, and pattern numbers are very useful in identifying these wares (see p. 375). However, pattern numbers were only used on wares with painted decoration, not on those dipped in coloured glazes or transfer-printed.

Spode collectors will want to join the Spode Society, which has regular meetings and outings, also publishing a very fine *Review*. The membership secretary is Mrs Rosalind Pulver, PO Box 1812, London NW4 4NW. The Spode factory (Church Street, Stoke-on-Trent ST4 1BX) has a fine museum and factory tours are also available by prior arrangement.

Further Reading

Leonard Whiter. *Spode* (Barrie & Jenkins, 1970, reprinted with new colour illustrations 1989).
The Spode Society. *Recorder & Review* (1986 to the present day).

Spode pale blue glazed teapot.

c.1810–33. Impressed mark 'SPODE/18'. 13 cm height   JJB

£550

This shape is also known decorated with Rockingham or green glazes, and in red stoneware with a smear glaze. The shape continued in production during the Copeland & Garrett years.

Spode earthenware dessert dish painted in polychrome enamels and gilded.

c.1822. Restored. Painted pattern number 3278; 'Spode' printed in blue; impressed mark 'SPODE 42'. 28 cm length
JM

£68

Spode earthenware dish with botanical painting in polychrome enamels.

c.1800–15. Impressed 'SPODE'; 'Christmas Rose' painted in red. 20 cm square   BG

£495

Pottery and porcelain with botanical paintings are very collectable, and as such are often more expensive than wares with floral patterns in a less exacting style.

Copeland earthenware bottle with transfer-print filled in with enamels.

c.1847–67. Crazed. Printed blue seal mark 'COPELAND LATE SPODE'. 23.5 cm height   JM

£60

WEDGWOOD
(1759 to the present day)

The 19th century saw great changes at Wedgwood. After the death of Josiah Wedgwood I in 1795, his son Josiah II, who took little interest in the business, went into partnership with Thomas Byerley. The firm declined under Byerley's management, although it was a difficult period for all businesses. In 1800 Josiah I's eldest son John, who had left the firm in 1793, returned and the firm was revitalised, introducing lustres, bone china and blue transfer-printed wares.

By 1840 the firm, which had always been slow to follow the latest fashions, preferring to trade on the strength of its 18th-century reputation, was again in a precarious financial position. In 1843 Francis Wedgwood took as his partner John Boyle, Herbert Minton's former partner. Boyle helped to raise the capital needed to modernise the factory before his death in 1845. Francis then took Robert Brown as partner, and Brown injected considerable capital into the firm, accelerated the modernisation programme and encouraged the introduction of new lines until his death in 1859.

This was the beginning of a new era for Wedgwood. In 1859 Francis took his eldest son Godfrey into partnership, and he was to act as art director for many years, during which he attracted several fine artists such as Émile Lessore to the factory. Clement Francis Wedgwood joined the firm in 1863 and became the firm's ceramic chemist.

Further Reading

Maureen Batkin. *Wedgwood Ceramics 1846–1959* (Richard Dennis, 1982).
Robin Reilly. *Wedgwood*, 2 vols (Macmillan, 1989).
Robin Reilly and George Savage. *The Dictionary of Wedgwood* (Antique Collectors' Club, Woodbridge, 1980).

Two plates from an ivory-glazed *Butterfly Tremblay* dessert service with *Card Motto* prints coloured with enamels and gilded.

c.1877. Painted pattern number T475. Impressed date code FXF (February 1877). Impressed 'WEDGWOOD'. 24 cm diameter   TA

£58 the pair

The full set of twelve *Card Motto* plates is illustrated in Batkin. The T pattern numbers are usually found on tiles, but occasionally on other wares decorated with prints designed for tiles.

Butterfly Tremblay refers to the relief-moulded border pattern. This border is usually found on wares with translucent coloured glazes, which sets them off to better advantage than does the opaque ivory glaze. They are made using a process known as *émail ombrant* invented by Baron Charles Paul Amable who went into partnership with Baron Hocédé Alexis de Tremblay in 1836. Wedgwood made a small number of similar wares in 1864. After purchasing 2,500 of the moulds and designs, recipes for shading enamels and the original patent in 1872, Wedgwood introduced nearly 175

Tremblay patterns, usually found with majolica glazes. The technique was also used by other contemporary French and English potters.

Wedgwood earthenware vase painted by Émile Lessore.

c.1861. Impressed mark 'WEDGWOOD'; impressed date code WVP (August 1861). 14.5 cm height   G

£200

Émile Lessore (c.1805–76) was a French painter who trained at Sèvres. In England he worked at Minton, and subsequently for Wedgwood. His distinctive style of painting influenced a number of contemporary ceramic artists.

Reverse.

Wedgwood *Triple Dolphin Centre* in pastel glazes.

c.1870. Painted pattern number 7035. Indistinct OPU or OPD impressed date code (October 1866 or 1875). 17.8 cm height   TA

£65

This comport was part of a dessert service which has been produced in various bodies and glazes since the Regency period. A 'Moonlight' lustre service c.1810 is illustrated in Geoffrey Godden's *Illustrated Encyclopaedia of British Pottery and Porcelain*. During the Victorian period the shape was revived for decoration in majolica glazes and in the 1870s with this pastel glaze treatment. During the 20th century the shapes were used for green-glazed wares and more recently have been decorated with matt black or white glazes. Various treatments of these shapes are illustrated in both Batkin and Victoria Bergesen's *Majolica* (Barrie & Jenkins, 1989).

OTHER MANUFACTURERS

Apart from his Parian wares, W. H. Goss made a range of items in terracotta. In 1867 he entered into a brief partnership with a Mr Peake. Terracotta wares marked 'GOSS &

PEAKE' date from this partnership and are more valuable than the subsequent terracottas which are marked 'W H Goss'. Goss continued terracotta production until 1876, at which time it fell out of fashion. For more information about the firm see chapter 19.

Terracotta *Cambridge Roman Jug* transfer-printed and painted in polychrome enamels.

c.1868–76 'W H GOSS' impressed. 12 cm height   GCC

£85

This jug was also made with a Britannia metal lid.

Terracotta bottle with incised decoration highlighted with enamels

c.1868–76. Missing stopper. 'W H Goss' impressed. 23 cm height   GCC

£65

This bottle is usually found without its stopper; with its stopper the asking price would be more like £100.

Brown-Westhead, Moore & Co. earthenware jug painted in polychrome enamels.

c.1879. Mark painted in red 'D3938'; diamond registration mark for 15 April 1879. 17 cm height   G

£40.

The bamboo handle is typical of *japonisme*, the Japanese-inspired designs of the 1870s.

Wood & Caldwell sprigged earthenware jug.

c.1790–1818. Impressed mark 'WOOD & CALDWELL'. 12 cm height   V

£75

This jug was made during a partnership between Enoch Wood and Ernest Caldwell, succeeded in 1818 by Enoch Wood & Sons. There are a great many such earthenware or stoneware sprigged jugs which are unmarked, and have a comparatively low value considering their quality.

While Carlton Ware of the 20th century (see chapter 14) is well known the Wiltshire & Robinson wares of the late 19th century often go unrecognised.

Wiltshaw & Robinson earthenware tobacco jar with match pot and striker in lid (three pieces), with green ground and white sprigging.

c.1898. Printed mark on base 'Rd. No. 330913' (1898); Wiltshaw & Robinson printed mark with bird; 'CARLTON WARE'. Printed mark on lid 'Rd. No. 313747' (also 1898). 14.5 cm height   CCC

£120

Wiltshaw & Robinson earthenware jug with green ground and white sprigging.

c.1896. Printed mark on base 'Rd. No. 289950 (1896); Wiltshaw & Robinson mark with bird; 'CARLTON WARE'. 17.5 cm height   CCC

£55

One of a pair of Charles Hobson earthenware plates with Shells pattern transfer-prints painted in enamels and gilded.

c.1865–80. Transfer-printed garter mark with 'C. H.' and pattern name 'SHELLS'. 23 cm diameter   G

£120 the pair

This a very fine print and is well decorated. Shells are a popular subject for collectors, and a similar plate with an unnamed landscape, for example, would be significantly less valuable.

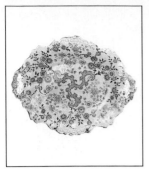

William Ridgway & Co. earthenware dessert service dish with *Helical* green transfer-print over a blue-glaze.

c.1834–54. Green transfer-printed mark of anchor and urn 'HELICAL'; 'W. R. & CO.', 30 cm length   JJB

£65

This pattern is number 63 in the William Ridgway pattern book. The page from the pattern book is illustrated in Geoffrey Godden's *Ridgway Porcelain* (Antique Collectors' Club, Woodbridge, 1985). Godden also illustrates part of a dessert service in this shape with a different pattern. Similar shapes also occur in John Ridgway porcelain.

UNATTRIBUTED EARTHENWARES

Unusual lady's head earthenware jug painted in polychrome enamels.

c.1800–20. 14 cm height   BG

£500

Elaborate pottery pipes such as the four shown below are vulnerable to breakage, and are very valuable, even with damage or restoration. Elaborate coils would have served to cool the smoke. It is not likely that these pipes would have been meant for everyday use.

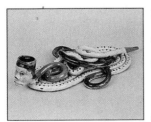

Prattware type pipe.

c.1790. 20 cm length   AS

£1,200

Prattware type pipe with green, blue and yellow decoration, signed B.

c.1790. Repairs. 19 cm height   AS

£1,200

Prattware pipe, John Bull with his lion, possibly Yorkshire.

c.1800. Sponging on vase. Restored pipe bowl and end of stem. 18 cm length   LR

£850

Earthenware swan pipe painted in polychrome enamels.

c.1800. 21 cm length   AS

£2,500

This interesting subject of a swan swallowing a fish also adds to the value.

Earthenware plate with sponged decoration in green, with relief-moulded edge coloured in green and painted bird in yellow and brown, probably Welsh.

c.1820. Incised heart mark. 24 cm diameter   AD

£320

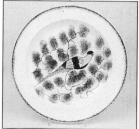

Cow creamers have been popular since the late eighteenth century. They have been made in earthenware with a wide variety of decorations until the present day. The largest collection of cow creamers in the world can be seen at the City Museum & Art Gallery, Stoke-on-Trent.

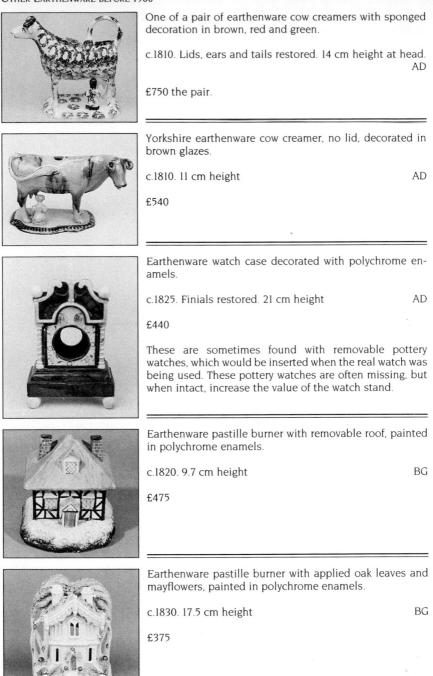

One of a pair of earthenware cow creamers with sponged decoration in brown, red and green.

c.1810. Lids, ears and tails restored. 14 cm height at head.
AD

£750 the pair.

Yorkshire earthenware cow creamer, no lid, decorated in brown glazes.

c.1810. 11 cm height   AD

£540

Earthenware watch case decorated with polychrome enamels.

c.1825. Finials restored. 21 cm height   AD

£440

These are sometimes found with removable pottery watches, which would be inserted when the real watch was being used. These pottery watches are often missing, but when intact, increase the value of the watch stand.

Earthenware pastille burner with removable roof, painted in polychrome enamels.

c.1820. 9.7 cm height   BG

£475

Earthenware pastille burner with applied oak leaves and mayflowers, painted in polychrome enamels.

c.1830. 17.5 cm height   BG

£375

Staffordshire earthenware castle spill vase painted in coloured glazes with applied foliage.

c.1825. Small chip on turret restored. 17 cm height   AD

£325

This type of foliage was made by forcing clay through a strainer and applying it to the pot. The technique was often used on animal figures to give them a furry appearance.

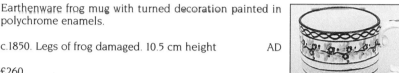

Earthenware frog mug with turned decoration painted in polychrome enamels.

c.1850. Legs of frog damaged. 10.5 cm height   AD

£260

Frog mugs have small figures of frogs inside them, either lurking at the bottom or crawling up the side. These were meant to startle the drinker who would uncover them after a large draught. Frog mugs are popular with collectors, so beware. Some unscrupulous persons have been known to add frogs to mugs which did not originally have them. In some cases these fake frogs are actually plastic! So examine the frogs carefully to see that they are original.

Many of these mugs are quite crude and there are un-marked reproductions about, particularly a version with poor relief-moulding showing men drinking and badly painted polychrome enamels. The example here is of good quality. Note the careful engine-turning and the generous C-scroll handle.

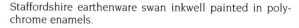

Staffordshire earthenware swan inkwell painted in poly-chrome enamels.

c.1820s. Neck repaired. 9.2 cm height   JM

£32

The price for this unusual piece is low, owing to the damage. An example in fine condition could fetch in excess of £75.

149

Relief-moulded earthenware jug painted in polychrome enamels.

c.1880s. 27 cm height   JJB

£87

Unusual earthenware plate with chinoiserie transfer-print painted in polychrome enamels.

c.1820. 25 cm diameter   JM

£78

The adjective 'Pratt' is applied to pearlwares with high-temperature underglaze colours, multicoloured transfer-prints and to printed terracotta wares such as the following. This is confusing, and nobody is really happy with this terminology, but it is so strongly ingrained in the collector's glossary that it is difficult to avoid.

The firm of F. & R. Pratt made many of these printed terracotta wares, but they were also made by other manufacturers. For some W. H. Goss examples see p. 144.

Pratt style terracotta urn with transfer-print painted in polychrome enamels and gilded.

c.1855–65. Marked 9131, painted in black. 18.5 cm height G

£95

Pratt style terracotta barrel with transfer-print painted in polychrome enamels and gilded.

c.1855–65. 10 cm height   G

£48

Unusual pair of jet ware vases with polychrome enamel paintings of shells and gilding.

c.1875–90. Gilding on handles slightly rubbed. 22 cm height
TA

£270

Jet wares are red wares with a cobalt blue lead glaze, which over the red body appears black. Mostly used for teapots c.1875–90.

Very rare Yorkshire earthenware elephant money box decorated with underglaze colours (black, green and yellow), some sponged.

c.1820. Impressed inscription in printer's type 'SAVE ALL'. 11.5 cm height
BG

£800

Earthenware cottage money box, probably Yorkshire.

c.1810. Typical buff walls. 13.3 cm height
LR

£400

This money box was reproduced by William Kent in the present century. The reproductions have two male figures.

Large Mexboro Chapel, Bank Street, Yorkshire earthenware money box decorated with coloured glazes and polychrome enamels.

c.1840. 18 cm height
JH

£1,100

Money boxes with the names of chapels are sometimes said to have been used as collection boxes in the chapels. It is more likely that they were issued for fund-raising.

9 EARTHENWARE FIGURES BEFORE 1900

RECENT research has shown that there were dozens of figure manufacturers, and we know little if anything about their products. It had been the practice in the past to attribute nearly every figure to one of the few potters who did occasionally mark their figures, e.g. the Wood family of Burslem (c.1754–1846) or John Walton. We now know that popular subjects were made by many potters, and it is dangerous to make attributions unless *every* detail is identical to that of a marked example. It should also be remembered that many of the firms had short lives, and their moulds were sold off when the businesses were dissolved. Thus figures made from the same mould could have been made by more than one firm. Changes in decoration and technique can help us to date figures approximately, but as few figures were marked, it is impossible to attribute most of them reliably.

There are three main parts to a figure, the base or plinth, the support and the figure itself. The figure may be made up from many separately moulded parts, e.g. head, arms, hands, hats, accessories. In general at the end of the 18th century and during the 19th century the factories reduced labour costs by casting the figures in fewer parts. For example, what had been an individually modelled arm held aloft became a relief-moulded arm resting on the lap or held across the breast, so that it could be made part of the body mould. Accessories were eliminated or again were relief-moulded against the body or the base.

The greatest challenge for the figure modeller is to design a figure which will not collapse in the kiln. It is easier to do this with seated figures, which can have a chair, bench or rock as a support. Standing figures may lean against a column, a tree or a bocage (a support decorated with applied leaves and flowers, or even tiny pieces of clay forced through a sieve). Bocages were introduced on pottery figures c.1810–15, but had been used on porcelain figures during the 18th century.

While some figures, particularly those of domestic or farmyard animals, were probably modelled from life, many figures were based on sculptures or engravings. The range of figures is enormous and only a small variety is illustrated below.

Early figures have great charm, and are very popular with collectors. Therefore even damaged examples can be quite valuable. As a rule I have avoided including damaged pieces in this book: however, in the case of early figures, it would be impossible to present a wide selection if all damaged or restored figures were excluded. The damage or restoration in each case is noted.

Further reading

It must be noted that Pat Halfpenny's excellent book has overturned many previous theories about earthenware figures of the period 1740–1840.

Reginald G. Haggar. *English Pottery Figures 1660–1860* (John Tiranti, 1947).

Pat Halfpenny. *English Earthenware Figures 1740–1840* (Antique Collectors' Club, Woodbridge, 1991).

Pat Halfpenny. *English Earthenware Figures 1740–1940* (City of Stoke-on-Trent Museum & Art Gallery, 1991).

Jonathan Horne. *A Collection of Early English Pottery,* Parts I–XII (Jonathan Horne, 1982–92).

Anthony Oliver. *Staffordshire Pottery. The Tribal Art of England* (Heinemann, 1981).

Julia Poole. *Plagiarism Personified? European Pottery and Porcelain Figures* (Fitzwilliam Museum, Cambridge, 1986).

Ross E. Taggart. *The Frank P. and Harriet C. Burnap Collection of English Pottery in the William Rockhill Nelson Gallery*, revised edn (Nelson Gallery/Atkins Museum, Kansas City, Missouri, 1967).

H. A. B. Turner. *A Collector's Guide to Staffordshire Pottery Figures* (Emerson Books, New York, 1971).

UNDERGLAZE AND COLOURED GLAZE DECORATION TO 1830

Earthenware figure of a cat with brown underglaze oxide colour.

c.1785. 20.7 cm height   JH

£2,650

This is an exceedingly rare figure, and figures of cats have always been most popular with collectors. Delftware examples in shapes similar to this have been recorded from the 17th century (see Horne, part V). For an example decorated with splashed pink lustre see p. 494.

Wood family Venus and Neptune pearlware figures decorated with coloured glazes and gilded.

c.1785. Venus's head restored, chip. 28 cm height   JH

£4,950

A figure of Admiral Van Tromp illustrated in Halfpenny, attributed to John Wood, has very similar medallions on the plinth. Venus and Neptune figures appear in John Wood's account book of 1786. However, figures from mythology were popular subjects in both pottery and porcelain, particularly Venus, who was sold paired with Apollo or Bacchus, as well as with Neptune. These were made by a number of manufacturers, including members of the Wood family.

Note how finely finished the backs of the figures are, a sure sign of the highest quality, as is evident in the modelling, particularly of the draperies. The squared neo-classical plinths of these figures help to date them.

Reverses.

Earthenware figure of old woman feeding birds, decorated with green, brown and blue glazes.

c.1780–1800. Some repairs. Impressed mark 'Ra Wood Burslem 70'. 20 cm height   AS

£15,000

This a particularly desirable figure because it is marked and there are two birds feeding. Notice the exceptionally fine moulding in the face and the way in which the woman seems to be caught in the midst of moving.

'70' represents the mould number for this figure. The mould number or 'Ra Wood' may be found together or separately on his figures. it is difficult to ascribe these figures specifically to Ralph Wood the Elder or Ralph Wood the Younger, as the younger Ralph used moulds which had been made by his father.

Staffordshire earthenware sheep, press-moulded hollow figure decorated with grey, brown, green and yellow glazes.

c.1780–1800. Repaired ear tips. 14 cm height   AS

£1,850

An identical figure with different colouring is illustrated in Halfpenny, colour plate 18. Compare the fine modelling of this figure with the coarse North Yorkshire enamelled version in the following section.

Staffordshire earthenware figures of stag and doe with coloured glaze decoration.

c.1780–1800. Stag's antlers re-stuck and neck cracked. Doe has a new left ear and neck crack. 15 cm height   LR

£3,000

The stag is illustrated in Halfpenny.

Staffordshire earthenware bagpiper with translucent brown, yellow and green glazes.

c.1780–1800. Restuck base. 20 cm height   LR

£1,650

Creamware vase with gardener figure in green and brown underglaze colours.

c.1785. Chips to top and edges of vase restored; spade restored. 17 cm height   AD

£740

Staffordshire earthenware monkey pounce pot decorated with brown, blue and green underglaze colours.

Late 18th century. Cracked in several places. Solid base with hole for filling at rear. 11.5 cm height   AS

£500

This is a very unusual item, as monkeys seldom appear in pottery until the 19th century. Thus it is quite valuable, despite the considerable damage.

155

The charming small animal figures shown below may have been made for children. They are certainly *very* rare, few having survived. The figures are hollow and the insides are roughly finished.

Staffordshire hollow press-moulded earthenware cat decorated with brown underglaze colour.

Late 18th century. Repaired ear. 15 cm height   AS

£2,250

Press-moulded earthenware rabbit decorated with brown and green underglaze colours.

Late 18th century. Unglazed hollow inside. 7 cm height AS

£5,500

Earthenware hollow press-moulded sheep with coloured glazes, brown stripes and green base.

c.1785. 10.8 cm length base   LR

£545

Earthenware brown dog on green base decorated with coloured glazes.

c.1780–1800. Repaired base. 8.9 cm length of base   LR

£550; £650 perfect.

Staffordshire press-moulded hollow earthenware horse decorated with green glaze.

Early 19th century. 7.5 cm height   AS

£1,850

This is a particularly well modelled figure, with a charming little dog relief-moulded under the horse's girth.

PEARLWARE UNDERGLAZE HIGH-TEMPERATURE COLOURS (PRATTWARE)
(c.1790–1840)

'Prattware' is a term commonly used to describe pearlware painted, sponged or stippled with underglaze high-temperature colours c.1790–1840. The colours (orange, yellow, green, blue, black, brown and occasionally a dark raspberry) were often used to highlight relief-moulding. They were produced from oxides which could withstand the high temperature necessary to fuse the glaze. The body is a cream coloured earthenware, and the lead glaze often has the blue tinge associated with pearlware. For more information about Prattware see chapter 4.

Further Reading

John and Griselda Lewis. *Pratt Ware: English and Scottish Relief Decorated and Underglaze Earthenware 1780–1840.* (Antique Collectors' Club, Woodbridge, 1984).
T. A. Lockett and Pat Halfpenny, eds. *Creamware and Pearlware.* (Stoke-on-Trent City Museum & Art Gallery, 1986).
Horne, Jonathan, A *Collection of Early English Pottery*, Parts I–XII (Jonathan Horne, 1982–92).

Prattware type Staffordshire pearlware lion with bluish glaze, decorated with brown, blue and yellow underglaze colours.

Late 18th century. 18.5 cm height   AS

£6,800

The lion with his paw resting on a ball is based on the marble lions which stand at the entrance of the Loggia dei Lanzi in Florence. Reproductions of these lions were also made in stone, marble, bronze and plaster. The lion was a popular symbol of British nationalism, deriving from its occurrence on the Royal Arms.

Prattware type multi-part moulded earthenware figure of St George and the Dragon.

c.1790–1800. Repairs to ears, reins and leg; missing spear; hollow base cracked. 28 cm height   AS

£1,750

St George and the Dragon has always been a popular subject for British artists and craftsmen. This particular figure is after an illustration of the Red Cross Knight from Edmund Spenser's allegory *The Faerie Queene*.

Prattware type Staffordshire 'Hurdy Gurdy Player' decorated underglaze in green, brown, blue, beige and yellow, possibly taken from a Ralph Wood original.

c.1785–1800. 26 cm height   LR

£600

A figure very like this one (but with overglaze enamel decoration) inscribed *Flemish Music* is illustrated in Halfpenny.

Prattware type ram decorated underglaze in brown and green.

c.1810. Very minor chip. 15 cm length   AD

£950

Prattware type long case clock, decorated underglaze in yellow, blue and green.

c.1820. 20.5 cm height   AD

£630

Prattware type Staffordshire earthenware watch holder with two figures, decorated in underglaze colours and painted in polychrome enamels.

Early 19th century. 24.5 cm height   AS

£850

These may also be found with removable pottery 'watches' to replace the real one during use. These have often been lost and a complete stand would be more valuable.

Yorkshire Prattware type figure group.

Early 19th century. Superb condition. 14.2 cm length of base; 14.5 cm height   JH

£1,250

Yorkshire earthenware rooster painted in yellow, pink, grey, black and green underglaze colours.

c.1820. 10 cm height   AD

£340

Yorkshire earthenware press-moulded rabbit figure with sponged black and manganese high-temperature underglaze colours.

c.1810. 12 cm height   JH

£990

North Yorkshire earthenware recumbent lamb painted in green and black high-temperature underglaze colours.

c.1800–15. 16.2 cm length of base   BG

£790

Compare the coarse modelling of this figure with the finer Staffordshire coloured glaze version in the previous section.

Yorkshire earthenware monkey, lion and bear group decorated with brown, grey and green high-temperature underglaze colours.

c.1800. 16.5 cm height   AS

£9,800

Yorkshire earthenware cow figure group painted in poly-chrome high-temperature underglaze colours.

c.1820. Bases and horns restored. 14.5 cm height   AD

£930

ENAMELLED DECORATION TO 1830

These figures were decorated with enamel colours after the glaze firing. They were then fired again at a much lower temperature. Two pioneers of this technique were Ralph Wood the younger (1748–95) and his cousin Enoch Wood (1759–1840). These figures were more expensive to produce as they required a second or third firing.

Figures from classical mythology, usually deities, were made by many manufacturers. Allegorical figures such as Faith, Hope, Charity, Prudence, Fortitude or The Four Seasons were very popular. In keeping with the neo-classicism of the period, these were generally portrayed in flowing draperies, and wearing sandals.

Staffordshire pearl-glazed earthenware *Hope* figure with overglaze enamel painted decoration in black, beige and orange.

c.1790–1800. 17.5 cm height   T

£150

While this figure is charming, notice how crude the modell-ing is compared with some of the figures illustrated above. A very similar, but *not* identical figure made by Theophilus Smith is illustrated in Halfpenny.

Earthenware Vestal Virgin figure, painted in polychrome enamels.

c.1810–20. 19.7 cm height   LR

£375

This is a rare figure in perfect condition. Halfpenny illustrates a very similar figure which is mounted on a low square base.

Pearl-glazed earthenware *Charity* figure painted in polychrome enamels.

c.1810–20. 18.5 cm height   HBW

£110

A Wedgwood version of *Charity* which is similar to this one is illustrated in Halfpenny (p. 169). It was a popular subject, and usually included two children and an infant, but sometimes appears with only two children. The cross and Bible carried by the child in this example appear to be unusual features.

Pomona earthenware figure painted in polychrome enamels.

c.1800. 19 cm height   HBW

£245

Leeds Pottery pearl-glazed earthenware figure of *Minerva*, with overglaze painted enamel decoration.

c.1790–1810. Hollow. 26.7 cm height   LR

£1,200

Another Leeds Pottery example with slightly different over-glaze enamel decoration is illustrated in Halfpenny.

Earthenware figure of *Summer* from *The Four Seasons*, possibly by Dixon, Austin & Co.

c.1820–6. 24 cm height   T

£390

A set of marked Dixon, Austin & Co.'s *Seasons* is illustrated in Halfpenny. Robert Dixon and Thomas Austin operated the Sunderland or Garrison Pottery under the style Dixon, Austin & Co. 1820–6.

Bull-baiting earthenware group, manganese, green, brown and yellow enamel decoration, possibly by John Wood.

c.1780–1800. Restored cracks in right foreleg, dog's tail and top left horn tip. 17 cm length; 14 cm height   LR

£1900

163

Staffordshire pearl-glazed earthenware bust with overglaze polychrome enamel decoration.

c.1790. 24 cm height   AD

£575

Earthenware bust of *Plato* by Enoch Wood, with polychrome enamel decoration.

c.1800. 'PLATO' impressed in rear of socle. 33 cm height
                                                              LR

£675

Early 20th-century copies of this bust are in existence.

FIGURES WITH BOCAGES

Bocages are most commonly found on earthenware figures c.1810–25. The moulding used on the leaves and flowers is often quite distinctive, and may be used to attribute unmarked figures in some cases. Pat Halfpenny has made a detailed study of this subject, and many photographs in her book point out details to look for.

Bocages are very vulnerable to damage, and should be examined carefully. Slight damage or restoration is not a serious problem, but the loss of the entire bocage or an entire branch reduces the figure's value dramatically. The loss of a branch will be evident because the symmetry of the bocage will be lost. Any strange stump behind a figure should be treated with suspicion. Sometimes the remaining stump will have been ground down to conceal the loss.

Staffordshire pair of figures *Show Woman* and *Show Man* painted in polychrome enamels.

c.1820. Restored. 15 cm height   JH

£880

Staffordshire pair of musicians painted in polychrome enamels with rococo bases.

c.1820. Restored. Woman 15.8 cm height; man 16 cm height
JH

£1,350

Staffordshire *Rural Pastimes* earthenware group decorated in polychrome enamels.

c.1815. Part of bocage missing and one head restored. 21.5 cm height   AD

£380

This is one of a group of figures which have Staffordshire porcelain counterparts. Others illustrated in Halfpenny are *Virgin Mary* and *Contest*.

Staffordshire earthenware mandolin player painted in polychrome enamels and gilded.

c.1815. Slight restoration to mandolin. 15 cm height HBW

£300

This figure is unusually finely modelled and painted.

Fruitboys Staffordshire earthenware figure decorated with polychrome enamels.

c.1820. No restoration. 14 cm height   AD

£360

Earthenware 'Birds in Branches' group decorated with green and yellow glazes.

c.1810. Restored bird tail and some leaf tips. 19.7 cm height
LR

£1,250

This subject was treated by several potters.

Tittensor earthenware figure group painted underglaze and decorated with coloured glazes.

c.1810–25. Large chips to bocage. 10 cm height. AS

£950

Charles Tittensor, who potted 1803–30 in a series of partnerships and on his own, is thought to be the manufacturer of the large group of underglaze painted figures marked 'TITTENSOR'. This figure has been attributed on the basis of close comparison with marked examples.

Staffordshire earthenware bird group painted underglaze.

Early 19th century. Repairs to bocage, one tail and nest. 19.5 cm height AS

£1,100

Staffordshire earthenware group painted in polychrome enamels.

c.1820. Restored. 23.2 cm height   JH

£3,300

This group is sometimes entitled *Perswasion* (*sic*). A very similar example with a pine-cone bocage is illustrated in Halfpenny.

Reverse.

Earthenware spill vase with figure groups of 'Shepherd Musicians' painted in polychrome enamels.

c.1820. Restoration to arms, flute, lyre and vase. 17.7 cm height   JH

£1,650

Staffordshire earthenware group painted in polychrome enamels.

c.1820. Bocage badly damaged. Height of spill 20 cm; length of base 33 cm   AS

£3,800

Staffordshire earthenware group, *Raising of Lazarus*, painted in polychrome enamels.

c.1830. Repairs to tree and tomb. 28 cm length   AS

£2,850

OBADIAH SHERRATT?

The figures which have in the past been attributed to Obadiah Sherratt (c.1775–1846) are characterised by their primitive charm. As the figures were all moulded separately before the whole group was assembled, there are many variations from one example to the next. Many of the figures found on the large groups may also be found as separate figures.

Sherratt potted at Hot Lane, Burslem from c.1810 until c.1828, when he moved to Waterloo Road. After his death his son Hamlet continued the business. In his *Staffordshire Chimney Ornaments* (Phoenix House, 1955) Reginald Haggar first suggested that Sherratt was responsible for the group of wares now generally attributed to him. However, apart from the fact that we know that Sherratt was making toys or figures in Burslem at the right period, there is *no evidence to tie this group to him*. Whether or not Sherratt actually did make this group of figures, the Hodkinsons have firmly established by close analysis that the group were made by the same potter.

Further Reading

Malcolm and Judith Hodkinson. *Sherratt? A Natural Family of Staffordshire Figures* (Chisquare, 1991).

Earthenware figure group *Sacrifice of Isaac*, table base with cartouche 'ABRAM STOP' painted in polychrome enamels and sponging in lines. Little oak bocage with mayflowers.

c.1825. Some restoration. 29 cm height   LR

£2,000

Halfpenny and Hodkinson illustrate more elaborate versions of this group with bocage and a text from Genesis on a scroll. The group is known on several versions of table bases and on square bases.

Earthenware figure group, 'TAM O'SHANTER SOUTER JOHNNY' in printer's type on cartouche, decorated with coloured enamels.

c.1830. Table made up, should be a cricket table. Black base with serpentine front. 17.8 cm height; 19 cm length   LR

£4,000

The statues of Tam O'Shanter and Souter Johnnie from which this design was taken are now at the Burns Monument, Alloway. The statues were sculpted by James Thom (1802–50) and toured Britain in 1829. Figures of Tam O'Shanter and Souter Johnny are rarely found separately, but the group is even rarer (see Hodkinsons). A relief-moulded stoneware jug also based on the statues is illustrated on p. 506.

Earthenware 'Baptism Group' with feather base and may-flowers on triple oak-leaf bocage, decorated with polychrome enamels.

c.1825. Replacement hat. 18.4 cm height   LR

£4,500

These groups are relatively common. Some are marked 'BAPTISM OF MARY' The Hodkinsons illustrate versions with other typical 'Sherratt' bocages. Halfpenny illustrates a version with a table base.

Large earthenware rural 'Musicians Group' on table base with twelve sheep and a dog painted in polychrome enamels.

c.1825. 33 cm length   LR

£5,500

The musicians are illustrated in Hodkinson as separate figures with the girl having a different head. The dog seated at the base of the tree is found on several other groups.

Earthenware 'Shepherd Musician with Rover', bocage with chrysanthemums.

c.1825. 12.7 cm height   LR

£450

It is unusual to find this figure with two sheep.

Earthenware Masonic mantel group of Craft and Tyler Mason on a table base.

c.1830. Restoration to top ornaments. 25.4 cm length; 31.7 cm height   LR

£1,800

This group is usually found with the top ornaments damaged or missing. Restorers sometimes ground down the remnants and painted over the blemishes.

169

Pair of earthenware figures, Neptune and Venus four-footed low table bases, Venus different head from ordinary figure. Black and white base.

c.1830. Venus 19 cm, Neptune 17.8 cm height   LR

£2,400

Pearl-glazed earthenware Village Maid figure on table base painted in overglaze enamel, triple oak-leaf bocage.

c.1825–30. 29.2 cm height   LR

£1,200

This figure is more often found titled Reading Maid. The subject was used by a number of manufacturers for a period of years.

WALTON

John Walton of Burslem (c.1780–1835+) was first known as a 'colour maker and earthenware manufacturer' in 1818. The colour works was in Burslem and the pottery in Haddereage. His work is widely known today because so many of his figures bear a strap mark 'Walton': The authentic Walton strap mark has letters with serifs, which are missing from reproductions. A common feature of many of his figures is a flat tree background. The leaves are usually six-lobed with a brightly coloured flower at the centre of each one. The colouring is heavy and opaque with brush marks visible. He was a highly successful commercial potter and many of his contemporaries copied his style, so that their work is now sometimes known as the Walton School. In 1835 Walton's pottery was taken over by George Hood, who is believed to have continued using the Walton moulds.

Walton pearl-glazed earthenware pair of Songsters with overglaze enamel decoration.

c.1815–25. Moulded 'WALTON' strap marks. Right-hand figure has restoration to hunting horn and swans' necks; left-hand figure has restorations to end of pipe and swans' necks. Lady 13.3 cm height; man 14 cm height   LR

£1,800 the pair

Reproductions of these groups will not have serifs on the titles. A similar group is illustrated in Halfpenny.

Walton pearl-glazed earthenware pair of 'Rustic Gardeners' with four-branch bocages and overglaze enamel decoration.

c.1815–25. Moulded 'WALTON' strap marks. 14.3 cm height
LR

£800 the pair

A similar pair of Walton gardeners with different modelled details and decoration is illustrated in Halfpenny.

Pearl-glazed earthenware 'Shepherdess' figure with overglaze enamel decoration, blind cartouche.

c.1815–25. Moulded 'Walton' strap mark. 14 cm height   LR

£350

Reproductions of this common figure are equally common. One is illustrated in William Kent's catalogue of 1955, reproduced in Halfpenny. These reproductions may bear the Walton strap mark.

VICTORIAN EARTHENWARE FIGURES

Although there are always carry-overs from one era to another, Victorian earthenware figures as a group are quite distinctive. The increased wealth of the nation and the concomitant growth of the middle classes considerably enlarged the market for ornaments at the cheaper end of the market. As a result the modelling is generally rather flat and lacking in detail. Compare the figures below with some of the 18th-century figures above: the faces have bland features and are smooth; there are fewer separately moulded arms and legs; the painting is generally in broad strokes which highlight moulded details in low relief. The figures of the Victorian era are delightful in their own right, but they did not employ the craftsmanship of the earlier figures. Very few of these figures were marked, and the vast majority cannot be attributed.

There were, of course, some very excellent figures made in the Victorian era. However, these were most often produced in porcelain, Parian or with majolica decoration: examples may be found in other chapters of this book.

Inexperienced collectors are advised to be wary, as the most popular subjects have been reproduced throughout the 20th century. These sometimes find their way into the antique shop or fair, but are quite easy to spot. A few visits to a reliable dealer specialising in these figures will soon acquaint the collector with the enormous differences between the antique and the reproduction. A specialist dealer will often have a few reproductions on hand (for reference not for sale) to show you the differences. The modern figures stand out as their glazes are too shiny, the colours border on the garish and the gilding is too bright. When artificial crazing is present it is usually grey and so regular as to form almost a mosaic effect.

It should be made clear that the modern commercial reproductions are not meant to deceive: and to reproduce the originals accurately would cost more than they are worth. Many reproductions are now decades old and are legally nearly antique themselves.

The best guide is to look for quality by examining the figure carefully. Even if the figure is Victorian a badly decorated example is less desirable. How was it made? Was it slip-cast in one piece or are there legs, tails, ears, arms or other features which would have been separately modelled? Are the enamels applied haphazardly, or are there carefully painted features, or patterns on the clothing?

Further Reading

Clive Mason Pope. A–Z of Staffordshire Dogs (Resego, Switzerland, 1990).

P. D. Gordon Pugh. Staffordshire Portrait Figures of the Victorian Era, revised edn (Antique Collectors' Club, Woodbridge, 1987).

Anthony Oliver. The Victorian Staffordshire Figure (Heinemann, 1971).

Amoret and Christopher Scott. Staffordshire Figures of the Nineteenth Century (Shire Publications, Aylesbury, 1989).

Staffordshire Portrait Figures. A Catalogue of the P. D. Gordon Pugh Collection in the City Museum & Art Gallery, Stoke-on-Trent (City of Stoke-on-Trent Museum & Art Gallery, n.d.).

Children seated on recumbent or standing dogs were a popular Victorian subject. Many examples are illustrated in Pope. The children are sometimes thought to be the children of Queen Victoria and Prince Albert, but the only definitely identified mounted children figures have been seated on ponies or riding in pony carts. Victorian boys and girls were dressed quite similarly, but can easily be distinguished by their poses. The girls will be riding side-saddle, the boy astride.

Rare and unrecorded earthenware figure of a girl riding a Newfoundland dog painted in polychrome enamels.

c.1835. 14 cm height   WA

£560

Staffordshire earthenware figure of a boy seated on a dog painted in polychrome enamels.

c.1830–40. 11 cm height   W

£175

This child is probably a boy, as the pose is not one which would have been thought proper for a girl (see previous item). Note that the figure has been modelled and decorated in the round.

Reverse.

Earthenware figure of *Plenty* painted in polychrome enamels.

c.1845. 18.5 cm height   WA

£225

Allegorical figures were still popular in the Victorian era, but the classical draperies and poses were largely abandoned. This figure was probably modelled after an engraving of a Continental peasant girl.

Earthenware 'Music Lovers' group painted in polychrome enamels.

c.1845. 17.5 cm height   WA

£390

This was a very popular subject produced in earthenware and porcelain throughout the 18th and 19th centuries. A number of porcelain examples are Illustrated in Halfpenny,

Daniel Defoe's *Robinson Crusoe*, first published in 1719, was the subject of a number of dramatisations during the 19th century. These figures may portray actors in one of the Victorian productions, but have not yet been identified.

Earthenware Robinson Crusoe figure painted in polychrome enamels and gilded.

c.1845. Minor restoration. 16 cm height   WA

£275

Very rare earthenware Man Friday figure painted in polychrome enamels.

c.1845. Firing crack to base. 17 cm height   WA

£585

This figure is much more valuable than the previous one, because it is rarer and in better condition.

Scottish earthenware shoe inkwell painted in polychrome enamels of yellow, pink, green and black.

c.1840. Two chips. 15 cm length   AD

£260

Earthenware swan with gilding.

c.1850. 15.5 cm length   AD

£250

Staffordshire earthenware nesting hen painted in polychrome enamels.

c.1855. 23 cm length   WA

£500

These nesting hens were used to hold boiled eggs at the breakfast table. Stoneware versions were made by Dudson. Reproductions were made by William Kent of Burslem, and appear in their catalogue of 1955 (reproduced in Half-penny).

Earthenware stag group with spill vase painted in polychrome enamels and gilded.

c.1845. 21.5 cm height   WA

£1,630

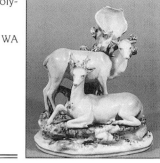

Unusual Staffordshire earthenware figure of a dog attack-
ing an eagle's nest, painted in polychrome enamels and
gilded.

Victorian. 16.5 cm height   HBW

£170

Gordon Pugh illustrates a similar figure which has a child
sleeping on the right-hand side of the rocks, with the dog
protecting her from the eagle. There were a number of other
figures showing dogs protecting children from snakes, and
also a figure with a mother rescuing her child from an eagle.

Staffordshire earthenware figure of a girl painted in polychrome enamels.

Late 19th century. 10.5 cm height   TA

£25

This figure is poorly modelled and has only the most rudi-
mentary enamel decoration.

Staffordshire earthenware Highland lass figure with basket of fruit and watering-can painted in polychrome enamels.

Victorian. Restoration to waist. 17.5 cm height   TA

£38

The Royal children were often portrayed in Tartan, and they were given their own gardens to work in, so this could be a portrait. This figure is not very well modelled, but has more detail and considerably more enamelled decoration than the preceding one. These two factors lead to a higher value.

Staffordshire earthenware *Babes in the Wood* spill vase, painted in polychrome enamels and gilded.

c.1850. One hand restored. 21 cm height   TA

£58

This subject was popular after 1847, when the painting *Children in the Wood* by J. H. Benwell and W. Westall was engraved and published in the *Art-Union*. Samuel Alcock & Co. and Cork & Edge made *Babes in the Wood* relief-moulded jugs using the subject. The original painting, the engraving and the jugs omit the angel figure.

PAIRS OF FIGURES

Many figures were made in pairs, sometimes identical except for the direction in which they face, often with complementary subjects, e.g. a male and female engaged in the same activity or two characters from a play or novel.

Rare pair of earthenware scarf dancers painted in polychrome enamel and gilded.

c.1850. 25 cm height   WA

£540

At Balmoral in 1849 Queen Victoria and her children took lessons in Scottish dancing, and this soon became a craze. Many theatrical productions included Scottish dancing, and some of the figures are taken from portraits of actors and actresses who performed in these.

Pair of Staffordshire milkmaid and boy figures with cows on gilded bases.

c.1865. 24.5 cm height   WA

£1,950

Reproductions of these figures were made by William Kent of Burslem, and appear in their catalogue of 1955 (illustrated in Halfpenny).

Pair of Staffordshire earthenware figures painted in polychrome enamels and gilded.

c.1850. *My Grandmother* 16.5 cm height; *My Grandfather* 15.8 cm height   BG

£855

PAIRS OF ANIMAL FIGURES

Animal figures were very popular in the 19th century, and remain popular with collectors today. The menagerie included exotic zoo and circus animals, but by far the most popular subjects were dogs. The animals usually came in matching pairs, designed to face one another across the mantelpiece. Such a pair is always more desirable than a single figure.

King Charles's spaniels were made in a large range of sizes and were always in pairs. These lapdogs are often called 'Comforter Dogs', or in Scotland are sometimes known as 'Wally' dogs, the derivation of which is much disputed. Queen Victoria had King Charles's spaniels, and this increased their popularity in the same way in which Queen Elizabeth II's love of corgis has increased theirs.

Spaniels are sometimes decorated with lustre, either with or instead of enamels. Those on raised bases or in combination with other figures are most desirable. One sign of quality is a separate front leg, which would have been moulded separately: another desirable feature is the addition of glass eyes which also added to the expense of production. These figures remain very popular today and there are many reproductions. Pope illustrates several of the latter, and points out the features which give them away.

Very rare pair of earthenware King Charles's spaniels on leaf bases painted in polychrome enamels.

c.1845. 24 cm height   WA

£4,650

177

Very rare pair of earthenware pipe-smoking King Charles's spaniels, painted in polychrome enamels.

c.1850. 26.7 cm height   WA

£3,250

Greyhound racing became popular in the 19th century. Pope illustrates many examples, including two named figures who were the principal contenders in the Waterloo cup in 1871.

Very rare earthenware running greyhound vases painted in polychrome enamels.

c.1855. 27.5 cm height   WA

£1,350

Pair of Staffordshire earthenware greyhounds painted in polychrome enamels.

c.1880. 26 cm height; 25 cm length of base   WA

£960

Pair of earthenware dalmatians painted in polychrome enamels.

c.1845. 17 cm height   WA

£1,680

The dalmatian was a popular breed during the 18th and 19th centuries. They were trained to run behind the rear axles of carriages, becoming elegant status symbols. Many potters made pairs of dalmatians, and several examples are illustrated in Pope.

The first giraffe to be seen in England was a gift to George IV by Mehemet Ali, Pasha of Egypt. The giraffe was given his own paddock and attended by two Arab keepers, who are sometimes portrayed with giraffes in figure groups.

A pair of Staffordshire earthenware giraffes painted in orange, brown and green enamels.

c.1850. 14 cm height JM

£370

Very rare earthenware giraffe vase painted in polychrome enamels.

c.1850. Restored. 30 cm height WA

£845

This originally would have been one of a pair.

Very rare earthenware camel painted in polychrome enamels.

c.1850. Tip of tail restored. 16.5 cm height WA

£1,670

Originally this would have been one of a pair.

Very rare pair of earthenware parakeets painted in polychrome enamels.

c.1850. 25 cm height WA

£1,800

A similar pair 34.5 cm height was priced at £2,800.

179

Pair of earthenware zebras painted in polychrome enamels.

c.1855. 16 cm height   WA

£1,630

These figures were reproduced by William Kent of Burslem and appear in their 1955 catalogue, reproduced in Half-penny.

Extremely rare pair of earthenware leopards painted in polychrome enamels.

c.1845. 18 cm height   WA

£6,400

Pair of Staffordshire earthenware spill vases with figures of foxes with geese in their mouths, painted in polychrome enamels.

c.1850. 23 cm height   WA

£1,280

FLATBACK FIGURES

Flatback figures were made for display on the mantelpiece. Figures had been made for this purpose for many years, but the flatbacks were an innovation, as the shape made it possible to place a much larger figure on the narrow ledge. If these figures had been modelled in the round they would be far too large.

The figures have a great deal of charm and are highly collectable, but they were made for the lower end of the market, and are not usually finely modelled or decorated. Much of the interest in them today stems from the history they represent. P. D. Gordon Pugh has written a comprehensive guide to these figures, often providing source material. The figures were taken from contemporary engravings which appeared in newspapers, periodicals, sheet music and theatre posters. Many were commemoratives, and some of these are illustrated in our chapter on that subject.

Harriet Beecher Stowe's novel *Uncle Tom's Cabin*, which was published in 1852, aroused the sympathies of abolitionists and inspired many portrait figures. See Gordon Pugh for illustrations of this figure and many other versions.

Earthenware *Uncle Tom* and *Little Eva* flatback figures decorated with polychrome enamels and gilded.

c.1852. Transfer-printed quotation on base reading 'Eva. Uncle Tom! What funny things you are making there!' 19.5 cm height   BG

£345

Earthenware George and Eliza Harris flatback figures, hair painted with black enamel, gilded.

c.1852. Gilding rubbed. 33.5 cm height   WA

£640

George and Eliza Harris are also characters from *Uncle Tom's Cabin*. This figure has never been recorded with coloured decoration.

Earthenware Highland flatback figure painted in polychrome enamels.

c.1850. 30 cm height   WA

£580

This is a particularly good example of a flatback figure. The modelling and painting are unusually well executed.

Staffordshire earthenware flatback figure group with *Sailor and his Lass* spill vase painted in polychrome enamels.

c.1850. 20 cm height   JM

£95

10 IRONSTONE AND OTHER STONE CHINA

Tᴴᴇ first stone china was apparently Turner's Patent, which was patented by John Turner's sons in 1800. Miles Mason's son Charles James Mason took out his patent for Ironstone China in 1813. This recipe called for ironstone, but it is now thought that this was intended to mislead competitors: several authorities have stated that the recipe would not make a workable ceramic body, and chemical analysis of the early Mason's Ironstone carried out at the behest of Geoffrey Godden has shown that there is no iron-stone in the ware at all.

Ironstone or stone china is not really a china or porcelain, but an earthenware body strengthened with silica. The body is highly vitreous and often has a greyish tinge. The wares are generally not translucent, although there are some exceptions, such as Spode's stone china. The body's strength and durability made it perfect for dinner services in im-itation of Chinese export wares, so most pieces found today are dinner plates, but it was also used for decorative items. Some pieces were transfer-printed, usually in blue, with no further decoration. The wares in this section have been painted in polychrome enamels, usually over an outline transfer-print. For ironstone decorated with a transfer-print only see chapter 7.

The name of Mason has become nearly synonymous with ironstone, but many con-temporaries produced ironstone-type wares, known as 'stone china' or 'granite'. A com-prehensive listing can be found in Geoffrey Godden's book (see Mason's below).

Further Reading

Geoffrey Godden. *Mason's China and the Ironstone Wares*, 3rd edn with many new colour plates (Antique Collectors' Club, Woodbridge, 1991).

G. L. ASHWORTH & BROS
(c.1861–1968)

Ashworth became the largest ironstone manufacturer after having acquired Mason's moulds, patterns, etc. The firm also continued to use Mason's transfer-printed marks, so wares marked *Mason's Patent Ironstone China* made after 1861 were actually produced by Ash-worth. In 1968 the firm's style changed to Mason's Ironstone China Ltd, continuing to make ironstone in traditional shapes and patterns to the present day.

One of a pair of Ashworth ironstone 'Double Landscape' pattern teapot stands. transfer-printed and painted in polychrome enamels.

c.1870. Impressed mark 'ASHWORTH'; painted pattern number B103. 18 cm diameter   VH

£130 the pair.

Double Landscape is one of the patterns still produced by Mason's Ironstone China in the late 20th century (illustrated in Godden). The original design shows the influence of *japonisme*, a wave of Japanese influence on European design which peaked in the 1870s. These types of landscape panels can be found on many English wares of the period.

Painted pattern numbers are not ordinarily found on Mason's Ironstone wares. When found, they are usually on post-1850 wares. High four-digit numbers occur on 20th-century Ashworth wares, usually marked 'ENGLAND'.

Ashworth ironstone plate, transfer-printed and painted in polychrome enamels.

c.1861–90. Impressed mark 'ASHWORTH/REAL/IRON-STONE/CHINA'. Printed mark with wreath 'REAL/STONE/CHINA'. 18.5 cm diameter   JJB

£38

This is a copy of a pattern used by Hicks & Meigh, illustrated in Godden.

Reverse.

Ironstone plate, probably Ashworth, with brown transfer-printed pattern painted in polychrome enamels.

c.1881–90. Printed mark in brown 'REAL IRONSTONE CHINA'; painted mark in red '212' and a crown. 26.5 cm diameter   G

£75

MASON'S IRONSTONE
(c.1813–53)

Miles Mason started as a Chinaman, a dealer in pottery and porcelain, principally dealing in the Chinese export wares which were flooding Britain in the 18th century. When these imports ceased in the 1790s, he decided to manufacture porcelain himself. In 1813 his sons succeeded him under the style George and Charles Mason, producing earthenwares and porcelain. They introduced Mason's Patent Ironstone China, which was to become the mainstay of the firm, in that same year. George Mason retired in 1830, and the firm was continued under the style C. J. Mason & Co. by Charles Mason c.1830–48 and c.1849–53. The moulds, pattern books, etc. were purchased by Francis Morley & Co., and subsequently passed to G. L. Ashworth & Bros (see above).

Most of Mason's Ironstone wares show a very strong oriental influence, particularly the many Japan-type patterns, using an Imari palette of iron red and cobalt blue.

Further Reading

Reginald Haggar and Elizabeth Adams. *Mason Porcelain & Ironstone, 1796–1853* (Faber & Faber, 1977).

JUGS

The *Hydra* shape jug was made by Mason's (and subsequently Ashworth) in many sizes over a long period of time. The shape was copied by many other ironstone china and earthenware manufacturers.

Mason's Ironstone *Hydra* shape jug, Japan pattern transfer-printed and painted in polychrome enamels with lustre handle.

c.1820. Printed mark 'MASON'S PATENT IRONSTONE CHINA'. 13.3 cm height   TA

£78

Early Mason's Ironstone *Hydra* shape jug with 'Waterlily' pattern painted in polychrome enamels with hydra handle.

c.1815. Impressed mark 'MASON'S PATENT IRONSTONE CHINA'. 13.5 cm height   VH

£320

Mason's Ironstone cider jug with chinoiserie pattern painted in polychrome enamels and red scale ground.

c.1825. Chip repaired. Black printed mark with crown 'MASON'S PATENT IRONSTONE CHINA'. 17 cm height   VH

£190

Ironstone jug with chinoiserie pattern painted in polychrome enamels and red scale ground, attributed to Mason's.

c.1820. Printed circular mark with lion and crown and in a garter 'ROYAL TERRA COTTA PORCELAIN'. 14 cm height

JM

£160

The scene here is similar to that shown on the cider jug above, but it is not identical. Note, for example, how the trees on this jug are much more clearly defined.

Reverse.

Mark.

Mason's Ironstone *Bandana Ware* jug, with transfer-printed sheet print coloured with black and yellow enamels.

c.1840–53. 19 cm height

VH

£165

The bandana was a printed Indian silk handkerchief. The patterns on these wares were all-over or sheet prints, coloured with enamels. Another typical example is illustrated in Haggar & Adams. *Bandana Ware* jugs were shown by Mason's at the Great Exhibition of 1851. Godden illustrates this jug in a different colour combination as well as an untypical example which is marked 'Mason's Bandana Ware. 1851. Patentee of the Patent Ironstone China.' *Bandana Ware* is sometimes marked with only a crown and 'MASON'S'.

Mason's Ironstone ewer and bowl with mazarine ground, painted with polychrome enamels and gilded.

c.1815–20. Spout restored. Impressed mark 'MASON'S PATENT IRONSTONE CHINA'. Bowl 21.5 cm diameter; Jug 18.5 cm height   VH

£465

Mason's Ironstone *Fenton* shape jug with 'Old Schoolhouse' pattern painted in polychrome enamels with mazarine ground, red, green and lustre handle.

c.1815. Restored. 20 cm height   VH

£260

This pattern is also known as 'Gay Japan', but is commonly referred to as 'Old Schoolhouse' by collectors. It is very popular but relatively uncommon.

TABLEWARES

Mason's Ironstone soup plate with unusual chinoiserie pattern transfer-printed and painted in polychrome enamels and gilded.

c.1825. Impressed mark 'MASON'S PATENT IRONSTONE CHINA'. 26 cm diameter   JM

£25

A jug with this pattern is illustrated in Godden.

Rare early Mason's Ironstone dessert sauce tureen, cover and stand with floral design painted in polychrome enamels, mazarine border and gilding.

c.1813–20. Firing cracks on bottom of tureen. Impressed mark on stand 'MASON'S PATENT IRONSTONE CHINA'. 23 cm height with stand   VH

£675

A dessert sauce tureen in this typical early shape with a similar pattern is illustrated in Godden. Two of these tureens would have been included in a dessert service.

Mason's Ironstone drainer painted in polychrome enamels on six feet.

c.1825. Mauve printed mark with crown 'MASON'S PATENT IRONSTONE CHINA'. 32 cm length   VH

£190

Pierced drainers, for insertion in meat dishes or drainer platters, were part of a standard service.

Mason's Ironstone dessert plate in 'Old Schoolhouse' pattern painted in polychrome enamels and gilded.

c.1815–20. Impressed mark 'MASON'S PATENT IRON-STONE CHINA'. 20 cm diameter   VH

£120

This pattern is also known as 'Gay Japan', but is commonly referred to as 'Old Schoolhouse' by collectors. It is very popular, but relatively uncommon.

Mason's Ironstone dessert dish in the 'Table and Flower' pattern, painted in polychrome enamels in the *famille rose* palette.

c.1815. Service comprising eighteen plates, comport, six dishes and two tureens. Impressed mark 'MASON'S PATENT IRONSTONE'. This dish 24 cm length   VH

£550 the service.

The pattern is based on an 18th-century *famille rose* Chinese pattern.

Mason's Ironstone dessert dish with mazarine ground border, painted with polychrome enamels and gilded.

c.1815. 28 cm length   VH

£150

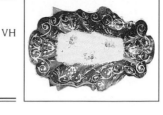

Mason's Ironstone Mogul pattern bowl transfer-printed and and painted in polychrome enamels.

c.1815–25. Printed mark, 21 cm diameter   VH

£480

This is one of the many chinoiserie patterns used by Mason's. It is mentioned in a Christie's sale catalogue in 1818. A larger bowl in this pattern is illustrated in Godden.

Mason's Ironstone mug with 'Old Schoolhouse' pattern painted in polychrome enamels over mazarine ground, green, orange and lustre handle.

c.1815. 14 cm height   VH

£320

Two mugs with this shape handle are illustrated in Godden.

Mason's Ironstone plate painted in blue and orange enamels.

c.1815–20. 24 cm diameter   JJB

£115

A dessert service in this pattern is illustrated in Godden.

Mason's Ironstone sauce tureen and stand in polychrome enamels and gilded.

1832–53. Printed mark with crown 'MASON'S PATENT IRONSTONE CHINA/J. ALLSUP/NO. 16/ST. PAUL'S CHURCHYARD/LONDON'. 14.5 cm height   JJB

£850

John Allsup was a London retailer operating 1832–58.

ORNAMENTAL WARES

Very rare Mason's Ironstone bottles and stoppers with Japan pattern with fence, transfer-printed and painted in red and blue enamels, unburnished gilding.

c.1815. Slight damage. 11 cm height   VH

£495

Very rare early Mason's Ironstone card rack with Japan pattern with fence, transfer-printed and painted in red and blue enamels, unburnished gilding.

c.1815. Slight damage. Impressed mark 'MASON'S PATENT IRONSTONE CHINA'. 11 cm height   VH

£980.

Mason's Ironstone potpourri vase and cover painted in polychrome enamels and gilded.

c.1820–5. 20 cm height   VH

£285

A potpourri vase in this shape but with a different pattern is illustrated in Godden.

One of a pair of Mason's Ironstone vases in a very rare shape, mazarine ground with rare griffin handles painted in polychrome enamels and gilded.

c.1815. Restored. 22.5 cm height   VH

£850 the pair

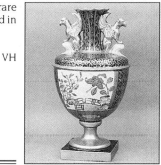

Mason's Ironstone vase in a very unusual shape painted in polychrome enamels and gilded.

c.1825. 17 cm height   VH

£275

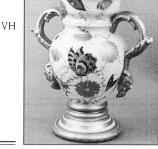

Early Mason's Ironstone inkwell in the 'Old Schoolhouse' pattern painted in polychrome enamels and gilded.

c.1815. Cover missing. 11.5 cm diameter   VH

£335

This pattern is also known as 'Gay Japan', but is commonly referred to as 'Old Schoolhouse' by collectors. It is very popular, but relatively uncommon.

Early very rare Mason's Ironstone double-shell inkstand with loose inkpots. Celadon ground and polychrome enamel floral painting and gilding.

c.1820–5. One stopper missing and one pot restored. Impressed mark 'MASON'S PATENT IRONSTONE CHINA'. 14 cm length   VH

£720

An inkstand in this shape with applied flowers on the base is illustrated in Godden.

Mason's Ironstone inkwell painted in polychrome enamels.

c.1820–5. Firing crack; hairline crack. 9 cm length   VH

£230

A lavishly decorated inkwell in this shape is illustrated in Godden. it is perhaps the 'shell inkstand' referred to in Mason's 1822 sale catalogue.

Mason's Ironstone inkstand with mazarine ground, transfer-print painted in polychrome enamels and gilded.

c.1835. Two of the lids are replacements. 31 cm length VH

£850

Mason's Ironstone chinoiserie pattern vase transfer-printed and painted with polychrome enamels.

c.1825. Printed mark. Restoration to top of handles. 24 cm height   VH

£395

A wide range of toy or miniature items was included in an 1822 sale of Mason's Ironstone. These included basins and ewers, candlesticks, cups and saucers, jars and covers, jugs, mugs, tea kettles, teapots and watering cans. All of these items are quite rare and much sought after, which is reflected in the high prices.

Mason's Ironstone toy argyle with Japan pattern with fence transfer-printed and painted in red and blue enamels, unburnished gilding.

c.1813. 7 cm height   VH

£250

An argyle (or argyll) is a gravy warmer, with a central tube to hold hot water. These are named after the 3rd Duke of Argyll who was said to have invented the form for silver c.1750.

Mason's Ironstone miniature watering can with Japan pattern with fence transfer-printed and painted in red and blue enamels, unburnished gilding.

c.1815. Handle has been restuck. Impressed circular mark 'PATENT IRONSTONE CHINA'. 6 cm height   VH

£420

Mason's Ironstone miniature candlestick with Japan pattern with fence transfer-printed and painted in red and blue enamels, unburnished gilding.

c.1815–20. 10 cm diameter   VH

£135

Small Mason's Ironstone vase of an unusual shape with Japan pattern with fence transfer-printed and painted in red and blue enamels, unburnished gilding.

c.1815. 12 cm height   VH

£250

RIDGWAY
(1802–54)

The ironstone wares made by the John & William Ridgway partnership (c.1814–30) were of a high quality. A variety of transfer-printed marks were employed incorporating the initials 'J. W. R.', 'J & W. R.' or 'J. & W. Ridgway'. Trade names for their ironstone included Stone China and Opaque China.

Both brothers continued fine ironstone manufacture after they parted ways. Transfer-printed marks used by John Ridgway (1830–55) on his ironstone wares often include the Royal Arms and the initials 'J. R.', 'J. R. & Co' (after 1841) or the name in full. Trade names used by John for his ironstone included Real Ironstone China, Superior Stone China and Imperial Stone China. Painted pattern numbers often in excess of 1000 may also be found.

193

William Ridgway's ironstone (c.1830–54) may have transfer-printed marks including the Royal Arms and 'W. Ridgway' or 'W. Ridgway & Co.' (from c.1834) or the initials 'W. R.' or 'W. R. & Co.' (from c.1834). Trade names employed for his ironstone included Opaque Granite China and Quartz China.

Further Reading

Geoffrey A. Godden. *Ridgway Porcelains*, 2nd edn (Antique Collectors' Club, Woodbridge, 1985).

Ridgway stone china dish painted in Japan pattern in polychrome enamels and gilded.

c.1815. 23 cm length   JJB

£195

Stone china plate possibly Ridgway, blue transfer-printed with enamel decoration and lustre rim.

c.1820. Printed mark in rectangle 'IRONSTONE CHINA'. Painted pattern number 995+. 22.6 cm diameter   JJB

£85

SPODE
(1770–1833)

Spode introduced their Stone China c.1813, the same year in which Mason's Patent Ironstone was introduced. Although Mason's wares have their charm, the Spode wares are more finely potted and decorated. Spode Stone China is translucent in strong artificial light, and the body is quite grey, an effect achieved by adding cobalt to the mix. Many of the patterns are direct imitations of earlier Chinese export porcelains. The body was suitable for blue transfer-prints and was frequently used for that purpose.

After the death of Josiah Spode III, the firm was purchased by William Taylor Copeland, who had been a partner in Spode's London retail business, and Thomas Garrett, under the style Copeland & Garrett, who continued production of many Spode Stone China patterns and shapes.

Spode marked most of its stone china with a mock Chinese seal mark with 'SPODE/Stone China'. Pattern numbers were only used on wares with on-glaze decoration, often over underglaze transfer-prints. A Spode pattern number list can be found on p. 375.

Spode collectors will want to join the Spode Society, which has regular meetings and outings, also publishing a very fine *Review*. The membership secretary is Mrs Rosalind Pulver, PO Box 1812, London NW4 4NW. The Spode factory (Church Street, Stoke-on-Trent ST4 1BX) has a fine museum and factory tours are also available by prior arrangement.

Further Reading

David Drakard and Paul Holdway. *Spode Printed Ware* (Longman, 1983).
Leonard Whiter. *Spode*, reprinted with new colour illustrations (Barrie & Jenkins, 1989)
The Spode Society. *Recorder & Review* (1986 to the present day).

Spode Stone China plate with underglaze blue painted outlines and border painted with polychrome enamels and gilded.

c.1815. 23 cm diameter   WG

£75

This is an interesting documentary piece as the pattern was later engraved as Spode's 'Punt and Mosque' pattern 2372. A printed example along with a Chinese painted prototype is illustrated in *Oriental Expressions, The Influence of the Orient on British Ceramics*, The Northern Ceramic Society, 1989.

Spode New Oval shape Stone China teapot and stand painted in polychrome enamels and gilded.

c.1815. Printed seal mark 'SPODE/Stone China'. Pattern number 2117 painted in red. Stand 20.5 cm length; teapot 17.5 cm height   LM

£420

Spode Stone China soup plate with *Mosaic* border and *Willis* centre painted in polychrome enamels and gilded.

c.1817–18. Printed seal mark 'SPODE/Stone China'; painted pattern number 2647. 24 cm diameter   VH

£50

The *Willis* centre was used in some seventeen permutations on Stone China, usually with a floral border. Some of these have been recorded with the inscription 'Willis Thatch'd House', a London Tavern, and a number of pieces in this pattern with the names of other hostelries have also been recorded.

Spode Stone China plate with blue transfer-printed *Ship Border* and *Star Centre*, enamelled in blue and gilded.

c.1823. Impressed mark 'SPODES/NEW STONE'. Pattern number painted in red 3701. 24 cm diameter   WG

£65

Spode introduced their New Stone body c.1822, more translucent than the earlier body, perhaps from the addition of china clay and the increase of flint. The border print is so named because it usually appears with a centre illustrating a chinoiserie scene with a sailing ship in the background (illustrated in Whiter). Presumably the *Star Centre*, which usually appears with a different floral border, takes its name from the fringed large flower.

Spode Stone China meat plate with blue transfer-print and painted with enamels.

c.1820. Combed back. Printed seal mark 'SPODE/Stone China'. Painted pattern number 2857. 37 cm length   JJB

£215

A Stone China plate in this pattern is illustrated in Whiter alongside a Chinese export porcelain plate which inspired the design.

OTHER MANUFACTURERS

R. Stevenson & Williams Royal Stone China relief-moulded dish.

c.1825–6. 25 cm diameter   G

£120

A plate in the same shape and pattern is illustrated in Godden.

Charles Meigh Stone China sauce tureen and stand.

c.1835–49. Impressed mark 'INDIAN STONE CHINA'. Painted pattern number 857. 14 cm total height; 22 cm diameter stand   JM

£185

Folch Improved Ironstone China plate, transfer-printed and painted in polychrome enamels.

c.1820. Printed mark. 20.6 cm diameter   JJB

£85

Stephen Folch (& Sons) of Stoke (1819–30) produced some interesting ironstone wares, as well as some rare bone chinas.

Reverse.

The imposing mark used by Folch makes the reverse of the plate nearly as attractive as the front.

Ironstone China plate attributed to Ridgway & Morley or Ridgway, Morley, Wear & Co.

c.1835–44. Transfer-printed mark with Royal Arms, 'IRON-STONE CHINA'; impressed mark (illegible). 23.5 cm diameter   RS

£68

Ridgway, Morley, Wear & Co (c.1835–42) and their successors Ridgway & Morley (c.1842–4) manufactured Ironstone China. This is a particularly fine example.

197

Mark on reverse.

One of a pair of stone china dishes, transfer-printed in blue and painted in polychrome enamels and gilded.

c.1820. Some staining. Printed mark 'BRITANNICUS/DRES-DEN/CHINA'. 28 cm length   BG

£195 the pair.

Hicks & Meigh Stone China sauce tureen, cover and stand decorated with polychrome enamels and gilding.

c.1830. Printed Royal Arms mark with lion and unicorn. 26 cm length of stand; 20 cm length of tureen   VH

£320

A tureen, cover and stand in this shape attributed to Hicks & Meigh is illustrated in Godden.

11 MAJOLICA

MAJOLICA is actually a trade name, which came to be the accepted name of all ceramics of a similar type. Minton introduced their Imitation Majolica at the Great Exhibition in 1851. This made an enormous impression on critics at the time, and was soon copied by many other potters both here and on the Continent, as well as in the United States a little later. For more than thirty years majolica enjoyed immense popularity, appearing in an enormous number of shapes and styles.

Maiolica was faenza, a tin-glazed earthenware made in Italy from the 15th century onwards, and painted in rich colours. An earthenware body, once fired was dipped into a white tin enamel. During the middle of the 19th century there was an enormous revival of interest in Italian maiolica, and both antique and reproduction pieces sold for high prices. The first Victorian majolica wares imitated the maiolica shapes and decoration, although the body, glaze and decorative technique employed were entirely different.

Majolica's translucent glazes are responsible for its unique brilliance. In most cases the wares were dipped into an opaque white glaze before being dipped into or painted with coloured glazes. The thickness of the glaze can be seen on the undersides of pots where it may have pooled. In many cases the glazes have a delicate iridescence. This cannot be duplicated with modern leadless glazes, and gives many reproductions away. The pieces were fired at temperatures high enough to cause a subtle fusing of colour.

Majolica usually has a simple earthenware body, but other bodies such as Parian or stoneware were sometimes used. Most majolica is relief-moulded, and however good the colour, glazes and decoration, a poorly moulded piece makes for a poor result. The importance of the modeller in this process cannot be overemphasised.

Majolica was not well suited for dinner wares, as it just did not stand up to hard usage, but it was ideal for serving pieces and salad or dessert services. Large tea services were not made, but many *tête-à-tête* or *déjeuner* services were offered, which one only used on special occasions.

There were more than 150 British manufacturers of majolica, most of whom did not mark their wares. In some cases shape or pattern numbers may give a clue to the identity of the maker: in others, shapes or glazes may help. However, in most cases you must choose a piece because it appeals, rather than for a particular provenance. Minton and some other major British potters did often mark their majolica. Copeland and Royal Worcester majolica are both uncommon, but as substantial quantities were made, I suspect that a great many remain unidentified because the small impressed marks are often difficult to detect beneath thick glazes.

Further Reading

Victoria Bergesen. *Majolica* (Barrie & Jenkins, 1989).
Nicholas M. Dawes. *Majolica* (Crown Publishers, New York, 1990).
Marilyn G. Karmison with Joan B. Stacke. *Majolica. A Complete History and Illustrated Survey* (Harry N. Abrams, New York, 1989).
Mariann K. Marks. *Majolica Pottery* (Collector Books, Paducah, Ky, 1983).
Mariann K. Marks. *Majolica Pottery*, Second Series (Collector Books, Paducah, Ky, 1986).

MINTON
(c.1796 to the present day)

Léon Arnoux, art director at Minton, began majolica manufacture in 1849 or 1850. His knowledge of Continental methods of lead glazing was invaluable. He also perfected the majolica colours through endless experimentation. The Minton palette was a major factor in the superiority of the ware, which was maintained throughout the majolica period.

Minton produced more figures in majolica glazes than any other manufacturer. A great many of these were revivals of earlier shapes, and may be found in other bodies apart from earthenware, such as porcelain painted with enamels or Parian.

Minton wares usually bear impressed factory marks and ornament numbers. They also usually bear impressed date ciphers.

Further Reading

Paul Atterbury and Maureen Batkin. *The Dictionary of Minton* (Antique Collectors' Club, Woodbridge, 1990).
Victoria Cecil. *Minton 'Majolica'* (Jeremy Cooper, 1982).

Minton *Girl Resting on Basket* majolica posy vase.

c.1861. Impressed marks 'MINTON'; erroneous shape number 421; date cipher for 1861. 24.2 cm height   TA

£375

There is a matching *Boy Resting on Basket* vase, which is properly shape number 421. The *Girl Resting on Basket* should have been impressed with shape number 431. It is easy to see how the mistake was made; however, it serves as a warning that workmen were not infallible and occasionally wrong shape numbers or pattern numbers were applied to pieces. This is quite a low shape number, indicating a date of introduction in the early 1850s. The vases are relatively common, and must have been popular as they were made at least until c.1870.

Minton majolica parrot.

c.1890s. Moulded mark 'MINTONS/ENGLAND'. Incised shape number 1847. 35 cm height   TA

£160

A pair of Minton majolica *Hen and Cockerel Flower Holders*, modelled by John Henk.

c.1876. Impressed 'MINTONS' and shape numbers 1982 and 1983. 35 and 31 cm heights   AF

£2,300

John Henk stayed with Minton for his entire working life, rising to be chief modeller. His speciality was animal models.

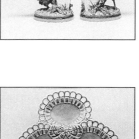

Minton majolica dish decorated with turquoise majolica glaze.

c.1871. Impressed mark 'MINTON 1543 34'; impressed date cipher for 1871. 25 cm length   AD

£55

Minton majolica oyster plate.

c.1806. Impressed mark MINTONS and shape number 1323. 25 cm diameter   AF

£85

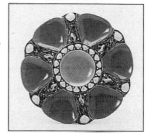

SHORTER
(c.1874–1974)

Arthur Shorter worked as an artist for Hope & Carter and Minton prior to establishing his own decorating workshop in Hanley c.1874. Around 1878 he established a partnership with James Boulton under the style Shorter & Boulton, principally manufacturing majolica. The style changed to Shorter & Son c.1906 and to Shorter & Sons c.1926. The firm became a limited company in 1933.

The firm specialised in novelty wares and 'fancies' for the middle market. The range produced is enormous, and like many firms they continued to use popular shapes for many decades, usually with new colours and glaze treatments to update them.

Unlike most manufacturers, Shorter continued to produce majolica into the 1930s. Many of the early shapes continued, but the palette changed with lavender and uranium orange appearing prominently in the 1920s. The majolica is not of very good quality but filled a need at the 'cheap and cheerful' end of the market. A great deal of it was made for export to the United States.

Further Reading

Irene and Gordon Hopwood. *The Shorter Connection* (Richard Dennis, 1992).

Shorter & Sons majolica 'Stork' jug.

c.1920s. Impressed mark 'Made in England'. Moulded shape number 89. 19 cm height   IGH

£75

Shorter & Sons majolica 'Oceanic' jug.

c.1935. Black stamped mark 'SHORTER & SONS LTD/STOKE-ON-TRENT/MADE IN/GREAT BRITAIN'. 18 cm height   IGH

£85

Shorter & Son majolica dragon jug.

c.1920s. Printed mark 'Shorter & Son/Stoke-on-Trent/England'. 16 cm height   IGH

£48

WEDGWOOD
(1759 to the present day)

The Wedgwood factory was experiencing considerable difficulties during the period when majolica was first introduced. Struggling to regain its former prestige, the firm hesitated before investing in the production of new ware, whose popularity might prove ephemeral. By 1861, however, Wedgwood decided that they had stood by and watched their competitors garner all the glory and profits associated with majolica for long enough.

None the less, they started production in a modest way. The vast majority of the early pieces in the Wedgwood Majolica Pattern Books are old shapes such as these here, with the new glazes applied.

The period 1875–80 was Wedgwood's peak majolica period, when approximately 1300 designs were introduced. The vast majority of Wedgwood majolica is marked.

Further Reading

Robin Reilly. *Wedgwood*, 2 vols (Macmillan, 1989).
Robin Reilly and George Savage. *The Dictionary of Wedgwood* (Antique Collectors' Club, Woodbridge, 1980).

Wedgwood *Pecten Japonicus* dessert plate with mottled green and brown majolica glazes.

c.1866. Impressed mark 'WEDGWOOD', date code for 1866. 22 cm length   AF

£25

See p. 298 for a Wedgwood green-glazed shell-shaped dish.

Wedgwood majolica argenta *Peacock* pickle dish.

c.1885. Impressed mark 'WEDGWOOD'; date code for 1885. 22 cm length   AF

£38

Majolica argenta has a white ground often decorated with Japanese inspired motifs in pastel colours. It was introduced by Wedgwood c.1879, but was soon copied by other manufacturers.

OTHER MANUFACTURERS

Royal Worcester turquoise majolica figure *Boys and Faggots*.

c.1865. Impressed Royal Worcester mark. 12 cm height TV

£185

Turquoise majolica was made in large quantities by Royal Worcester from the mid 1860s, to some extent supplanting polychrome majolica wares. They revived many shapes which had previously been made in polychrome majolica glazes for this new treatment. This figure (shape 10) was introduced in 1862.

Brown-Westhead, Moore & Co. majolica woven cane pattern dessert plate with mazarine border and gilding.

c.1875. Impressed mark 'BROWN WESTHEAD MOORE & CO.' with illegible diamond registration mark. 24.5 cm diameter   HBW

£75

Brown-Westhead, Moore & Co. (1861–1920) was the largest pottery in England by 1882. Manufacturers of both earthenwares and porcelain, majolica was one of their specialities. The wares are of a uniformly good quality.

George Jones majolica *Leaf* dessert plate.

c.1870s. Painted pattern number 2584H. 21 cm diameter
                                                           AF

£60

George Jones, a former Minton employee, founded his firm at the Old Bridge Works, Stoke-on-Trent in 1861. Soon after this Jones established himself as a maker of fine quality majolica and Palissy wares. His majolica vies with that of Minton and Wedgwood for the title of the best majolica ever produced.

Looking at the reverse we can see two of the firm's characteristics. One is the rich mottled glazes on the underside. Few firms took this much trouble to glaze the back of their pieces so well. Second, although many pieces are marked with one of the several George Jones marks, unmarked pieces such as this one may be identified by a reserve in the glaze into which has been painted a pattern number.

Reverse.

Majolica jug with brown ground.

c.1880s. 20.5 cm height   TA

£68

Trompe l'œil grounds resembling wood were very popular majolica designs, as were wild rose patterns.

Majolica garden seat in blue, green and brown majolica glazes.

c.1870s. Impressed mark 'J. M. D. & SON/BOSTON' (retailer's mark). 45 cm height   AF

£750

The impressed mark is for Jones McDuffee & Stratton, importers of Boston, Massachusetts.

Relief-moulded oak-leaf dish decorated with green, yellow and brown majolica glazes.

c.1880s. A few small chips to underside. Impressed mark with triangle in a circle. 31 cm length   AF

£10

This is a very common pattern and is found in a variety of glazes, probably made by a number of Staffordshire manufacturers. The reverse is covered with a streaky, pale brown majolica glaze, which is usually an indication of lesser quality manufacture. A similar dish is illustrated in Bergesen. In perfect condition these would cost around £20.

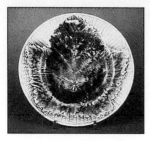

Relief-moulded dessert plate decorated with yellow, brown and green majolica glazes.

c.1860–80. 22.8 cm diameter   AF

£12

This is a very common pattern and is found in green glaze. In the author's collection is a green-glazed example impressed 'J. ADAMS & CO.', but the pattern was probably made by a number of Staffordshire manufacturers. The reverse is covered with a streaky, pale brown majolica glaze, which is usually an indication of poorer quality. Ordinarily these would cost around £20.

Majolica corn bread tray.

c.1860s. 34 cm length   AF

£135

This is a common pattern used by several manufacturers, most often found on corn cob shaped jugs.

12 TOBY JUGS

THE appeal of Toby jugs has continued unabated for over two centuries. Toby Fillpot was the nickname of Henry Elwes of Yorkshire (d.1761), who was said to have consumed 2,000 gallons of strong ale during his lifetime. Toby is now used generically as a name for jugs or mugs in the shape of seated or occasionally standing figures, generally holding a cup and jug. The hats of the early Toby jugs originally had a crown, which was detachable for use as a cup, but these have seldom survived.

Jugs in human form have origins going back to earliest times. In England medieval jugs and early stoneware Bellarmine jugs reflect the human figure. A small group of character jugs in various poses, drinking, smoking, ironing, drawing a sword or playing a fiddle, c.1800 had at one time been thought to be mid 18th century. An example of these is illustrated in Horne IV (see below).

Most early Toby jugs are slip-cast earthenware with coloured glaze. These are often attributed to the Wood family, but there were several other Staffordshire manufacturers of Toby jugs in the late 18th century. Prattware examples with underglaze pigments and a pearlware glaze were also made, as were examples decorated with coloured enamels. Modern examples are slip-cast with few if any individually modelled accessories such as a jug or cup.

Named figures used for early Toby jugs were Bluff King Hal, Admiral Howe, Martha Gunn, Bacchus (illustrated in Horne II) and the Hearty Good Fellow (a standing figure). There are a number of other early figures used such as the rare Rodney's Sailor (illustrated in Horne II). During the 20th century character jugs portraying the faces of a wide variety of persons, real or imaginary, have been very popular, the most prolific manufacturer being Royal Doulton at Burslem. W. T. Copeland issued an immensely successful Winston Churchill Toby jug designed by Eric Olsen in 1940. Several other manufacturers, including Minton, made Churchill Toby jugs, all of which are collected today both by Toby jug collectors and by collectors of Churchilliana.

Further Reading

John Bedford. *Toby Jugs* (Cassell, 1968).
Jonathan Horne. *A Collection of Early English Pottery*, Parts I–XII (Jonathan Horne, 1982–92).
V. Schuler. *Toby Jugs* (Pearson, 1986).

Staffordshire earthenware Toby jug with hat cup, painted in polychrome coloured glazes.

c.1785. The miniature jug is hollow. 26 cm height   JH

£1,150

Toby jugs with their original hat cups are very rare. This is an exceptionally fine example in very good condition.

Pratt type Martha Gunn Toby pearlware jug decorated with yellow, blue and brown underglaze colours.

c.1800. Solid miniature bottle and cup. Filled chip to rim. 25.7 cm height   JH

£2,500

Martha Gunn was said to have given the Prince of Wales (later George IV) his first dip in the sea at Brighton, where she was the keeper of a bathing machine. Martha Gunn holds a gin bottle and gill rather than an ale jug. For more about Pratt type wares see p. 68.

Earthenware Toby jug painted in green, blue, brown and yellow glazes.

Late 18th century. Hollow miniature jug. Cracks in base, chips to base. 24 cm height   JH

£1,500

Staffordshire pearlware Toby jug with brown jug.

c.1790. Pipe cracked; star crack in base. 25 cm height   AD

£485

The very finely modelled features of the face, the nostrils and mouth with the teeth visible are the signs of excellent workmanship typical of the 18th-century Toby jugs.

Staffordshire earthenware Toby jug decorated with coloured glazes.

c.1800. The jug on his knee is open. 25 cm height   BG

£895

Spotty-faced earthenware Toby jug sometimes known as Dr Johnson or the Unfrocked Parson decorated with polychrome enamels.

Early 19th century. 20 cm height   BG

£895

This example is not as meticulously modelled as the earlier examples above, but the mouth and nostrils are still more finely modelled than the following example.

Hearty Good Fellow earthenware Toby jug.

c.1820. Restored front of tricorn hat; jug. 29 cm height LR

£750

A very similar Hearty Good Fellow jug at the Victoria & Albert Museum marked Walton (see p. 170) is illustrated in Bedford. Another example at Stoke-on-Trent City Museum & Art Gallery is marked Lakin & Pool. The model was copied in Staffordshire during the late 19th century. Compare the features of the face with the much more finely modelled examples above. A perfect example will cost about £900.

Staffordshire Paul Pry earthenware jug decorated with polychrome enamels.

c.1825. 14.5 cm height   BG

£500

This jug portrays the central character in John Pool's comedy *Paul Pry* (1825). The character was played by John Liston, a well-known comic of the period.

Allerton's earthenware Toby jug painted in polychrome enamels.

c.1891–1912. Printed mark 'ALLERTONS ENGLAND' and crown. 10.5 cm height   G

£50

Charles Allerton & Sons (1859–1942) made a wide variety of china, earthenwares and lustre decoration. The firm was taken over by Cauldon Potteries Ltd in 1912, after which they operated under the style Allerton's Ltd.

Compare this 20th-century Toby with earlier examples above. The entire piece has been slipcast, with no independently modelled and applied parts. The features of Toby are bland and the enamelling is crudely painted. None the less, the jug is relatively valuable, because many Toby jug collectors are interested in examples from all periods and manufacturers.

Torquay red earthenware Toby jug decorated with green, blue and black glazes, inscribed 'BILL BREWER'.

c.1920s. A few chips to glaze. 15 cm height   BK

£30

Bill Brewer of the 'Widdecombe Fair' ballad, was a popular character in Torquay wares.

Large Devonmoor earthenware Toby jug with polychrome enamels.

c.1924. One chip to enamel. Impressed mark 'DEVON-MOOR MADE IN ENGLAND; painted in black 'ORH'. 16.5 cm height   BK

£55

Devonmoor Pottery was established in 1922, and made a speciality of Toby jugs, the smallest of which was only 3.8 cm high. They also made Judy jugs, bird jugs and Devon jugs – a series of seven different faces modelled to represent the characters of the 'Widdecombe Fair' ballad. Other novelties included double-faced mugs Full and Empty; Bacchus mugs and a Toby jug to serve as a cigarette container.

The jug shown here was illustrated in the *Pottery Gazette and Glass Trade Review*, June 1924 and on several subsequent occasions.

Torquay Punch Toby mug, earthenware decorated with black and brown slip and a honey glaze.

c.1920s. 9 cm height   BK

£35

Birks, Rawlins & Co. china Bagpiper jug painted in polychrome enamels.

c.1930s. Printed mark 'SAVOY CHINA/MADE IN ENGLAND'. 12.5 cm height   CCC
◀
£120

The high price of this jug reflects the market for Crested China, of which Birks, Rawlins & Co. made a speciality.

211

Three miniature bone china Toby jugs painted in polychrome enamels.

c.1950s. Printed mark 'ARTONE/ENGLAND'. Old man, 7.6 cm height. Fat man, printed mark with artist's palette, 6.5 cm height. Young man, 7.8 cm height   CCC

£24 each

Shorter produced a wide range of Toby jugs in both traditional and novelty shapes. The amusing novelty shapes such as the two shown below are more desirable than the copies of traditional designs. For more about Shorter see entry in chapter 14.

Shorter slip-cast earthenware *Long John Silver* Toby jug painted in polychrome enamels.

c.1941+. Moulded mark 'LONG JOHN SILVER. SHORTER.-ENGLAND'; printed black mark 'GENUINE/STAFFORD-SHIRE/HAND PAINTED/SHORTER & SON LTD/ENGLAND'. 23 cm height   IGH

£75

Shorter slipcast earthenware *Father Neptune* Toby jug painted in polychrome enamels.

c.1949+. Moulded marks 'FATHER NEPTUNE/SHORTER/ENGLAND' and 'L/S' (large size); green printed mark 'GENUINE/STAFFORDSHIRE/HAND PAINTED/SHORTER & SON LTD/ENGLAND'. 24 cm height   IGH

£75

13 ART POTTERY (1870–1920)

A WIDE variety of wares were called art pottery during the period 1870–1920. 'Art' was the operative word in three important movements in the decorative arts of the period, all of which influenced the potters of the period: the Aesthetic Movement, the Arts and Crafts Movement and Art Nouveau.

The earliest art wares were the stonewares as made at Doulton & Co., Lambeth and by the Martin Brothers, and the terracottas, such as those made at the Watcombe Terra-Cotta Co. These wares were initially historicist, although they did evolve styles of their own. The second major group were the painted wares closely associated with the Aesthetic Movement. These 'china' paintings (which were usually done on earthenware) included Doulton's Lambeth Faience, the wares decorated by Minton's Art Pottery Studio and many wares produced in small studios and by amateurs and exhibited at Howell & James and other china retailers and art galleries. The third group were the wares made at country potteries which combined traditional forms and methods with new styles to produce a vigorous range of wares, such as those of C. H. Brannam. The fourth movement was that of the chemists, who increasingly used glaze effects as the sole decoration on their pots. The last was the hand-painting movement, which would carry on well into the 20th century, adapting itself to industrial production. These wares were distinct from the earlier china painting, in that they employed increasingly abstract decoration, usually floral, suited to pottery, especially tablewares.

Further Reading

Victoria Bergesen. *Encyclopaedia of British Art Pottery* (Barrie & Jenkins, 1991).
Malcolm Haslam. *English Art Pottery 1865–1915* (London Antique Dealers' Club, 1975).
E. Lloyd Thomas. *Victorian Art Pottery* (Guildart, 1974).

DOULTON (LAMBETH)
(1858–1956)

Having apprenticed at the Fulham Pottery, where he became noted as a big ware thrower, John Doulton purchased the Vauxhall pottery in 1815. After John Watts, foreman and manager of the pottery, became Doulton's partner, they traded as Doulton & Watts (1820–1858). In 1828 they moved their pottery to High Street, Lambeth.

After Watts's death, John Doulton carried on the business in partnership with his sons John and Henry, under the style Doulton & Co. Henry Doulton (1820–97) was an inventive and innovative businessman. In 1846 he introduced the manufacture of stoneware pipes, which were soon in great demand for the thousands of miles of waterpipes and sewers which were being laid all over Britain.

In 1854 Canon Gregory, later dean of St Paul's, established the Lambeth School of Art to teach drawing and art in its elementary stages. John Sparkes was appointed director. During the next decade Henry Doulton was approached several times by his friend Edward Cressy and John Sparkes about a co-operative venture between the school and the pottery. Although Henry was very actively engaged in religious, intellectual and artistic pursuits outside business hours, he was not initially enthusiastic about these proposals.

Finally Cressy and Sparkes won him over and during the late 1860s, Doulton fired some of the students' efforts. The idea was to imitate the *Grès de Flandres* stonewares, which were

Cressy's passion. However, their earliest efforts were far from successful, as most pigments dissolved in the fierce heat of the stoneware kilns. Consequently the early wares only used brown and blue. At the 1867 International Exhibition in London, Doulton's included a few of these pots in their display, where they met with unexpected success. Efforts were redoubled and a display of some sixty specimens shown at the 1871 South Kensington Exhibition was greeted with great acclaim.

In 1873 the Art Studio's marginal existence ended with the official opening of specially appointed studios and the arrival of the first major contingent of Lambeth students. Lambeth Faience was introduced, and decorated in a separate workshop from the Doulton Ware stonewares. By 1874 thirty lady artists were employed under the superintendence of Mr Sparkes, aided by Mr Bennet who directed the painting. The studio produced some 2,000 pieces in that year alone.

In 1877, against all advice, Henry Doulton acquired an interest in Pinder & Bourne, Nile Street, Burslem. Some Pinder & Bourne blanks were imported to the Lambeth Studio for decoration, probably when due to pressure of work the Lambeth factory could not supply enough blanks.

In the 1880s the technical problems had been resolved. In consequence the pottery threatened to be swamped with overly elaborate decoration, including gilding. Numerous novelty wares were introduced. Yet the reputation of the firm continually grew. In 1887 Henry Doulton became the first potter ever to be knighted. Even a severe fire in 1888 did not set them back too badly, for the works were quickly rebuilt. By 1890, 350 artists and assistants were employed.

Upon Henry Doulton's death in 1897, the firm was carried on by his staff and heirs. At the Paris Exhibition of 1900, Doulton's once again surpassed itself with George Tinworth's fountain twelve and a half feet high, with a circular basin twelve feet in diameter. However at St Louis in 1904 they emphasised the useful side of their Lambeth productions, by a display of jugs, tankards, flowerpots, spills, spirit bottles, candlesticks etc. and the old time 'Toby Fillpot figure jug – a Lambeth speciality'. The pottery was in decline, and by 1913 there were fewer than 100 artists and assistants employed. In these latter years their advertisements in the *Pottery Gazette* list shape numbers beside the illustrations, indicative of the mass production of wares.

The art pottery wares are highly collectable and usually well marked, and signed by the artists and their assistants. Doulton encouraged the careers of these artists, many of whom made their reputations in the fine arts, alongside their achievements in decorating and designing pottery. A few Doulton artists went on to establish their own art potteries or to follow careers in design.

Hannah Barlow (1851–1916) is probably the most famous of the Doulton artists. Her sgraffito decorations, especially of animals, are greatly valued. Hannah's sister Florence and her brother Arthur were also fine decorators. Despite the enormous output of the art studios, Doulton art pottery is highly priced today, because there are so many avid collectors. Most pieces are profusely marked.

It should always be remembered that Doulton's greatest production was in stoneware sewer pipes, bottles and other utilitarian wares. Although the art wares brought great acclaim, they were not responsible for the financial success of Henry Doulton. See chapter 5 for more Doulton stonewares and chapter 21 for Doulton Burslem wares.

A fine collection of Doulton wares may be seen at the Henry Doulton Gallery at the Royal Doulton works, Nile Street, Burslem, Stoke-on-Trent.

Doulton Lambeth salt-glazed stoneware vase with griffin handles, incised and modelled with mauve and blue floral decoration.

c.1895. Some minor firing faults in glaze. Impressed mark DOULTON LAMBETH ENGLAND. Incised F. C. P. (Frank C. Pope); JH monogram (Jane S. Hurst). 42 cm height   G

£600

Frank C. Pope worked as an artist and designer at Doulton c.1873–1923. He was well known for his vases decorated with grotesques. Jane S. Hurst was a Doulton Ware Senior Assistant c.1879–1906. This vase is a unique piece and as such is quite valuable.

Doulton Lambeth salt-glazed stoneware jug.

Dated 1875. Impressed Doulton Lambeth mark with rosette. Incised mark ELH (Eliza L. Hubert). 26 cm height
G

£220

Eliza L. Hubert was a Doulton Ware Artist c.1876–83. She assisted George Tinworth and Frank Butler.

The following are series designs, and many of them would have been made.

Doulton Lambeth salt-glazed stoneware tobacco jar, Chiné ware with sprigged decoration.

c.1886–90. Impressed rosette mark; 'DOULTON & SLATERS PATENT'; 1110; incised mark ER (Ellen Rumbol). 41 cm height   G

£45

Chiné wares, also known as Doulton & Slater's Patent, were produced 1886–1914. Using a process developed by John Slater, fabrics such as lace were impressed into the soft clay. The fabric burned away in the kiln, leaving an impressed pattern on the body of the wares. These were then enamelled and sometimes gilded.
  Ellen Rumbol was a Doulton Ware Senior Assistant by 1882.

215

One of a pair of Doulton Lambeth Faience vases, green ground with slip decoration in blue, white and yellow.

c.1880s. Printed circular mark DOULTON/LAMBETH; impressed DOULTON and shape number 2617; painted artist's mark KBS (Katherine Blake Smallfield). 21 cm height   MB

£60 the pair.

Katherine 'Katie' Blake Smallfield worked as a Lambeth Faience Senior Assistant and later Artist c.1881–1912. She is best known for her figure subjects, which would be much more valuable than this attractive floral design.

Doulton Chiné stoneware jardinière.

c.1902–14. Impressed lion and crown mark with '7185t/bw/ DOULTON/SLATERS PATENT'. Incised artist's initials LB. 19.5 cm height   HBW

£150

Doulton Marqueterie Ware cream jug and sugar bowl.

c.1887. Printed mark '12-7-1887/DOULTON/& RIX'S/ PATENT' in shield with 'MARQUETERIE' beneath. Painted mark '643B (1)'. Sugar bowl 6.3 cm height; jug 10.3 cm height   HBW

£250

Marqueterie ware was patented by Wilton P. Rix and Doulton in 1887 and produced until 1906. They used thin slices of different coloured clays to obtain marbling effects (similar to 18th-century agate ware) or unique patchwork effects.

Doulton salt-glazed brown stoneware ewer decorated with white slip.

c.1882–90. Impressed Doulton rosette mark and 391; incised mark JeR, monogram HP. 21.5 cm height   HBW

£135

EWENNY POTTERIES

The Ewenny area has been the site of a pottery industry since the early 18th century. There were several potteries in Ewenny, two of which began to make art pottery in the 1880s. The Ewenny Pottery has been owned by the Jenkins family since c.1820. it is still operated today by Alun Jenkins, using many of the shapes which have been associated with the pottery for decades, but he has developed very glassy mottled glazes, which are quite distinctive from the softer streaky or mottled glazes used earlier in the century.

The Ewenny Pottery was a country pottery making traditional wares when it was first visited by Horace Elliott, a London designer and retailer. Initially content with retailing their rustic pottery in his Bloomsbury shop, Elliot soon began to spend several months at Ewenny annually. The Jenkins family executed his highly original designs, some of which were exhibited at the Arts and Crafts Exhibitions of 1889 and 1893.

Ewenny wares have a red clay body coated with white slip and decorated with coloured glazes. They are invariably incised on the base 'Ewenny Pottery', very occasionally with a date. The wares made today also have the mark 'Wales'.

Just across the road from Ewenny is the Claypits Pottery, today operated by studio potter Leonard Edger. Here from the beginning of the 20th century Evan Jones made red-bodies earthenwares, usually decorated with green or blue glazes. Some of these have incised Welsh mottoes. The shapes are often quite similar to those used at Ewenny, but who copied whom is impossible to determine. The wares have incised or impressed marks incorporating 'JONES', until the late 1930s when a 'CLAYPITS POTTERY' stamp was acquired, still in use today.

Ewenny Pottery red earthenware fluted neck vase with green glaze.

c.1907. Incised mark '1907/Ewenny/Pottery'. 8.5 cm height
CG

£15

Ewenny Pottery red earthenware tankard with streaky yellow, rust and green glazes.

c.1920s. Incised mark 'Ewenny Pottery'. 12 cm height   AF

£12

Ewenny Pottery red earthenware basket with mottled brown and green glazes.

c.1910s. Incised mark 'Ewenny Pottery'. 24.7 cm length AF

£18

This has a particularly rich glaze effect, and when held to the light small metallic flecks can be seen in the glaze. These were probably caused by brass pin dust, imported from Belgium, which was a by-product of pin manufacture.

Claypits Pottery red earthenware basket with green glaze.

c.1910s. Inscribed Welsh motto, 'Can moled pawb y bwyd fel y caffo'. Impressed mark 'JONES'. 18.8 cm length   AF

£15

Note the similarities between this basket and the one above. Not surprisingly, considering their proximity, many of the shapes made at Ewenny Pottery were also made at Claypits Pottery.

MARTIN BROTHERS
(1873–1915)

In January 1873, Robert Wallace Martin took a lease on Pomona House, Fulham to serve as a residence for his parents and siblings, as well as his pottery: a second kitchen served as his laboratory, and the stables as his studio. He was soon joined in the business by his brothers Walter Fraser, Edwin and Charles. For the first eighteen months, their wares were fired by C. J. C. Bailey, Wallace's former employer. John Patterson, an employee of Bailey's and later to become Walter Martin's father-in-law, retrieved an old wheel from Bailey's yard and built the Martins' first pug mill.

In the early years, the mainstay of the firm was architectural work, supplied by architects whom Wallace had met in his previous employ, or to whom he boldly introduced himself. These included J. P. Seddon (whose commissions Wallace had carried out while with Bailey), Frederick Pepys Cockerell and George T. Robinson. The brothers also made clock cases for Lund & Blockley of Pall Mall.

In December of 1874 they broke off their relationship with Bailey, who was charging exorbitant prices for the firing of their wares. They briefly used the kilns at Ruel Bros Crucible Works, but in 1876 resorted to Bailey's kilns again. In 1877 they moved to Southall, and with the finance of several patrons, most notably the ironmonger Frederick Nettlefold, they set up their own pottery.

The brothers' early work was influenced by the Gothic revival, but conventional ornament as proposed by Christopher Dresser was also used. As the 1880s progressed, they developed what Charles Beard called the Canal Bank style. Malcolm Haslam has shown that while the brothers may have been inspired by the flora and fauna of their rural Southall situation, many of their designs were taken from 18th-century botanical and zoological illustrations; their execution of these was very much influenced by the *japonisme* of the period. The use of a few powerful lines to convey the essence of a flower, bird or fish was well suited to the stoneware medium.

After H. F. Fawcett had taught Edwin and their assistant W. E. Willy to draw, they decorated some wares in a painterly fashion enhanced by new colours developed by Walter which gave a richness not seen before in stoneware. Renaissance designs, inspired by maiolica, were a speciality of Willy and Fawcett, although some were executed by Edwin. As Edwin and Willy developed their decorating skills, Wallace devoted himself to modelling. Although he is most admired today for his grotesques and 'Wally' birds, he modelled a wide range of figures and conventional portrait plaques and busts.

The Martin Brothers, celebrated as they were, never achieved a wide popularity. Although the Martin wares were appreciated by connoisseurs, they were an acquired taste. After a visit to the Brownlow Street gallery, Edward Spencer commented, 'I do not say that all pieces of their ware are beautiful, or that any of it is *pretty*, but every piece possesses individuality of character, so that even those which are downright ugly have the fascinating interest similar to that which is to be found in the face of a plain but intellectual-looking man. Indeed, at first sight, every one is disappointed by this sombre coloured, severely shaped, salt-glazed ware: after a time, however the disappointment wears off and interests takes its place, then the latest beauties disclose themselves and at last, the fact that no hands save only those of the artist have touched it produces a subtle charm, and leaves the spectator in a state of delight.'

The brothers experimented with earthenware 1896–8. There were only two partially successful earthenware firings in a new kiln, and consequently these pots are extremely rare. Perhaps inspired by ceramics seen at the Paris Exhibition in 1900, Walter experimented with lustre and crystalline glazes, but he was largely unsuccessful.

The 20th century brought increasing recognition to Edwin. He had for several years been making small pots to fill the spaces in the kilns. These were simply decorated with abstract patterns, sometimes in shapes inspired by animal or vegetable forms. This new style was encouraged by Edwin's friend Sidney Greenslade, who also provided sketches. Edward Spencer, who would later become involved with the Upchurch Pottery, sold these wares through his Artificer's Guild.

R. W. Martin & Bros are listed in Morris's Business Directory 1880–1914 as having their showroom at 16 Brownlow Street, Holborn, but they had probably used these premises for some time before that. This London retail outlet was vital after their removal to Southall, and it was skilfully run by Charles Martin, who managed the finances of the firm as well. Charles's contribution and the degree to which he dominated his brothers is usually underestimated. Apart from the business management, which took some doing in precarious years, he cultivated connoisseur patrons, and frequently sent his own designs for execution at Southall. When the showroom caught fire in 1903, resulting in the death of three persons living above, as well as the loss of a large amount of stock, Charles suffered a breakdown from which he never recovered. He died insane from tuberculosis seven years later.

After Charles's breakdown, marketing became uncertain and the brothers lacked the direction he had provided. Despite the success of Edwin's new wares, the brothers were consumed by internal squabbles and firings became less and less frequent. Wallace's son

Clement had joined the firm c.1900, and Edwin and Walter feared he would succeed to the business. Walter died in 1912, and with him many of his ceramic formulae. Edwin continued by firing in a small muffle kiln, but he suffered cruelly from cancer of the jaw and his output before his death in 1915 was small. Wallace modelled sporadically, but the pottery was only fired, presumably in Edwin's muffle kiln, twice more before his death in 1923.

In 1921, the *Pottery Gazette and Glass Trade Review* reported that there were 'over a thousand pieces still in clay on the pottery, but no kiln has been fired since Walter's death in 1912, and although offers have been made by practical men to undertake the firing of it in their own kilns, arrangements to do so are still pending, and it is quite possible that a different effect would result without the guiding and experienced presence of Walter.' The arrangements to have the wares fired elsewhere failed and in 1928, Clement tried to revive the pottery with a Captain H. Butterfield who had worked there as a boy. They fired at least some of the wares decorated by Walter and Edwin, but these can be recognized by the poor colouring. The quality of the new wares was inferior, and they found few customers in the Jazz Age. Nevertheless, the revival lasted until at least 1937.

Further Reading

Malcolm Haslam. *The Martin Brothers* (Richard Dennis, 1978).

Martin Brothers stoneware beaker.

c.1873. Early incised mark 'R W Martin/Pomona House/Fulham'. 10 cm height   HBW

£185

Martin Brothers brown salt-glazed stoneware 'Wally' bird.

c.1892. Head incised 'R. W. M. Martin Brothers/London & Southall'; base painted mark 'MARTIN BRO's LONDON & SOUTHALL'. 33.5 cm height   S

£5,500

Martin Brothers miniature stoneware vase.

c.1902. Incised mark '4 1902/Martin Bros./London & Southall'. 6.5 cm height   TV

£450

Martin Brothers brown salt-glazed stoneware Face jug.

c.1901. Incised mark 'Martin Bro.s/London & Southall'.
21.5 cm height   S

£1,750

JAMES MACINTYRE & CO.
(1852–1940)
WILLIAM MOORCROFT
(1913 to the present day)

William Moorcroft became a designer for James Macintyre's Washington works at Burslem
in 1897, and was made Manager of Ornamental Ware in 1898. He developed the art nouveau tube-lining techniques brought to Macintyre by Harry Bernard. Most pieces bear
Moorcroft's signature or a facsimile, but this is only meant to indicate that he personally
supervised the workshops where the pieces were made.

In 1912, Macintyre decided to discontinue decorative pottery in order to expand production of electrical porcelains. Moorcroft took Liberty & Co. (the largest retailers of his
wares) as his partner and built his own factory. Although retaining his own distinctive
style, Moorcroft changed with the times and his pottery, always hand-crafted, remained
popular. His experiments with reduction glazes and coloured lustre glazes produced
many very attractive wares. William was succeeded by his son Walter, who was a fine designer capable of bringing Moorcroft into the Contemporary design of the 1950s. Walter
Moorcroft retired in 1987 and the firm, now owned by the Dennis and Edwards families,
has flourished during the late 1980s and 1990s, due to the imaginative work of Sally Tuffin,
chief designer.

Further Reading

Paul Atterbury. *Moorcroft*, revised edn (Richard Dennis & Hugh Edwards, Shepton Beauchamp, 1990).

James Macintyre earthenware vase designed by William Moorcroft and decorated with tube-lined cornflower design.

c.1900–2. Printed mark with JM monogram. Signed W. MOORCROFT in green. Impressed shape mark 166. 23 cm height   GCC

£385

A group of wares decorated in this pattern is illustrated by Atterbury.

James Macintyre Florian Ware earthenware vase designed by William Moorcroft decorated with tube-lined poppies and panels of forget-me-nots.

c.1902–4. Painted mark WM (William Moorcroft); pattern number M955. Printed mark in orange 'Florian Ware/ JAS. MACINTYRE & CO LD/BURSLEM/ENGLAND'. 29 cm height   GCC

£450

A group of wares decorated in this pattern is illustrated by Atterbury.

Moorcroft rouge flambé earthenware vase.

c.1922–45. Impressed 'MOORCROFT/MADE IN ENGLAND/ M358' with a paper label reading 'W. Moorcroft' [facsimile signature]/HAND   MADE/POTTERY/REGISTERED/N0.10'. 32 cm height   MH

£650

William Moorcroft built a special kiln for flambé wares which was completed in 1922. He continued to experiment with these wares until his death in 1945. Like many contemporary chemist potters, he carried his secret processes and formulae to his grave. Some vases such as this one were decorated with only the flambé glaze, others with tube-lined patterns beneath the glaze.

PILKINGTONS TILE & POTTERY CO.
(1893 to the present day)

An unsuccessful attempt to drive a new mine shaft at the Clifton Colliery led to the discovery of red marl clay. The Pilkington family, who owned the colliery, sent samples to William Burton, then a chemist for J. Wedgwood and Sons, asking his opinion as to whether it would produce satisfactory bricks. In fact, Burton recommended that they produce decorative tiles, and the Pilkingtons soon secured the services of him and his brother Joseph as Manager and Assistant Manager. William was given a free hand to design the efficient and modern works, which began production in January 1893.

The firm soon established a wide reputation for these tiles (see chapter 25). The Burton brothers decided that the Sunstone glaze (developed by Joseph in 1893) which had small gold flecks in a green, yellow or brown glaze, would be seen to better advantage on hollow wares than it was on the flat surface of tiles.

Pilkingtons produced two lines of pottery. Lancastrian, simple classical shapes designed by Lewis F. Day decorated only with the Burton brothers' magnificent glaze effects, was introduced at the Graves Gallery, London in June 1904. The glaze effects exhibited in 1904 included orange peel, eggshell, metallic, transmutation and fruit-skin glazes. Lewis F. Day also mentions that flambé wares were being produced at this time.

Lancastrian Lustre Wares were introduced shortly after. These were 'true lustre', that is lustres with a smoky iridescence, as opposed to what William Burton referred to as 'metallised' or 'plated' wares in an address to the Northern Art Workers Guild at the Manchester School of Art in 1908. Burton also pointed out that having mastered the technical side of lustre production, they then set about gathering the finest collection of young artists from the art schools possible, as well as employing the established talents of Walter Crane and Lewis F. Day.

In 1907, the *Pottery Gazette* commented: 'All the pieces are painted by different artists, for it is one of the merits of this Lancastrian lustre ware that no two pieces are decorated alike. All the artists are left free to treat each vase, plate or dish on its merits, and while there is a unity of purpose through the works as a whole, there is endless variety in detail and treatment.' This is not entirely true, for there were certainly set designs carried out to order by whichever artist happened to be available. In fact, designs were ponced on to the pots using tissue paper tracings of the designer's original drawing, which necessarily limited the creativity of the painter. Nevertheless, there is no doubt that the artists were strongly encouraged to develop their own ideas, within the stylistic canon of Walter Crane's, and later Gordon Forsyth's work.

The year 1913 saw a Royal Warrant issued, and the firm's productions were thereafter known as Royal Lancastrian. This was really the peak of the fame of Lancastrian wares. In 1915, William Burton retired, leaving Joseph as manager. There is no doubt of Joseph Burton's talent and competence, but he does not seem to have possessed the innovative flair of his brother. The pottery further suffered from the loss of several of its principal artists who were serving in the armed forces. Most crippling was the loss of Gordon Forsyth, who only returned briefly after the First World War.

All tile manufacturers suffered a severe drop in demand during the war but afterwards the tile side of Pilkingtons increasingly dominated the firm. In 1928 Lapis Ware was introduced, being first exhibited at the British Industries Fair 1929. This was decorated on the biscuit ware 'in underglaze colours of special composition, which change in the firing and soften and merge to a certain extent with the glaze' (*Pottery Gazette and Glass Trade Review*, March 1934). The pottery side of the business slowly wound down, the last firing taking place in 1938.

In 1948 William Barnes set up a pottery studio at Pilkingtons, which made attractive decorative wares in the Contemporary style of the 1950s. This studio closed in 1957. In December 1964 the firm merged with Carter and Co. In 1971 the amalgamated firm was taken over by Thomas Tilling Group. There was another revival of pottery production in 1972–5. Although these wares were sometimes taken from Carter & Co. and Pilkingtons originals, the glaze effects used were entirely different, being commercially supplied. The colours most often used were green, orange and blue. In March 1983 Thomas Tilling was bought by the finance group British Tyre and Rubber. The firm continues as a tile manufacturer to this day.

Further Reading

A. J. Cross. *Pilkington's Royal Lancastrian Pottery and Tiles* (Richard Dennis, 1980).
Geoffrey Godden and Michael Gibson. *Collecting Lustre Ware* (Barrie & Jenkins, 1991).
Abraham Lomax. *Royal Lancastrian Pottery, 1900–1938* (Abraham Lomax, Bolton, 1957).

Pilkingtons Kingfisher glaze earthenware vase.

c.1914–23. Impressed mark 'ROYAL/LANCASTRIAN/ENG-LAND' with rose tree; '3277'. 23 cm height   D

£195

Pilkingtons Royal Lancastrian earthenware vase with uranium orange glaze.

c.1930–8. Impressed mark with rose 'ROYAL LANCASTRIAN MADE IN ENGLAND'. 16 cm height   T

£46

These uranium orange glazes are literally uranium glazes and are radioactive. The level of radiation is not dangerous, although it has been suggested by experts that one should not store a large number of such pieces in a closed cabinet. Opening the door after a prolonged period could be equivalent to receiving an X-ray!

CADBOROUGH POTTERY
(c.1834–76)
BELLE VUE POTTERY
(1869–1939)
RYE POTTERY
(1947 to the present day)

William Mitchell was manager of Cadborough Pottery, where typical Sussex Rustic wares were made. These were usually green or brown glazed and often decorated with inscriptions impressed with printer's type and sprigging. Mitchell established the Belle Vue Pottery on Ferry Road, Rye in 1869, specialising in rustic ware whose surface imitated tree bark, and sprigged pieces, often bearing hops. The pots were glazed with green or brown lead glazes.

William's sons, Henry and Frederick, had been helping him at the Cadborough Pottery for many years, and Frederick succeeded him at Belle Vue. When Frederick Mitchell died in 1875, his widow Caroline, who is said to have been a skilled potter, continued the pottery. She favoured copies of Continental wares but also produced Trojan Ware, which consisted of some eighteen different shapes after the pottery excavated at Troy by Dr Schliemann.

In 1882, Frederick's nephew, F. T. Mitchell, joined the firm and continued after Mrs Mitchell's death in 1895. He returned to the traditional wares produced by his uncle. Although his work was of a higher standard than that of his predecessors, some feel that it lacks the naïve charm of the earlier Rye wares. In 1930 the pottery was purchased by Mrs Ella D. Mills who produced Sussex Art Pottery for the tourist trade. The pottery was shut down in 1939 but was reopened in 1947 as Rye Pottery by the studio potters John and Walter Cole.

Cadborough Pottery earthenware green-glazed plate with impressed inscription in printer's type and sprigged border.

c.1853. Hairline crack. Incised mark 'Rye Pottery'. 16 cm diameter   HBW

£80

Belle Vue Pottery earthenware vase with applied hops, decorated in brown and green glazes.

c.1876–1930. Incised mark SRW in arms of an X, 'Rye'. 9 cm height   GCC

£45

MINTON, HOLLINS & CO,
(1845–1968)

Minton, Hollins & Co was established at Stoke in 1845 to produce encaustic tiles. In 1870 production was expanded to wall tiles (see chapter 25). During the First World War, Hollins experienced a slump in demand for their tiles: they countered by introducing Astra

Ware c.1917, sometimes advertised as 'reproduced from the antique'. This was made in simple, classical shapes decorated with glaze effects, which were admired for their beauty and restraint. The firm continued to advertise Astra ware until the late 1920s, but Cynthia Weaver has collected oral evidence that it continued in production until 1934.

Until the publication of Bergesen's *Encyclopaedia of British Art Pottery* and the article by Cynthia Weaver, Astra Ware had been virtually ignored by researchers. Consequently the prices one can expect to pay for these wares vary wildly as can be seen below. Certainly, with increasing recognition of the wares, values will increase. The collector should look for interesting glaze effects, for the single colour vases, while attractive, are of less interest.

Further Reading

Cynthia Weaver, 'The "Astra" Ware of Minton, Hollins & Co.', *Antique Collecting*, November 1991, pages 8–14.

Large Minton Hollins Astra Ware earthenware vase with streaky blue and green glazes.

c.1920s. Chip on base with pieces replaced. Printed circular mark 'MINTON, HOLLINS & CO./STOKE-ON-TRENT' with 'ASTRA WARE' in centre. 29.7 cm height   AF

£8

A perfect vase like this one would normally cost about £40.

Small Minton Hollins Astra Ware earthenware bottle-shaped vase with pink glaze.

c.1920s. Printed circular mark 'MINTON, HOLLINS & CO./STOKE-ON-TRENT' with 'ASTRA WARE' in centre. 13 cm height   AF

£18

This shape was illustrated in *Pottery Gazette and Glass Trade Review* in 1920. This vase would be more valuable if it had a more interesting glaze.

Minton Hollins Astra Ware earthenware vase with blue glaze.

c.1920s. Printed circular mark 'MINTON, HOLLINS & CO./ STOKE-ON-TRENT' with 'ASTRA WARE' in centre. 19.5 cm height   AF

£26

WILLIAM HOWSON TAYLOR
(RUSKIN POTTERY)
(1898–1933)

William Howson Taylor established the Ruskin Pottery at Smethwick in 1898, with the financial backing, artistic guidance and moral support of his father Edward Taylor. By 1903, they were receiving good notices in the arts press for their coloured lustre and transmutation glazes. They won the Grand Prize at the Louisiana Purchase exhibition In St Louis in 1904. The firm made tea wares as well as vases. The tea wares are beautifully potted: although they are made of stoneware they are as light as Japanese eggshell porcelain. There were several classes of ware:

(1) Soufflé Wares with a single colour glaze mottled, clouded or shaded.

(2) Lustre Wares in a wide variety of colours, the most beautiful being the Kingfisher lustre. The lustre wares, especially the orange and yellow, are prone to scratching. Many pieces today can be expected to have a few minor scratches, but disfiguring scratches or rubbed areas decrease the value of the piece dramatically.

(3) Flambé wares are Taylor's transmutation glazed wares. These are made in a reduction atmosphere in the kiln, with the chemical interchange of ions between the atmosphere and the glaze causing each piece to be unique. These have always been the most valuable of Ruskin wares. William Howson Taylor restricted access to the special kiln where these were made, and closely guarded his notes, which he burned before his death in 1935.

(4) Matt glazed slip-cast wares were made in the early 1930s in an effort to bolster the firm's failing fortunes. Some of them have angular Art Deco shapes, but these are the least desirable and least valuable Ruskin wares to be found today.

(5) Crystalline glazes, in which minute crystals, like the starbursts of frost on a window, can be seen were introduced as early as 1908.

Ruskin Pottery also produced 'enamels', which were small stoneware plaques decorated with various glaze effects. These were set as jewellery in beaten copper mounts of mirrors, fire screens etc., and sold to other potteries to set into art pottery (see p. 230).

Further Reading

James H. Ruston. *Ruskin Pottery*, 2nd edn (Sandwell Metropolitan Borough Council, 1990).

Ruskin stoneware vase with high-temperature red and purple transmutation glaze.

c.1919. Impressed mark 'RUSKIN/ENGLAND/1919'. 12 cm
height   HBW

£165

Ruskin stoneware blue lustre vase.

c.1920. Impressed mark 'RUSKIN/ENGLAND/1920'. 15 cm
height   HBW

£105

Ruskin stoneware bowl with high-temperature transmutation glaze.

c.1927. Impressed mark 'RUSKIN/ENGLAND/1927'. 13 cm
diameter   HBW

£210

Ruskin crystalline glaze stoneware vase in blue, green and pearl.

c.1931. Incised signature 'W. Howson Taylor'; impressed mark 'RUSKIN ENGLAND 1931' arranged in a triangle. 25 cm height   MH

£325

Three Ruskin miniature stoneware bowls with coloured lustre glazes.

All 6 cm diameter. Rear: Kingfisher blue lustre, impressed mark 'ENGLAND/RUSKIN 1914'. CG £35. Left: pale blue lustre, impressed mark 'RUSKIN'. CG £25. Right: pink lustre, unmarked. AF £5.

This is an example of how three very similar items can vary drastically in price, according to the cost to the dealer, and the popularity of the item with their clientele. In each case the dealer had correctly identified the piece. Which is the correct price? Whatever price the buyer and seller can agree upon!

HENRY TOOTH & CO.
(1887 to the present day)

In 1882 Henry Tooth (1842–1918) and William Ault established the Bretby Art Pottery under the style Tooth & Ault at Church Gresley, Burton-on-Trent, Derbyshire. In 1887 Ault departed, leaving Tooth to continue. In 1933 Fred Parker acquired the firm and they continue to produce figures and novelties to the present day.

Although Tooth's was clearly a commercial pottery that employed modern methods such as slip-casting, as opposed to a purist's art pottery that would only produce thrown pots, the firm's work was universally acknowledged as art pottery by contemporaries. Very little is known of Tooth's employees. He did a great deal of the design work himself and his son, W. E. Tooth, also had his own studio at the works. In 1929, W. E. Tooth acknowledged the contribution of his sister Florence (Mrs J. B. Rigg) as a modeller.

The early wares were relief-moulded with lead glazes as decoration. There were some fine pieces of barbotine (slip painting) such as the ewer below. The firm specialised in large wares such as umbrella stands and pots with pedestals. However, nearly every type of ornamental ware was made, down to ash and pin trays. Figures, including grotesques, were also made. Some of the figurines were very finely modelled. Another speciality was *trompe l'œil* wares known as 'deception' pieces. These included nuts, biscuits, tomatoes, reels of cotton, cigars and pipes with matches and scissors on trays. They also produced many wares whose surfaces imitated materials such as ivory, wood and metals. The word which appears most often in the many reviews of Bretby Ware is 'novelty'.

The Bretby rising sun mark was registered in 1882, and is still used as a trademark by the firm today. Clanta Ware was registered as a trademark in 1914 and was used for some twenty years.

Large Bretby barbotine earthenware ewer, signed Manson.

c.1892. Impressed Bretby rising sun mark; shape number '957/ENGLAND'. 32 cm height   CCC

£275

This is a very important piece as the only other recorded signed piece of Bretby is a similar vase signed by G. L. Parkinson at the Derby Art Gallery.

Bronze and Jewelled Ware was introduced in 1905. At least some of these ceramic jewels were purchased from Ruskin Pottery (see above).

Bretby Bronze and Jewelled Ware earthenware vase with a matt bronze effect glaze with two inserted 'jewels' in turquoise and brown.

c.1907. Moulded Bretby mark with sunrise, shape number 1612 and 'ENGLAND'. 30 cm height   GCC

£175

A Bretby Bronze and Jewelled Ware earthenware vase with matt bronze effect glazes on slip-cast shape with two applied 'jewels'.

c.1907. Moulded Bretby mark and shape number '1667'. 21.6 cm height   G

£175

Bretby slip-cast vase with brown glazes sprayed with gold.

c.1922. Impressed Bretby rising sun mark; shape 2022. 40 cm height   GCC

£325

This vase was illustrated in Tooth's advertisements in 1922.

TORQUAY POTTERIES

Although the Torquay area of Devon had an abundance of fine red clay, exported to other areas of the country, it was not until the second half of the 19th century that a pottery industry developed there. The Watcombe Terra-Cotta Co. established in 1869 was soon followed by the Torquay Terracotta Co., both of whom excelled in fine terracotta vases, busts and figures. They were joined by John Phillips who had established the Aller Vale Pottery as an ordinary concern in 1868. When the undecorated terracotta wares were losing popularity, Watcombe and Torquay countered with enamel decoration on the terracotta body, but Aller Vale answered the public's demands for brightly coloured ware by introducing slip decoration. By dipping the red earthenwares in a white slip, they had the freedom to use various colours effectively. For example if they had put a blue or green glaze on a red earthenware pot, it would appear black. The extra labour involved in coating the wares was necessary because most of the clay in the district was red, and importing white ball clay from Devon would have incurred extra expense. By coating the red clay, which they dug on the premises, with a thin coating of white slip they could minimise this expense.

Aller Vale's technique and patterns were copied by many potteries which sprung up in the district in the early 20th century. When Aller Vale was purchased by the local conglomerate Hexter, Humpherson, many of the workers were disaffected and left to start their own potteries or to work for others. This further disseminated the patterns and techniques throughout the district.

Motto ware was another introduction of Aller Vale, which was eventually copied by most Torquay potteries and continued in production at Watcombe and Longpark into the 1950s. It is difficult for the novice to differentiate between these wares, but if you want to collect Torquay pottery you must learn to do so. You may like the more recent wares, and they are collectable, but you should not have to pay very much for them. As certain patterns were made by many firms over a long period, Deena Patrick's marks book can be very useful.

Today Torquay Pottery and motto wares, of the sort sold as cheap souvenirs, are nearly synonymous. However, some very fine art pottery was produced in the region. The Torquay Pottery Collectors' Society (TPCS) actively promotes the appreciation of these wares through their publications, seminars and meetings. Their membership secretary is Mrs Shirley Everett, 23 Holland Avenue, Cheam, Sutton, Surrey.

Further Reading

Virginia Brisco. *Torquay Mottowares* (The Torquay Pottery Collectors' Society, Torre Abbey, 1989).

Virginia Brisco. *Torquay Commemoratives and Advertising Wares* (The Torquay Pottery Collectors' Society, Torre Abbey, 1991).

Deena Patrick. *Torquay Pottery Marks Book* (The Torquay Pottery Collectors' Society, Torre Abbey, 1986).

E. Lloyd Thomas. *The Old Torquay Potteries* (Arthur Stockwell, Ilfracombe, 1978).

The Torquay Pottery Collectors' Society Magazine.

ALLER VALE (ART) POTTERY (c.1868–1901)

John Phillips began to produce art pottery at Aller Vale c.1881. He employed students from the Kingskerswell School of Art, which he had patronised since its establishment in 1879. Phillips drew nearly all his labour force from the local community. It was believed that this local character was responsible for the distinctive style of Aller Vale pottery. At Aller Vale all pots were made from clay dug on the site, thrown and decorated by hand with slips and glazes prepared by the pottery.

Although the earlier wares were amateurish, by the mid 1880s the quality had improved. Most wares had a deep red body, but some pieces had a white body or a combination of red and white. These wares were heavily glazed and decorated with barbotine flowers and insects on blue, yellow, green or reddish-brown grounds. Small decorative items predominated, often with quaint shapes, including features such as filled rims, skewed handles and flower vases with several necks, known as udder vases. Many of these shapes were copied by the other Torquay potteries. It is believed that Aller Vale was the first to introduce motto wares to the Torquay area. These were soon copied widely in the region.

When John Philips died in 1897, the business was taken over by Hexter Humpherson & Co. who later purchased the Watcombe Terra-Cotta Co. (see below) and amalgamated the two firms in 1901 under the style Royal Aller Vale & Watcombe Pottery Co. Although motto wares continued to be marked 'Aller Vale' the works at Aller Vale closed in 1924.

Aller Vale wares are often marked with 'ALLER VALE' or incised shape and pattern numbers. Most potters paint their pattern numbers at the time of decoration, leaving the flexibility to use whatever pattern is required at the time. Because Aller Vale incised the intended pattern number before biscuit firing, one will occasionally find a pot whose pattern does not match the number.

Very rare Aller Vale green-glazed vase with a South American inspired design in the manner of Christopher Dresser.

c.1880s. Impressed 'ALLER VALE'; incised shape number 46. 18 cm height   BK

£120

Christopher Dresser is not known to have designed for Aller Vale. This design is typical of his work and quite unlike other Aller Vale wares. It thus remains an unusual, mysterious piece.

Aller Vale red earthenware vase with green ground, polychrome slip decoration.

c.1890s. 18 cm height   BK

£45

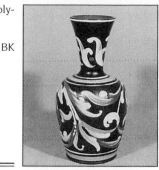

Aller Vale buff earthenware *Sandringham* pattern vase.

c.1890s. 25.5 cm height   BK

£68

Unlike most Aller Vale pottery, the *Sandringham* pattern is made with a buff body. The design is then painted with blue slip, and coated with a clear glaze.

Aller Vale red earthenware motto ware jug decorated with the *Scandy* pattern on a cream ground.

c.1897–1902. Incised mark '906/N1'; impressed mark 'ALLER VALE HH&Co' (Hexter, Humpherson & Co.). 18 cm height
                                                         BK

£30

This simple jug is well potted and well decorated, an example of the better quality of motto wares. The very popular *Scandy* pattern was copied by many other Torquay potters. It is thought that the name may be an abbreviation for Scandinavian.

Aller Vale buff earthenware jug with pierced rim, *Normandy* decoration with green glaze running down over a clear glaze.

c.1900. Impressed mark 'ALLER VALE'; incised shape and pattern numbers '648 G1'. 14.5 cm height   TPCS

£28

This very attractive shape was copied by other Torquay potteries. The green glaze was also used on its own, pattern M1.

LONGPARK POTTERY (c.1903–57)

William and James Brewer operated the Longpark Pottery in partnership with Ralph Willott (1895–1903). The Longpark Pottery was acquired by a group of Aller Vale (Art) Pottery employees disgruntled with Hexter Humpherson & Co., possibly in 1903. The wares produced by Longpark were, not surprisingly, quite similar to those produced at Aller Vale. In some cases even the same pattern numbers were used. Nevertheless, some good quality original designs were produced and there are a number of distinctive features of Longpark wares. The lettering on Longpark motto wares is particularly thick. Some Longpark motto wares with coloured grounds have slip-trailed writing.

Pots marked Tormohun were made 1907–13. The Royal Tormohun Pottery Co. Ltd seems to have been an art studio within Longpark rather than a separate pottery, although it did appear as such in some directories.

The pottery closed in 1943, after which it was acquired by Hexter, Humpherson & Co.'s Mid-Devon Trading Co. The wares were mostly motto wares in Scandy, Black Cockerel and cottage patterns and daffodil wares.

A *Longpark Pottery Co. Illustrated Catalogue and Revised Price List* c.1930s has been reprinted by the Torquay Pottery Collectors' Society.

Longpark red earthenware tobacco jar decorated with polychrome slip-painted scene.

c.1903. Small chip to rim. Impressed marks 'LONGPARK. TORQUAY'; circular mark reading the same. Incised mark '2SS'. 13 cm height   AF

£10

A vase with a similar decoration is illustrated in Lloyd Thomas, who surmised that the 'SS' might have been the initials of the artist. The dating of this piece is problematical, as the circular mark is generally attributed to the Brewer Brothers period at Longpark, while the impressed mark is attributed to Longpark c.1903–9. One would normally expect to pay about £25 for a perfect example of this type.

Longpark red earthenware udder vase with a green ground and yellow slip-painted daffodils.

c.1907–13. Incised 'Tormohun Ware 3242'. 11.5 cm height
                BK

£52

Daffodil Ware was still being made at Longpark in the 1950s.

Longpark three-handled red earthenware vase with blue ground and polychrome slip decoration.

c.1907–13. Impressed marks 'LONGPARK/TORQUAY';'TORMOHUM WARE'; '3B3'. 19.5 cm height   BK

£35

Red earthenware candlestick with polychrome slip decoration, attributed to Longpark.

c.1910s. 15 cm diameter   BK

£20

Ships were another very popular motif in Torquay. Although there were variations within individual potteries, many unmarked pieces such as this one can be attributed according to the colours employed.

Longpark red earthenware motto ware puzzle jug with *Coloured Cock* slip decoration.

c.1903–30. Incised shape and pattern numbers 222 N2; 'LONGPARK POTTERY'. 11 cm height   BK

£52

Puzzle jugs were an 18th-century novelty which have survived to the present day. They were often the subject of wagers in taverns, as all but one of the openings must be sealed with the fingers in order to drink successfully.

Coloured Cock motto ware puzzle jugs were still being made at Longpark in the 1930s. The firm continued to use the pattern on their motto wares after the Second World War. These later wares usually had a black stamped mark, rather than an incised mark.

235

Longpark *Kingfisher* red earthenware vase with slip decoration on blue ground.

c.1920–30s. 37 cm height   BK

£65

Watcombe, Hart & Moist and Daison Art Pottery also used the Kingfisher designs, but the Longpark birds can be distinguished by their eyes (which are simply a dot in a circle) and long tails which begin at the neck. Longpark still made Kingfisher Ware in the 1930s.

Longpark red earthenware pot with two handles and three feet, blue green glaze with *art nouveau* ribbon and ring slip-decoration.

c.1914–23. Incised mark 'Longpark/Torquay'. 7.4 cm height
AF

£6

WATCOMBE TERRA-COTTA CO. (1869–1903)

ROYAL ALLER VALE & WATCOMBE POTTERY CO. (1903–62)

George Allen established Watcombe with six other investors in 1869. Within three years the firm had won a reputation for fine quality terracotta wares. These included figures and busts (see p. 540), plaques, baskets of finely modelled flowers and decorative wares with barbotine decoration.

Upon Allen's death in 1883 the firm went into liquidation. Frances R. Evans acquired the firm, changing the nature of the wares (although many old moulds continued in use). Slip-painted wares in the manner of Aller Vale were introduced.

In 1900 Hexter, Humpherson (already owners of Aller Vale) acquired Watcombe and in 1903 amalgamated the two firms under the style Royal Aller Vale & Watcombe Pottery Co. After the merger, Watcombe continued to make slip-decorated wares in the manner of Aller Vale.

One of a pair of Watcombe 'Jewel' shape terracotta vases with apple blossoms painted in enamels and turquoise-glazed interiors.

c.late 1880s. 18 cm height BK

£110 the pair

Watcombe red earthenware vase with barbotine decoration and clear glaze.

c.1880s. Impressed mark 'WATCOMBE/TORQUAY/184'. 15.5 cm height BK

£35

Watcombe red earthenware green-glazed owl bowl.

c.1900. Incised mark 'Watcombe'. 22 cm diameter TPCS

£75

Rare Watcombe two-handled red earthenware vase with silver ground and bronzed handles and interior, enamel painting of ferns.

c.1880s. Impressed mark 'WATCOMBE'. 13.5 cm height
TPCS

£38

Watcombe red earthenware vase with slip decoration portraying Anne Hathaway's Cottage.

c.1901–20. Incised 'Watcombe'; shape number 164. 11 cm height   BK

£32

Watcombe red earthenware *Windmill* pattern vase.

1920s–1945. Rubber-stamped mark 'WATCOMBE/TORQUAY/ENGLAND'. 25 cm height   BK

£58

Many Torquay potteries made *Windmill* patterns. Royal Aller Vale & Watcombe Pottery advertised the *Windmill* pattern as early as 1908. The large size of the vase explains its relatively high value for a common pattern and late date.

Watcombe red earthenware *Devon Pixie* mug.

Late 1920s+. Incised mark 62; black stamped mark 'WATCOMBE/TORQUAY/ENGLAND'. 12 cm height   BK

£30

OTHER TORQUAY POTTERIES

Unusual red earthenware two-handled vase with slip decoration, blue-glazed.

c.1900. Painted pattern number 630. 15.5 cm height   BK

£110

Large Hart & Moist red earthenware 'udder' vase with polychrome slip decoration.

c.1904. Impressed mark 'HM EXETER'. 19 cm height   BK

£48

Hart & Moist (1897–35) succeeded Cole & Trelease's Exeter Art Pottery, for which they had both worked. The wares are distinguished by their brown body, as opposed to the usual red body found in Torquay wares. For the most part Hart & Moist copied the successful shapes, patterns and mottoes used by other Torquay firms. A vase similar to the one shown here was illustrated in a 1904 advertisement.

Devon Tors red earthenware jug with 'Pevensey Castle' sgraffito decoration.

c.1960s. Impressed mark 'DEVON TORS POTTERY'; 'B' incised. 13 cm height   BK

£16

Devon Tors (1921–70s) was established by four former employees of the Bovey Pottery. They mainly produced small souvenir wares in the typical Torquay style.

UPCHURCH POTTERY
(1913–63)

Seymour Wakeley established an art pottery at Upchurch, near Rainham in 1913. He hired Edward J. Baker (1876–1955) to run the pottery. Baker had previously worked at the Chelsea Pottery with studio potter Reginald Wells, who was a friend of Wakeley's. By 1915,

Upchurch Pottery was exhibiting interesting examples of matt glazed wares at the British Industries Fair. The Pottery was quite successful in the following decade, although it was never large enough for Baker to employ more than one of this three sons.

The glaze recipe books of Edward J. Baker reveal that he used a large proportion of boracic, which intensifies colour and reduces the expansion of the glaze to prevent crazing. Indeed Upchurch wares are *very rarely* crazed. During the late 1920s the quiet tones of the Upchurch glazes were unpopular with the Jazz Age customers. The wares were described by the press as sombre and stolid.

From 1936 the pottery passed through successive owners, but Edward J. Baker continued to pot, always experimenting. He finally purchased the pottery c.1953. His eldest son William Baker returned from London where he had been working for the Fulham Pottery to assist his father. William carried on with his youngest brother James, until 1963. The wares produced from the late 1930s were considerably different from earlier wares. The glazes are more often pastel, and tablewares were made.

During the Wakeley period, the Bakers impressed or incised their wares indiscriminately. The 'MADE IN ENGLAND' was added after the Second World War, when Upchurch joined the national drive to bolster exports. The 'HANDMADE' impressed mark also dates from after the Second World War, as does the impressed name of 'SEEBY', a retailer in Reading.

Rare Upchurch two-handled earthenware bottle with a matt white glaze subtly streaked with blue and pale pink.

c.1920. Incised mark 'UPCHURCH'. 21 cm height   CG

£65

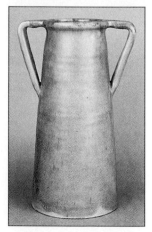

Tall Upchurch two-handled earthenware vase with green matt glaze.

c.1925. Impressed 'UPCHURCH'; painted glaze batch number 687. 27 cm height   CG

£55

This shape was illustrated in *Pottery Gazette and Glass Trade Review* in April 1925.

Large Upchurch globular earthenware vase with blue glazes running over a grey glaze.

c.1928. Incised mark 'Upchurch'; painted glaze batch 'PB BC'. 16.5 cm height   CG

£45

According to Edward Baker's notebooks, this glaze batch was used c.1928.

Upchurch *Shell* shape earthenware vase with green interior and yellow and brown exterior.

c.1950s. Impressed marks 'MADE IN ENGLAND'; 'UPCHURCH'; 'HANDMADE'. 30.5 cm length   CG

£45

Newspaper articles from the 1950s show these *Shell* vases being made. They are very common and can be found in many sizes, with and without handles. As most have a single colour matt glaze, this example is more valuable.

OTHER ART POTTERY MANUFACTURERS

Minton Secessionist Ware earthenware vase, tube-lined and coloured with polychrome majolica glazes.

c.1904. Restored rim. Printed mark 'Minton Ltd/NO 1'. 25 cm height   GCC

£70

Mintons' Secessionist wares designed by Léon Solon and John W. Wadsworth were introduced in 1902. The outlines were slip-trailed, or relief-moulded to appear slip-trailed (an economy measure). Some pieces were also block-printed. Majolica glazes in art colours were used: mustard, pink, olive green, purple, red, indigo blue, pale lime and copper brown. Seccessionist Wares had a special back-stamp 'Mintons Ltd.', often accompanied by a stamped shape number. The wares were discontinued in 1914. See Paul Atterbury and Maureen Batkin, *The Dictionary of Minton* (Antique Collectors' Club, Woodbridge, 1990).

Large earthenware owl jug with red body and green glaze.

c.1910. Some wear on raised surfaces. 25 cm height   RS

£120

Green-glazed owl jugs were made at country potteries such as A. Harris & Sons at Farnham, and C. H. Brannam at Barnstaple. The owl motif was also used at Watcombe.

Small green-glazed earthenware owl jug.

c.1910. Small chip to rim. 11.5 cm height   RS

£38

Red earthenware vase coated with white slip and green glaze with very fine sgraffito decoration.

c.1880s. Incised mark of a horseshoe and 'Green'. 19 cm height   GCC

£125

Reverse.

Pair of Wilkinson Oriflamme miniature earthenware vases with commercial liquid lustre over lavender and pale green glazes and gold rims.

c.1924. Printed Oriflamme mark. Both 6.7 cm height   G

£45

Arthur J. Wilkinson (Ltd) of Burslem (1885–1964) introduced Oriflamme wares designed by J. Butler in 1910: these were described as 'a series of splashed, veined, and lustrous glazed effects'. Production of Oriflamme was halted during the First World War, but was resumed in 1919.

Thomas Fradley slip-decorated earthenware plaque with applied portrait, tan and brown ground.

c.1890s. Impressed mark 'T. FRADLEY'. 24 cm diameter TV

£100

Thomas Fradley (1844–c.1900) worked as an artist at Minton. He also had his own pottery on Copeland Street, Stoke, where he made slip-decorated wares. Most of these wares were sold in public houses locally.

Wessex red earthenware bottle with polychrome slip decoration.

c.1915. Incised mark 'WESSEX/POOLE'. 14 cm height   BK

£40

Wessex Perfumery and Pottery started c.1915, and is believed to have employed some of the employees from Charles Collard's Crown Dorset Pottery, when it shut down in 1915. The patterns employed were 'Scandy' and others similar to early Crown Dorset wares.

One of a pair of Lovatt's Potteries stoneware vases with running blue and mauve glazes.

c.1937. Marked 'PATENT NO 803679' (registered in 1937). 24 cm height   MH

£55 the pair

Lovatt & Lovatt of Langley Mill, Nottinghamshire (1895–1931) specialised in fireproof and domestic wares using only leadless glazes. Their predecessors Calvert & Lovatt had introduced Langley Art Ware in the mid 1880s. Many of these wares used a technique similar to Doulton's Chiné wares (see Doulton above). They were succeeded by Lovatt's Potteries (1931–67) and Langley Potteries (1967–82).

Large Forester earthenware vase with hand-painted rural scene signed Dean.

c.1900. Lip restored. Printed mark 'T F & S LD/ENGLAND' with picture of phoenix, for Thomas Forester & Sons Ltd. 31.5 cm height   CCC

£300

Thomas Forester (& Sons) (1877–1959) was a Longton majolica manufacturer who turned to art pottery during the 1880s. The wares consisted of flower pots, vases and toilet pieces, often hand-painted, but the only known artist was A. Dean whose work was shown at Forester's stand at the Paris International Exhibition of 1900. This vase is of unusual excellence, and may have been one of the pieces Dean painted for the Exhibition.

Dicker Ware three-handled miniature red earthenware vase with mauve and blue metallic glaze.

c.1915. Impressed mark 'DICKER WARE/SUSSEX'. 6.2 cm height   CG

£15

Uriah Clark & Nephew (1845–1959) acquired the Dicker Pottery, which had been established c.1774. The early art wares had a red body which was incised, impressed with printer's type or sprigged. Some pieces were decorated with inlays of white clay, and a thick honey glaze was used. These were all techniques typical of the traditional Sussex potter; many of these pots were deliberate reproductions of antique wares.

Pieces such as the one shown here in quaint historic shapes with metallic and coloured lustre glazes had been introduced by 1917. In the early 1920s the firm introduced their black ironstone lustre, which is the treatment most commonly encountered. The pottery closed in 1941, re-opened after the Second World War, and finally closed in 1959. The post-War pieces bear an impressed or printed circular mark 'DICKER WARE/MADE IN ENGLAND'.

Ault shell-shaped earthenware vase with yellow and green lead glazes.

c.1892. Small crack. Moulded mark 'AULT' in ribbon. Impressed mark RD195324 (registered in 1892). 9 cm height

AF

£8

William Ault & Co. (1887–1922) was established at Swadlincote after William Ault left his partnership at Bretby Pottery with Henry Tooth (see above). The firm produced a wide variety of art wares until the 1930s, when production was devoted to useful wares. The firm specialised in pots and pedestals and other large items.

This shape was illustrated in Ault's advertisement in the *Pottery Gazette* January 1895. It was possibly designed by Christopher Dresser, who designed for Ault 1892–1900. The advertisement mentioned 'NEW DESIGNS by Dr. Dresser in course of preparation.' In 1911 Ault's advertisement in the *Pottery Gazette* illustrated a vase with three of these shell-shaped vases on an ornate base. Should this design be certainly identified as one of Christopher Dresser's the value for a perfect example would be about £70.

Linthorpe Art Pottery relief-moulded earthenware plate with thick green, gold and cream lead glazes, reverse with green glaze.

c.1880s. Impressed mark 'LINTHORPE' superimposed on a base; shape number 1835. Painted mark (possibly indicating colour combination) 'Ad 471'. 24.5 cm diameter   CE

£35

Linthorpe Pottery, Middlesbrough, Cleveland (1879–89) is almost inextricably linked with the name of Christopher Dresser. In fact he had nothing to do with the actual production: there is no evidence that he even visited the works. He only designed for the firm for a brief period 1879–82. From that time most of the pots were designed by Henry Tooth (see above).

The Linthorpe moulds were purchased by William Ault (see previous item), Henry Tooth and Torquay Terra-Cotta Co. in 1890. Many of these were put into production at these potteries, with Ault using some of them as late as the 1920s. Designs which can be definitely identified as those of Christopher Dresser are highly desirable and much more valuable. See Clive W. Hart, *Linthorpe Art Pottery* (Aisling Publications, Cleveland, n.d.).

14 20TH-CENTURY EARTHENWARE

DURING the first years of the 20th century, British industrial potters seemed to have lost their way artistically, although enormous artistic and technical advances were made by the art potters or in the art studios of the industrial potters (see chapter 26). In the early years of the century, art nouveau designs, particularly those with strong Celtic lines, were among the best and most original. Production continued during the First World War with the export trade (especially to the United States) providing much-needed foreign currency. However, tile manufacturers in particular experienced a decline in demand, possibly because by this time the United States had a large and advanced tile industry of its own. Several of the English tile manufacturers, including Carter & Co. at Poole, Candy & Co. at Newton Abbot and Minton Hollins at Stoke, turned to the manufacture of decorative pottery. Many major factories such as Copeland, Wedgwood and Minton relied heavily on revivals of earlier designs.

Immediately after the war, many firms brought out designs with black grounds relieved by stencilled floral treatments. Popular colours were bright pink, orange and yellow, sometimes with black and white check borders. In an article in 1921, the *Pottery Gazette and Glass Trade Review* noted: 'As everybody knows, however, the ornamental trade, after the Armistice, began to wane, and it was necessary to bring out a variety of lines of a more utilitarian character in order to keep the factory busily employed.' Popular treatments mentioned included plain white, white and gold, lithograph borders and gilt, and mazarine blue bands and gold.

It was not until the 1920s that Art Deco with its bold colours and geometric shapes and patterns revived British ceramic design. The work of Clarice Cliff is the best known of the Art Deco period, but most firms produced some designs in the style. Art Deco took its name from the Exposition des Arts Décoratifs et Industriels held in Paris in 1925, whose architecture incorporated some of the elements which were soon reflected in ceramics. Art Deco wares were consciously modern, rebelling against the 18th-century revival which had gripped British ceramic design in the early years of the 20th century. The muted, 'tasteful' colours which had been dominant since they were popularised by the Aesthetic movement in the 1870s were superceded by brilliant colours. The energy and movement in the patterns and shapes reflected the Jazz Age. Hand-painting enjoyed a revival during the First World War, when lithographic transfers (which had largely been imported from Germany) became unavailable. After the war German imports remained unpopular, and the hand-painting movement burgeoned.

The Streamline style predominated as the 1930s progressed. Although these wares are sometimes lumped together with Art Deco, they are in fact quite distinctive. The brilliant reds, oranges, yellow and greens were now replaced with quiet pastels, often with matt glazes. Angularity began to disappear from both pattern and shape design. The designs of Susie Cooper exemplify this style.

Not all wares of the 1920s and 1930s fit neatly into these two categories. The work of Charlotte Rhead, for example, was influenced by the trends around her, but always maintains a strong individuality. Novelty manufacturers produced cottage wares (portraying idyllic thatched cottages), often humorous teapots and salad wares in the shape of lettuce leaves.

With the advent of the Second World War, the industry was completely disrupted as labour and raw materials were diverted to the war effort. Manufacturers were restricted to the austere, undecorated utility wares, with the exception of wares destined for export, principally to the United States. Only some firms were licensed to produce utility and/or export wares: other firms devoted their workforce to different products for the war effort.

In 1948 the 'Britain Can Make It' exhibition was called the 'Britain Can't Have It' exhibition by the public, as many of the wares displayed were still only available for export.

The Festival of Britain in 1951, celebrating the centenary of the Great Exhibition of 1851, showed wares which would soon be available, as in 1952 all restrictions on ceramic production were lifted. It is often impossible to distinguish the wares of the late 1930s from the early 1950s. Perusal of trade journals shows that when restrictions were lifted, most firms initially continued lines abandoned in 1939. However, after an initial boom caused by more than a decade of pent-up demand, the industry was forced to search for a new style.

The Contemporary style, inspired by American tablewares, and introduced to Britain by Roy Midwinter, soon appeared in the designs of most British potters. The modern housewife demanded the sleek rimless coupe shape plate. Most of the patterns were simply expressed florals or abstracts. Many popular motifs of the period also appear: poodles, rock and roll dancers, Parisian street scenes, tropical beaches and, in the case of Ridgways' famous 'Homemaker' pattern, television sets, potted plants and coffee tables. Small items are still readily available in boot fairs and flea markets for under £3. The tasteful floral subjects are usually less valuable than poodles etc., but look for any piece where the backstamp names the designer. The most collected designers include Susie Cooper and Midwinter designers Terence Conran, Hugh Casson and Jessie Tait.

The later 1960s brought in a new geometric style and a brighter palette, largely achieved with improved lithographic transfers. On the other hand, industrial manufacturers began to imitate the simple shapes and oatmeal glazes of studio potters. These wares too, are becoming collectable and are available for a pittance.

The collector should keep in mind that most British factories have been dependent on exports, especially to the United States, throughout the 20th century. Therefore the bulk of the manufactures have been imitations of earlier styles, which are popular abroad. Even if manufactured by a 'collectable' factory, these wares are of little value. It is wiser to choose wares with strong contemporary design, whether Art Deco, Streamline, Contemporary or even the geometric designs of the late 1960s and 1970s. Even the soft pastel floral designs of the 1980s will eventually become collectable.

Another field for the collector is contemporary studio pottery. For relatively small sums, there are many marvellous pots to be found that were literally made yesterday. This field is treated in chapter 26.

Further Reading

Decorative Art, The Studio Yearbook 1949.
Gordon Forsyth, Twentieth Century Ceramics (The Studio, 1950).
Geoffrey Godden and Michael Gibson. Collecting Lustrewares (Barrie & Jenkins, 1991).
Frances Hannah. Ceramics, Twentieth Century Design (E. P. Dutton, New York, 1986).
Kathy Niblett. Dynamic Design, The British Pottery Industry 1940–90 (Stoke-on-Trent City Museum & Art Gallery, 1990).
Judy Spours. Art Deco Tableware (Ward Lock, 1988).

BESWICK
(c.1894 to the present day)

J. W. Beswick began potting in Longton in 1894. The earlier wares were majolica and other earthenwares typical of the late Victorian period. These were not marked and have not been identified. In the 20th century Beswick began production of animal figures, for which they became well known. The firm became John Beswick (Ltd) in 1938. They were taken over by Doulton in 1969 and have since been known as John Beswick Studio of Royal Doulton. Beswick is popular with collectors, and for that reason it is worth looking out for their ornamental and tablewares of the 1930s, 1950s and 1960s.

Further Reading

Harvey May. *The Beswick Collectors' Handbook* (Kevin Francis Publishing, 1986).

Beswick earthenware slip-cast relief-moulded vase with green matt glaze.

c.1936. Green printed mark 'Beswick Ware/Made in England'; impressed 'MADE IN ENGLAND/675'. 24 cm height   RS

£28

Beswick earthenware vase with blue and lavender matt glazes.

c,1936. Printed mark 'Beswick Ware/England'; impressed shape number 186. 23.5 cm height   MH

£48

Beswick earthenware figure of a horse, painted in brown, black and white enamels.

c.1950s. Printed circular mark 'BESWICK ENGLAND'. 15 cm height   HA

£22

Beswick earthenware figure of a donkey with mottled green, blue and yellow glazes.

c.1936. Moulded marks 'MADE IN ENGLAND' and shape number 369. Printed mark 'Beswick/Ware/MADE IN ENGLAND'. 21.5 cm height; 22.5 cm length of base   HA

£125

Largest of a flight of five Beswick earthenware ducks.

c.1950s. Printed mark in circle 'BESWICK ENGLAND'. Impressed mark 'MADE IN ENGLAND/BESWICK' and shape number 596-0. Largest 29 cm length; smallest (shape number 596-4) 13.5 cm length   HA

£174 for the five

BOOTHS
(c.1845–1948)

During the 20th century Booths made many table and ornamental wares typical of the era at Tunstall. During the early 1920s they produced their popular Fruit Bowl range, and in the late 1920s a range of quirky novelty wares. From c.1930 they produced Cornucopia embossed floral ornamental ware. They introduced Ribstone, ribbed slipcast wares in imitation of thrown wares with a wide variety of Art Deco decoration in c.1933.

In 1948 Booths & Colcloughs hired two Hungarian refugees Endre Hévézi and Dr Gyula Bajo to design a line of wares inspired by Hungarian folk pottery. After 1953 the Booths factory concentrated on producing 'fine quality dinner ware' in traditional patterns.

As the history of this firm is exceedingly complex, the following table may be of assistance.

c.1845	Thomas Booth & Co.
1872	Thomas Booth & Son(s)
1876	T. G. Booth
1883	T. G. & F. Booth
1891	Booths
1898	Booths Ltd
1948	Booths & Colcloughs Ltd
1954	Ridgway, Adderley, Booths & Colcloughs Ltd
1955	Ridgway Potteries Ltd (now part of Royal Doulton)

Booths earthenware Fruit Orient pattern bough pot with removable lid. Matt orange glaze with transfer-printed fruits and flowers filled in with enamels.

Early 1920s. Some chips to glaze and rubbing on edges. Marked 'BOOTH'S SILICON CHINA/FRUIT ORIENT/Rd. No. 674316'; painted marks '9/R/2383'. 20.3 cm length; 10.2 cm height.   G

£75

Booths introduced Silicon China, a semi-porcelain type earthenware, c.1900. Fruit Bowl or Bowl of Fruit patterns were originally made with a white ground. These were marketed by Heals.

Booths earthenware *Roma-Bronze* wall plaque.

c.1937. Black stamped mark 'ROMA-BRONZE/BOOTHS LTD/MADE IN ENGLAND'. 32.5 cm diameter   AF

£4

Booths introduced *Roma-Bronze* wares in 1936. This plaque was illustrated in an advertisement in *Pottery Gazette and Glass Trade Review*, February 1937. Some pieces may bear the Roman *fasces* mark, an axe and a bundle of rods, with ROMA-BRONZE/BOOTHS/ENGLAND'. The wares were purportedly: 'Faithful reproductions in genuine Ceramics, of examples of Roman and Old British Pottery in useful and ornamental shapes including Vases, Fruit Dishes, Placques, Bulb Bowls, Lamps, Candlesticks and numerous other articles.' One seldom finds these interesting Roma-Bronze items, so they do not have an established value.

JOSEPH BOURNE & SON
(DENBY)
(1812 to the present day)

Joseph Bourne of Denby, Derbyshire has always specialised in good quality utilitarian stonewares. Danesby art wares were introduced in 1904. During the 1920s glaze effects such as that shown below were made in large numbers. The Electric Blue wares produced during the 1930s have matt blue and orange glazes and other glossy ones. Some well-designed wares were made in the Contemporary style during the 1950s. Their blue and green cottage range is now collected, as are their hand-painted patterns. They have greatly profited from the popularity of oven-to-tablewares since 1960. Few factories' patterns become collectable so soon after withdrawal, so any Bourne wares are worth looking out for. The trade name Denby can occur without Bourne in marks after 1948.

Bourne's Danesby Ware Electric Blue stoneware vase with blue and orange matt glazes.

c.1930s. Marked 'Danesby Ware BOURNE DENBY ENGLAND'. 20 cm height   RS

£28

Bourne stoneware rectangular dish, hand-painted.

c.1952+. Signed 'Glyn Colledge' on reverse. 32 cm length
MH

£45

Glyn Colledge designed two ranges of ware for Joseph Bourne & Son, Glyn Ware and Cheviot Ware, during the 1950s, These hand-painted stonewares are rapidly becoming recognised and increasing in value. Glyn Colledge now pots independently.

Reverse.

BURGESS & LEIGH
(BURLEIGH WARE)
(c.1867 to the present day)

Burgess & Leigh have been producing good quality tablewares for over a century. The firm's production took on a new individuality when they acquired the services of Charlotte Rhead 1926–31. She trained decorators at Burgess & Leigh in the technique of tube-lining required for her designs, which the firm continued to produce after her departure.

Harold Bennett, who became art director during the 1930s, also designed some tube-lined patterns, some of which appear stilted in comparison with Rhead designs. Burleigh Ware in the 1930s also included designs with strong sculptural lines such as the first vase below. In the following years the firm employed a number of talented designers whose work is of interest, but the bulk of their wares remained utilitarian and dull.

The firm has always made a good deal of transfer-printed tableware, and it continues to be an important part of their production. They made some interesting Contemporary style tablewares and vases in the 1950s.

Further Reading

Bernard Bumpus. *Charlotte Rhead, Potter & Designer* (Kevin Francis Publishing, 1987).

Burleigh Ware earthenware vase, tube-lined and hand-painted with lustres, designed by Charlotte Rhead.

c.1926. Printed Burgess & Leigh globe mark with 'LRhead' signature. Painted pattern number 40/16/32. 17.5 cm height

MH

£75.

Another vase in pattern 4016 is illustrated by Bumpus.

Burleigh Ware earthenware hat-shaped vase with mottled grey and cream ground painted in orange and blue enamels, probably designed by Harold Bennett.

c.1930s. Printed beehive mark 'BURGESS & LEIGH LTD/ MADE IN ENGLAND'. Painted pattern number 5606. 5.5 cm height; 15 cm diameter   MH

£16

Burleigh Ware earthenware slip-cast relief-moulded jug painted in polychrome enamels.

c.1930s. Printed mark 'Burleigh Ware/B & L Ltd/MADE IN ENGLAND'. Painted pattern number 5076/A. 18 cm height

MH

£65

Many manufacturers made jugs, vases and planters like these with 'cute' animal motifs (see SylvaC under Shaw & Copestake below). Compare them with the Art Deco and Streamline designs with which they are contemporary. To those interested in the history of modern design, these types of wares are not very desirable, but many collectors today, as in the 1930s, find them appealing.

Burleigh Ware earthenware budgerigar-handled jug with yellow ground and polychrome enamels.

c.1930s. Hairline crack. Printed beehive mark 'BURGESS & LEIGH LTD/EST'D 1851/MADE IN ENGLAND'. Painted pattern number 4902/B. 19 cm height   MH

£35

Jugs and mugs with animal handles have a long history. Hound handles are frequently found in salt-glazed stoneware, and 'hydra' serpentine handles are often found on 19th-century ironstone wares. Here we have a 1930s interpretation of the tradition.

Burleigh Ware flower trough with fish, painted in yellow, green, brown and blue glazes.

c.1930s. Printed beehive mark 'BURGESS & LEIGH LTD/EST'D 1851/MADE IN ENGLAND'. Painted pattern number 6244. 22 cm length   HA

£125

Burleigh Ware earthenware relief-moulded vase in matt green glaze highlighted with brown enamel.

c.1940–60. Printed beehive mark 'Burleigh Ware/BURGESS & LEIGH LTD/ESTD. 1851/BURSLEM ENGLAND'. Impressed shape number 204; painted pattern number in brown 'b. 114 P'. 21.5 cm height   RS

£28

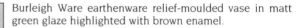

Burleigh Ware earthenware vase in the Contemporary style with red interior and red and black enamel decoration.

c.1958. Printed beehive mark 'BURGESS & LEIGH LTD/MADE IN ENGLAND'. Moulded shape number 75. 22 cm height   MH

£45

CANDY & CO.
(WESCONTREE WARE; CANDY WARE)
(c.1850–1991)

Candy Pottery was established at Newton Abbot by Frank Candy c.1850. The pottery came under the control of J. Howard Fox, a member of the well-known banking family, in the late 1880s. The firm specialised in tiles and fire surrounds. When demand for these wares declined during the First World War, Candy began the production of Wescontree art wares as a sideline. The early wares were slip-cast in simple shapes and decorated with various matt glaze effects. In 1936, the firm employed Sid Dart to throw the art wares, now known as Candy Ware. These were manufactured until 1960.

The firm manufactured tiles until their closure in 1991. During the 1980s they made screen-printed copies of William De Morgan's 19th-century hand-painted tiles in 'Persian' colours. They also produced Delta mural tiles with modern pictures or abstract designs.

Candy earthenware slip-cast vase decorated with brown and blue sponged glazes on a buff body.

c.1922. Stamped circular mark 'WESCONTREE/WARE/CANDY'. 16 cm height   AF

£6

This shape was illustrated in *Pottery Gazette and Glass Trade Review* in 1922.

Large Candy thrown earthenware vase with streaky light blue glazes.

c.1952. Stamped circular mark 'CANDY WARE/MADE IN ENGLAND'. 21 cm height   AF

£12

A vase in this shape, thrown by Sid Dart, was illustrated in *Pottery Gazette and Glass Trade Review* in 1952.

CARTER, STABLER & ADAMS
(POOLE; STUDIO WARE)
(1921 to the present day)

Carter & Co. specialised in tiles and architectural ceramics. They also made some art pottery, supplying blanks to William De Morgan and the Omega Workshops. They produced some fine lustreware and in-glaze painted wares. The firm became Carter, Stabler & Adams in 1921. The new partners radically changed the nature of the firm's wares. Phoebe and Harold Stabler and John and Truda Adams brought modern design to Poole, and their hand-painted wares are highly valued today. The stylish in-glaze hand-painted wares, most often with floral patterns, are still made in a special studio.

Several figures designed by the Stablers, some of which they had also made earlier at their London workshops, were produced at Poole.

The firm also produced many well-designed tablewares, always in the vanguard of fashion. The matt glazed two-tone pastel tablewares were introduced in the late 1930s, and revived after the Second World War under the name Twintone. This was stylishly updated on the Streamline shape with coupe-shaped plates.

The 1950s also saw the introduction of 'free form' vases with abstract patterns designed by A. B. Read. These very attractive wares are already avidly collected.

The firm has operated under the style Poole Pottery Ltd since 1962. During the 1960s and 1970s, they produced a brightly coloured range with bold patterns known as Studio Ware. Initially the wares were made in a small studio at the factory, but by the early 1970s a large part of the factory's production was devoted to the wares.

Throughout its history the larger part of Poole Pottery's production has been devoted to tiles (see chapter 25). Some very fine and important architectural ceramics were also made. Their hand-painted tiles are much sought after by collectors today. These include not only bright, sometimes amusing pictorial tiles, but entire murals. Today Poole Pottery uses some of the most advanced technology in the United Kingdom. A wide range of table and ornamental wares are also made.

The Poole Pottery Museum is well worth a visit and factory tours can be arranged. There is also a crafts gallery, with demonstrations of pottery painting.

Further Reading

Jennifer Hawkins. *The Poole Potteries* (Barrie & Jenkins, 1980).

Leslie Hayward. *Collectors' Guide to Poole Pottery* (to be published in 1993). Leslie Hayward is the Curator at the Poole Pottery Museum. His book has been exhaustively researched and promises to be indispensable to those interested in the productions at Poole Pottery from the time of Carter & Co. until the present day.

Poole Pottery is best known for its hand-painted wares. The body, which has varied in colour over the years, was covered in a creamy white slip (the earliest slip used was grey-white). The paintresses followed pounced outlines. Some of the designs have continued in use for decades.

Poole earthenware vase painted in polychrome colours underglaze.

c.1925–78. Impressed mark 'POOLE ENGLAND' in rectangle. Painted pattern code SND (or P?). Incised shape number 959 (or 4?). 10.5 cm height   G

£95

Poole earthenware vase painted in polychrome colours underglaze.

c.1925–78. Impressed mark in rectangle 'POOLE/ ENGLAND'; incised shape number 337; painted pattern code MZ. 10 cm height   G

£250

Poole earthenware vase painted in polychrome colours underglaze.

Post-1952. Impressed mark 'POOLE ENGLAND' with dolphin in centre; painted pattern code 'CS X'. 16 cm height
                                                        T

£63

Poole earthenware slip-cast candelabra with matt light blue glaze.

c.1935. Impressed mark 'POOLE ENGLAND/962/C100'. 16.9 cm height   HA

£47

Poole earthenware plate with *Black Pebble* print under semi-matt Alpine White glaze.

c.1959. Printed backstamp with dolphin 'BLACK PEBBLE/ POOLE/ENGLAND/DES. REGD. NO. 890,632 APP. FOR' (1958) 18 cm diameter   AF

£1.50

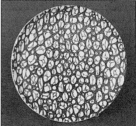

Poole introduced their first and only underglaze printed patterns *Black Pebble* and *Grey Pebble* in 1959. The patterns were designed by R. B. Jefferson especially for printing by the Murray-Curvex machine, developed by Dr G. L. Murray in collaboration with the Spode factory in 1955, which lifts the print from a copper plate with a 'bomb', a large sack filled with a gelatine-type substance. This has the

257

advantage of being able to print on curved surfaces. The process was discontinued at Poole due to technical difficulties. It is still in use at a few factories today.

Poole earthenware dish in brown glazes, *Aegean* ware.

c.1970. Printed dolphin mark 'POOLE/ENGLAND' with stamped range name AEGEAN and shape number '91'. 31 cm length.   MH

£38

Poole Studio Ware earthenware charger with red, orange, black and blue enamels.

c.1970+. Black stamped mark 'POOLE/ENGLAND/54'. 41 cm diameter   HA

£150

CAULDON POTTERIES
(ROYAL CAULDON)
(1920–62)

Cauldon Potteries was the successor to Cauldon (1905–20), which had previously been Brown-Westhead, Moore & Co., at the Cauldon Place works in Hanley. Although the firm is best known for their useful wares, they produced a number of interesting decorative lines.

Cauldon earthenware vase, *Blue Lagoon* pattern with blue ground painted in polychrome enamels and gilded.

c.1930s. Printed mark 'Royal Cauldon/England/Est 1774' with crown. 29 cm height   CCC

£120

Cauldon earthenware vase with blue ground painted in polychrome enamels and gilded.

c.1930s. Printed mark 'Royal Cauldon/England/Est 1774' with crown. 35 cm height   CCC

£200

This pattern is more unusual than *Blue Lagoon*.

GEORGE CLEWS & CO.
(CHAMELEON WARE)
(1906–61)

Although best known for their teapots, Clews began to product art pottery with a wide range of glaze effects in 1914. During the 1920s they began to produce hand-painted wares with matt glazes, which are not well known, but are worth looking for.

Further Reading

Victoria Bergesen. *Encyclopaedia of British Art Pottery* (Barrie & Jenkins, 1991).

Clews earthenware jug with matt white glaze painted underglaze with blue and orange pigments.

Late 1930s. Printed mark in circle 'CHAMELEON WARE/ CLEWS & CO. LTD/TUNSTALL/MADE IN ENGLAND/HAND PAINTED'. Painted pattern number 224/114. 23 cm height   GCC

£185

Clews earthenware slip-cast relief-moulded vase. Turquoise glaze with brown glaze sprayed over.

Late 1930s. Hairline crack. Printed mark in circle 'CHAMELEON WARE/CLEWS & CO. LTD/TUNSTALL/MADE IN ENGLAND/HAND PAINTED'. 23 cm height   GCC

£95

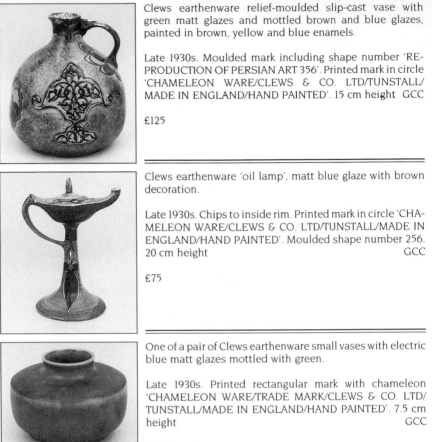

Clews earthenware relief-moulded slip-cast vase with green matt glazes and mottled brown and blue glazes, painted in brown, yellow and blue enamels.

Late 1930s. Moulded mark including shape number 'RE-PRODUCTION OF PERSIAN ART 356'. Printed mark in circle 'CHAMELEON WARE/CLEWS & CO. LTD/TUNSTALL/MADE IN ENGLAND/HAND PAINTED'. 15 cm height GCC

£125

Clews earthenware 'oil lamp', matt blue glaze with brown decoration.

Late 1930s. Chips to inside rim. Printed mark in circle 'CHAMELEON WARE/CLEWS & CO. LTD/TUNSTALL/MADE IN ENGLAND/HAND PAINTED'. Moulded shape number 256. 20 cm height   GCC

£75

One of a pair of Clews earthenware small vases with electric blue matt glazes mottled with green.

Late 1930s. Printed rectangular mark with chameleon 'CHAMELEON WARE/TRADE MARK/CLEWS & CO. LTD/TUNSTALL/MADE IN ENGLAND/HAND PAINTED'. 7.5 cm height   GCC

£24 the pair.

These pieces without hand-painted decoration are very commonly found. The electric blue glaze was introduced by Clews c.1920, and seems to have been produced in large quantities over a number of years. Small items can frequently be found for under £10.

SUSIE COOPER

Susie Cooper has been in the forefront of ceramic design for five decades. She worked for Gray's Pottery from 1922–9 (see below) when she established her own decorating studio, from which the illustrated pieces come. Her wares range from bright and dynamic Art Deco designs to pastel Streamline shapes which she designed in the 1930s. After the

Second World War, Susie Cooper designed Contemporary style shapes and patterns, which proved very popular; (see p. 491).

Further Reading

Cheryl Buckley. *Potters and Paintresses. Women Designers in the Pottery Industry* 1870–1955 (The Women's Press, 1990)
Ann Eatwell. *Susie Cooper Productions* (Victoria & Albert Museum, 1987).

Two Susie Cooper small earthenware *Kestrel* shape coffee pots.

c.1932. Printed mark on both 'A SUSIE COOPER PRODUC-TION/CROWN WORKS/BURSLEM/ENGLAND'. Right: Painted pattern number 1017. Decorated with *Dresden Spray* transfer-print which was popular both before and after the Second World War. 13 cm height   MH

£45 each

Susie Cooper earthenware *Kestrel* shape covered vegetable dish painted in pastel enamels.

c.1933. Printed mark 'A SUSIE COOPER PRODUCTION/ CROWN WORKS/BURSLEM/ENGLAND'. Painted pattern number 1161/2Rubber-stamped mark in black 'BRITISH PATENT 781916' (1933). 21 cm diameter excluding handles.
HA

£225 for the service.

Part of a complete dinner service including two covered vegetable dishes, three meat plates, a sauceboat and saucer, eighteen plates (three sizes) and six soup bowls and stands.

W. T. COPELAND & SONS
(1847–1970)

W. T. Copeland, formerly Copeland & Garrett (1833–47), continued to use many of the shapes and patterns used by the previous firm, and by Spode, who preceded Copeland & Garrett. The firm made both earthenwares and porcelains, including Parian wares. Copeland is one of the exceptions to the rule that period designs are most desirable. Examples of their *Blue Italian* pattern, first produced by Spode c.1815, from all periods are avidly collected, and are still produced by Spode Ltd, the name of the firm since 1970 when the Copeland family sold their controlling interest.

From the 1930s Copeland employed a number of very talented designers who introduced Streamline and Contemporary style designs. These included Harold Holdway,

Eric Olsen and Ted Hewitt. They also introduced new glazes and bodies: during the 1930s there were two new matt glazes, Royal Jade and Velamour, and in the 1950s Spode introduced two bodies coloured with a stain, Flemish Green and English Lavender. They produced a number of humorous and stylish patterns on their *Tricorn* shape c.1957–9.

The *Royal College* shape designed by the Royal College of Art was introduced in 1959. The shape was, perhaps, too progressive for contemporary taste; a great success with the critics, but a poor seller. Examples are now rare.

Copeland used a series of impressed and printed marks. They also introduced a system of impressed date codes in 1870. The last two digits of the year are surmounted by a letter for the month. The system was used on earthenwares until 1957.

Copeland rectangular earthenware comport, transfer-print coloured with polychrome enamels.

c.1919. Printed seal mark 'COPELAND LATE SPODE'; 'Rd. no. 667947' (1919). Painted pattern number 7613/EH. 29 cm length   CD

£36

Copeland Royal Jade earthenware *Wicker* embossed dessert plate, decorated with green matt glaze.

c.1935. Impressed mark 'COPELAND'; printed mark 'SPODE'S/Royal Jade/ENGLAND'. 22 cm diameter   AF

£5

Royal Jade, introduced c.1935, was a range of green matt glazed giftwares. The dessert set for twelve persons was the only item of tableware produced. The complete dessert set consisted of twelve plates (shape J16), two round dessert dishes (shape J19), two square dessert dishes (shape J17) and two oval dessert dishes (shape J42). The shape is similar to one used by Spode in the early 19th century. However, the original had a pierced border, which has been eliminated to reduce costs.

Copeland *Tean* shape earthenware teapot with *Olympus* pattern, Flemish Green body lid, spout and handle.

c.1956. Printed seal mark with 'COPELAND/SPODE/ENGLAND/OLYMPUS'; impressed size mark 24. 13.5 cm height   AF

£5

Copeland introduced their Flemish Green body in 1955, used both alone and in combination with a white body. Flemish Green was obtained by staining the clay, but many manufacturers copied the effect by using a pale green glaze. Two new shapes were introduced for Flemish Green: *Tean*, a 'moderately contemporary' shape and *Kaga*, which was 'markedly traditional'. The *Olympus* pattern, designed by Harold Holdway, was introduced In 1956. The simple, but extremely elegant lines of the pattern are typical of his fine work.

Copeland earthenware *Tricorn* shape plate with *Barbeque* design.

c.1957. Special printed backstamp 'BARBEQUE/SPODE/ COPELAND/ENGLAND'; impressed mark 'Copeland/ Spode/Imperial'; painted pattern number 5/3252. Impressed date code N/57 (for November 1957). 26 cm width

SG

£12

Spode introduced the *Barbeque* series of four humorous designs for Christmas 1957. They retailed at 6/11d each. The other three designs feature a monkey riding a kangaroo in a steeplechase, footsteps circling a lamp post and swimming chickens. Spode also produced *Kutie Kitten* nursery ware in the *Tricorn* shape.

S. FIELDING & CO.
(CROWN DEVON)
(1870–1982)

Simon Fielding established himself in 1870 at the Railway Pottery on Sutherland Street in Stoke. The pottery was not successful and in 1878 his son Abraham took over. Under the direction of Abraham, who was a skilled colour maker, the firm became a major majolica manufacturer. During the 1920s and 30s they made many of the popular novelty wares. Their Musical Novelties, which play a tune when lifted from the table, were produced 1930s–1950s. Garden and Salad ware were relief-moulded tableware ranges. They also produced Ruby-and Devon Silverine lustre wares from the 1920s and a wide variety of Art Deco giftware.

In the 1950s they quickly took up the Contemporary style, with their *Karen* pattern perhaps the most successful line. In 1976 Fielding was purchased by a Liverpool company, and the works closed in 1982. The works were later demolished.

The 20th-century trade name Crown Devon may confuse the new collector, as the firm was not located in Devon.

Further Reading

Ray Barker. *The Crown Devon Story* (Warwick Printing Co., Warwick, 1991).

Originally Crown Devon dogs, known as *Perky Pups* and *Woeful Willies*, had glass eyes; these were later omitted.

Three Crown Devon earthenware *Perky Pups* with matt glaze.

c.1930s+. Printed mark with crown 'CROWN DEVON/MADE IN ENGLAND/TRADE MARK'. Largest 12 cm height, smallest 7 cm height   CCC

£40 each

Two Crown Devon earthenware *Perky Pups* with matt glaze.

c.1930s+. 10 and 12 cm height   CCC

£40 each

Crown Devon earthenware *Woeful Willie* with matt glaze.

c.1930s+. Printed mark with crown 'CROWN DEVON/MADE IN ENGLAND/TRADEMARK'. 14 cm height   CCC

£40

Crown Devon earthenware figure of a woman with cream and pink glazes.

c.1930. Printed mark with crown 'CROWN DEVON/MADE IN ENGLAND/TRADE MARK' and 'Rd applied for'; impressed shape number 226. 24.2 cm height   CCC

£200

A series of twenty-five of these Hollywood-style figures was modelled by Kathleen Parsons, and produced at Crown Devon from 1930. Their elegance has made them much sought after. Slightly smaller, matt-glazed versions were also made, but are not considered as desirable by collectors.

The firm also made two Sutherland series of figures. The first were expensive with a high glaze (shape numbers 129–40 recorded by Barker). The second series was painted overglaze and sprayed with cellulose, which means that the decoration has often been damaged.

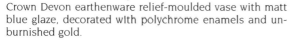

Crown Devon earthenware relief-moulded vase with matt blue glaze, decorated with polychrome enamels and unburnished gold.

c.1930s. Printed mark 'Crown Devon/FIELDINGS/MADE IN ENGLAND'. Paper label with shape number 254/6 and pattern number M119. 15.5 cm height   GCC

£135

Crown Devon earthenware dish with cream matt glaze sprayed with orange matt glaze to create a mottled effect, painted in yellow and green enamels.

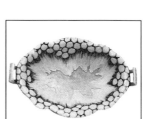

c.1930s. Printed mark 'CROWN DEVON/MADE IN ENGLAND'; impressed shape name and number 'MAVIS 534'; painted pattern number (illegible). 30 cm diameter   GCC

£75

265

Crown Devon earthenware wall plaque with transfer-printed design in red filled in with enamels and surmounted by a gold print, gilded rim, matt cream glaze sprayed to create celadon effect.

c.1930s. Gold printed paper label with shape and pattern numbers 'Shape 703, Deco M.199'. Printed mark 'CROWN DEVON/FIELDING'S/MADE IN ENGLAND'. Painted pattern number M199. 30 cm diameter   G

£95

Crown Devon earthenware vase with *Karen* lithograph decoration.

c. 1956. Moulded shape number A594. Printed mark 'CROWN DEVON/FIELDING'S/MADE IN ENGLAND'. 24 cm length   MH

£30

Crown Devon earthenware breakfast cup and saucer with printed *Wedding Scene* pattern in black.

c.1950s. Printed mark 'WEDDING SCENE CROWN DEVON/ FIELDING'S/MADE IN ENGLAND'. Painted pattern number 5543. Cup 9.2 cm height; saucer 17 cm diameter   MH

£27

GIBSON & SONS
(1885–1970s)

This was a large firm at Burslem employing some 500 hands in 1905, when they kept 15,000 dozen teapots in stock. Primarily a producer of general earthenware including jet, Rockingham, russet and mosaic-bodied wares, the firm also produced several art wares and ornamental wares.

Pottery Gazette and Glass Trade Review reported in August 1950: 'Gibson & Sons Ltd, are perhaps best known as one of the largest and oldest-established manufacturers of earthenware teapots in the world.'

Gibson & Sons platinum lustre earthenware jug with a band of green glaze painted in green and white slip.

c.1930. Printed mark 'Silvoe Art Ware'. 15 cm height   G

£25

Gibson & Sons advertised their Silvoe Art wares, which were platinum lustres, from 1918.

Gibson & Sons earthenware figure of *Sarah Gamp*.

c.1930s. Printed mark 'SARAH GAMP' and 'G & S LTD/ BURSLEM/MADE IN ENGLAND'. 19 cm height   CCC

£75

Gibson & Sons earthenware figure of *Tony Weller*.

c.1930s. Printed mark 'TONY WELLER' and 'G & S LTD/ BURSLEM/MADE IN ENGLAND'. 19 cm height   CCC

£75

W. H. GOSS
(ROYAL BUFF; COTTAGE POTTERY)
(1858–1939)

W. H. Goss is best known for their Parian and crested wares (see chapters 19 and 20). However during their Third Period (1930–9) they made earthenware tablewares.

Further Reading

Nicholas Pine. *The Concise Encyclopaedia and Price Guide to Goss China* (Milestone Publications, Horndean, 1992).

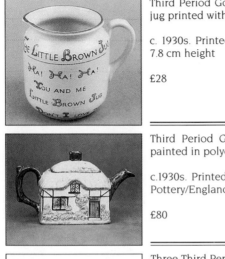

Third Period Goss Royal Buff earthenware upright cream jug printed with Little Brown Jug verse and enamelled.

c. 1930s. Printed mark 'Royal Buff/W H Goss/ENGLAND'. 7.8 cm height   CCC

£28

Third Period Goss Cottage Pottery earthenware teapot painted in polychrome enamels over cream glaze.

c.1930s. Printed Goshawk mark with 'W. H. Goss/Cottage Pottery/England.' 17.5 cm length   GCC

£80

Three Third Period Goss earthenware teacups.

c.1930s. All with printed Goshawk mark and 'ENGLAND'. Rear left: relief-moulded 'Cottage' cup marked 'Cottage Pottery', 6.8 cm height. Rear right: 'Royal Buff' with transfer-print filled in with enamels, 6.4 cm height. Front: 'Cottage Pottery' cup with hand-painted crocus. 7.2 cm height.GCC

£6–12 each

Matching cups and saucers will cost £15–25, according to the rarity of the shape and pattern.

A. E. GRAY & CO.
(1902–62)

A. E. Gray & Co. was a decorating firm, who used the blanks from a number of Staffordshire manufacturers. The range of pottery decorated by Gray's is enormous. Paul and Kathy Niblett remark in their book: 'Reviewing the type of pottery that A. E. Gray & Co Ltd did not produce would be considerably easier than reviewing that which they did produce.' They employed a wide range of decorative techniques including lustre, banding, enamelling, transfer-printing and lithographic transfers. With the exception of a range of stonewares 1933–50, the body was earthenware. Gray's used several talented designers, including Gordon Forsyth and Susie Cooper (working at Gray's 1922–9).

Further Reading

Ann Eatwell. *Susie Cooper Productions* (Victoria & Albert Museum, 1987).
Paul and Kathy Niblett. *Hand-painted Gray's Pottery*, 3rd edn (Stoke-on-Trent City Museum & Art Gallery, 1987).

Gray's earthenware bowl painted in polychrome enamels in various shades of blue and gilded.

c.1930. Printed yellow and green mark 'HAND-PAINTED/ GRAY'S POTTERY/MADE IN/STOKE-ON-TRENT/ENGLAND'. 23 cm diameter   MG

£75

Large Gray's earthenware plate painted in bright orange, yellow, grey, black and brown enamels and gilded.

c.1933. Small chip to rim reverse. Printed yellow and green mark 'HAND-PAINTED/GRAY'S POTTERY/MADE IN/ STOKE-ON-TRENT/ENGLAND'. Painted pattern number A1546. 27 cm diameter   MB

£52

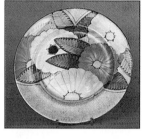

Rare Gray's earthenware jug inscribed 'Ross's Belfast Ginger Ale' with *Cubist* pattern painted in polychrome enamels, designed by Susie Cooper.

c.1929. Printed yellow and green mark 'HAND-PAINTED/ GRAY'S POTTERY/MADE IN/STOKE-ON-TRENT/ ENGLAND'. Impressed mark 'ENGLAND'. 12 cm height   HA

£175

T. G. GREEN & CO.
(CORNISH KITCHEN WARE; DOMINO WARE)
(1864 to the present day)

T. G. Green & Co., Church Gresley, Derbyshire are best known for their good quality yellow wares and the blue-banded Cornish Kitchen Ware. Another popular line introduced in the 1930s was Domino Ware with a blue ground and white dots painted in slip. These wares was copied by many other firms, especially in South Devon. During the 1950s they made

269

two ranges of wares in Contemporary shape. The *Patio Modern* shape was introduced in 1955. Popular patterns included *Central Park* (c.1955), *Flaire* (c.1956), *Gingham Ware* (a copy of Midwinter's *Homeweave*, c.1958), *Samba* (c.1958) and *Blue Domino* (c.1958). In 1959 they introduced their *Gay Day* shape designed by Audrey Levy. This was decorated with geometric patterns such as *Harlequin* (c.1959), among others.

T. G. Green Cornish Kitchen Ware earthenware teacup and saucer.

c.1950s+. Printed shield mark in black 'T. G. GREEN & CO. LTD/MADE IN ENGLAND/CORNISH KITCHEN WARE'. Cup 7.5 cm height; saucer 13.6 cm diameter   MB

£6.50

During the First World War, T. G. Green had built up a large trade in turned beer mugs. As these were replaced with glass mugs in the 1920s, the turners found themselves on short time and the management was looking for a new market. The solution to their problem was a line of storage jars, dipped in blue slip and then turned to reveal white bands. The name is thought to have come from a comment by the firm's South of England representative who said that the ware portrayed the blue of Cornish skies and the white crests of the waves. Over the decades, a wide variety of table and kitchen wares have been produced. In the 1950s a range of refrigerator storage wares were made. These have flat lids to facilitate stacking.

The ware has always been relatively expensive as the process required skilled labour. Cheaper imitations such as Chef's Ware have bands in painted blue.

Cornish Kitchen Ware is very popular with collectors. It is most commonly found with blue bands, but yellow bands can be found occasionally. The tablewares are still made today, so look for more unusual items such as rolling pins or milk jugs.

T. G. Green earthenware *Patio Modern* coupe shape plate with tiger-skin pattern lithograph.

c.1960. Printed mark with picture of a church 'T. G. GREEN & CO. LTD./CHURCH GRESLEY/MADE IN ENGLAND'. 23.8 cm diameter   AF

£1.50

GRIMWADES
(ROYAL WINTON)
(1900–1970s)

Grimwades Ltd (formerly Grimwade Bros 1886–1900) at Stoke used the Royal Winton trade name from the 1930s. They specialised in tablewares, many of which are not very interesting. However, some of their novelty wares such as the teapot below are becoming collectable.

Grimwades earthenware figure with 'MR MICAWBER' impressed on base.

c.1930s. Printed Grimwades globe mark. 19 cm height
CCC

£80

Grimwades earthenware figure with 'MR. PECKSNIFF' impressed on base.

c.1930s. Printed Grimwades globe mark. 19 cm height
CCC

£80

Grimwades earthenware beehive teapot with wrapped wicker handle, painted in polychrome enamels.

c.1930s. Printed mark 'ROYAL WINTON/GRIMWADES ENGLAND'. 13.5 cm height
MH

£85

S. HANCOCK (& SONS)
(MORRIS WARE; RUBENS WARE; TITIAN WARE; CORONA WARE; IVORY WARE)
(1881–1937)

The firm was established as B. & S. Hancock in 1857. From 1881, Sampson Hancock continued alone. Until the early 20th century the firm specialised in good quality useful wares. Morris Ware, designed by George Cartlidge, was introduced in 1918. F. X. Abraham designed several interesting ranges in the 1920s including Rubens Ware, Titian Ware and the Woodland range. Molly Hancock, Sampson Hancock's granddaughter, designed several ranges in the 1920s and 1930s including Cherry Ripe.

Further Reading

Victoria Bergesen. *Encyclopaedia of British Art Pottery* (Barrie & Jenkins, 1991).

Hancock earthenware relief-moulded plate with matt green glaze.

c.1930s. Printed mark 'CORONA WARE S. HANCOCK & SONS/STOKE-ON-TRENT/ENGLAND.' 21.5 cm diameter
GCC

£15

Hancock Rubens Ware earthenware vase with underglaze coloured *Pomegranate* pattern.

c.1920s. Printed mark with crown 'S. HANCOCK & SONS/ STOKE-ON-TRENT/ENGLAND/POMEGRANATE'. 24 cm height
MH

£48

F. X. Abraham, art director, designed the Rubens Ware range. He had previously worked as art director for W. T. Copeland & Sons.

Hancock retailer's earthenware display plate inscribed 'Corona Ware/Langtry Rose' with transfer-print painted in polychrome enamels.

c.1929. Printed mark with crown 'ROYAL CORONA WARE/S. HANCOCK & SONS/STOKE-ON-TRENT/ENGLAND'; 'Rd No. 750182' (1929); painted pattern number 7243. 26 cm diameter ·   CCC

£38

Corona Ware was a trademark first introduced in 1912 and continued until the factory's closure.

Ivory Ware was Hancock's cream coloured body with a clear glaze used for tablewares during the 1930s.

Hancock Ivory Ware earthenware butterfly dessert plate decorated with green, brown and beige enamels.

1930s. Printed mark on an artist's palette 'IVORY WARE/ HANCOCK'S ENGLAND' with 'HAND PAINTED'. Painted pattern number 7769/X. 21.5 cm diameter   MH

£50

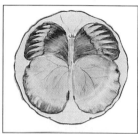

Hancock Ivory Ware earthenware bowl painted in poly-chrome enamels.

1930s. Painted mark 'Ivory Ware/Hancock's/ENGLAND/ HAND PAINTED'. Painted pattern number 8316x. 21 cm diameter   MH

£65

HORNSEA POTTERY
(1949–80s)

The Rawson brothers established the Hornsea Pottery at Hornsea, Yorkshire in 1949. It was not until 1951 that they took on their first employee. At this time the first animal posies were introduced, which evolved into the Fauna range, in which there were over 100 items. The range was redesigned by Alan Luckham c.1960–2, produced as Fauna Royale. These remained in production until 1967.

Although Hornsea wares are already avidly collected for their striking Contemporary style design and their cute animal figures, these wares can still be found quite cheaply at boot fairs etc.

Further Reading

Lawrie Dex. *Hornsea Pottery. A Collector's Guide*, 1949–1967 (L. Dex, 1989).

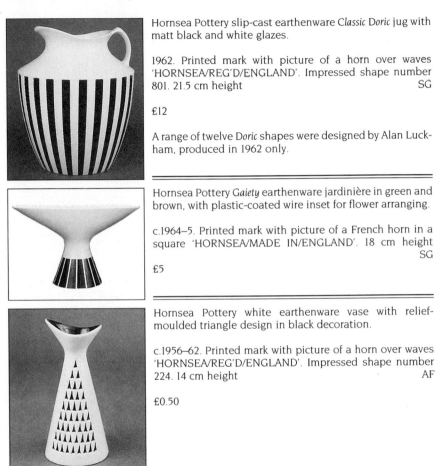

Hornsea Pottery slip-cast earthenware *Classic Doric* jug with matt black and white glazes.

1962. Printed mark with picture of a horn over waves 'HORNSEA/REG'D/ENGLAND'. Impressed shape number 801. 21.5 cm height   SG

£12

A range of twelve *Doric* shapes were designed by Alan Luckham, produced in 1962 only.

Hornsea Pottery *Gaiety* earthenware jardinière in green and brown, with plastic-coated wire inset for flower arranging.

c.1964–5. Printed mark with picture of a French horn in a square 'HORNSEA/MADE IN/ENGLAND'. 18 cm height   SG

£5

Hornsea Pottery white earthenware vase with relief-moulded triangle design in black decoration.

c.1956–62. Printed mark with picture of a horn over waves 'HORNSEA/REG'D/ENGLAND'. Impressed shape number 224. 14 cm height   AF

£0.50

C. T. MALING & SONS
(1853–1963)

C. T. Maling purchased a small pottery at Maling near Newcastle upon Tyne in 1853. By the time of his death in 1901, he had created what he claimed to be the largest earthenware manufacturer in the world. The firm's production was fairly mundane until the 1920s, when bold, original designs came to the fore. These were introduced by C. N. Wright and continued by Lucien Émile Boullemier, at the firm 1926–36.

Boullemier brought the use of gold register printing and rich lustres to the firm. These lustre wares usually had an Oriental theme. His son Lucien George Boullemier continued with the firm until its closure in 1963. Maling lustre wares with apple green or pink grounds produced in the 1950s are much collected. They can be distinguished from the lustre wares made in the 1920s and 1930s as the colours are brighter and more metallic.

Further Reading

Steven Moore and Catherine Ross. *Maling: The Trademark of Excellence!* (Tyne and Wear Museums Service, Newcastle upon Tyne, 1989).

Maling earthenware bowl painted with polychrome enamels.

c.1930–2. Maling printed mark. Painted pattern number 5479. 23.5 cm diameter   MH

£275

Maling earthenware teapot with *Vine* lithograph print.

c.1940. Printed mark in orange 'Ringtons Ltd./Newcastle-upon-Tyne/Maling Ware'. 16.5 cm height   MH

£45

Ringtons Ltd was a local tea merchant for whom Maling produced several teapots and tea caddies. The *Vine* print was used in the late 1930s and 1940s.

Maling earthenware plaque painted in polychrome enamels over a transfer-print.

c.1955–60. Printed Maling castle mark with 'NEWCASTLE-UPON-TYNE/ENGLAND'. Painted pattern number 6575. 29 cm diameter   MH

£250

W. R. MIDWINTER
(STYLECRAFT)
(1910–87)

Midwinter made a wide range of toilet, table and ornamental wares at Burslem which were typical of their period throughout the first half of the century. The firm did not become a design and market leader until W. Roy Midwinter became active in the firm after the

Second World War. On a sales trip to Canada and the United States in 1952, he found that the North American market was demanding the modern coupe shape dinner wares. Within six months, Midwinter introduced their Stylecraft range, with forty entirely new shapes for tea and dinner wares. Some three dozen patterns were available, all designed by Miss Jessie Tait.

The daring of the firm in risking so much of their production was greeted with amazement and admiration by the industry. The new wares were featured on television in 'About the Home'. Other innovations included the twenty-piece Starter Set, which could be enhanced from open stock of all patterns. In 1954 Midwinter introduced the *Riviera* range, with patterns designed by Sir Hugh Casson. Terence Conran was also employed to design new patterns. In 1955, they introduced the *Fashion* shape tablewares, which were even more modern, eliminating the rims entirely from their coupe shape plates.

Again taking their lead from the American industry, Midwinter introduced Melmex plastic tablewares in 1957. The following year they brought out the 'tea set with the extra cup' in a carry-home pack. Like many of their contemporaries, Midwinter faltered in 1959. It seemed that they had carried the Contemporary style as far as it could go. They reverted to a revival of earlier styles with their *New Classic* shape. This was not very successful, but in 1962 Midwinter again led the way by inviting David Queensberry, Professor of Ceramics at the Royal College of Art, to design a new modern shape. The *Queensberry* shape proved so popular that in 1963 Midwinter published advertisements apologising for the long delays in delivery dates for the wares. The same year Midwinter introduced coordinated cutlery, designed by David Carter. *Queensberry* was followed by MQ2 shape, which was a failure, and pieces are now *very* rare.

In 1966 the firm introduced the *Portobello* shape, designed by studio potter David Long. The Wedgwood Group took over Midwinter in 1970. In 1972 they introduced *Stonehenge* shape made in stoneware, designed in collaboration with studio potter Robin Welch. Roy Midwinter retired in 1981, and in 1987 the factory closed, although the patterns were continued by another Wedgwood Group factory. Roy Midwinter died in 1991.

The role of Midwinter as a design pioneer is now appreciated by many connoisseurs of 20th-century industrial pottery. At the present time a band of devoted collectors roams boot fairs, flea markets and jumble sales purchasing the wares for minute sums. These wares are likely to increase dramatically in value over the next decade. The collector should look for the early Stylecraft shapes with hand-painted patterns, any patterns designed by Terence Conran or Sir Hugh Casson, and the bird patterns designed by Peter Scott.

Midwinter also produced figures: rarest are the Contemporary figures designed by Colin Melbourne decorated with white, fawn or black matt glazes. Known figures are the camel, polar bear, giraffe, bison, seal, jaguar, otter, brontosaurus and African Figures. Abstract flower vases were also produced with these glazes.

Further Reading

Alan Peat. *Midwinter: A Collector's Guide* (Cameron Books, 1992).

Four Midwinter earthenware figures.

c.1950s. Printed mark with crown 'W. R. Midwinter Ltd./ Burslem/England'. Fawn 13.3 cm height; hare 11 cm height; seated doe 6.3 cm height; lying bear cub 12 cm length. AF

£8 each

Midwinter earthenware *Stylecraft* shape plate, *Riviera* pattern designed by Sir Hugh Casson ('hand-engraving' filled with underglaze colours).

c.1954. Special backstamp (see below). 22 cm diameter

AF

£0.50

Having admired Sir Hugh Casson's sketches of the coronation route, Roy Midwinter commissioned some sketches for use on tablewares. A set of seven different scenes was chosen for *Riviera*. An article in *Design* magazine in 1954 commented, 'The pieces shown here are relatively inexpensive; a quality which assists their bold attack on a section of the trade long used to traditional landscapes, sequestered cottages and picturesque ruins in sepia and grey. The Riviera patterns are colourful and unlaboured in a manner which has made Sir Hugh Casson's work well known.'

Mark on reverse.

Midwinter earthenware *Fashion* shape plate, *Cannes* pattern designed by Sir Hugh Casson ('hand-engraving' filled with underglaze colours).

c.1959. Special backstamp (see below). 15.5 cm diameter

AF

£0.10

Sir Hugh Casson's *Cannes* pattern was introduced in 1959. The picture, one of those employed on the *Riviera* series on the *Stylecraft* shape introduced in 1954, was now adapted for use on *Fashion* shape. These are already being avidly collected, and a dinner plate from the earlier Riviera range in fine condition often fetches around £10.

Mark on reverse.

Midwinter earthenware *Fashion* shape plate with *Plant Life* transfer print designed by Terence Conran, filled in with underglaze colours.

c.1961. Printed mark 'Midwinter/Stylecraft/STAFFORD-SHIRE ENGLAND/FASHION SHAPE/6-61' (6-61 is a date code for June 1961). 22 cm diameter   AF

£0.50

Plant Life was introduced in 1956. Terence Conran designed a number of patterns for Midwinter including the Collectors' Series which were coasters boxed in sets of four. There were four sets portraying antique modes of transportation: cars, ships, trains and bicycles. These are uncommon and if the collector should be fortunate enough to find a boxed set, he should be *very* careful to preserve the packaging! Conran's other tableware patterns included *Chequers* (c.1957), *Melody* (c.1957) and *Nature Study* (c.1959).

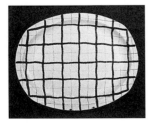

Large Midwinter earthenware *Stylecraft* shape meat plate with hand-painted *Homeweave* pattern in red and black underglaze colours.

c.1954. Special printed mark "HOMEWEAVE"/A GENUINE HANDPAINTED DESIGN IN PERMANENT ACID RESISTING UNDERGLAZE COLOURS/stylecraft by MIDWINTER/ STAFFORDSHIRE/SEMI-PORCELAIN/MADE IN ENGLAND/ REG'D 711843; 868695' (latter registration 1952 for *Stylecraft* shape). 45 cm length   AF

£4

Homeweave was one of Jessie Tait's early patterns for the *Stylecraft* shape. It was copied by several other firms, some of whom did not mark their wares, but Midwinter always did.

Midwinter earthenware *Fashion* shape teapot with lithographed *Riverside* pattern designed by John Russell.

c.1960. Printed mark 'MIDWINTER/Stylecraft/STAFFORD-SHIRE/ENGLAND/FASHION SHAPE'. 16.5 cm height   AF

£2

This pattern sometimes appears with a special backstamp with a bulrush reading 'RIVERSIDE BY JOHN RUSSELL'. It is easily the most common Midwinter pattern found.

NEWPORT POTTERY
(CLARICE CLIFF; BIZARRE; FANTASQUE)
(1920–64)

Clarice Cliff (1899–1972) received training and worked as a paintress, a lithographer, a gilder and designer before she was allowed her own decorating studio at Newport Pottery in 1926. Initially she was given old warehouse stock to decorate. The wares were market tested in 1928 and the Bizarre range was launched with its own backstamp (1928–34). After only one year of trading the wares were so popular that the entire Newport Pottery was given over to their production. Her *Crocus* pattern was so popular that it remained in production until 1963!

Cliff changed with the time, producing Streamline style designs in the late 1930s and Contemporary style tablewares in the 1950s. She remained a well respected designer until her retirement in 1965, when the firm was taken over by W. R. Midwinter. Collectors today have little interest in the later wares, but as interest in the Contemporary style grows they will increase in value.

The recognition of Clarice Cliff's Art Deco wares during the late 1970s and 1980s and their rocketing prices are instructive for the collector. These had been 'cheap but cheerful' wares at the time they were made. They are not, as a group, rare. Nevertheless, the enthusiasm of collectors has pushed prices to ludicrous levels. The wares are routinely sold at prices far surpassing those fetched by far older, rarer and more finely crafted pots. However, they are clearly marked, easily recognised and fine examples of the design of the period.

Further Reading

Cheryl Buckley. *Potters and Paintresses. Women Designers in the Pottery Industry* 1870–1955 (The Women's Press, 1990).

Leonard Griffin and Louis K and Susan Pear Meisel. *Clarice Cliff, The Bizarre Affair* (Thames & Hudson, 1988).

H. Watson. *Collecting Clarice Cliff* (Kevin Francis Publishing, 1988).

H. Watson. *The Colourful World of Clarice Cliff* (Kevin Francis Publishing, 1992).

Newport Pottery earthenware vase with *Butterfly* pattern painted in polychrome enamels, designed by Clarice Cliff.

c.1930. Printed mark 'Hand Painted Fantasque by Clarice Cliff' [facsimile signature]; incised shape number 366. 15 cm height   MH

£880

The *Butterfly* pattern was copied from Edouard Benedlctus in 1930. The stepped vase shape is known by its shape number 366. The trade name Fantasque was used 1929–34.

Rare Newport Pottery earthenware footed bowl with *Sliced Circle* pattern, designed by Clarice Cliff.

c.1930. Impressed shape number 382. Printed mark 'HAND PAINTED/Bizarre/by/Clarice Cliff [facsimile signature] /HAND PAINTED/ENGLAND/MADE IN ENGLAND'. 23 cm diameter   MH

£2,200

Newport Pottery earthenware *Daffodil* shape vase with *Bridgewater Orange* pattern painted in polychrome enamels (mostly yellow and orange), designed by Clarice Cliff.

c.1934. Printed mark 'HAND PAINTED/Bizarre/by/Clarice Cliff [facsimile signature] /NEWPORT POTTERY/ENGLAND'. Moulded 'MADE IN ENGLAND' and shape number 450. Label with pattern number T75. 12 cm height; 33 cm length   MH

£750

The *Daffodil* shape number 450 was introduced c.1931. *Bridgewater* pattern, which also had a green version, was produced only briefly in 1934.

A. J. Wilkinson earthenware rectangular plate with *Viscaria* pattern, designed by Clarice Cliff.

1934. Printed mark 'The Biarritz/Royal Staffordshire/Great Britain/Registered number 784849' (for 1933). Impressed date mark 7/34 (July 1934). 23 cm length   MH

£195

A. J. Wilkinson was owned by the Shorter family, as was Newport Pottery. Although this plate bears the Royal Staffordshire trade name used by Wilkinson, the Clarice Cliff wares were all decorated at Newport Pottery.

Viscaria is a predominantly pink version introduced in 1934 of the earlier *Rhodanthe* pattern; a predominantly green version also introduced then was named *Aurea*. All three versions were decorated using the 'etching technique', which is actually the laying on of brush strokes of different colours to build up the pattern. This was cheaper than the earlier outlined and banded patterns.

Newport Pottery earthenware *Tee Pee* teapot painted in polychrome enamels, designed by Clarice Cliff.

c.1930s. Printed green mark 'Clarice Cliff [facsimile signature]/NEWPORT POTTERY CO. ENGLAND'; 'Greetings from Canada'. '30s' size moulded mark. 18 cm height   MH

£750

Newport Pottery earthenware My Garden vase painted in polychrome enamels, designed by Clarice Cliff.

c.1935. Printed mark 'HAND PAINTED'; BIZARRE BY CLARICE CLIFF [facsimile signature] NEWPORT POTTERY/ ENGLAND'; stamped mark 'MADE IN ENGLAND'. 17 cm height   MH

£250

The My Garden range was produced in an effort to cut decorating costs. It required painting only to highlight the relief-moulded shapes, eliminating the more expensive banding and hand-painting of patterns.

Newport Pottery earthenware Water Lily bowl, designed by Clarice Cliff.

c.1938. Green printed mark with facsimile signature 'Clarice Cliff'; 'NEWPORT POTTERY CO. ENGLAND'. 22.3 cm length

G

£140

This bowl was the best-selling shape from the Water Lily range. Its pastel colouring and smooth rounded shape is typical of the Streamline style which superseded Art Deco. As with the My Garden range (above), the range could be decorated more cheaply than earlier designs.

Newport Pottery earthenware *Lotus* shape jug with brown crackle glaze, designed by Clarice Cliff.

c.1936–9. Printed mark CLARICE CLIFF |facsimile signature|/- NEWPORT POTTERY/ENGLAND'; MADE IN ENGLAND. 26 cm height

MH

£275

Newport Pottery earthenware *Circus* plate with pink transfer-print filled in with polychrome enamels and gilded, designed by Laura Knight.

c.1934. Printed mark (see below). 23 cm diameter

MH

£850

The artist Dame Laura Knight (1877–1970) was one of the designers commissioned by E. Brain & Co. and Newport Pottery's 'Exhibition of Contemporary Art for the Table' at Harrods in 1934. Among the many subjects she covered in her long and varied career, she was fascinated by circuses, which she portrayed in numerous paintings during the late 1920s and 1930s. Unlike most of the artists involved in the exhibition, who provided only surface patterns, she designed an entire range of shapes for her *Circus* dinner ware made by Newport.

Mark on reverse.

R. H. & S. L. PLANT
TUSCAN FAIENCE
(1898 to the present day)

Best known for its Tuscan China, this Longton firm produced Tuscan Faience after the First World War. Their speciality was china figures and novelties. The firm became part of the Wedgwood Group in 1966, and was renamed Royal Tuscan in 1971. In 1976 Tuscan China Holdings was formed from R. H. & S. L. Plant and Susie Cooper, under the style Wedgwood hotelware. The factory was once again renamed Royal Tuscan in 1989.

Plant Tuscan Faience two-handled earthenware vase with pale yellow ground, painted in subdued purple, dark red, yellow, green and blue enamels.

c.Late 1930s. Printed mark 'PLANT/TUSCAN/FAIENCE/ MADE IN ENGLAND'. 19 cm height   GCC

£100

Plant Tuscan Faience earthenware vase painted with enamels underglaze in subdued mauve, grey and green on pink ground.

c.Late 1930s. Printed mark 'PLANT/TUSCAN/FAIENCE/ MADE IN ENGLAND'. 24 cm height   CCC

£95

A. G. RICHARDSON
(CROWN DUCAL)
(1915–74)

Albert Goodwin Richardson, formerly works manager for S. Fielding & Co., founded this firm, primarily manufacturers of medium quality table earthenwares at Tunstall, and after c.1934 at Cobridge. Charlotte Rhead worked for A. G. Richardson 1931–c.1942, although the firm used some of her designs before that period. Her characteristic tube-lined art wares soon brought prosperity to the firm. However, these and her tablewares were only a small part of the firm's output. The firm was acquired by Enoch Wedgwood in 1974, which was in turn taken over by Wedgwood in 1980 and renamed Unicorn Pottery.

Further Reading

Bernard Bumpus. *Charlotte Rhead, Potter & Designer* (Kevin Francis Publishing, 1987)
Cheryl Buckley. *Potters and Paintresses. Women Designers in the Pottery Industry 1870–1955* (The Women's Press, 1990).

Crown Ducal earthenware ornamental plaque with *Omar* pattern designed by Charlotte Rhead, tube-lined and painted in polychrome enamels on a matt oatmeal glaze.

c.1935. Inscribed 'Rubyat of Omar Kayam'. Signed 'C. Rhead'; printed Crown Ducal mark. 24.5 cm diameter
GCC

£450

This *Omar* plaque (pattern number 4036) was shown at the British Industries Fair 1935. As it was expensive to produce, it is not very common.

Uncommon Crown Ducal earthenware vase with shiny greyish glaze over tube-lined decoration painted in polychrome enamels designed by Charlotte Rhead.

c.1930s. Facsimile signature mark 'CRHEAD' with pattern number 5411 and tube-liner's mark 'J' for Dora Jones; printed Crown Ducal mark. 21 cm height   GCC

£350

A plaque in pattern 5411 is illustrated in Bumpus.

Crown Ducal earthenware jug without a spout with a matt cream glaze, tube-lined and painted in pink and grey enamels and gilded, designed by Charlotte Rhead.

c.1930s. Printed Crown Ducal mark; painted pattern number 6778 and 'L' tube-liner's mark; impressed shape number 146. 21 cm height   GCC

£200

Crown Ducal earthenware jug with matt white glaze and sprayed mottled orange ground, with tube-lined *Byzantine* decoration painted in rust, orange and blue enamels, designed by Charlotte Rhead.

c.1932 Painted mark 'CRhead' with shape number 185 and pattern number 2681; printed Crown Ducal mark. 21.5 cm height   GCC

£250

This pattern was also produced in two other colour versions (pattern numbers 2801 and 3052).

Crown Ducal earthenware jug with grey and white mottled glaze and tube-lined decoration painted in pink and blue enamels and gilded, designed by Charlotte Rhead.

c.1930s. Impressed shape number 198; painted pattern number 6569; printed mark 'TRADEMARK/CROWN DUCAL WARE/MADE IN ENGLAND'. 19 cm height   MH

£95

Crown Ducal earthenware Petit Pierre pattern celery vase with 'original' lithograph over a matt Snow glaze.

c.1958. Lithographed green and yellow mark 'Crown Ducal/ Ware/MADE IN ENGLAND'. Moulded shape number 292. 15.8 cm height   AF

£4

Petit Pierre salad ware was introduced in 1958. Mexican themes were also popular during the 1950s, as were the cacti which appear on the reverse of this vase. In 1959 A. G. Richardson introduced Arizona pattern, which also featured cacti.

RIDGWAY(S)
(1879 to the present day)

This pottery has undergone many changes of ownership and style:

1879–1920	Ridgways
1920–52	Ridgways (Bedford Works) Ltd
1952–4	Ridgway & Adderley Ltd
1955	Ridgway, Adderley, Booths & Colcloughs Ltd
1955–present day	Ridgway Potteries Ltd

By 1957 Ridgway Potteries controlled eight factories in the Staffordshire Potteries: Booths Church Bank Pottery, Colcloughs, Paladin Works, North Staffordshire Pottery, Portland Pottery, Bedford Works, Adderley Floral China Works, and Gainsborough Works. They centralised design for all eight works in one design studio, with Tom Arnold as chief designer. Arnold, at only 28 years of age, injected a youthful contemporary boost into the designs, some of which are now held up as the best of Contemporary style. The average age of the designers working for him was 25, which Pottery Gazette and Glass Trade Review noted 'confers a vigorous and dynamic outlook to the department, and bodes well for design to continue over the years.' Ridgway is now part of the Royal Doulton Tableware group.

Ridgways earthenware mug with honey glaze over a transfer-print, silver lustre handle.

c.1920–52. Printed backstamp 'SCENES/FROM/COUNTRY WAYS BY SPECIAL PERMISSION/OF/MACMILLAN & CO LTD./RIDGWAYS/ENGLAND/'. 12 cm height   TA

£45

Ridgways earthenware bowl with *Homemaker* pattern lithograph.

c.1950s. Special backstamp (see below). 18 cm diameter

AF

£0.50

This pattern is highly collectable and although it is very common, pieces often fetch £3–5.

Mark on reverse.

SHAW & COPESTAKE
(SYLVAC, FALCON WARE)
(c.1894–1982)

SylvaC was the trade name used by Shaw & Copestake Ltd at the Sylvan Works Longton from c.1935. Today Shaw & Copestake are best known for their matt-glazed animal figures, but the firm made a wide range of decorative pottery throughout their operation. The trade name Falcon Ware was used for some wares produced at the Falcon Pottery purchased from Thomas Lawrence Potteries in 1938. The wares made at the two factories were similar and during the Second World War, when the Sylvan Works were requisitioned, SylvaC wares were made at the Falcon Pottery. SylvaC wares are widely collected, but are still widely available, making perfect condition essential to the collector.

Further Reading

Susan J. Verbeek. *The SylvaC Story* (Pottery Publications, 1989).
Susan J. Verbeek. *The SylvaC Companion* (Pottery Publications, 1991).

SylvaC earthenware dog with beige matt glaze with dark brown highlights.

c.1950s–82. Impressed shape number 1379; impressed mark 'SYLVAC/MADE IN ENGLAND'. 19 cm height   MH

£50

This model was made 1939–82. Shape 1379 is shown in a 1960 SylvaC catalogue – reproduced in Verbeek 1989. The impressed mark on this figure is believed to have been used from the 1950s.

SylvaC earthenware rabbit with beige matt glaze.

c.1940s–50s. Impressed shape number 990; impressed mark 'MADE IN ENGLAND'. 12.5 cm height   MH

£40

Shape 990 was made c.1930s–75, and is shown in a 1940 SylvaC catalogue – reproduced in Verbeek 1989. The bunnies were offered in a wide range of colours and in seven sizes from 2 to 9¾ inches (5–25 cm).

SylvaC earthenware planter with sprayed pink, orange and green glazes.

c.1955–65. Impressed shape number 353; impressed mark 'SYLVAC/ENGLAND'. 21 cm length   GCC

£35

This planter was illustrated in the *Pottery Gazette and Glass Trade Review*, February 1956. Shape 353 is shown in a 1960 SylvaC catalogue – reproduced in Verbeek 1989.

SylvaC relief-moulded earthenware coffee pot, brown glazed.

c.1970. Impressed shape number 4204; impressed mark 'SYLVAC/MADE IN ENGLAND'. 28 cm height   AF

£1.50

SHELLEY
(FOLEY; SHELLEY)
(1928 to the present day)

Formerly Wileman & Co. at Foley Works, Fenton from c.1870, this firm was incorporated as Shelley Potteries Ltd in 1928. The firm's owners the Shelley family had adopted the Shelley tradename in 1910. During the Second World War, the firm ceased earthenware production, thereafter specialising in bone china tablewares, especially for export markets. The name was changed to Shelley China in 1965. It was taken over in 1966 by Allied English Potteries, and is now part of Royal Doulton Tablewares Group. Today the firm's wares are widely collected, most especially their Art Deco china tea wares (see chapter 21).

The trade name Foley was also used by E. Brain & Co. (1903–67). Old Foley was the trade name used by James Kent (1897–present day) from 1913.

Further Reading

Susan Hill. *The Shelley Style* (Jazz Publications, 1990).
Chris Watkins, William Harvey and Robert Senft. *Shelley Potteries* (Barrie & Jenkins, 1986).

Shelley earthenware vase painted with orange, turquoise and grey glazes.

c.1930s. Printed mark 'Shelley/MADE IN ENGLAND'; 14 painted. 19 cm height   RS

£85

Shelley earthenware jug painted with yellow, orange and brown bands.

c.1930s. Printed mark 'Shelley/MADE IN ENGLAND'. 16.5 cm height   RS

£38

SHORTER
(c.1874–1974)

Arthur Shorter worked as an artist for Hope & Carter and Minton before establishing his own decorating workshop in Hanley c.1874. Around 1878 he established a partnership with James Boulton under the style Shorter & Boulton, principally manufacturing majolica (see chapter 11). The style changed to Shorter & Son c.1906 and to Shorter & Sons c.1926. The firm became a limited company under the style Shorter & Son Ltd in 1933.

The firm specialised in novelty wares and 'fancies' for the middle market. The range of these wares produced is enormous, and like many firms they continued to use popular shapes for many decades, usually with new colours and glaze treatments to update them.

Mabel Leigh's work as a ceramic designer for Short & Sons is just beginning to be appreciated by collectors. Like her contemporaries, Clarice Cliff, Susie Cooper and Charlotte Rhead, she has a distinctive style which was later copied by other firms. Many of her sgraffito designs reveal an ethnic source, often reflected in the pattern name. These patterns were introduced in the 1930s, but some, including *Aztec*, *Jardinière*, *Medina* and *Khimara*, continued in production into the 1960s. Many of her designs bear backstamps with the name of the pattern and her name.

Further Reading

Irene and Gordon Hopwood. *The Shorter Connection* (Richard Dennis, 1992).

Shorter earthenware jug in *Basra* pattern with sgraffito decoration painted in polychrome enamels, designed by Mabel Leigh.

c.1933–9. Black stamped mark 'SHORTER & SON LTD/ STOKE-ON-TRENT/MADE IN/GREAT BRITAIN'; incised mark 'BASRA'; decorator's monogram painted in blue. 18.8 cm height   IGH

£80

Basra pattern pots are often marked 'MABEL LEIGH'.

Shorter earthenware jug in *Aztec* pattern with sgraffito decoration painted in polychrome enamels, designed by Mabel Leigh.

c.1933–9. Impressed mark 'SHORTER/ENGLAND'; incised marks 'AZTEC' and 'by MABEL LEIGH'; black stamped mark 'SHORTER & SON LTD/STOKE-ON-TRENT/MADE IN/ GREAT BRITAIN'. 21.9 cm height   IGH

£90

Shorter slip-cast earthenware *Pagoda* teapot painted in coloured glazes, designed by Mabel Leigh.

c.1933–9. Printed mark 'SHORTER & SON LTD/STOKE-ON-TRENT/MADE IN/GREAT BRITAIN'. 16 cm height   IGH

£85

Shorter slip-cast earthenware vase in *Kandahar* pattern.

c.1930s. 21.8 cm height   IGH

£70

Shorter earthenware plaque in *Mecca* pattern with incised decoration and painted in polychrome enamels.

c.1936. Black stamped mark 'SHORTER & SON LTD/STOKE-ON-TRENT/MADE IN/GREAT BRITAIN'; moulded shape mark 60; painted decorator's mark. 31 cm diameter   IGH

£110

Shorter slip-cast earthenware *Pyramus* vase with matt green and crystalline running glazes.

c.1926–33. Black printed mark 'Shorter & Sons/Stoke-on-Trent/England'; moulded mark 'PYRAMUS/ENGLAND'. 26.2 cm height   IGH

£65

This Art Deco architectural shape is one of several produced by Shorter.

Shorter earthenware vase with streaky and mottled red and black glazes.

c.1950s. Printed mark SHORTER & SON LTD/STOKE-ON-TRENT/ENGLAND'; impressed shape number 650; 'L/S' (large size). 30 cm height   AF

£29

Shorter earthenware *Katisha* figure painted in polychrome enamels.

c.1950. Moulded mark 'Katisha/SHORTER ENGLAND'; printed mark 'REPRODUCED BY/PERMISSION OF THE/DOYLY/CARTE/OPERA CO./SHORTER & SON LTD/STAFFORDSHIRE/MADE IN ENGLAND'. 25 cm height   IGH

£150

This *Katisha* figure after the character in Gilbert and Sullivan's *Mikado* is one of a series of figures from their operas introduced by Shorter in 1949 and reissued in the 1960s. A smaller size was also made, and these were reproduced from the original moulds during the 1980s.

Shorter shell shape slip-cast earthenware flower holder with matt glazes.

c.1950s. Moulded marks 'SHORTER/ENGLAND'; shape number 321; 'L/S' (large size). 27.5 cm length. IGH

£38

A range of shell-shaped flower holders were introduced by Shorter in the 1930s, continuing in production well into the 1950s.

Shorter fish sauceboat and stand (2 pieces), painted in coloured glazes.

c.1950s. Printed mark in black on stand and sauceboat 'SHORTER & SON LTD/STOKE-ON-TRENT/ENGLAND'. Stand 17 cm length IGH

£30

This shape also appears in matt and more subdued glazes, which are earlier in date. It is part of a fish service designed in the 1930s which includes fish-shaped plates and a larger fish-shaped platter.

Shorter slip-cast earthenware cheese dish painted in coloured glazes.

c.1950s. Black stamped mark 'GENUINE/STAFFORDSHIRE/HAND PAINTED/SHORTER & SON LTD/ENGLAND'. Stand 20 cm length IGH

£35

This Kate Greenaway type shape was used by Shorter for majolica in the 19th century. The straw hats with ribbons and flowers which appear in Kate Greenaway illustrations were used for earthenware shapes by a number of 19th-century manufacturers including Wedgwood who produced a *Kate Greenaway* umbrella stand in the shape of a straw hat.

Shorter Contemporary style slip-cast earthenware vase with black glaze and yellow enamels.

c. Early 1960s. Black stamped mark 'SHORTER & SON LTD/ STOKE-ON-TRENT/ENGLAND'; moulded shape number 747 and 'M/S' (medium size). 30.7 cm height   IGH

£45

Shorter slip-cast earthenware cow creamer in polychrome enamels.

c.1960s. Black stamped mark 'GENUINE/STAFFORDSHIRE/ HAND PAINTED/SHORTER & SON/ENGLAND'. 19.8 cm length   IGH

£38

Cow creamers have been popular since the late 18th century and even later 20th-century examples are quite collectable.

WADE
(FLAXMAN WARE; BRITISH ROSKYL POTTERY)
(1927 to the present day)

J. W. Wade & Co. established the Flaxman Art Tile Works in Burslem in 1892, producing majolica and transfer-printed tiles. Early in the 20th century they produced art pottery. The company operated under the style Wade, Heath & Co. from 1927. They produced Flaxman Ware from c.1936. Roskyl Pottery was ware tube-lined or painted in imitation of tube-lining made in the late 1930s. These wares do not usually bear a Wade, Heath mark. The firm operated as Wade Potteries until 1990, and now uses the style Wade Ceramics. Today they are best known for their miniature figures, which are widely collected.

Further Reading

I. Warner and M. Posgay. *The World of Wade* (c.1988).
Bernard Bumpus. 'Tube-line variation', *Antique Collector*, December 1985.

Wade Heath earthenware vase with brown and green ground and polychrome enamels.

c.1934–9. Printed mark with lion 'WADE HEATH/ENGLAND'. Moulded shape number 129. 16 cm height
MH

£35

Wade Heath earthenware jug with brown and polychrome enamels.

c.1934–9. Printed mark 'FLAXMAN WARE/HAND PAINTED POTTERY/BY WADE HEATH/ENGLAND'; painted pattern number [illegible]; moulded shape number 110. 23 cm height
MH

£35

Wade Heath earthenware jug painted in imitation of tube-lining.

c.1934–9. Marked 'BRITISH ROSKYL POTTERY'; 'DE4/E'. 14 cm height
MH

£30

Tube-lining was a very expensive method of decoration and some firms imitated it with relief-moulded patterns and painting. Collectors should study carefully any wares which appear to be tube-lined for the characteristic irregularities of genuine tube-lining.

Earthenware rabbit with matt blue glaze, possibly Wade Heath.

c.1930s. Printed mark 'MADE IN ENGLAND'. 9.5 cm height
MH

£28

WEDGWOOD
(c.1759 to the present day)

Many of Wedgwood's designs during the 20th century were in the forefront of modern design. These are of much greater interest today than the revivals of earlier patterns and shapes, e.g. 18th-century creamwares. During the 1930s Wedgwood employed a number of innovative outside designers, including Keith Murray and Eric Ravilious.

For Wedgwood porcelain wares of the 20th century see chapter 21.

Further Reading

Maureen Batkin. *Wedgwood Ceramics, 1846–1959* (Richard Dennis, 1982).
Robin Reilly. *Wedgwood*, 2 vols (Macmillan, 1989).
Robin Reilly and George Savage. *The Dictionary of Wedgwood* (Antique Collectors' Club, Woodbridge, 1980).

Wedgwood earthenware jug with transfer-print filled in with polychrome enamels.

c.1908. Painted pattern number C36534; impressed marks 'WEDGWOOD', '3TK' (date code for 1908). 14 cm height
JM

£48

This is an example of the Wedgwood wares in traditional style popular early in the century. To the present day, one of the firm's greatest assets is its pattern and shape books, from which revivals have been drawn. The C series was used for Queensware Fancies 1875–1957. Queen's Ware was the trade name given by Josiah Wedgwood to his creamwares (see chapter 3).

Keith Murray (1892–1981) trained as an architect, but had difficulty finding work in the field during the 1930s. He turned to industrial design, working as an outside designer at Etruria from 1932 until 1948, when he returned to architecture. His training as an architect is evident in the shapes of these wares. Many of his shapes continued to be produced into the 1950s.

Wedgwood earthenware tankard with matt green glaze designed by Keith Murray.

c.1932–3. Printed mark 'Keith Murray/WEDGWOOD/MADE IN ENGLAND'. 12.2 cm height
MH

£48

Wedgwood earthenware bowl with matt green glaze, designed by Keith Murray.

c.1932–3. Printed mark 'Keith Murray/WEDGWOOD/MADE IN ENGLAND'. 16 cm height   MH

£275

Wedgwood creamware plate with underglaze print of 'Josiah Wedgwood FRS'.

1930. Impressed marks 'WEDGWOOD MADE IN ENGLAND'; 4U30 (date code for April 1930). 22.5 cm diameter   V

£38

This plate commemorates the bicentenary of Wedgwood's birth in 1730.

Wedgwood earthenware plate with *Persephone* pattern designed by Eric Ravilious.

c.1938. Printed mark 'Persephone/Designed by Ravilious'; 'WEDGWOOD OF ETRURIA & BARLASTON'. 25.5 cm diameter   MH

£33

Eric Ravilious (1903–42) worked as an outside designer for Wedgwood from 1936–40, although many of his designs could not be produced in quantity until the 1950s. The elegance of his designs has made them highly collectable.

Wedgwood black basalt teacup, saucer and plate (this last not shown).

c.1954. Impressed marks 'WEDGWOOD/MADE IN ENGLAND'; shape number 687; date 1954. Cup 6.2 cm height; saucer 14 cm diameter; plate 19 cm diameter.   CE

£16.50

This is a good example of Wedgwood's ability to adapt basalt, which they introduced in the 18th century, to the 20th-century taste. The clean lines give the black stoneware body a severe modernist look.

Wedgwood relief-moulded green-glazed *Pholas Aestatus* shell shaped dish.

Impressed marks 'WEDGWOOD'; '5 M 56' (date code for 1956). Printed circular mark 'WEDGWOOD/OF ETRURIA/& BARLASTON/MADE IN/ENGLAND'. 32.8 cm length   AF

£6

Wedgwood has made green-glazed wares continuously since the 18th century (see chapter 6). This shell shape was first introduced at the beginning of the 19th century and has been produced with many types of decoration. The later wares should have impressed date marks and printed marks as above. Green-glazed shell wares are very common and all recorded examples have been of a post-Second World War date.

WILTSHAW & ROBINSON
(CARLTON WARE)
(1890–1957)
CARLTON WARE
(1957–89)

Established in 1890 as an earthenware manufacturer, Wiltshaw & Robinson began to produce Carlton Heraldic China, in competition with W. H. Goss, in 1902 (see chapter 20). They developed their lustres after the First World War, having perfected twelve colours by 1924. The firm went into receivership in 1931 and merged with Birks, Rawlins & Co. Ltd the following year.

Renamed Carlton Ware in 1957, the firm was purchased by Arthur Wood & Son (Longport) in 1966. The firm was then purchased by County Potteries Plc in 1987, going into receivership in 1989. The trade name, pattern books and some moulds were purchased by Grosvenor Ceramic Hardware in 1989, and the trade name was relaunched in 1990.

Wiltshaw & Robinson used many techniques assimilated from other factories, generally offering a cheaper alternative: for example their lustre wares were certainly inspired by Wedgwood's Fairyland Lustres and their Handcraft range utilized the underglaze painting techniques employed by Carter, Stabler & Adams at Poole and Charles Collard at Honiton. Nevertheless, their designs were often striking and original and executed to a very high standard. Today Carlton Ware is widely collected and highly esteemed.

Further Reading

Nicholas Pine. *The Price Guide to Crested China* (Milestone Publications, Horndean, 1992).

Wiltshaw & Robinson earthenware plate with vellum glaze, unburnished gilt edge, lithograph decoration.

c.1894. Printed mark with design registration numbers 236722 (1894) and 226167 (1894); painted pattern number 683R. 23.5 cm diameter   GCC

£110

Marks on reverse.

Carlton Ware earthenware vase with red matt glaze over black and white lithograph.

c.1927. Printed mark 'W & R' with swallow; 'Carlton Ware/ Made in England'; painted pattern number 2907; impressed shape number 217. 20.5 cm height   GCC

£125

This vase was illustrated in a Carlton Ware advertisement in the *Pottery Gazette Diary* 1927.

Carlton Ware earthenware hot water jug with matt cream glaze and underglaze painted decoration in blue, mauve, yellow and green.

c.1929. Printed mark 'Carlton Ware/MADE IN ENGLAND/ "TRADE MARK"/Handcraft'; 'Registered no. 742986' (1929). 20.5 cm height·   GCC

£350

One of a pair of Carlton Ware earthenware vases with underglaze painted decoration.

c.1930. Painted pattern number 4/474/3291. Printed mark 'Carlton Ware/MADE IN ENGLAND/''TRADE MARK''/Handcraft'. 20 cm height   GCC

£500 the pair

Carlton Ware earthenware relief-moulded plaque with matt beige glaze with enamels in autumnal tones.

c.1935. Printed mark 'Carlton Ware/MADE IN ENGLAND/''TRADE MARK''.' 32 cm diameter   GCC

£300

Carlton Ware earthenware dish with black exterior, yellow interior, gilded rim.

c.1960. Printed mark 'Carlton Ware/Handpainted/MADE IN ENGLAND/''TRADEMARK''.' Impressed shape number 2362 Z. 31 cm length   GCC

£45

Carlton Ware earthenware vase with apple green ground painted in polychrome enamels and gilded.

c.1930s. Printed mark 'Carlton Ware/MADE IN ENGLAND/''TRADE MARK'' ', painted pattern numbers 3/5061 and 3587. 18 cm height   GCC

£450

Carlton Ware earthenware jug with orange, yellow and black 'Jazz' pattern painted decoration with lustre glaze and gilded.

c.1930s. Printed Carlton Ware mark; painted pattern numbers O/3680 and 3655. 20 cm height   GCC

£1,000

Carlton Ware earthenware covered jar with ruby lustre and gilded.

c.1930s. Printed Carlton Ware mark. 30 cm height with lid.
                                                                GCC

£1,500

Carlton Ware earthenware jug with orange ground and lustre painted in polychrome enamels over a transfer-print.

c.1930s. Printed Carlton Ware mark; painted pattern numbers A28/4875 and 4247. 21 cm height   GCC

£300

Carlton Ware earthenware 'Egyptian' covered jar with blue ground and gold transfer decoration.

c.1920s. Special printed hieroglyphic backstamp and Carlton Ware mark. Painted pattern number 2710. 40 cm height
                                                                GCC

£2,200

The discovery of the tomb of King Tutankhamun in 1922 inspired many Egyptian designs during the 1920s.

Base with marks.

Carlton Ware Confederation of Canada commemorative earthenware jug painted in polychrome enamels.

c.1927. Printed mark 'CONFEDERATION OF CANADA' with three paragraphs of history and 'Production limited 350'; 'This jug is No. 9.'; 'Carlton Ware/MADE IN ENGLAND/ "TRADE MARK" '. 25 cm height   GCC

£12,950

Carlton Ware earthenware dish with green ground, gilded and painted in polychrome enamels.

c.1920s. Printed Carlton Ware mark and 'Bert Royale'. Impressed shape number 1633. 17.5 cm length   GCC

£110

OTHER MANUFACTURERS

Thomas Forester 'Jazz' shaped earthenware bowl painted in polychrome enamels and gilded.

c.1930s. Printed circular mark 'TF&S LTD/PHOENIX/MADE IN ENGLAND'. 11.5 cm height   MH

£225

Thomas Forester (& Sons) (1877–1959) was a majolica manufacturer at Longton turned art pottery (see chapter 26). This is an especially fine example of the Art Deco style, and so is more valuable than most Forester wares.

Myott earthenware flower holder with removable inset painted in grey, yellow, orange and brown enamels.

c.1930s. Printed gold mark with pattern number 'Myott, Son & Co./MADE IN ENGLAND/HAND PAINTED/8662'. 14.5 cm height   MH

£75

Myott, Son & Co. produced a wide variety of earthenwares at Stoke from 1898. This vase has a typical Art Deco reversed Aztec pyramid shape.

Buchan stoneware bowl painted in blue and brown.

c.1952. Printed marks 'BUCHAN/PORTOBELLO/SCOT-LAND' with a thistle; 146; M1/28. 12 cm diameter   MH

£45

A.W. Buchan & Co. (1867 to the present day) made a number of attractive stonewares in the Contemporary style. These tastefully designed, free-hand painted wares are destined to become better appreciated in the coming years. The firm experienced a boost from the growth of the oven-to-tableware market in the 1960s, as did many stoneware manufacturers. This bowl was illustrated in the *Pottery Gazette and Glass Trade Review* in September 1952, along with other examples of their Thistle Ware.

Radford Handcraft earthenware jug with pastel matt glazes.

c.1936–64+. Crack in handle. Printed script mark 'E. Radford Handpainted'. 10 cm height   MH

£20

This jug was one of the range of Edward Radford wares produced at Burslem by H. J. Wood 1933–64+ under the style Radford Handcraft Pottery at Amicable Street, Burslem. Their matt pastel glazes with hand-painted patterns, usually floral, are much admired and the number of collectors is rapidly growing. This jug would be worth about £35 in perfect condition.

Kensington Ware earthenware budgie vase with matt glazes.

1930s. Moulded mark 'MADE IN ENGLAND/No.2/CHESTER'. Printed mark with Staffordshire knot. 'KENSINGTON WARE' with 'KPH' inside knot; 'ENGLAND'. 20.5 cm height
MH

£48

Kensington Pottery Ltd (1922–62) specialised in novelties for the lower end of the market such as piggy banks and vases. During the 1950s they made a wide range of vases to accommodate the craze for flower arranging. In 1962 they amalgamated with an associated firm, Price Bros, under the style Price & Kensington Potteries.

Vulcan Ware earthenware *Genda* vase with relief-moulded design highlighted with black matt glaze.

c.1950s. Moulded mark with shape name 'MADE IN ENGLAND/GENDA'; Printed mark 'VULCAN WARE/MADE IN ENGLAND'. 17 cm height
MH

£35

Vulcan Ware was a trade name for Elektra Porcelain Co. Ltd (founded 1924) from c.1940. Despite the firm's name they were earthenware, not porcelain, manufacturers. Vulcan Ware included some very poor quality majolica-type wares. Their matt-glazed wares often had poor quality stencil-sprayed decoration. The vase shown here is not typical of the firm's wares, most of which would sell in the £3–7 range. The firm was associated with Avon Art Pottery, another manufacturer of cheap decorative pottery.

James Kent earthenware bowl painted with *Peony* pattern in blue enamels.

Printed mark with pattern name 'PEONY/JAMES KENT LTD./LONGTON/STOKE-ON-TRENT/ENGLAND'. 22 cm diameter MH

£95

James Kent (1897 to the present day) is well known for their reproduction Staffordshire figures. They also produced a wide range of pottery and china decorative and tablewares. From 1981 they were subject to a number of acquisitions, and are now owned by M. R. Hadida Ltd.

Earthenware vase decorated in yellow, green and black.

Printed mark 'HAND PAINTED/B. A. G. Co. Ltd./ENGLAND'; painted pattern number P9591. 21 cm height MH

£25

Losol Ware earthenware lustre vase.

Printed mark 'Losol Ware/KEELING & CO. LTD./BURSLEM/ENGLAND'. Painted pattern number 97/K2. 28 cm height CCC

£250

Keeling & Co. (1886–1936), primarily a manufacturer of table and toilet wares, introduced their Losol Ware trademark c.1912. This was used on the tablewares as well as their decorative pottery.

Earthenware *Ye Daintee Lady* teapot in yellow and green.

c.1937. Painted pattern number 850; printed mark 'AS PURCHASED BY HER MAJESTY THE QUEEN'; moulded mark 'Ye Daintee Lady Teapot/Reg'd no. 824571/MADE IN ENGLAND' (design registered in 1937). 19.5 cm height MH

£50

Large Devonmoor earthenware mug with broken green glazes.

c.1928. Impressed mark 'DEVONMOOR ENGLAND'. 10 cm height   AF

£1.50

Devonmoor Art Pottery Co. at Liverton near Newton Abbot operated from 1922. They produced wares with interesting glaze effects, Toby and character jugs, and hand-painted wares.

Meakin coupe shape earthenware plate with lithographed French street scene.

c.1955–60. Stamped mark with crown 'ALFRED MEAKIN/ ENGLAND'. 17.2 cm diameter   AF

£0.50

Alfred Meakin (1875–1970s) was a tableware manufacturer whose designs generally copied those of the leading manufacturers. This plate is of interest for its typical 1950s drawing of a Parisian street scene complete with poodle. The poodle was a very popular motif at the time, and it is worth looking out for any items decorated with poodles.

Johnson Bros coupe shape earthenware plate with *Fish* transfer-printed design illuminated with underglaze colours.

c.1961. Special printed backstamp (see below). 26.2 cm length   AF

£2.50

Johnson Bros (1883 to present day) was a tableware manufacturer whose designs generally copied those of the leading manufacturers. The firm has been a part of the Wedgwood Group since 1968. This plate is of interest because of the fine quality of the transfer-print. Johnson Bros introduced this technique of underglaze illuminated transfer-prints in 1961. Other patterns made using this technique were *Friendly Village* and *Dreamtime*.

Mark on reverse.

Swinnertons coupe shape earthenware plate with red, green, black and grey lithographic print.

c.1958. Printed mark with picture of an oil lamp 'SWINNER-TONS/STAFFORDSHIRE/MADE IN ENGLAND/"NESTOR VELLUM" '. 22.8 cm diameter   AF

£0.30

Swinnertons (1906–59) also made a *Philodendron* pattern c.1957, which is quite similar to this pattern. Compare this treatment with Terence Conran's *Plant Life* pattern on p. 278. The Conran design has more potential on the collectors' market, but patterns such as this anonymous one by Swinnertons will also increase in value as typical of 1950s design.

15 PORCELAIN BEFORE 1780

THE first commercial imports of porcelains came to England from China during the 17th century. It was not until the beginning of the 18th century that porcelain was produced in Europe. The first European manufacturer was Meissen c.1710, followed by several others. Porcelain manufacture in England did not begin until the 1740s. The early English porcelains were of a soft-paste type as opposed to the hard-paste porcelains produced by most of the Continental manufacturers. After 1750 porcelain manufacture spread widely throughout Europe.

The style of decoration of the early English porcelains is generally described as chinoiserie, Kakiemon or European. Chinoiserie designs are inspired by, or more often very close copies of, designs found on Chinese export porcelain. The Kakiemon designs are inspired by Japanese Kakiemon patterns which use simple motifs such as blossoms, twigs with bird, or quails. European designs incorporate European landscapes, figures or flowers.

The Seven Years War dislodged the Meissen factory from their pre-eminence, and the principal Western influence on English porcelains became France. The French Royal porcelain factory was moved from Vincennes to Sèvres in 1856. The most important evidence of this influence was the use of rich ground colours and elaborate rococo gilding.

Further Reading

Paul Atterbury, ed. *The History of Porcelain* (William Morrow, New York, 1982).
Michael Berthoud. A *Compendium of British Cups* (Micawber Publications, Bridgnorth, 1990).
G. Coke. *In Search of James Giles* (Micawber Publications, Wingham, 1983).
Robin Emerson. *British Teapots & Tea Drinking* (HMSO, 1992).
Geoffrey Godden, ed. *Staffordshire Porcelain* (Granada, 1983).
Geoffrey Godden. *English China* (Barrie & Jenkins, 1985) (1985a).
Geoffrey Godden. *Eighteenth-century English Porcelain* (Granada, 1985) (1985b).
Geoffrey Godden. *Encyclopaedia of British Porcelain Manufacturers* (Barrie & Jenkins, 1988).
Philip Miller and Michael Berthoud. An *Anthology of British Teapots* (Micawber Publications, Broseley, 1985).
John Sandon. *English Porcelain of the 18th and 19th Centuries* (Merehurst Press, 1989).
Bernard Watney. *English Blue & White Porcelain of the Eighteenth Century*, revised edn (Faber & Faber, 1973).

BOW
(c.1748–74)

Thomas Frye and Edward Heylyn took out a patent for the use of a new substance in a porcelainous body in 1744. However, there is no evidence that Frye started commercial production at Bow in east London until 1748. Significant production did not begin until after Frye's second patent, which included calcined bones in the paste, taken out in November 1749.

The factory's output was large and covered a very wide range of wares. The porcelain was often thickly potted, heavy and not very translucent. The glaze, which was often laid on thickly, was greyish or bluish, with a creamy colour being achieved c.1750. The majority of Bow's porcelain tablewares were painted in underglaze blue. This was not a method of decoration usually employed by their chief rivals at Chelsea. The blue was very bright before 1752, afterwards becoming grey-blue and still later a dull royal blue.

The factory called itself New Canton to emphasise their efforts to emulate Chinese porcelains. Much of the output, especially in the early years, was inspired by these and by the Japanese Kakiemon style of decoration. Western styles later became more evident, particularly those influenced by Meissen.

Nicholas Sprimont, owner of the Chelsea factory, described Bow as the makers of 'the more ordinary sort of ware for common use'. Bow is thought to have undercut Chelsea's prices for tablewares, and doubtless Sprimont was disgruntled. Bow also made some very fine ornamental wares, particularly figures from 1750 (see chapter 18).

Further Reading

Elizabeth Adams and David Redstone. *Bow Porcelain*, 2nd edn revised (Faber, 1991).
Anton Gabszewicz. *Bow Porcelain: The Collection formed by Geoffrey Freeman* (Lund Humphries, 1982).

Blanc-de-Chine is the term originally used to describe the Chinese white wares, particularly the 'prunus-moulded' wares made in Fukien province towards the end of the 17th century. *Blanc-de-Chine* constituted a large proportion of Bow's early tablewares. The sprigged prunus decoration is typical. Tea and coffee wares, plates and sauceboats are the most common shapes. Many examples are illustrated in Adams & Redstone.

Bow porcelain bell-shaped, *blanc-de-chine* mug with sprigged prunus decoration.

c.1756. Hairline crack. 9.5 cm height   AD

£520

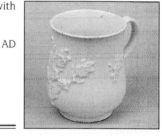

Bow porcelain *blanc-de-chine* octagonal plate with sprigged prunus decoration.

c.1755. 21.5 cm diameter   V

£385

Bow porcelain plate painted in underglaze blue.

c.1769. Mock Chinese marks painted in underglaze blue. 19 cm diameter   W

£335

This pattern is moving away from the Chinese influence, although the reverse is an imitation of the Chinese.

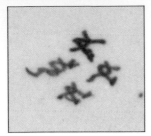

Reverse.

Bow porcelain bell-shaped tankard with powdered blue ground, chinoiserie scenes in fan-shaped and circular medallions painted in underglaze blue.

c.1762. 15 cm diameter   V

£630

A plate with very similar decoration is illustrated in Gabszewicz. Several other examples are illustrated in Adams & Redstone.

Rare Bow porcelain ribbed mug with borders painted in underglaze blue.

c.1758–62. Crescent mark. 9 cm height   B

£1,000

Bow porcelain sauceboat with chinoiserie scene painted in underglaze blue.

c.1755–60. Two chips. 19.5 cm length   TA

£225

A similar sauceboat is illustrated in Adams & Redstone.

Rare Bow porcelain plate with chinoiserie pattern painted in polychrome enamels in the *famille rose* palette.

c.1758. 24 cm diameter   KK

£750

The Bow factory's earliest wares were painted in the Chinese *famille rose* palette, and these were popular for about fifteen years. This is an unusual pattern, with the Chinese tiger-lily and lotus flower prominent in the centre.

Bow porcelain pickle dish painted in polychrome enamels.

c.1760. Tiny nick filled. 11 cm length   KK

£475

This flower-painting in the Meissen style reflects the move away from Oriental towards Western design.

Pair of Bow porcelain ornamental pots missing lids, painted in polychrome enamels with relief-moulded ring handles.

c.1760. 4 cm height   AD

£780

A garniture of three of these pots with *Aloe vera* lids is illustrated in Gabszewicz. An example with realistically modelled flowers on the lid is illustrated in Adams & Redstone. The pots would be much more valuable with these beautifully modelled lids.

Bow porcelain potpourri encrusted with flowers and painted in polychrome enamels.

c.1765. Bird missing from knop, chipped but no restoration. Height with lid 26 cm   AD

£680

Even with the damage, this is a very decorative and desirable pot.

CAUGHLEY
(c.1775–99)

Ambrose Gallimore established a pottery at Caughley in Shropshire c.1754. In 1772 he took as his partner Thomas Turner, who it is believed had experience in porcelain manufacture at Worcester. Turner rebuilt and expanded the works, which were producing porcelains by c.1775.

These were good quality durable tablewares with a soapstone-type porcelain body similar to that used at Worcester. The wares were for the medium-priced market and were often in the style of contemporary Worcester. Caughley made a speciality of blue-printed wares. In the late 1780s and early 1790s much of their ware was sent for decoration to Chamberlain's decorating shop in Worcester.

The hybrid hard-paste bodies introduced c.1796 were not very successful. These wares were heavily potted and the body was prone to tears. In 1799 Turner sold the works to the Coalport partnership, who continued production at the factory until c.1814.

Further Reading

Geoffrey Godden. *Caughley and Worcester Porcelains*, 1755–1800, 2nd edn (Antique Collectors' Club, Woodbridge, 1981).

Caughley porcelain bread and butter plate with chinoiserie *Temple* pattern blue transfer-print and gilding.

c.1780–5. Slight rubbing to gilded edge and inner border. 19 cm diameter   TV

£120

Very rare Caughley porcelain tea cup and saucer with basket-weave moulded border painted in underglaze blue and gilded.

c.1790. Cup 5.7 cm height; saucer 12.3 cm diameter   G

£220

A similar cup is illustrated in Berthoud.

Caughley porcelain plate with an Imari pattern painted in polychrome enamels and gilded.

c.1780s. Slight surface rubbing to decoration. 20.6 cm diameter   V

£215

This is a rare enamelled design.

Caughley porcelain cabbage-leaf jug with mask spout, with 'Birds in a Tree' blue transfer-print and painted monogram in underglaze blue.

c.1785, 24.5 cm height   V

£695

Caughley porcelain plate with blue 'Fisherman' transfer-print.

c.1785. Impressed mark 'Salopian'; 'S' printed in underglaze blue. 19.8 cm diameter   V

£215

This popular pattern, also known as 'Pleasure Boat' or 'Fisherman and Cormorant', was also used by Worcester. The Caughley version may be distinguished by the fat fish held by the man in the boat and the straight line of the fisherman sitting on the island in the background. The impressed mark 'Salopian' was also used by an art pottery in the late 19th century, but Caughley never made earthenwares and the art pottery never made porcelains, so there should be no cause for confusion.

Very rare Caughley porcelain butter tub painted in underglaze blue with flower knop.

c.1785. Marked with 'c' painted in underglaze blue. 10.3 cm diameter   V

£220

Rare Caughley porcelain spittoon with *Temple* pattern blue transfer-print.

c.1785. 11 cm height   TV

£1,200

Unusual shapes like spittoons are always very desirable.

Caughley porcelain melon-shaped dessert dish with blue transfer-print 'Full Nankin' pattern and gilding.

c.1785–90. Some rubbing to gilding. 26.5 cm length   TV

£140

CHELSEA
(c.1744–69)

The Chelsea porcelain factory was founded c.1744 by Nicholas Sprimont, a Huguenot silversmith. The factory was patronised by courtiers and aristocrats, but declined when Sprimont's health failed. In 1769 the factory was taken over by William Duesbury. The factory continued to produce soft-paste porcelains of the Chelsea type, often using old Chelsea models and continuing to use the gold anchor mark. However, to confuse things, the term Chelsea-Derby is sometimes used to refer to wares made at Derby during the period when Duesbury owned both factories. Furthermore some porcelain tablewares may be found with a mark containing the Chelsea anchor and the Derby script 'D'. The Chelsea factory was shut down in 1784.

Chelsea, whose wares were very fashionable, was among the first porcelain manufacturers to mark their wares. This has enabled collectors to divide them into periods according to marks. This is a useful way to refer to the pots, but it should be remembered that many wares would have spanned more than one period, continuing in production for a number of years. The earliest wares, when marked, bear an incised triangle mark. These are quite rare. For Chelsea porcelain figures see chapter 18.

Further Reading

Elizabeth Adams. *Chelsea Porcelain* (Barrie & Jenkins, 1987).
F. Severne Mackenna. *Chelsea Porcelain: The Triangle and Raised Anchor Wares* (F. Lewis, Leigh-on-Sea, 1948, reprinted 1969).
F. Severne Mackenna. *Chelsea Porcelain: The Red Anchor Wares* (F. Lewis, Leigh-on-Sea, 1951).
F. Severne Mackenna. *Chelsea Porcelain: The Gold Anchor Period* (F. Lewis, Leigh-on-Sea, 1952).

RAISED ANCHOR PERIOD (c.1749–52)

The period during which Chelsea occasionally marked their wares with a moulded raised anchor saw a considerable refinement in their porcelain. The soft-paste porcelain body was thick and white, for the first time displaying the 'moons', which would characterise Chelsea porcelain until a new body was introduced c.1758. These moons are lighter spots of transparency in the body caused by air bubbles trapped in the paste. They can be seen when the pot is held up to a strong light. Stylistically there was a very strong Japanese influence on the wares of this period. Any marked Chelsea wares from this period are rare and desirable.

Chelsea porcelain plate with 'Lady and Pavilion' pattern painted in polychrome enamels.

c.1750. Chips restored. 22 cm diameter   KK

£660

A cup and saucer in this pattern is illustrated in Adams. There is considerable variation in the pattern, such as the placing of the large urn, presumably to cover up flaws in the body.

Chelsea hexagonal porcelain teapot painted in the Kakiemon style in polychrome enamels and gilded.

c.1750. Restored. 14.6 cm height   KK

£4,950

A Chelsea hexagonal teapot and its Chinese counterpart are illustrated in Miller & Berthoud, and another in Emmerson.

RED ANCHOR PERIOD (c.1752–8)

The Chelsea porcelains produced during this period are considered their best. The wares were often painted with a small red anchor in enamel over the glaze: this anchor has since appeared on forgeries and reproductions, but is usually too large (so that you can't miss it!). The genuine mark should never be more than 0.7 cm in height. A brown anchor has also been recorded, and is thought to date from c.1755–60, overlapping the period during which the red anchor mark was used.

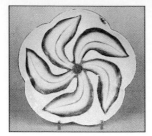

Chelsea porcelain Scolopendrium-moulded lobed plate painted in green, pink and yellow enamels with a red rim.

c.1752–8. Tiny chip and rubbed rim. Red anchor mark. 21 cm diameter   D

£2,400

This shape was also made in the earlier Raised Anchor period (illustrated in Adams). The small insect seen in the upper right hand corner was painted by the manufacturers to hide a flaw in the porcelain. Because the flaws occurred at random, other examples may have insects or flowers painted in other places, or none at all.

Chelsea relief-moulded porcelain plate painted in polychrome enamels.

c.1757. Brown anchor mark. 21 cm diameter   KK

£660

Chelsea porcelain relief-moulded lobed plate painted with European floral motifs in polychrome enamels with mauve rim.

c.1754. 24 cm diameter   KK

£355

This moulding is known as Gotskowsky moulding. Adams illustrates two examples with Kakiemon patterns.

GOLD ANCHOR PERIOD (c.1759–69)

During this period Chelsea wares were increasingly influenced by French porcelains, with rich coloured grounds and elaborate rococo gilding. This style is not now as popular with collectors as the earlier Red Anchor style, but the quality continued to be very high. The wares were often marked with a small gold anchor. This anchor has since appeared on forgeries and reproductions, but is usually too large (so that you can't miss it!). The genuine mark should never be more than 0.7 cm in height. The mark was carried over into the Chelsea-Derby period when the factory was managed by William Duesbury (see Derby below).

Chelsea porcelain relief-moulded plate painted in poly-chrome enamels and gilding.

c.1759–69. Gold anchor mark. Tiny chip. 24 cm diameter D

£375

The rococo moulding of the plate and the European style of painting are typical of this period.

DERBY
(William Duesbury I 1756–86)

William Duesbury's ceramic career may have started when a decorator in London; his account book of the 1751–3 period has been preserved. He seemingly moved to Stafford-shire and it is assumed that he was working with William Littler at the Longton Hall fac-tory from c.1754 before he moved to Derby c.1756. The porcelains of the Derby factory are of a uniformly high quality. Fine tablewares, ornamental wares and figures (see chapter 18) were produced. In 1770 he purchased the Chelsea factory (see above), which he ran until 1784, when all staff and materials were moved to Derby. Upon his death in 1786, the firm was continued by his son William Duesbury II (see chapter 16).

Further Reading

John Twitchett. *Derby Porcelain* (Barrie & Jenkins, 1980).
Gilbert Bradley. *Derby Porcelain 1750–98* (Thomas Heneage & Co., 1990).

Derby porcelain tankard painted with Kakiemon style scenes in panels in underglaze blue.

c.1770. 13 cm height V

£440

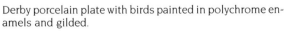

Derby porcelain plate with birds painted in polychrome en-amels and gilded.

c.1760. 24 cm diameter AF

£300

Derby porcelain Bacchus mug painted in polychrome enamels and gilded.

c.1790. Crown, crossed batons, dots and 'D; mark painted in puce. 10 cm height   T

£365

Derby was the only English porcelain manufacturer to make these mugs in the 18th century. However, they were popular in the 18th century and may be found in a variety of other bodies. Quite a number of 20th-century reproductions are around, so beware.

Derby porcelain leaf-shaped dish with relief-moulded basket border painted in polychrome enamels and gilded.

1758–60.

28.5 cm length   D

£695

Two smaller dishes in the same shape, with different paintings are illustrated in Twitchett.

Derby porcelain dish painted in polychrome enamels and gilded.

c.1760. 23 cm length   KK

£465

Derby porcelain 'Dolphin Ewer' cream boat painted in polychrome enamels.

c.1765. 8 cm height   TV

£665

LIVERPOOL FACTORIES
(c.1760–85)

Liverpool was an important port and became a centre of pottery manufacture during the early 18th century (see chapter 2). Various types of pottery continued to be made in Liverpool well into the 19th century. There were also a number of porcelain manufacturers from the 1760s onwards.

The Liverpool makers were classified by Dr Watney into the products of Reid, Ball, Gilbody, Chaffers, Christian and Christian/Pennington. Recent research has reattributed some of these groups. Robert Chaffers began porcelain manufacture at Shaw's Brow, Liverpool c.1755, succeeded on his death in 1765 by his partner Philip Christian. After the first couple of years, Chaffers used a soapstone-type porcelain body of the sort used by Worcester.

John Pennington manufactured porcelain at Copperas Hill, Liverpool c.1769–79, and at Folly Lane, Liverpool 1779–94. Pennington's widow Jane carried on the business after his death in 1786.

Seth Pennington, brother of John, took over Philip Christian's pottery at Shaw's Brow in 1778. As both Pennington brothers produced a bone-ash porcelain, most of their wares cannot yet be distinguished.

The group of wares formerly attributed to William Reid at Liverpool are now attributed to the Limehouse factory in London on the evidence of factory 'wasters'.

Recently the group of wares formerly attributed to William Ball have been reattributed to the Vauxhall factory in London, based on the findings of excavations.

Due to the reattributions, the whole field of Liverpool porcelains is being reassessed, and for the purposes of this book, one can only say with confidence that a pot was made by one of the Liverpool potters, and give an approximate date.

Liverpool porcelain globular teapot, possibly Christian's, with floral decoration painted in mauve and red enamels.

c.1770. 16 cm height   V

£395

Liverpool porcelain coffee pot painted in underglaze blue.

c.1780. 20 cm height   V

£450

Pennington Liverpool porcelain saucer with chinoiserie pattern painted in underglaze blue.

c.1780. 13 cm diameter   V

£41

Very rare Pennington Liverpool porcelain eye bath.

c.1770–5. 6 cm height   B

£1,500

Eye baths are very rare and collectable. There would have been little original demand for such a utilitarian object in porcelain

LONGTON HALL
(c.1749–60)

William Littler (& Co.) established a porcelain factory at Longton in 1751. Littler was an experienced potter, whose partners were a lawyer and William Jenkinson who had obtained a recipe for porcelain manufacture. The firm had financial difficulties throughout its short life. In 1753 Jenkinson withdrew from the partnership. Despite various attempts to increase their markets, the partnership did not prosper and was dissolved in 1760. In 1764 William Littler established a porcelain factory at West Pans near Musselburgh in Scotland.

Longton Hall porcelains are often thickly potted and occasionally clumsy. Leaf-shaped dishes and leaf relief-moulding were particularly popular. During the last three years of its existence the firm concentrated on the manufacture of useful wares and figures (see chapter 18).

Further Reading

Arnold R. Mountford. 'Porcelain comes to The Potteries: the pre-1760 period', Geoffrey Godden ed., *Staffordshire Porcelain* (Granada, 1983).
Bernard Watney. *Longton Hall Porcelain* (Faber, 1957).

Longton Hall or West Pans porcelain leaf-shaped dish painted in polychrome enamels.

c.1765. 28.5 cm length   V

£700

It is often difficult to differentiate between the wares made by William Littler at Longton Hall in its last years and the early West Pans wares.

Longton Hall porcelain relief-moulded sauceboat with chinoiserie pattern painted in underglaze blue.

c.1755. 10 cm length   V

£1,300

A Longton Hall sauceboat in this shape with a different handle but very similar decoration is illustrated in Mountford. A waster in this shape has been found on the factory site.

Longton Hall porcelain vase with flowers decorated in polychrome enamels.

c.1755. Large chip on neck restored. Marked '12' in blue enamel on base. 14 cm height   KK

£530

LOWESTOFT
(c.1757–99)

This small Suffolk factory made soft-paste porcelains with bone-ash. For the first ten years production was confined to underglaze blue painted wares, usually in chinoiserie patterns. Most of the factory's output was useful wares, especially tea wares.

Further Reading

Geoffrey Godden. *Lowestoft Porcelains* (Antique Collectors' Club, Woodbridge, 1985).

Lowestoft porcelain globular teapot, painted in polychrome enamels.

c.1785. Slight chips to lid. 14 cm height   V

£490

The globular shape teapot originated in Chinese porcelain. It was made by a variety of English porcelain manufacturers. Miller & Berthoud illustrate a number of these along with Chinese examples. This European style of flower-painting with swags and cross-hatched diapers is typical of the 1785 period. Miller & Berthoud illustrate a number of Lowestoft teapots in the globular shape, including one with very similar decoration (plate 293). Another with an inscription dated 1787 is illustrated in Godden 1985a.

These simple chinoiserie patterns painted in underglaze blue and then painted over the glaze in coloured enamels are associated with the Redgrave family of china painters.

Lowestoft porcelain Redgrave-style tea bowl and saucer painted with a chinoiserie pattern in underglaze blue and red enamel overglaze.

c.1775. Saucer 12.7 cm diameter; tea bowl 4.7 cm height V

£198

A saucer in this pattern is illustrated along with a Chinese export porcelain saucer in the same pattern in Godden 1985a.

Lowestoft porcelain Redgrave-style chinoiserie pattern tea bowl and saucer painted in underglaze blue and red enamel overglaze and gilded.

c.1775–80. Saucer 13 cm diameter; cup 4.6 cm height   KK

£200

Representative pieces from a tea and coffee service in this pattern are illustrated in *Lowestoft Porcelains* (in colour) and Godden 1985a.

Lowestoft porcelain cream jug painted in pink, green and red enamels.

c.1785. Usual minute stress crack by spout. 8.3 cm height

G

£240

Fine Lowestoft porcelain relief-moulded waste bowl with chinoiserie pattern painted in underglaze blue.

c.1764. Old crack. 13 cm diameter

G

£550

Relief-moulded wares of this type are attributed to designer or modeller James Hughes, who sometimes included his initials in the design. Several other examples are illustrated in Godden 1985a.

Lowestoft porcelain mug painted in underglaze blue.

c.1765. Long hairline crack. 14.2 cm height

LM

£500

Very rare Lowestoft porcelain spoon painted in underglaze blue.

c.1765. 11 cm length

BG

£675

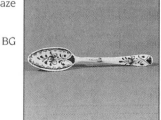

Reverse of spoon.

Lowestoft porcelain relief-moulded sauceboat printed and painted in underglaze blue.

c.1770. 16 cm length   TA

£225

The floral panels are printed, and the borders etc. are painted. A sauceboat in the same shape with different relief-moulding is illustrated in Godden 1985a.

WORCESTER
(c.1752–83)

Dr John Wall took over the soapstone formula for soft-paste porcelain from Benjamin Lund's short-lived factory at Bristol (c.1749–52). Worcester porcelains were of a consistently high quality until Dr Wall's retirement in 1774. Afterwards the firm was managed by William Davis, and declined to some degree. However, even these later wares are often charming and highly collectable.

Worcester sometimes bears marks, but many unmarked pieces may be identified by shape, pattern and colour thanks to the exhaustive researches of scholars, especially Henry Sandon.

A visit to the Worcester factory and the Dyson Perrins Museum in the factory grounds is a must for anyone interested in pottery and porcelain. Reservations for factory tours should be made in advance: (0905 23221).

Further Reading

Lawrence Branyan, Neal French and John Sandon. *Worcester Blue & White Porcelain 1751–1790*, revised edn (Barrie & Jenkins, 1989).

R. L. Hobson. *Catalogue of the Frank Lloyd Collection of Worcester Porcelain of the Wall Period* (Victoria & Albert Museum, 1923).

H. Rissik Marshall. *Coloured Worcester Porcelain of the First Period* (1954; facsimile edn, Ceramic Book Co., Newport, 1977).

Henry Sandon. *Worcester Porcelain 1751–1793*, 2nd edn (Barrie & Jenkins, 1974).

BLUE UNDERGLAZE PAINTED WARES

Branyan, French & Sandon catalogue and illustrate all recorded Worcester patterns painted in underglaze blue. All of the patterns shown below appear in that invaluable book, unless otherwise noted.

Rare Worcester porcelain feather-moulded coffee cup with 'Feather Mould Birds' pattern painted in underglaze blue.

c.1765. 5.5 cm height   T

£185

The only recorded examples of this pattern appear on feather-moulded wares.

Worcester porcelain saucer with uncommon 'Circled Landscape' pattern painted in underglaze blue.

c.1775+. Painted mock Chinese blue mark. 12.3 cm diameter   JJB

£125

This pattern is uncommon and has been recorded with the border here illustrated (catalogued as 'T') and another border (catalogued as 'U'). The pattern has also been recorded with a non-Worcester border. A pattern named *Circl'd Landscape* has been found in Chamberlain's Worcester records, which may refer to this pattern, or a very similar one.

Worcester porcelain jug with 'The Walk in the Garden' pattern painted in underglaze blue.

c.1756. 17 cm height   B

£2,800

This pattern was used by Derby, but with an elaborate border. The Worcester examples are usually without a border, as here.

Worcester porcelain gugglet (or bottle) and basin painted with 'Willow Bridge Fisherman' pattern in underglaze blue.

c.1765. Bottle 27.3 cm height; basin 26.7 cm diameter   B

£2,000

A bottle in this pattern appears in Sandon along with a waster from an excavation at the factory site. The pattern was used over a long period and noticeable variations may be found.

Worcester porcelain pickle dish painted with 'Pickle Leaf Vine' pattern in underglaze blue.

c.1770. Crescent mark painted in underglaze blue. 8.5 cm length   W

£165

This pattern was used c.1758–70, and considerable variations occur. A similar example is illustrated in Sandon.

Rare early Worcester porcelain cabbage-leaf jug with unusual handle and no spout, with floral pattern painted in underglaze blue.

c.1758–62. Slight chip. 21.4 cm height   G

£495

This is painted in the soft blue typical of the period. The pattern is uncommon and is always found on cabbage-leaf ware, which may or may not have spouts. A variety of different handle shapes have been recorded.

Small Worcester porcelain relief-moulded sauceboat with the 'Little Fisherman' pattern, painted in underglaze blue.

c.1765. Two minor rim chips. 13 cm length   TV

£350

This pattern has only been recorded on these small sauceboats. A very similar pattern known as 'Fisherman and Billboard Island' is used on larger sauceboats. Both versions are uncommon.

BLUE UNDERGLAZE TRANSFER-PRINTS

Branyan, French & Sandon catalogue and illustrate all recorded Worcester patterns transfer-printed in underglaze blue. All the patterns shown below appear in that invaluable book, unless otherwise noted.

Worcester porcelain globular teapot printed in underglaze blue in the uncommon 'Three Ladies' pattern.

c.1770. Hatched crescent mark. Slight chip to cover. 15 cm height   TV

£925

The globular shape teapot originated in China, and was copied by several English porcelain manufacturers. Miller & Berthoud illustrate Chinese and Worcester examples side by side for comparison.

Worcester porcelain two-handled leaf dish with 'Pine Cone' transfer-print in underglaze blue.

c.1775. Some damage to modelled flowers. Crescent mark painted in underglaze blue. 26.5 cm length. excluding handles.   W

£365

The Pine Cone group of Worcester blue transfer-prints was one of the most popular floral groups of patterns. It occurs on many forms. The pattern has since been revived several times by the Worcester company and is in production by Royal Worcester today as *Rhapsody*. Close versions of the pattern were used by Caughley and Lowestoft.

Worcester porcelain relief-moulded cabbage-leaf dish with 'Wispy Chrysanthemum Sprays' blue transfer-print.

c.1770. Small firing crack. 25.7 cm length   W

£275

This is an uncommon pattern, and no examples with a border print have been recorded. It is usually only found on this shape of dish. A dish in this shape painted with polychrome enamels is illustrated in the next section (Enamelled Decoration).

Worcester porcelain drainer with 'Fisherman and Cormorant' blue transfer-print with gilding.

c.1780. 9 cm diameter, excluding handle.   AD

£285

This popular pattern was also used by Caughley. The Worcester version may be distinguished by the thin fish held by the man in the boat and the curved line of the fisherman sitting on the island in the background.

Worcester porcelain mug with uncommon 'European Landscape' print in underglaze blue.

c.1775. Crescent mark. 14.5 cm height   BG

£750

ENAMELLED DECORATION

Worcester 'Dry Blue' porcelain plate, painted in overglaze blue enamel and gilded.

c.1770. 22 cm diameter   AD

£300

Worcester porcelain globular shape teapot with 'Mosaic' pattern painted in polychrome enamels and gilded.

c.1770. Cracked. 17 cm height   KK

£275

The globular shape teapot originated in China, and was copied by several English porcelain manufacturers. Miller & Berthoud illustrate Chinese and Worcester examples side by side for comparison. The dark blue panels with medallions are set off with fine gilding.

Rare Worcester porcelain elongated globular shape teapot painted in polychrome enamels.

c.1760. Spout restoration. 13 cm height   KK

£395

The elongated globular shape teapot, which first appeared on the Continent, is an adaptation of the Chinese globular shape teapot.

James Giles was a china dealer, who operated an independent decorating studio in London c.1760–78. The standard of decoration was much higher than that of some manufacturers, and the output was considerable. These plates are attributed to the Sliced Fruit Painter at James Giles's London decorating workshop. A number of examples are illustrated in Rissik Marshall.

A pair of Worcester porcelain plates in the so-called 'Lady Mary Wortley Montague' pattern with underglaze scale-blue grounds painted in polychrome enamels and gilded.

c.1768–70. One with a star crack. Fretted square mark painted in underglaze blue. 23 cm diameter.   BG

£2,500 the pair.

The Dishevelled Birds in the border reserves are associated with the Sliced Fruit Painter, who did not always include cut fruit in his work.

Rare Worcester porcelain coffee cup and saucer with green ground painted in polychrome enamels.

c.1765–70. Coffee cup 6.4 cm diameter; saucer 12 cm diameter   B

£1,200

Attributed to the Spotted Fruit Painter at James Giles's London studio.

Worcester porcelain dessert dish.

c.1775. 21 cm diameter   V

£650

This is part of a Giles-decorated combined Worcester and Caughley service, c.1775.

Worcester porcelain armorial plate. Painted in polychrome enamels.

c.1770.   B

£2,500

From a service made for Warwick Calmody, MP for Worcester, decorated by James Giles in London.

Rare Worcester porcelain coffee pot painted in pink enamel and gilded.

c.1770. Crack and restored knop. 22 cm height   KK

£990

Fewer coffee pots were made than teapots, thus making them quite rare today. This piece possibly decorated at Giles's studio.

The popular, colourful 'Dragons in Panels' pattern (also known as 'Bishop Sumner' or 'Kylin') was made by many factories including Chamberlain's Worcester, Spode, Minton and Coalport. The pattern is based on a Chinese *famille verte* dish, but the palette is not limited to *famille verte* colours. It continued to be used in the early 19th century.

Worcester porcelain vertically fluted coffee cup and saucer painted in polychrome enamels with the 'Dragons in Panels' pattern and gilded.

c.1770. Cup 7.5 cm height; saucer 13.5 cm diameter   KK

£540

Worcester porcelain dessert service dish painted in poly-chrome enamels with the 'Dragons in Panels' pattern and gilded.

c.1770. 27.5 cm length   V

£770

Rare Worcester porcelain cup and saucer with crest in centre surrounded by Kakiemon pattern panels, painted in underglaze blue with polychrome enamels and gilded.

c.1768–70. Crescent mark painted in underglaze blue. Cup 5.8 cm height; saucer 15.5 cm diameter   BG

£600

This is a relatively common pattern, but the shape is unusual and the crest makes the item more desirable as it could be traced to a particular service. A fine dish in this pattern is illustrated in Sandon; a fluted cup and saucer are illustrated in Hobson.

Worcester porcelain hexagonal fluted spoon tray with rare pattern painted in polychrome enamels, *bleu du roi* border and gilded.

c.1775. Blue open crescent mark. 14 cm length   B

£1,850

Small spoon trays of this type are very popular with collec-tors. For some reason the spoon tray disappeared from tea services in the 19th century, probably to the chagrin of those who had to wash the table cloths! A covered sugar bowl and stand in this pattern are illustrated in Hobson.

The 'Fan' pattern is relatively common. The simple and bold design is complemented by intricate gilding.

Worcester polychrome dish with 'Fan' pattern painted in underglaze blue with polychrome enamels and gilded.

c.1765–68. Mock Chinese seal mark painted in underglaze blue. 24 cm length   B

£900

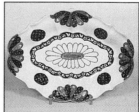

Worcester porcelain tea canister with 'Fan' pattern painted in underglaze blue with polychrome enamels and gilded.

c.1765–8. Mock Chinese seal mark painted in underglaze blue. 15.9 cm height B

£1,100

Worcester porcelain fluted tea canister painted in polychrome enamels and gilded.

c.1770. Knop restored. 16 cm height AD

£840

Worcester porcelain sparrow-beak jug painted in polychrome enamels.

c.1770. 8.3 cm height V

£120

Worcester porcelain twelve-foil edge plate painted in polychrome enamels with gold rim.

c.1770. 22 cm diameter V

£165

Worcester porcelain plate painted in polychrome enamels and gilded.

c.1780. Blue crescent mark. 23 cm diameter   AD

£450

One of a pair of Worcester porcelain plates with scale-blue ground, painted in polychrome enamels in reserves and gilded.

c.1770. Mock Chinese seal mark painted in underglaze blue. 19 cm diameter   V

£990 the pair.

The combination of a fine dark blue ground, elaborate gilding and beautiful painted panels, makes these plates highly desirable and decorative as well. This style of decoration with three vase-shaped reserves and three larger reserves was used at Worcester c.1760–76. Other examples are illustrated in Sandon. The Worcester scallop-edged plates have twenty-four lobes.

Worcester porcelain sauceboat relief-moulded with cos lettuce leaves, handle curved for right-hand pouring, painted in polychrome enamels.

c.1758. 18.5 cm length   V

£650

Other examples of this shape are illustrated in Rissik Marshall.

Worcester basket-weave relief-moulded porcelain junket dish, with pale green ground, recesses painted in polychrome enamels by James Rogers.

c.1760. Heavy spitting in the body. 23 cm length   B

£800

A similar example with a canary yellow ground and a factory waster are illustrated in Sandon.

Worcester porcelain partridge-shaped tureen naturalistically painted in on-glaze colours.

c.1760–5. Rare uncharacteristic incised triangle mark. 19 cm length   B

£4,000

These were once thought to be Chelsea, but Worcester factory wasters have confirmed a Worcester attribution for this version. Two sizes were made. The Bow version has applied rather than relief-moulded nesting material (illustrated in Adams & Redstone, see Bow above). Similar Continental inspired tureens were made at several English factories.

Worcester porcelain ovoid vase with 'Telephone Box' pattern painted in polychrome enamels.

c.1770. Missing lid. 23 cm height   B

£900

This pattern also appears painted in underglaze blue. Only a very limited number of Worcester pieces were decorated in both manners with the same patterns.

Worcester porcelain green ground relief-moulded cabbage-leaf dish painted in polychrome enamels.

c.1770. 30.5 cm excluding handle.   W

£950

A dish in this shape printed in underglaze blue is illustrated in the previous section (Blue Underglaze Transferprints).

Large Worcester porcelain jug painted in polychrome enamels.

c.1754. Scratch cross incised mark. Lip restored. 25.5 cm
height   KK

£8,800

This is a stunning jug with very fine painting on the round.
The spout with a scroll is unusual and particularly attractive.

View two.

View three.

335

OTHER DECORATION

Worcester porcelain elongated globular shape teapot with on-glaze black print.

c.1770. Painted mark on lid in gold 'C'. 14.5 cm height LM

£500

A Worcester elongated globular shape porcelain teapot with the 'Tea Party' on-glaze black print, c.1770 is illustrated in Miller & Berthoud. This too has a flower knop.

Small Worcester porcelain barrel-shape *blanc-de-chine* teapot, gilded.

c.1765. 9 cm height, excluding knop.   V

£320

The barrel shape was used from the 1760s and was particularly popular in the 1780s, when it was often fluted.

Worcester porcelain jug with green ground and gilding.

c.1770. Graze on spout restored. 12 cm height   KK

£290

OTHER MANUFACTURERS

William Cookworthy set up the short-lived Plymouth Porcelain Manufactury (c.1768–70), which was the first British firm to produce hard-paste porcelain. He experienced considerable technical difficulties, and commonly found faults in the wares include smoke stains, discoloration and warping. Figures had a tendency to lean or show open firing cracks in the thicker parts. In 1770 Cookworthy moved his hard-paste works to Bristol. Richard Champion of Bristol was a partner and appears to have played an important part in the manufacture. When Cookworthy retired in 1774, he transferred the patent for producing the hard-paste porcelain to Champion, who sold it to the New Hall partnership in 1781 (see chapter 16).

Some of the difficulties that were encountered at Plymouth persisted in the Bristol wares, but they were a great improvement over the earlier wares, and are very collectable, representing an important part of British ceramic history. In the early 20th century marked fakes were manufactured, sometimes in a soft bone china body.

Plymouth hard-paste porcelain dish with modelled shells.

c.1770. Two cracks and two shells repaired. 11.5 cm height

D

£475

Bristol hard-paste porcelain coffee cup painted in under-glaze blue.

c.1775. Painted mark in underglaze blue 'X'. Cup 6.3 cm height

BG

£400

16 PORCELAIN 1780–1830

THE period 1745–80 saw the establishment of porcelain in England. During this period English porcelains were rare and expensive objects manufactured mainly for the wealthy. The period 1780–1830 saw many new developments, culminating in the production of porcelains which were affordable by the middle classes. The most important development was the introduction of bone china, for which England is renowned even today. This very white, very fine but durable body had the advantage of firing more consistently than the earlier soft-paste bodies, reducing kiln wastage and the cost to the consumer.

Stylistically, there were several great changes during the period. At the beginning the neo-classical revival can be seen in the shapes and the modest decoration of the wares. With the beginnings of the 19th century there were many influences. The Regency period 1800–20 saw a great exuberance in decoration, with elaborate gilding and use of enamel painting. The first tea ware shapes to predominate were the New Oval and Bute, whose simple, graceful lines were ideal for setting off the increasingly complex decoration. By 1815 the London shape with its sharper, angular lines began to hold sway. During the 1820s more relief-moulded decoration began, and the lines softened, culminating in the full-blown neo-rococo of the 1830s.

Although the earlier porcelains have their charms for collectors, there is little doubt that this era was the first to produce large quantities of consistently excellent quality wares.

Further Reading

Michael Berthoud. A *Compendium of British Cups* (Micawber Publications, Bridgnorth, 1990).
Geoffrey Godden. *British Porcelain* (Barrie & Jenkins, 1974).
Geoffrey Godden. *Staffordshire Porcelain* (Granada, 1983).
Geoffrey Godden. *English China* (Barrie & Jenkins, 1985).
Geoffrey Godden. *Encyclopaedia of British Porcelain Manufacturers* (Barrie & Jenkins, 1988).
Geoffrey Godden. *Godden's Guide to English Porcelain* (W. H. Smith, 1992).
Philip Miller and Michael Berthoud. An *Anthology of British Teapots* (Micawber Publications, Broseley, 1985)

CHARLES BOURNE
(c.1817–30)

Charles Bourne was one of the many small Staffordshire porcelain manufacturers during the first half of the 19th century. He is exceptional in that he sometimes marked his wares (in a fractional form with a 'CB' over the pattern number). The known pattern numbers range from 1 to 1017. Bourne specialised in good quality bone china tea wares and dessert services, although some stunning ornamental wares were also made. Some Bourne animal figures as well as a selection of tablewares are illustrated in Godden 1983. Although the name Charles Bourne is not well known among the general public, the scarcity of the wares, due to the short period of operation, has made them collectable.

Further Reading

Geoffrey Godden. 'Charles Bourne, the Foley Potteries, Fenton, c.1817–c.1830', *Staffordshire Porcelain* (Granada, 1983).

Charles Bourne bone china sucrier, painted floral decoration in polychrome enamels and gilding.

c.1825. Painted initials 'CB' over pattern number 525. 14.5 cm height   W

£285

This is a previously unrecorded pattern.

Charles Bourne bone china vase with blue ground, painted in polychrome enamels (pink roses) and gilded.

c.1820–5. Painted mark in red 'CB'. Hairline crack. 13 cm height   AD

£105

An identical vase is illustrated in Godden 1983. The pattern number is unknown.

Rare Charles Bourne bone china shell-shape dessert dish with floral relief-moulded border, painted in polychrome enamels and gilded.

c.1820. Painted initials 'CB' over pattern number 60. 21 cm length   TV

£700

Charles Bourne bone china tea cup and saucer, part of London-shape trio, painted in polychrome enamels and gilded.

c.1820. Painted initials 'CB' over pattern number 208. Saucer 14.5 cm diameter; cup 5.8 cm height   TV

£400 for the trio.

CHAMBERLAIN'S WORCESTER
(c.1791–1851)

Robert Chamberlain was the head of the decorating department at the Worcester porcelain factory (see chapter 15) before he established his own china decorating studio c.1786. At first the firm decorated blanks from Caughley, but by c.1791 Chamberlain's had begun to manufacture *some* of their own porcelains. The first wares were hybrid hard-paste porcelains with a hard, glassy glaze. An enormous range of fine quality porcelains were manufactured over the next six decades.

It should be remembered that pattern numbers were sometimes repeated over a long period of time, and the dates given here are only approximate dates of *introduction*.

Pattern numbers	Dates of introduction
1–200	1791–1800
200–380	1800–c.1805
380–860	c.1805–20
860–1000	1820–2
1000–1350	1822–30
1350–1820	1830–40
1820–2450	1840–8
2450–5109	1848–51

Numbers apparently not used: 1822–1999, 2625–2999, 3100–3999, 4100–4999.

A visit to the modern Royal Worcester factory, still on the site of the Chamberlain works, and the Dyson Perrins Museum in the factory grounds is a must for anyone interested in pottery and porcelain. Reservations for factory tours should be made in advance: (0905) 23221.

For later Chamberlain's Worcester wares see chapter 17.

Further Reading

Geoffrey A. Godden. *Chamberlain-Worcester Porcelain 1788–1852* (Barrie & Jenkins, 1982).

Chamberlain's Worcester porcelain plate, centre painted in polychrome enamels and border gilded.

c.1819. Signature ED:1819 (with two dots below ED). 23.5 cm height   V

£185

This is possibly the work of Enoch Doe, who joined Chamberlain's in 1805 and left to establish his own decorating firm in the Worcester High Street in partnership with George Rogers from 1820.

Early Chamberlain's Worcester porcelain footed dish (possibly the centre from a sandwich service) painted in brown enamel (pattern 258) and gilded.

c.1805–10. Some firing cracks. 11.5 cm height   G

£85

Illustrated in Godden.

Chamberlain's Worcester porcelain plate with unusual decoration painted in green and black enamels and gilded.

c.1800. Painted mark in red 'Chamberlain Worcester'. 22 cm diameter   D

£320

The gadroon edge was frequently used by manufacturers during the 1820s and 1830s for armorial services. A number of Chamberlain's Worcester porcelain gadroon-edged dessert wares are illustrated by Godden.

Chamberlain's Worcester porcelain gadroon-edged crested dessert service dish with green ground, painted in polychrome enamels and gilded.

c.1820–40. Small chip restored. Motto 'Gloria Quo Collum Que Vocant'. Painted mark in green 'Chamberlain's Worcester'. 27 cm length   AD

£280

One of a pair of Chamberlain's Worcester porcelain Royal Gadroon shape armorial plates with green ground, painted in polychrome enamels and gilded.

c.1820–40. Motto 'Vive et vivere sinas'. Red script mark 'Chamberlain's Worcester'. 26 cm diameter   TV

£650 the pair

Chamberlain's Worcester porcelain plate with painted picture of Chamberlain's Royal Porcelain factory, with pale blue ground rim.

c.1830. Slight crack on rim. 26 cm diameter JJM

£250

The centre portrays Chamberlain's Royal Porcelain Factory with Worcester Cathedral behind. The present day Royal Worcester factory occupies this site. In 1818 a fine dessert service with similar, but better quality paintings of the factory was produced. This is a later edition, possibly produced as a souvenir item for visitors to the works.

Chamberlain's Worcester porcelain plate with green ground, painted in polychrome enamels and gilded.

c.1830. 23.5 cm diameter TA

£155

Chamberlain's Worcester porcelain Old Oval cream jug with Japan pattern painted in polychrome enamels and gilded.

c.1820. Painted pattern number 886. 14.5 cm length TV

£175

Chamberlain's Worcester porcelain comport with painted Dresden flowers pattern in polychrome enamels and gilded.

c.1818. Painted pattern number 707. 25.7 cm length JJB

£395

Miniature porcelain vase attributed to Chamberlain's Worcester with mazarine ground, painted in polychrome enamels and gilded.

c.1810. Hairline crack. 9 cm height   JJB

£110

Chamberlain's Worcester porcelain mug with gilding and initials.

c.1795. 8 cm height   HBW

£195

A similar gilded and initialled mug is illustrated in Godden. Apart from the shape, note the distinctive concentric half-circles in gold on the thumb-rest of the handle.

Chamberlain's Worcester porcelain jug with unusual dry blue ground and gilding.

c.1820. Painted mark 'Chamberlain's Worcester'. 4.9 cm height   HBW

£195

COALPORT
(c.1790s–1926, continued in the Potteries to the present day)

John Rose established the Coalport factory on the east bank of the Severn in Shropshire in the 1790s. The availability of both clay and coal in the district as well as its connections by water made it an ideal location. In 1799, Rose took over Thomas Turner's porcelain factory at Caughley. John Rose's Coalport firm continues until the present day in Staffordshire as part of the Wedgwood group, but the history is very complicated.

In 1803 his younger brother Thomas established a second Coalport factory on the other side of the Shropshire Canal. This firm often produced shapes and patterns which are nearly identical to those produced by John Rose. In some cases it is only the differing pattern numbers which enable us to distinguish between the wares of the two firms. In other cases we can only generically identify the wares as 'Coalport'.

In 1814 John Rose took over the Thomas Rose works and combined it with his own. The firm traded under a number of different styles, which Godden (1988) lists as follows:

John Rose Pottery

c.1795–1803	Rose & Co., also known as
	Blakeways or Rose Blakeway & Rose
c.1800–13	Colebrook (or Coalbrook) Dale China Company
c.1803–89	John Rose & Co.

Thomas Rose Pottery

c.1800–3	Reynolds, Horton & Rose
c.1803–14	Anstice, Horton & Rose

As mentioned above different pattern numbers were used by the two Coalport factories. John Rose porcelains very rarely have pattern numbers before 1810. The numbers are as follows:

Date of introduction	Pattern numbers
1795–1810	1–600
1810–c.1822	600–999

The Anstice, Horton & Rose Porcelains (c.1803–14) are numbered 1–1419+. The numbers used by the combined factories are fractional as follows:

Date of introduction	Pattern numbers
c.1822–30	$\frac{2}{1} - \frac{2}{676}$

Visitors to the Ironbridge Gorge complex in Shropshire can see the Coalport museum, where many fine examples of the factories' wares are on display. The Clive House Museum, Shrewsbury also has a fine collection of Coalport wares.

For later Coalport wares see chapter 17.

Further Reading

Geoffrey Godden. *Coalport & Coalbrookdale Porcelains*, revised edn (Antique Collectors' Club, Woodbridge, 1981):
Michael Messenger. *Shropshire Pottery and Porcelain* (Shrewsbury Museums, 1976).

Coalport porcelain French-style inkstand and quill holder painted in polychrome enamels and gilded.

c.1810. 14 cm length   W

£385

Pair of Coalport porcelain gadroon-edged plates. Left: 'Belvoir Castle, Leicestershire, The Seat of his Grace the Duke of Rutland'. Right: 'Guy's Cliff, Worcestershire, The Seat of Bertie Greathead, Esquire'.

c.1825. 24 cm diameter   V

£525

Early Anstice, Horton & Rose Coalport porcelain Japan pattern (number 1339) dish.

c.1810–14. 24 cm length including handle   G

£120

A part tea service in pattern 1339 is illustrated in Godden.

Coalport porcelain sauce tureen with cover and stand.

c.1810. Stand 21 cm length; tureen 13.5 cm high with knop
                W

£300

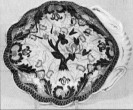

Coalport porcelain mug, painted in polychrome enamels and gilded.

c.1810–20. Hairline crack. 'WTP' initials painted in gold. 8 cm height   D

£175

A mug with this unusual shape handle is illustrated in Godden.

345

Coalport porcelain dessert tureen, stand and cover, painted in polychrome enamels on gold ground.

c.1815. Cracked lid with riveted repair. 15 cm height complete   AD

£450

Coalport porcelain shanked teacup and saucer painted in red and green enamels.

c.1800. Cup 6 cm height; saucer 14 cm diameter   WG

£45

One of a pair of John Rose & Co. Felt Spar Porcelain trios painted in green, yellow and blue enamels and gilded. Teacup is illustrated in Berthoud 1990, plate 621.

c.1820–5. Printed mark; painted pattern number $\frac{2}{253}$. Teacup 7.2 cm height; coffee cup 9 cm height; saucer 15 cm diameter   JJB

£175 the pair

Printed mark.

This mark refers to the Society of Arts Gold Medal, won in 1820 by John Rose & Co. for a leadless feldspathic glaze. Other marks used by Coalport read 'Feldspar' or 'Feltspar'.

Coalport porcelain plate blue transfer-printed.

c.1805. 24.5 cm diameter   JJB

£115

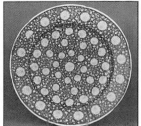

Coalbrookdale is used to describe floral-encrusted Coalport porcelain, usually of the 1820–50 period.

Coalbrookdale style porcelain chamber candlestick with applied modelled flowers, painted in polychrome enamels and gilded.

c.1825. Painted mark in blue 'Coalport'. 12 cm length excluding handle   G

£460

Coalbrookdale style porcelain inkstand decorated with polychrome enamels and gilding.

c.1825. Some damage to applied flowers. Tray 25.5 cm length   JJB

£475

One of a set of six porcelain plates probably by Coalport with polychrome enamels and gilding.

c.1825. 21.5 cm diameter   HBW

£450 for six.

John Rose Coalport porcelain sucrier with scenes painted in pink and gilding.

c.1810. Gilding slightly rubbed. 15 cm length   HBW

£190

DANIEL
(c.1826–46)

Daniel & Son were a Stoke decorating firm contracted to decorate Spode's bone china. Henry and Richard Daniel set up as potters in their own right c.1826. Not surprisingly their wares (mostly porcelain, but some earthenware after 1835) are finely decorated. After Henry Daniel's death in 1841, his son Richard (in partnership with Nathaniel Solomon) continued until 1846.

Recorded pattern numbers run from 3500 to 8925, although not all patterns within that range have been recorded or identified. Berthoud (1982) has also recorded a fractional pattern number $\frac{1}{124}$. It should be remembered that pattern numbers were sometimes repeated over a long period. Dates of introduction given below are approximate.

Pattern numbers	Date of introduction
3500–4700	1826–30
4700–6800	1830–40
6800–8925	1840–46

Further Reading

Michael Berthoud. *H. & R. Daniel 1822–1846* (Micawber Publications, Wingham, 1980).
Michael Berthoud. *The Daniel Tableware Patterns* (Micawber Publications, Wingham, 1982).
Geoffrey Godden. 'H. & R. Daniel of Stoke, c.1822–1846', *Staffordshire Porcelain* (Granada, 1983).
Leonard Whiter. *Spode* (Barrie & Jenkins, 1970, reprinted with new colour illustrations, 1989).

Rare Daniel porcelain coffee cup and saucer painted in red enamel and gilded.

c.1827+. Saucer 14 cm diameter; cup 6 cm height   G

£50

Porcelain box attributed to Daniel with threaded lid painted in polychrome enamels and gilded.

c.1830. Hairline crack. 8 cm diameter   AD

£340

Reverse.

Daniel porcelain 'Savoy' shape plate painted in polychrome enamels and gilded to highlight elaborate relief-moulding.

c.1840. Painted pattern number 8766. 24 cm diameter   G

£140

Savoy is a name assigned by Berthoud (1980) to a 'conjectural group' of later shapes with elaborate moulded scrolls. 8766 is a previously unrecorded pattern.

Daniel porcelain miniature octagonal shape teapot with a pear knop, painted in polychrome enamels and gilded.

c.1830. 4.6 cm height   G

£300

This shape is a close imitation of the Spode octagonal shape, which can be distinguished by its apple knop. Examples of both shapes are illustrated in Miller & Berthoud.

DAVENPORT
(1794–1887)

Primarily an earthenware manufacturer, Davenport made hybrid hard-paste porcelains c.1800–8 and bone china afterwards. The earlier porcelain wares were seldom marked, and many have yet to be identified.

Tea wares and dessert wares had separate runs of pattern numbers. The tea ware pattern numbers and approximate dates of introduction for this period are as follows:

Pattern numbers	Date of introduction
1–500	c.1794–1820
500–800	c.1820–30

349

The dessert ware pattern numbers for this period were:

Pattern numbers	Date of introduction
1–150	c.1800–15 (none recorded)
150–200	c.1815–20
200–300	c.1820–5
300–400	c.1825–35

For later Davenport porcelains see chapter 17.

Further Reading

Terence A. Lockett. *Davenport Pottery and Porcelain, 1794–1887* (David & Charles, 1972).

Terence A. Lockett. 'The Davenport Porcelains, 1794–1887', *Staffordshire Porcelain* (Granada, 1983).

Terence A. Lockett and Geoffrey A. Godden. *Davenport China, Earthenware, Glass* (Barrie & Jenkins, 1989).

Davenport bone china plate with polychrome 'Table Pattern'.

c.1805–10. Painted mark 'Longport'. 23 cm diameter   W

£185 for plate; £385 for rectangular stand.

The stand is illustrated in Lockett & Godden.

Davenport bone china coffee cup with 'Old English' handle and saucer painted in polychrome enamels and gilded.

c.1830. Printed ribbon mark with anchor and 'DAVENPORT'; painted pattern number 781. Cup 6.5 cm height; saucer 15 cm diameter   BG

£375

A Davenport coffee cup in this shape is illustrated in Berthoud.

Davenport bone china plate painted in polychrome enamels and gilded.

c.1850. Blue printed ribbon mark with anchor 'DAVEN-PORT'. 24 cm diameter   JJB

£125

DERBY PORCELAINS

There was a confusing number of firms and works operating in the city of Derby during this period. In many cases wares made by earlier partnerships were carried on by subsequent partnerships, and it is not always possible to attribute the unmarked wares certainly.

I have followed the lead of Geoffrey Godden by dividing porcelain production into the following periods:

The first, or Planché period, c.1748–56
William Duesbury I, c.1756–86
William Duesbury II, c.1786–95
Duesbury & Kean, c.1795–1811
Robert Bloor, c.1811–48
The King Street Partnerships, c.1848–1935
Derby Crown Porcelain Co., 1876–90
Royal Crown Derby Co. Ltd, c.1890 to the present day

There are fine collections of Derby porcelains at the Royal Crown Derby Museum at the factory and at the Derby Art Gallery.

Further Reading

Gilbert Bradley. *Derby Porcelain* 1750–98 (T. Heneage, 1990).
John Twitchett. *Derby Porcelain* (Barrie & Jenkins, 1980).

WILLIAM DUESBURY II (c.1786–95)

Derby tureen with blue enamel and gilt, raised white enamel beading.

c.1790. Red painted Derby mark with crown, crossed batons, six dots and script 'D'. 13 cm diameter   KK

£220

DUESBURY & KEAN (c.1795–1811)

Duesbury & Kean porcelain wine cooler painted in purple and green enamels and gilded.

c.1795–1800. Handles repaired; some rubbing of gilding, liner missing. Red painted Derby mark with crown, crossed batons and script 'D';'775' beneath. 33 cm height including lid   D

£775

A wine cooler in this shape by Duesbury & Keane is illustrated by Twitchett.

Duesbury & Kean porcelain teacup and saucer with mazarine ground and gilding, 'Vitta of Horace' painted scene by Robert Brewer.

c.1810. Red painted Derby mark with crown, crossed batons, six dots and script 'D'. Cup 5.5 cm height; saucer 14 cm diameter   TV

£800

Twitchett illustrates a trio with identical border and very similar scenes (plate 287). Robert Brewer (1775–1857) joined Derby c.1797, remaining until the factory's closure in 1848.

ROBERT BLOOR (c.1811–48)

Robert Bloor was working at the New Works Derby from 1811 and at the Old Works, Derby from 1815. In 1828 his mental health deteriorated so badly that the management of the firm was assumed by James Thomson. In 1844, Bloor's sole surviving descendant took out a statute of lunacy on Bloor, and managed the firm herself until 1848. Much of the equipment was sold to Robert Boyle in Fenton, and some of the moulds then passed to Copeland.

352

Rare Bloor Derby porcelain garniture with bombé-shaped bough pot decorated with applied flowers and polychrome enamels.

c.1835. Considerable damage to flowers. Vases 15.5 cm height; centre 16.5 cm height   D

£2,500

A complete set such as this one is rare, and always desirable. A pair of William Duesbury & Co. bombé-shaped bough pots, c.1775–80 are illustrated in Twitchett. He also illustrates a later Bloor example filled with porcelain flowers similar to the example here.

Bloor Derby porcelain jug with mazarine ground and gilded decoration.

c.1815–20. Printed circular mark with crown 'BLOOR DERBY'. 11.8 cm height excluding handle   T

£240

Gilding on a mazarine ground in this manner was done at Bloor c.1815–20, and is illustrated in Twitchett.

Bloor Derby porcelain plate 'View in Devonshire'.

c.1820. Red painted Derby mark with crown, crossed batons, six dots and script 'D'; gilder's number 44 in red. 22 cm diameter   W

£250

Bloor Derby porcelain plate, pink ground with birds painted in polychrome enamels and gilded by John Whitaker.

c.1810–25. Red painted Derby mark with crown, crossed batons, six dots and script 'D'; decorator's number 37 in red. 22 cm diameter   D

£600

John Whitaker left Derby in 1826.

Bloor Derby porcelain round shape cream jug decorated with blue, green and red enamels and gilding.

c.1830. Red painted Derby mark with crown, crossed batons, six dots and script 'D'; 'c6'. 10 cm height   TV

£60

A round shape teapot with an identical handle to that of this cream jug is illustrated in Miller & Berthoud.

The following two cream jugs are in a silver shape which matches the teapot which follows (shape also illustrated in Miller & Berthoud). Note the exact reproduction of a silver shape including the rivet at the base of the handle.

Bloor Derby porcelain cream jug with a silver shape.

c.1815. Red painted Derby mark with crown, six batons, six dots and script 'D'. 13.3 cm height   TV

£80

Bloor Derby porcelain silver shape cream jug with hand-painted scene 'In Sutherland' and fine gilding.

c.1815. Small hairline crack. Red painted Derby mark with crown, crossed batons, six dots and script 'D'. 13.3 cm height   HBW

£265

This Derby porcelain cream jug is the same shape as the one above; however, the hand-painted scene makes it considerably more valuable.

Bloor Derby porcelain silver shape teapot painted in pink, blue and green enamels and gilded.

c.1810–20. Gilding slightly rubbed. Red painted Derby mark with crown, crossed batons, six dots and script 'D'. 13 cm height   G

£220

354

Like many of their contemporaries Bloor Derby introduced Imari or Japan patterns. These patterns were immensely popular and are still in production today at the Royal Crown Derby works. The most popular was, and remains, the 'Witches' pattern.

Bloor Derby porcelain 'Witches' pattern dish painted in polychrome enamels and gilded.

c.1825. Red painted Derby mark with crown, crossed batons, six dots and script 'D'. 22 cm diameter　　WG

£120

Bloor Derby porcelain Japan pattern cup and saucer painted in polychrome enamels and gilded.

c.1825. Red painted Derby mark with crown, crossed batons, six dots and script 'D'. Cup 5 cm height; saucer 14.6 cm diameter　　WG

£95

Bloor Derby porcelain Japan pattern sucrier painted in polychrome enamels and gilded.

c.1825. Red painted Derby mark with crown, crossed batons, six dots and script 'D'. 10 cm height　　WG

£195

FLIGHT & BARR WORCESTER
(1783–1840)

The various Flight and Barr partnerships can be very confusing, and so have been grouped together in chronological order. The only work dealing exclusively with these wares is Henry Sandon's volume.

　　After the retirement of Dr Wall from the Worcester Porcelain Co. in 1774 (see chapter 15), the firm deteriorated under the management of William Davis. Thomas Flight purchased the factory in 1783. Five years later his son John began to take an active part in the management of the firm, and laid the groundwork for the vast improvement in the firm's productions. It was in 1788, on the occasion of his visit to Worcester, that George III gave the factory its first Royal Warrant.

John Flight died prematurely in 1792, leaving the management of the firm to his elder brother Joseph, who took as a partner Martin Barr. The firm was then styled Flight & Barr (1792–1804). Martin Barr junior became a partner in 1804, occasioning another change of style to Barr, Flight & Barr (1804–13). William Billingsley, the famous ceramic artist, arrived in 1812.

Martin Barr senior died, and his son George joined the firm as a junior partner, the style changing to Flight, Barr & Barr (1813–40). In 1815 Thomas Baxter arrived at Worcester, although he had previously decorated some of their wares in his London studio. Joseph Flight died in 1838, and when his will was proved in 1840, the firm was amalgamated with their arch rival Chamberlain's (see above).

A visit to the Royal Worcester factory and the Dyson Perrins Museum on the factory grounds is a must for anyone interested in pottery and porcelain. Reservations for factory tours should be made in advance: (0905) 23221.

Further Reading

Henry Sandon. *Flight and Barr Worcester Porcelain*, 1783–1840 (Antique Collectors' Club, Woodbridge, 1978).

FLIGHT PERIOD (1783–92)

Early Flight period Worcester porcelain plate with Imari pattern of 'Prunus and Chrysanthemums' painted in polychrome enamels and gilded.

c.1783–5. Crescent mark painted in underglaze blue. 23.5 cm diameter   B

£200

FLIGHT & BARR (1792–1804)

Flight & Barr porcelain shanked sucrier with gilded pattern.

c.1792–6. 14 cm height   JJB

£135

A part tea service in this shape is illustrated in Sandon.

Porcelain beaker attributed to Flight & Barr with pink ground, painted with polychrome enamels and gilded.

c.1800. 10 cm height   D

£650

A similar beaker with a matching jug, part of a set for cider, wine or lemonade is illustrated in Sandon. Another beaker of the Barr, Flight & Barr period is also illustrated.

BARR, FLIGHT & BARR (c.1804–13)

Barr, Flight & Barr porcelain bow-fronted desk stand with pink ground, painted rural scene in polychrome enamels and gilding.

c.1804–7. One inset chipped. Painted marks 'Flight & Barr Coventry Street London'; 'Barr, Flight & Barr Worcester Manufacturers to Their Majesties and Royal Families'. 18 cm length   D

£950

The gilded Greek Key border appears on a number of Flight & Barr pieces (c.1800) illustrated in Sandon. The gold vermiculi used in conjunction with the border seem to appear during the Barr, Flight & Barr partnership. Sandon illustrates an identically shaped Barr, Flight & Barr desk stand. The confusing marks are explained by the fact that the London retail operation continued to operate as Flight & Barr after the younger Barr had joined the Worcester partnership occasioning the restyling of the firm there as Barr, Flight & Barr.

Barr, Flight & Barr porcelain teapot and stand painted with orange and black enamels and gilded.

c.1805. Cover repair. Painted mark 'Barr, Flight & Barr Worcester Manufacturers to Their Majesties'. Teapot and lid 18.5 cm height; stand 18 cm length   D

£395

A breakfast service with a teapot in this shape is illustrated in Sandon.

Barr, Flight & Barr porcelain plate with grey marbled ground, painted with red enamel and gilded.

c.1807–13. Impressed mark 'BFB' with crown; printed mark with Prince of Wales feathers 'BARR FLIGHT & BARR/Royal Porcelain Works/WORCESTER/London House/FLIGHT & BARR/Coventry House' surrounded by the words 'Manufacturers to their Majesties Prince of Wales and Royal Family Established 1751'. 21 cm diameter   D

£75

This type of false marble ground was copied from the Continental porcelain manufacturers. Sandon illustrates a number of pieces.

Barr, Flight & Barr porcelain candlestick with beaded border, painted with polychrome enamels and gilded.

c.1804–13. Restored chip. Impressed mark with crown 'BFB'. 11 cm length   HBW

£175

A hexagonal candlestick with a London shape handle, with similar gilding and beaded border, is illustrated in Sandon.

Barr, Flight & Barr porcelain cream jug with interesting rustic bat-prints after Pyne on a yellow ground.

c.1806–13. Impressed mark with crown 'BFB'. 11.5 cm height   HBW

£120

The reverse shows two men scything the wheat and a woman and two children carrying sheaves from the field. Sandon illustrates a beaker with the former bat-print. Barr, Flight & Barr introduced bat-prints to the Worcester factory. According to Sandon, 'A fairly large amount of bat printing was done by Barr, Flight & Barr, perhaps not as much as was done by some of the Staffordshire factories, and the process did not seem to retain its popularity at Worcester for very long.' Unfortunately the Worcester bat-prints have not been as well documented as those of some other factories.

Barr, Flight & Barr porcelain bowl with pink ground and gilding.

c.1810. Slightly rubbed gilding. 18.5 cm diameter   G

£75

FLIGHT, BARR & BARR (c.1813–40)

A pair of Flight, Barr & Barr low porcelain urns, painted with sea shells in polychrome enamels on a pink ground with beaded rims and gilding.

c.1825. 10 cm height   LM

£1,400

It is often thought that most of these fine shell-paintings were done by Thomas Baxter (1782–1821), but Sandon points out that there were a number of shell-painters at Worcester. Several other examples of shell-paintings are illustrated in Sandon. He also illustrates an urn in this shape painted with a goldfinch. Shells and feathers, which required considerable skill to paint well, are particularly sought by collectors. Both were motifs in which the Flight, Barr & Barr firm excelled.

Flight, Barr & Barr porcelain gadroon-edged dish, with painted sprays of flowers in red, pink and blue enamels and gilded.

c.1830. Impressed crown mark 'FBB'. 30 cm length   WG

£90

This pleasing gadroon-edged shape was used a great deal by Flight, Barr & Barr c.1820–40. A number of examples with various decorative treatments are illustrated by Sandon.

Flight, Barr & Barr porcelain coffee cup and saucer with mazarine ground and gilding.

c.1817–25. Cup 7.7 cm height; saucer 15 cm diameter   JJB

£135

This handle shape is illustrated in Berthoud, plate 708. Gilding on a mazarine ground in a similar pattern is illustrated by Sandon.

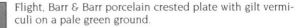

Flight, Barr & Barr porcelain crested plate with gilt vermiculi on a pale green ground.

c.1830. Chip to reverse. Printed mark with crown 'Royal Porcelain Works/Flight, Barr & Barr/WORCESTER/& COVENTRY ST. LONDON'. 22 cm diameter   HBW

£95

Sandon says that Flight & Barr and Chamberlain probably produced the greater proportion of the armorial and crested services made in England. The gadroon shape was often used by Flight, Barr & Barr and other manufacturers for armorials. An armorial service in this shape and a border with gilt vermiculi on a salmon ground, as seen here, is illustrated in Sandon. The crest is not one of those listed in Sandon, nor does it appear in the standard work on crests, *Fairbairn's Crests*.

GRAINGER'S WORCESTER
(c.1805–1889)

Thomas Grainger was born in 1783 and apprenticed to his uncle Robert Chamberlain in 1798. He was admitted Freeman of Worcester in 1805, and the earliest signed and dated piece of Grainger porcelain is dated 1807, so he must have established his own manufactory between 1805 and 1807. Grainger's original partners were John Wood and Stephen Wilkins.

The Grainger family were involved in porcelain manufacture at Worcester under a succession of partnerships as follows. It has been noted by Geoffrey Godden and by the Sandons that throughout these partnerships the firm was sometimes referred to simply as Grainger & Co. or Thomas Grainger & Co.

Grainger, Wood & Co.	c.1805–11
Grainger & Co.	1811–14
Grainger, Lee & Co.	1814–37
George Grainger (& Co.)	1837–1902

Thanks to the exhaustive research of Henry and John Sandon we can attribute and date these porcelains by their pattern numbers, which were often painted on the reverses or bases of the pots. The approximate dates of introduction of the earlier pattern numbers were:

Pattern numbers	Date of introduction
1–390	c.1805–12 (Pattern book 1, now lost)
391–1642	1812–25 (Pattern book 2)
1595–2019; 1x–464x	1825–31 (Pattern book 3)

Henry and John Sandon report a number of early Grainger pots with pattern numbers which do not match the factory pattern books at the Dyson Perrins Museum. The problem is further obscured as pattern book 1 is lost. Patterns up to the middle of pattern book 5 have been transcribed and printed in Sandon & Sandon (see chapter 17 for post-1830 patterns). One possible solution is that there must have been another early pattern book which was abandoned and numbering begun again.

A visit to the Worcester factory and the Dyson Perrins Museum on the factory grounds is a must for anyone interested in pottery and porcelain. Reservations for factory tours should be made in advance: (0905) 23221.

For later Grainger porcelains see chapter 17.

Further Reading

Henry and John Sandon. *Grainger's Worcester Porcelain* (Barrie & Jenkins, 1989).

Rare early Grainger & Co. hybrid hard-paste porcelain plate with Japan pattern painted in blue and orange enamels and gilded.

c.1807–10. The body is marred by 'spitting' and grit, caused by impurities in the body. Hairline crack. Painted pattern number in red 140. 21.5 cm diameter   G

£85

Sandon & Sandon illustrate a New Oval shape tea service in this pattern.

Grainger, Lee & Co. porcelain Japan pattern dessert dish, painted in enamels over a blue transfer-print and gilded.

c.1825. Painted mark in blue Grainger, Lee & Co. Worcester. 21 cm length   G

£90

HICKS & MEIGH
(c.1803–22)
HICKS, MEIGH & JOHNSON
(c.1822–35)

Hicks & Meigh at Shelton produced porcelains only after c.1816, and under the style Hicks, Meigh & Johnson after c.1822. These are unmarked, but pattern numbers may identify some of their wares. The approximate dates of introduction of the porcelain pattern numbers were:

Pattern numbers	Date of introduction
128–1100	1816–25
1100–2094+	1825–35

Further Reading

Geoffrey Godden 'The Hicks & Meigh Porcelains, c.1817–1835'. *Staffordshire Porcelain* (Granada, 1983).

Hicks, Meigh & Johnson porcelain teacup and saucer, red ground with painted scenes in polychrome enamels and gilded.

c.1830. Pattern number 1924 painted in red. Saucer 15 cm diameter; cup 5 cm height   G

£95

Berthoud illustrates a teacup in this shape (which he has named 'Bee Moulded') in pattern 1955.

Hicks, Meigh & Johnson porcelain teapot with pink ground painted in polychrome enamels and gilded.

c.1835. Spout slightly damaged. Painted pattern number 2054. 13 cm height   HBW

£250

A teapot in this shape in pattern 2094 is illustrated in Godden 1983. The cream jug shape which would match this teapot is illustrated below.

Hicks, Meigh & Johnson porcelain cream jug painted in polychrome enamels and gilded.

c.1835. Painted pattern number 2094. 8 cm height   HBW

£225

A most unusual shape, which can be associated with the teapot above.

MACHIN
(c.1802–38)

Joseph Machin was involved in a number of different Machin partnerships at Burslem:

Joseph Machin (& Co.) also known as Machin & Co., c.1802–18
Machin & Baggaley, also known as Machin & Co., c.1814–33
Machin & Potts, c.1834–8

Few Machin wares are marked and so only slowly has a representative selection been assembled by specialists. At this time only Machin tea wares have been identified, but it is assumed that they made other wares. The approximate dates of introduction of porcelain pattern numbers were:

Pattern numbers	Date of introduction
1–681	c.1809–31
681–1263+	c.1831–8

Further Reading

Philip Miller. 'The Machin porcelains, c.1809–1840', *Staffordshire Porcelain* (Granada, 1983).

Machin porcelain Old Oval shape cream jug painted with red, green and blue enamels.

c.1810. Painted pattern number 1. 14.5 cm length   WG

£42

Machin bone china ring-handled teacup and saucer with blue ground, painted in blue enamel and gilded.

c.1815. Painted pattern number in red 172. Cup 5.8 cm height; saucer 14 cm diameter WG

£65

MASON
(c.1800–53)

Miles Mason started as a Chinaman, a dealer in pottery and porcelain, principally dealing in the Chinese export wares which were flooding Britain in the 18th century. In the 1790s when these imports ceased, Mason decided to manufacture porcelain himself. At first he entered into a partnership with Thomas Wolfe and Thomas Luckcock at Liverpool, under the style Thomas Wolfe (& Co.). They manufactured a hybrid hard-paste type china 1796–1800. Given the brief duration of this partnership, the wares are not common. Despite the style of the company, these wares are often referred to as Wolfe-Mason porcelains.

Miles Mason then moved to Lane Delph in Staffordshire, manufacturing hybrid hard-paste porcelain and earthenwares and, later, bone china. In 1813 his sons succeeded him under the style George & Charles Mason, producing earthenwares and porcelain. They introduced Mason's Patent Ironstone, which was to become the mainstay of the firm, in that same year (see chapter 10). George Mason retired in 1830, and the firm was continued under the style C. J. Mason & Co. by Charles Mason c.1830–48 and after a bankruptcy c.1849–53.

Most of the Mason wares showed a very strong Chinese influence, although some of the wares such as the bat-printed tea wares were entirely European in design. Porcelain manufacture was eventually phased out in favour of Mason's successful Ironstone.

Miles Mason's most commonly found wares are bone china with a pale blue transfer-print of the chinoiserie pattern variously known as 'Broseley', 'Temple' or 'Pagoda'. These sometimes bear a mock Chinese seal mark. It is common practice to attribute all similar wares to Mason, but there were literally dozens of factories making them. Many Mason's wares are unmarked, as it was then usual to mark only one piece out of a service, so painted pattern numbers can be useful for identification. The pattern numbers and approximate dates of introduction are as follows:

Firm	Pattern numbers
Miles Mason, 1800–10	1–c.986
G. & C. Mason, 1810–20	none
C. J. Mason, 1830–40 tea wares and ornaments	1–824
C. J. Mason, 1840+ tea wares and ornaments	824+
C. J. Mason, 1830+ dinner wares	1008–3355

Further Reading

Geoffrey Godden. *Godden's Guide to Mason's China and the Ironstone Wares*, 3rd edn (Antique Collectors' Club, Woodbridge, 1991).

Reginald Haggar. 'Miles Mason's porcelains, c.1803–1813, and continued by his sons', *Staffordshire Porcelain* (Granada, 1983).

Reginald Haggar and Elizabeth Adams. *Mason Porcelain & Ironstone, 1796–1853* (Faber & Faber, 1977).

Miles Mason 'Veranda' pattern porcelain saucer, transfer-printed in blue underglaze and gilded.

c.1810. 14 cm diameter　　　　　　　　　　　　G

£25

This is a good example of the type of wares produced to satisfy the market for Chinese porcelains. Underglaze painted blue porcelains were eventually replaced with blue transfer-printed wares. A tea set in this pattern is illustrated in Godden.

One of a pair of George & Charles Mason porcelain plates with relief-moulding highlighted in pink and orange enamels and gilded.

c.1813–18. Two chips on rim restored. 21.5 cm diameter
　　　　　　　　　　　　　　　　　　　　　　VH

£140 the pair.

A dessert service in this shape with botanical paintings in the centres is illustrated in Godden.

George & Charles Mason porcelain teacup and saucer, relief-moulded with blue ground hand-painted rural scene and gilding.

c.1815. Hairline crack. Saucer 14 cm diameter; cup 6 cm height　　　　　　　　　　　　　　　　　　VH

£180

A matching coffee can with this shape handle is illustrated in Berthoud.

Miles Mason porcelain dish with a 'Shepherd' bat-print coloured with enamels.

c.1805–8. Restored. 21 cm diameter   VH

£160

A teapot with this pattern is illustrated in Godden. He has noted the 'unnatural looking trees favoured by Mason's engraver, particularly those on the right which look rather like two haystacks one on top of the other, and the three tier effort in the centre.'

MINTON
(c.1793 to the present day)

From the time that Thomas Minton founded this firm at Stoke c.1793 until 1884, the firm went under a number of styles, passing through various Minton partnerships. Thomas Minton had worked as an engraver for the Caughley factory, and blue transfer-printed earthenwares were among his earliest productions. Minton's first period of porcelain production was c.1800–16. These earlier wares are typical of their period and many patterns and shapes are quite similar to those made by Spode, just a few hundred yards away. Porcelain production recommenced c.1824, continuing until the present day. Minton produced fine porcelains, often with magnificent gilding and hand-painting. By the time of the Great Exhibition of 1851, Minton was on its way to its reputation as the finest porcelain manufacturer of the Victorian period. The dates given below are approximate dates of introduction of the Minton pattern numbers. Early Minton porcelains are seldom marked with their pattern numbers.

Pattern numbers	Date of introduction
1–560	c.1793–1809
560–948	c.1809–15
1–2865 (new series)	c.1824–35

Further Reading

Elizabeth Aslin and Paul Atterbury. *Minton 1798–1910* (Victoria & Albert Museum, 1976).
Paul Atterbury and Maureen Batkin. *The Dictionary of Minton* (Antique Collectors' Club, Woodbridge, 1990).
N. Robert Cumming. *Minton Bone China in the Early Years* (N. Robert Cumming, 1988).
Geoffrey Godden. *Minton Pottery & Porcelain of the First Period, 1793–1850* (Barrie & Jenkins, 1968).
Geoffrey Godden. 'The Minton porcelains, 1793 to the present day', *Staffordshire Porcelain* (Granada, 1983).
Joan Jones. *Minton* (Shire Publications, Princes Risborough, 1992).

Minton porcelain Old Oval shape cream jug, with painted scenes in polychrome enamels and gilded.

c.1805. Painted pattern number in gold 58. Hairline crack. 10 cm at spout   AD

£85

Quite a number of pieces in this pattern are recorded by Cumming. The matching sugar box is illustrated in Geoffrey Godden's An *Illustrated Encyclopaedia of British Pottery and Porcelain*, and the pattern book drawings for this tea service are illustrated in Godden's *Minton*.

Minton bone china gilded ring-handled teacup and saucer.

c.1810. Painted pattern number in gold '197'. Some rubbing to gilding. Cup 6 cm height; saucer 14 cm diameter   G

£75

Minton ring-handled cups are illustrated in Berthoud and in Godden's *Minton*.

Minton porcelain mazarine ground plate painted in polychrome enamels and gilded.

c.1810. Painted blue Minton crossed swords mark. Painted pattern number 780. 18.5 cm diameter   HBW

£220

367

Minton porcelain dessert dish.

c.1825. Pattern number 34 painted in red. 22 cm length G

£70

Minton 'Oxford embossment' porcelain dessert service dish with birds in compartments painted in polychrome enamels.

c.1830. 26.5 cm length   V

£170

A number of pieces from a service in this shape painted with landscapes, rather than birds, is illustrated in Godden's *Minton*. Godden noted that such elaborately moulded and decorated services are often erroneously attributed to the Rockingham factory. Today it is the fashion to attribute them to Ridgway (see below). The fact of the matter is that many firms, some of them small and relatively unknown, were producing wares like these at the time.

Minton porcelain hot water jug or coffee pot, painted in polychrome enamels and gilded.

c.1830. 21.6 cm height   G

£685

The rare and unrecorded shape and the very fine quality of decoration justify this rather high price.

Minton porcelain coffee cup with 'French Loop' handle and saucer with green and yellow grounds painted in polychrome enamels and gilded.

c.1830. Painted pattern number in red 1567/B. Saucer 15 cm diameter; cup 6.5 cm height   G

£85

A Minton teacup with a 'French Loop' handle is illustrated in Berthoud.

Minton porcelain coffee can with rare pinched loop handle painted in orange enamel and gilded.

c.1800–10. 6.3 cm height   TA

£28

Pinched loop handle Minton cups are illustrated in Berthoud and in Godden's *Minton*.

Minton porcelain dish painted in green enamels over a transfer-print and gilded.

c.1830. Very slight chips to reverse. 24 cm length   G

£55

Minton porcelain mug with gilding and red transfer print.

c.1830. Initialled in gold 'TMG'. 12.6 cm height   JJB

£445

369

Reverse.

NEW HALL
(c.1782–1835)

The New Hall pottery was operated at Shelton by a series of five partnerships c.1782–1835. Not very long ago, any porcelains with floral sprays of a 'cottagey' sort were automatically attributed to New Hall. Thanks to exhaustive research into pattern numbers, it is now appreciated that the factory made a wide range of table wares, from the less expensive tea wares with the simple floral decorations to fine dessert wares with painted landscapes. Likewise the shapes changed with the times, the earlier wares often in neo-classical shanked shapes, succeeded by Bute shape, the London shape and the more ornate shapes which became fashionable after the Regency period. The body was a hybrid hard-paste type porcelain until c.1814 when bone china was introduced. The pattern numbers and their approximate date of introduction are:

Pattern numbers	Date of introduction
1–200	c.1782–90
200–c.350	c.1790–5
c.350–c.500	c.1795–1800
c.500–c.650	c.1800–5
c.650–c.850	c.1805–10
c.850–1100	c.1810–15
1100–2350	c.1815–25
2350–c.3639	c.1825–35

Further Reading

David Holgate. New Hall Porcelain (Faber, 1987).

David Holgate. 'New Hall porcelains (c.1781–1835) and some contemporary manu-facturers', Staffordshire Porcelain (Granada, 1983).

A. de Saye Hutton. A Guide to New Hall Porcelain Patterns (Barrie & Jenkins, 1990).

New Hall hybrid hard-paste type porcelain coffee can and saucer with underglaze blue transfer chinoiserie print.

c.1800, saucer 13 cm diameter; can 6.2 cm height   V

£60

New Hall hybrid hard-paste type porcelain teapot stand with blue 'Trench Mortar' transfer-print.

c.1795. Some rubbing on gilding. 19.5 cm length   JM

£70

This pattern is also known as 'Malayan Village' or 'Pearl River House'. Robert Copeland illustrates an example painted in underglaze blue on Chinese export porcelain and a contemporary engraving of a Malayan village which shows a house with a similar construction. (*Spode's Willow Pattern & Other Designs after the Chinese*). This pattern was also used on earthenware by Spode and on porcelain by Caughley.

New Hall bone china plate with black overglaze Adam Buck print.

c.1815. Painted mark 1109. 21 cm diameter   G

£125

Adam Buck (1759–1833) was a painter and engraver who exhibited regularly at the Royal Academy and the British Institute at Suffolk Street c.1795–1833.

New Hall hybrid hard-paste type porcelain saucer with blue bat-print and gilding.

c.1800. 13.5 cm diameter   G

£70

New Hall hybrid hard-paste type porcelain teacup and saucer, painted chinoiserie scene in polychrome enamels (pattern number 789).

c.1810. Saucer 14 cm diameter; cup 5 cm height   G

£140

A boat-shape cream jug in this pattern is illustrated in de Saye Hutton.

New Hall bone china jug with relief-moulded hunting scene highlighted with polychrome enamels.

c.1820–30. Marked with painted black X. 16 cm height excluding spout and handle   T

£145

Illustrated in Holgate and in de Saye Hutton.

New Hall bone china relief-moulded dessert dish, blue ground border with white floral reserves, centre painted in polychrome enamels and gilded.

c.1820. Some slight rubbing to gilding. Pattern 1478. Printed mark New Hall in double circle. 22.9 cm length   G

£240

Rare New Hall bone china relief-moulded dessert dish, blue ground border with white floral reserves, with scene painted in enamels and gilded.

c.1820–5. Painted pattern number 2229. 28 cm length   G

£325

New Hall bone china teapot stand with charming Adam Buck black bat-print and black rim, c.1815. Painted pattern number 1109. 19 cm length   G

£325

RIDGWAY
(1802–54)

The brothers Job and George Ridgway were partners at the Bell Works, Shelton from 1792 until 1802 when Job founded the Cauldon Place factory. Little is known of the wares made by the Ridgway brothers at Bell Works, although in 1797 they were in a partnership with William Smith. Job Ridgway's sons joined the firm and then c.1830 split up, with William Ridgway moving to the Bell Works, and John Ridgway continuing at Cauldon Place. Although few Ridgway porcelains have a factory mark, most have pattern numbers, which can be helpful in identification. Ridgway's fractional pattern numbers used on tea wares are quite distinctive, but it is important to remember that fractional pattern numbers with a 2 denominator were used by Samuel Alcock, Coalport, Grainger's Worcester and briefly at Rockingham.

The dates of the early 19th-century Ridgway firms and the pattern numbers introduced on porcelain are as follows:

Date	Firm	Pattern numbers
c.1802–08	Job Ridgway	none recorded
c.1808–14	Job Ridgway & Sons	1–487
c.1814–30 ·	John & William Ridgway, John Ridgway & Co. or J. & W. Ridgway & Co.	

1814–20	teawares $\dfrac{2}{xxx} - c.\dfrac{2}{900}$
	dessert wares c.650 – 1000
	ornamental wares $\dfrac{3}{xxx} - \dfrac{3}{700}$
1820–30	teawares $\dfrac{2}{900} - \dfrac{2}{2500}$
	dessert wares 1000 – 2000
	ornamental wares $\dfrac{3}{700} - \dfrac{3}{800}$

The first designs to appear in William Ridgway's pattern books after 1830 were relief-moulded stonewares, of which he was one of the earliest manufacturers (see chapter 23). However William did make some porcelain. For later John Ridgway porcelains see chapter 17.

Further Reading

Geoffrey A. Godden. *Ridgway Porcelains*, 2nd edn (Antique Collectors' Club, Woodbridge, 1985).

Geoffrey Godden. 'The Ridgway porcelains, 1808–1856', *Staffordshire Porcelain* (Granada, 1983).

Ridgway porcelain sucrier in Old Oval shape, peach ground with gilding.

c.1815–20. Pattern number painted $\frac{2}{434}$. 13 cm height   W

£235

A sucrier in this shape is illustrated in Godden.

Ridgway porcelain relief-moulded sauce tureen and attached stand, with pink ground and gilding.

c.1815. Painted pattern number $\frac{2}{277}$. 17 cm height   VH

£190

Several of these tureens with different decorations and part of a dessert service in this elaborately moulded shape are illustrated in Godden 1985.

Superb John Ridgway porcelain dish, with a transfer-print painted in polychrome enamels.

c.1820. 21.5 cm length   G

£200

Godden 1985 illustrates a plate with the same print, also coloured with polychrome enamels.

Ridgway porcelain dessert plate with blue ground, finely painted scene in the centre in polychrome enamels and gilded.

c.1822–5. Painted pattern number 941. 22.5 cm diameter   TV

£225

Godden 1985 illustrates part of a dessert service in this shape in pattern 892.

SPODE
(1770–1833)

Josiah Spode II is credited with the introduction of bone china to Staffordshire. However, there are a few very rare examples of Spode hybrid hard-paste porcelains, which may have been experimental. After the death of Josiah Spode III, the firm was purchased by William Taylor Copeland (who had been a partner in Spode's London retail business) and Thomas Garrett, under the style Copeland & Garrett from 1833–1847 (see chapter 17).

Spode marked many of its wares, most often with 'SPODE' painted in red, although many other marks can be found. However, like many other manufacturers of the period, they frequently only marked a few pieces in a service, and pattern numbers are very useful on wares which have some on-glaze decoration. Some of these may also have underglaze transfer-print, if they were embellished with enamels. The following pattern list is taken from Robert Copeland's article.

Pattern numbers	Date of introduction	Pattern numbers	Date of introduction
1–150	1800–1	2601–2700	1817–18
151–300	1802	2701–2800	1819
301–450	1803	2801–3000	1820
451–600	1804	3001–3250	1821
601–750	1805	3251–3500	1822
751–900	1806	3501–3750	1823
901–1050	1807	3751–4000	1824
1051–1200	1808	4001–4150	1825
1201–1350	1809	4151–4300	1826
1351–1500	1810	4301–4450	1827
1501–1650	1811	4451–4500	1828
1651–1800	1812	4501–4600	1829
1801–1950	1813	4601–4700	1830
1951–2100	1814	4701–5050	1831
2101–2200	1815	5051–5200	1832
2201–2500	1816	5201–5350	1833
2501–2600	1817		

Spode collectors will want to join the Spode Society, which has regular meetings and outings, also publishing a very fine *Review*. The membership secretary is Mrs Rosalind Pulver, PO Box 1812, London NW4 4NW. The Spode factory (Church Street, Stoke-on-Trent ST4 1BX) has a fine museum and factory tours are also available by prior arrangement.

Further Reading

Robert Copeland. 'Spode porcelains, c.1797–1833, and the succeeding firms', *Staffordshire Porcelain* (Granada, 1983).

David Drakard and Paul Holdway. *Spode Printed Ware* (Longman, 1983).

Leonard Whiter. *Spode* (Barrie & Jenkins, 1970, reprinted with new colour illustrations 1989).

The Spode Society. *Recorder & Review* (1986 to the present day). Referred to as SSR in the text.

Spode Bute-shaped teacups and coffee cans usually have handles, like those shown below. Indeed, this shape handle was used at other factories, but is so commonly found in Spode that they are often referred to as Spode-type handles. Many of these are illustrated in Berthoud and in Whiter.

Spode bone china coffee can and saucer with mazarine ground, painted in polychrome enamels and gilded.

c.1806. Can 6.5 cm height; saucer 13.5 cm diameter   TA

£75

Berthoud illustrates this Spode can (pattern 893) and an unidentified can in this pattern, which he conjectures may be a Spode can with a 'non-conforming handle'.

Spode bone china coffee can and saucer, gilded.

c.1804. Painted mark in red 'SPODE'; painted pattern number 471. Saucer 14 cm diameter; cup 6 cm height   G

£90

Spode bone china coffee can and saucer with landscapes painted in polychrome enamels and gilded.

c.1810. Cup 6.2 cm height; saucer 14 cm diameter   JJB

£255

Spode bone china coffee can with bat-print and gilding.

c.1803. Some rubbing to gilding. 6.3 cm height   TA

£40

This romantic scene has been recorded by Drakard & Hold-way as P212. The print was included on the Hester Savory service which was made by Spode in 1802 or 1803.

Spode's pattern 488 (shown in the two illustrations below) is a typical example of an English factory copying a design from the Chinese. The pattern was used at several factories which would have used different pattern numbers.

Spode bone china Bute-shape teacup and saucer with chinoiserie pattern (number 488) painted in orange and blue enamels and gilded.

c.1804. Saucer 14 cm diameter; cup 6 cm height   G

£50

Spode bone china plate with chinoiserie pattern painted in red and blue enamels and gilded.

c.1804. Painted in red 'SPODE'; pattern number 488. 18 cm diameter   WG

£45

Early Spode bone china cache-pot and stand painted in pink and green enamel on black ground and gilded.

c.1803. Painted pattern number 311. Rubbing on vase. Height with stand 12.5 cm   W

£215

Spode bone china New Oval cream jug painted in iron red and magenta enamels and gilded.

c.1806. Painted mark 'SPODE'; pattern number 889. 14 cm length   TV

£150

Part of a tea service in pattern 889 is illustrated in SSR (vol. 1, p. 187).

Spode bone china sucrier in New Oval shape with 'Bamboo' pluck-and-dust print in red with gilding.

c.1807. Painted pattern number 981 in gold. 11 cm height
                                                                     W

£195

This 'Bamboo' pattern also appears in blue and yellow or black overwashed in green. It was one of only six all-over 'pluck-and-dust' patterns produced at Spode. The technique was costly, and was usually confined to borders. Several examples are illustrated by Drakard & Holdway.

Spode bone china vase painted in Spode's *Japan* pattern in polychrome enamels and gilded (pattern number 967).

c.1807+. 16.4 cm height WG

£500

Whiter writes that Spode's *Japan* was the most popular of the firm's Japan patterns. Its immense popularity led to its continuation for well over a century, being produced on earthenwares as well as bone china. The pattern was imitated by several other potters. Whiter illustrates several Spode examples.

One of a pair of Spode bone china potpourris or violet baskets with polychrome enamel painted flowers and gilding on mazarine ground.

c.1808+. Painted mark 'SPODE'; painted pattern number 1166. 11 cm length including handles D

£1,450 the pair.

The beautiful pattern 1166 was extremely popular and continued for decades. It remains popular and Whiter has called it the most sought after Spode pattern. He points out that the gilding in graduated scales took extreme skill. He also mentions that at one time, disreputable dealers removed the marks from Spode's 1166, in the hope of passing them off as products of what were then more fashionable factories. Whiter illustrates several examples.

Spode bone china New Shape jar painted in polychrome enamels and gilded.

c.1809. Slight rubbing to gilding. Painted mark 'SPODE'; painted pattern number 1227. 16 cm height G

£350.

Vases in pattern 1227 are illustrated in SSR (vol. 1, p. 50) and Whiter. A New Shape jar in pattern 1444 is also illustrated in Whiter.

379

Spode bone china sucrier in New Oval shape, blue ground with gilding.

c.1810. 11 cm height   W

£245

Pair of Spode bone china spill vases with bat-printed flower sprays coloured with green enamels, beaded borders and gilded.

c.1812. Painted mark 'SPODE'; painted pattern number 1676. 11.5 cm height   D

£695

Most factories applied their beaded borders in moulded groups of four or five. Spode's beads are each individually modelled and applied. Spode introduced bat-prints in 1803. These prints could convey exceptionally fine detail. The bat-print on the left is number P107 and that on the right is P106 (both illustrated and numbered by Drakard & Holdway).

Garniture of three Spode bone china vases with named ornithological subjects painted in polychrome enamels and gilding.

c.1813. The two small vases have painted pattern numbers 1805. One small vase has damaged rim. Large vase 15.5 cm height; small vases 12 cm height   LM

£2,500

A complete garniture of this kind is rare, and as a decorative item, as well as a collector's item, it is very desirable. Named ornithological, entomological or botanical paintings always give the item an added interest.

Spode bone china envelope shape dessert plate, with flower embossment reserved on a pale blue ground, painted flowers in enamels and gilded.

c.1814. Painted mark 'SPODE'. Painted pattern number 2027. 23.5 cm diameter V

£200

An envelope plate in pattern 2057, which is quite similar to pattern 2027, is illustrated in Whiter.

Here we have an interesting example of a Spode pattern with the Chinese *famille rose* pattern which it copied (below). The pattern was later engraved and printed on Spode's Stone China, filled in with polychrome enamels, illustrated in Whiter.

Spode bone china plate painted in polychrome enamels in a *famille rose* palette.

c.1814. Painted mark 'SPODE'; painted pattern number 2083. 21 cm diameter RS

£58

Chinese *famille rose* porcelain plate.

c.1760–70, reign of Emperor Chien Lung, Ching Dynasty. Riveted repair. 21 cm diameter RS

£24

Bone china footed bowl with ornithological subjects painted in polychrome enamels and gilded, possibly Spode.

c.1815. 22 cm diameter LM

£750

Spode bone china New Dresden shape relief-moulded coffee pot painted in polychrome enamels and gilded.

c.1817. Knop restored. Painted mark in red 'SPODE'; painted pattern number 2527. 27 cm height   AD

£680

The shape here Is known as Vase shape when not embossed. Coffee pots are scarce, and are more valuable than teapots.

Spode dessert tureen with cover and stand with butterfly handles and knop, painted in pink and green enamels and gilded.

c.1818. Painted mark 'SPODE'. 15 cm height   LM

£300

This shape was revived by W. T. Copeland & Sons during the early 20th century (see chapter 21).

Spode bone china plate with painted scene of Monmouth.

c.1825. Painted mark in grey 'SPODE/Monmouth'. 23.5 cm diameter   V

£198

A plate in this shape is illustrated in Whiter.

Spode embossed china twig-handled dessert centre with flowers painted in polychrome enamels and gilded.

c.1821. Mark painted in red 'SPODE'; painted pattern number 3127. 25 cm length without handles   G

£300

A twig-handled comport in pattern 2102 is illustrated in Whiter.

Spode introduced their Feldspar Porcelain in 1821. It often carries a special transfer-printed backstamp. The feldspar replaced part of the Cornish stone in the body, giving the ware extra strength. Robert Copeland has noted that it was frequently used for dinner services with armorial bearings, possibly because such services would undergo heavy use.

Spode Feldspar Porcelain dessert dish with red ground and gilding, some of it 'raised paste'.

c.1824. Printed Spode Feldspar Porcelain mark. Painted pattern number 3997. 21.2 cm length   JJB

£345

One of a pair of Spode Feldspar Porcelain armorial plates painted in polychrome enamels and gilded.

c.1821–33. Printed Spode Feldspar Porcelain mark. 25.4 cm diameter   JJB

£355 the pair

Spode bone china London shape cup and saucer painted in polychrome enamels and gilded.

c.1822. Painted pattern number 3404. Cup 6.2 cm height; saucer 14 cm diameter   JJB

£145

Unusual Spode bone china covered jar with applied moulded flowers, painted with polychrome enamels and gilded.

c.1830. Painted mark in brown 'SPODE'. 8 cm height   B

£350

OTHER MANUFACTURERS

Factory Z porcelain sucrier, with pink ground and gilding.

c.1810. Incised mark 'No 204'. 14 cm height including knop
T

£220

You will not find any porcelains marked 'Factory Z'. This is a name assigned by scholars to a group of porcelains which appear to have been made by one manufacturer, whose identity remains uncertain c.1800–20 or earlier. There have been a number of suggestions, and it now seems possible that the group were manufactured at Stoke by the Wolfe & Hamilton partnership.

Rare Yates bone china bowl with floral decoration painted in polychrome enamels and gilded.

c.1820. 18 cm diameter
G

£125

John Yates, an earthenware manufacturer was established by 1770. He began production of a hard bone china c.1820. The firm was succeeded by Yates & May in 1835. This is a recently recognised class of porcelains: see Geoffrey Godden, 'John Yates and the Yates & May porcelains, c.1822–1843', *Staffordshire Porcelain* (Granada, 1983).

Rathbone bone china 'London' shape cup and saucer with pale blue transfer-printed 'Broseley' or 'Temple' pattern.

c.1820–5. Transfer-printed mark in blue 'R' in a sunburst. Saucer 14 cm diameter; cup 5.5 cm height
G

£45

Samuel and John Rathbone operated at Tunstall 1812–35, with their brother William 1818–23. It is not certain whether they manufactured porcelains before 1818. These Broseley pattern wares are very common, although they are not often marked. Unlike most blue transfer-prints, Broseley was almost always used on porcelain or bone china, rather than earthenware. Many of these wares were very poor quality. However the pattern was also produced by some of the best firms, so look for clear prints and crisp body detail.

Swansea porcelain plate with garden flowers painted in enamel by William Pollard and gilded.

c.1820. 21 cm diameter   TV

£1,250

This plate was probably decorated by T. & J. Bevington during the period when they were decorating Dillwyn white ware.

UNATTRIBUTED PIECES

One of a pair of porcelain dessert plates painted in polychrome enamels and gilded.

c.1825. 22.5 cm diameter   JJB

£475 the pair

'Coalbrookdale' porcelain pen tray encrusted with flowers and painted in polychrome enamels.

c.1825. Some damage to applied flowers and one crack. 28 cm length   W

£185

The term 'Coalbrookdale' is applied to any pieces encrusted with flowers after the manner used at Coalport, where some pieces were actually marked 'Coalbrookdale'.

Very unusual porcelain dish on feet with modelled yellow birds and flowers painted in polychrome enamels and gilded. 25 cm length   W

£750

385

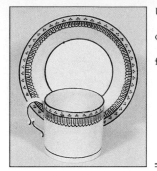

Unusual English porcelain coffee can and deep saucer.

c.1800. Saucer 13 cm diameter; can 6 cm height   G

£120

Porcelain shanked coffee cup and saucer with floral decoration painted in polychrome enamels and gilded.

c.1795. Cup 6.5 cm height; saucer 13.5 cm diameter   G

£110

Staffordshire porcelain cream jug decorated in polychrome enamels and gilded.

c.1820. Painted mark 'No 776' (the 6 is indistinct) in grey. 9.5 cm height   G

£70

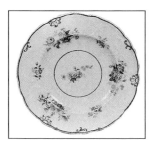

Embossed bone china dessert plate bat-printed with gilding.

c.1820. 21 cm diameter   RS

£65

Porcelain cache-pot painted in polychrome enamels and gilded.

c.1815–20. 14.5 cm height   AD

£680

Unusual large porcelain vase with blue ground, painted in polychrome enamels and gilded, with applied flowers.

c.1830. Some damage to flowers, no restoration. 45 cm height   AD

£1,050

Porcelain patch box with threaded lid painted with fruit and flowers in polychrome enamels and gilded.

c.1830. Small chip restored. 8 cm diameter   AD

£320

Reverse.

Porcelain plate with blue ground painted with fruit and flower cartouches and landscape centre in polychrome enamels and gilded.

c.1820. 23 cm diameter   JM

£160

Porcelain ale jug, mazarine ground with a scene painted in polychrome enamels and gilded.

c.1824. 21.5 cm height   BG

£675

Porcelain jug with lavender sprigging, claret band at neck and gilding.

c.1820. Sprigged mark with 75. 11.7 cm height   G

£120

Porcelain teacup and saucer painted with blue and orange enamels and gilded.

c.1810. Cup 5.6 cm height; saucer 14 cm diameter   JJB

£85

Porcelain coffee can with purple ground and brown enamelling and gilding.

c.1805. 5.8 cm height   JJB

£145

Porcelain cream jug with transfer-printed outline filled with polychrome enamels.

c.1810. Small chip at base. 10 cm height   TA

£68

Porcelain cream jug painted in orange, green and pink enamels.

c.1810. Painted pattern number 401. 10.3 cm height   TA

£68

One of a pair of porcelain plates with blue ground, painted botanical centres in polychrome enamels and gilded.

c.1820. Painted pattern number 865. 24 cm diameter   TV

£300 the pair

Porcelain tureen stand with mazarine and yellow grounds and gilding.

c.1825. Painted pattern number $\frac{2}{1082}$. 31.5 cm length   JJB

£185

Porcelain plate with mazarine ground, centre landscape painted in polychrome enamels and gilded.

c.1830. 23 cm diameter   JJB

£245

Porcelain coffee can with 'Dragons in Panels' pattern painted in polychrome enamels and gilded.

c.1805. Painted pattern number 281. 6.4 cm height   JJB

£125

This popular colourful pattern (also known as 'Bishop Sumner') was made by many factories including Chamberlain's Worcester, Spode, Minton and Coalport.

Pastille burners for the burning of aromatic pastilles were usually in novelty forms such as cottages. The pastilles were made of mixtures of cinnamon, aromatic oils, gum and willow charcoal.

Porcelain pastille burner flower-encrusted and painted in polychrome enamels.

c.1830. Stress crack to base; small repair. 9.5 cm height D

£150

Large porcelain pastille burner painted in polychrome enamels and gilded with applied modelled decoration.

c.1840. 13.5 cm height   D

£195

Staffordshire porcelain pastille burner painted in polychrome enamels with applied decoration.

c.1830. 18 cm height   BG

£875

Porcelain jug with sprigged lavender flower sprays.

c.1830. Inscribed initials 'M. W.' in gold. Lavender applied pad mark with 'No. 1'. 20 cm height   G

£125

Stirrup cups were handed to people in saddles during a hunt, and thus did not need a base on which to rest. The Greeks called these *rhytons*. The fox and the hound were the shapes most often made in England.

Porcelain fox stirrup cup painted in red and black enamels, and gilded.

Hairline cracks. 11.5 cm length   D

£475

Porcelain hound stirrup cup painted in black and red enamels and gilded.

12 cm length   D

£475

17 PORCELAIN 1830–1900

A LTHOUGH the artistic and technical achievements of the British porcelain manufacturers before 1830 were considerable, it was only after 1830 that the wares developed to the point that they became internationally renowned for their excellence.

The early part of this period was dominated by the neo-rococo style. Later tablewares
were often simple and quite 'modern'. *Japonisme*, a craze which pervaded the ceramics industry after exhibition of Japanese wares at South Kensington in 1862 and Paris in 1867
will be seen in any number of the pieces in this section.

Technical developments were very important. The chief development of the period was
Parian, which is covered in chapter 19. Another important porcelain development was
pâte-sur-pâte. In general, the industry considerably refined their porcelain bodies.

Disruptions in Europe during 1848 and later during the Franco-Prussian War (1870–1)
brought many French and German ceramicists to Britain. The best known of these was
Léon Arnoux, perhaps the greatest ceramicist of the Victorian period. His notebooks in
the Minton Archives show an unremitting search for improvements of glazes, enamels
and bodies. Many of the most famous designers, modellers, painters and decorators of
the period were immigrants, including Marc Louis Solon, Albert Carrier de Belleuse, Louis
M. Jahn, Pierre Émile Jeanest, Émile Lessore, W. William Mussill and Hughes Protât.

At the cheaper end of the market lithographs, mostly imported from Germany, aerography and liquid gold were introduced. These wares were under considerable pressure
from foreign imports, and many of the firms producing them might not have survived if
W. H. Goss had not created a craze for crested china (see chapter 20).

Further Reading

Geoffrey Godden. *Encyclopaedia of British Porcelain Manufacturers* (Barrie & Jenkins, 1988).
Geoffrey Godden ed. *Staffordshire Porcelain* (Granada, 1983).
Geoffrey Godden. *Victorian Porcelain* (Herbert Jenkins, 1961).

SAMUEL ALCOCK
(c.1826–59)

Samuel Alcock started as a potter at Burslem and Cobridge c.1826. He produced china,
Parian and earthenwares at Burslem until 1859 and at Cobridge until 1853. Although the
wares were not generally of the class made at some of the major factories, some of the
wares were very fine. The firm's relief-moulded Parian jugs are of excellent quality.

Few of Alcock's porcelains bear factory marks, but painted pattern numbers are frequently found, given here with approximate dates of introduction:

Pattern numbers	Date of introduction
400–9999	1822–c.1840
$\frac{1}{xxxx}$	first half of the 1840s
$\frac{2}{xxxx}$	second half of the 1840s
$\frac{3}{xxxx}$	first half of the 1850s
$\frac{4}{xxxx}$	second half of the 1850s

Further Reading

Dr Geoffrey and Mrs Alma Barnes. 'The Samuel Alcock porcelains, c.1822–1859', in Godden 1983.

Samuel Alcock porcelain low comport with scene of 'Kelso Abbey' painted in enamels with red and pink grounds, and gilding.

c.1845. 24 cm length   G

£120

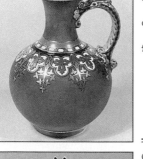

Samuel Alcock porcelain cup with serpent entwined handle and saucer painted in polychrome enamels with pale green ground and gilded.

c.1840. Saucer 17 cm diameter; cup 7 cm height   G

£75

Samuel Alcock porcelain jug, painted in polychrome enamels on matt orange ground and gilded.

c.1850. Painted pattern number $\dfrac{3}{9079}$. 19 cm height   T

£118

One of a pair of unusual porcelain starburst dishes attributed to Samuel Alcock, painted in polychrome enamels and gilded.

c.1830s. Small chip. 15 cm diameter   AD

£230 the pair.

Pieces of dessert services with this pattern are illustrated in Godden, *Encyclopaedia of British Porcelain Manufacturers* (1988).

Large Samuel Alcock porcelain vase with flowers and rural scenes on reverse, painted in polychrome enamels and gilded.

c.1840. Painted pattern number $\frac{2}{877}$. 13.5 cm height   G

£450

Samuel Alcock porcelain low comport painted in polychrome enamels and gilded.

c.1855. Painted pattern 'No $\frac{3}{7575}$'; diamond registration mark for 6 January 1855, parcel 4. 25 cm length   G

£220

Porcelain inkstand with blue ground, painted in polychrome enamels and gilded, attributed to Samuel Alcock.

c.1840s. 1 knop restored, one inkwell without liner. Tray 37 cm length; candlestick 12 cm height; wells 11 cm height.
    BG

£780

Samuel Alcock porcelain candlestick painted in polychrome enamels and gilded.

c.1845. Painted pattern number $\frac{2}{5995}$;   painter's   tally number 7. 7.2 cm height   TA

£68

BELLEEK
(1863 to the present day)

Belleek Pottery (Ltd) are best known for their eggshell-glazed Parian wares with fine marine inspired decorations, applied flowers or woven into baskets although they produce unglazed Parian figures. The Belleek Collectors' Society publishes *The Belleek Collector* c/o The Belleek Pottery Ltd, Belleek, Co. Fermanagh, Northern Ireland.

Further Reading

G. M. Smith. *Belleek Porcelain and Pottery* (Toucan Press, Guernsey, 1979).

Belleek glazed Parian vase with view of 'The River Erne, Ballyshannon' painted in polychrome enamels and gilded.

c.1880s. Printed mark. 25.2 cm height   S

£880

Belleek glazed Parian jardinière.

c.1890. Printed mark with dog, tower and harp reading 'BELLEEK/CO. FERMANAGH IRELAND'. 27 cm height   BG

£1,275

BROWN-WESTHEAD, MOORE & CO.
(1861–1904)

In 1861 the partnership between Thomas Chappell Brown-Westhead and William Moore took over the Cauldon Works (formerly associated with the Ridgway family). When William Moore died in 1866, his brother James Moore took his place. A major reorganization was completed in 1882, with the new works covering eight acres and employing 1,500 people, making it the largest pottery in England. The firm continued until 1920 when it became Cauldon Potteries Ltd.

Brown-Westhead, Moore & Co. made a wide variety of good quality earthenwares and porcelains. Relatively few factory marks appear, which makes identification difficult. However, they registered quite a few of their designs and fractional pattern numbers with denominators from B to L are frequently found.

Brown-Westhead & Moore porcelain plate painted in polychrome enamels.

c.1870–5. Marked $\dfrac{B}{\dfrac{4995}{7}}$. 22.5 cm diameter

T

£46

Brown-Westhead & Moore porcelain pierced dessert plate
painted in enamels and gilded.

c.1865. Printed diamond registration mark for 3 July 1865,
parcel 7. Painted pattern number $\dfrac{B}{2126}$. 24 cm diameter

JJB

£165

This plate would be less expensive if the rim were not
pierced. Pierced rims require careful work, and always add
to the value of a pot.

Brown-Westhead & Moore porcelain plate painted in polychrome enamels and raised paste gilded border, pale blue
ground.

c.1870. Painted pattern number $\dfrac{B}{4240}$. 23.7 cm diameter

JJB

£72

COALPORT
(c.1790s and continued in The Potteries to the present day)

The early history of the Coalport factories is given in chapter 16. The united firm's styles
after 1830 are as follows:

c.1803–89	John Rose & Co.
c.1889–1951	Coalport China Company (John Rose & Co.) Ltd
1951 to present day	Coalport China Ltd (part of the Wedgwood Group)

397

The pattern numbers used by the combined factories after 1830 are fractional as follows:

Pattern numbers	Date of introduction
$\dfrac{2}{67} - \dfrac{2}{999}$; $\dfrac{3}{1} - \dfrac{3}{999}$; $\dfrac{4}{1+}$	c.1830–40
$\dfrac{4}{1} - \dfrac{4}{999}$; $\dfrac{5}{1} - \dfrac{5}{999}$; $\dfrac{6}{1}$	c.1840–50
$\dfrac{6}{1+} - \dfrac{6}{999}$; $\dfrac{7}{1} - \dfrac{7}{486}$	c.1850–60
$\dfrac{7}{486} - \dfrac{7}{999}$; $\dfrac{8}{1+}$	c.1860+

Visitors to the Ironbridge Gorge complex in Shropshire can see the Coalport museum, where many fine examples of the factory's wares are on display. The Clive House Museum, Shrewsbury also has a fine collection of Coalport wares.

Further Reading

Geoffrey Godden. *Coalport & Coalbrookdale Porcelains*, revised edn (Antique Collectors' Club, Woodbridge, 1981).
Michael Messenger. *Shropshire Pottery and Porcelain* (Shrewsbury Museums, 1976).

Coalport porcelain plate with green ground, painted in polychrome enamels and gilded.

c.1850–60. 24 cm diameter   AD

£110

Coalport porcelain 'Brewer Vase' with bright blue ground, painted in polychrome enamels (attributed to Thomas Dixon) and gilded. Modelled by Francis Brewer.

c.1840. 15 cm height   TV

£240

A drawing of this shape from a traveller's book is illustrated in Godden. The basic shape was made in various sizes.

Coalport porcelain teapot with gilding.

c.1891–1920. Printed mark with crown 'ENGLAND.COAL-
PORT/AD 1750'. 21 cm diameter   AF

£165

Coalport porcelain vase with mazarine ground painted in
polychrome enamels with raised paste gilding and enamels.

c.1881–91. Painted pattern number B1439. Printed green
mark with crown 'COALPORT/AD 1750'. 16 cm height HBW

£185

This design reflects the *japonisme* popular in the 1870s and
1880s.

Coalport porcelain mazarine ground dish with scene
painted in polychrome enamels with raised pasted gilding
and jewelling.

c.1881–91. Painted pattern number A9341. Printed mark
with crown 'COALPORT/AD 1750'. 13 cm length   HBW

£135

COPELAND & GARRETT
(1833–47)

The Copeland & Garrett partnership took over the Spode factory in 1833. They continued to produce many of the shapes and patterns used by Spode, but also produced many contemporary designs. They particularly excelled in coloured transfer-prints.

Many of the Copeland & Garrett bone china wares have painted pattern numbers which continued the Spode series (see chapter 16). The numbers as given in Robert Copeland's article are:

Pattern numbers	Date of introduction	Pattern numbers	Date of introduction
5351–5466	1834	6509–6700	1841
5467–5662	1835	6701–6819	1842
5663–5738	1836	6820–6991	1843
5739–5841	1837	6992–7128	1844
5842–6138	1838	7129–7342	1845
6139–6367	1839	7343–7547	1846
6368–6508	1840	7548–7747	1847

Further Reading

Robert Copeland. 'Spode porcelains, c.1797–1833, and the succeeding firms', *Staffordshire Porcelain* (Granada, 1983).

The Spode Society. *Recorder & Review* (1986 to the present day).

One of a pair of Copeland & Garrett bone china plates with green transfer-printed borders and polychrome enamel painted centres.

c.1843. Transfer-printed Copeland & Garrett mark; painted pattern number 6824/O. 24 cm diameter   JJB

£195 the pair

Copeland & Garrett bone china coffee can with pale blue 'Broseley' transfer-print.

c.1830s. Transfer-printed Copeland & Garrett mark with crown. 6.3 cm height   JJB

£52

This is a standard Spode shape and print continued by Copeland & Garrett.

DAVENPORT
(1794–1887)

Primarily an earthenware manufacturer, Davenport made hybrid hard-paste porcelains c.1800–8 and bone china after c.1808. Uniquely for a ceramics factory, Davenport also made glassware.

The tea ware pattern numbers for this period are as follows:

Pattern numbers	Date of introduction
800–1200	c.1830–40
1200–2200	1840–50
2200–3000	1850–65
3000–6000	1865+ (very few 4000+ and 5000+ patterns recorded)

The dessert ware pattern numbers for this period were:

Pattern numbers	Date of introduction
400–700	c.1835–45
700–1200	c.1845–55
1200–1700	c.1855–75
upper limit not known	

For earlier Davenport porcelains see chapter 16.

Further Reading

Terence A. Lockett. *Davenport Pottery and Porcelain, 1794–1887* (David & Charles, 1972).
Terence A. Lockett. 'The Davenport Porcelains, 1794–1887', *Staffordshire Porcelain* (Granada, 1983).
Terence A. Lockett and Geoffrey A. Godden. *Davenport China, Earthenware, Glass* (Barrie & Jenkins, 1989).

Davenport specialised in Japan pattern porcelains in the 1870s and 1880s. The patterns tend to be in the 3000–6000 range, so those with lower pattern numbers are slightly earlier examples.

Davenport bone china plate painted with Japan pattern in orange and blue enamels and gilded.

c.1850. Printed mark with crown; painted pattern number 1931. 22.5 cm diameter   JJB

£165

Davenport bone china teacup and saucer with Japan pattern painted in blue and orange enamels and gilded.

c.1860. Printed mark with crown 'DAVENPORT/LONGPORT/ STAFFORDSHIRE'. Painted pattern number 2614. Cup 5 cm height; saucer 14.5 cm diameter   JJB

£75

Davenport bone china pepper pot and miniature bowl painted with Japan pattern in orange and blue enamels and gilded.

c.1875. Pepper pot painted pattern number 4471/2; bowl 4471/6. Bowl also with printed mark 'DAVENPORT/LONG-PORT/STAFFORDSHIRE'. Pepper pot 8.3 cm height; bowl 6.5 cm diameter   JJB

£55 the pair.

Davenport bone china plate with sepia 'Duchess' painting and enamel and gold decoration, pierced border.

c.1880–7. Impressed mark 'DAVENPORT'. 23.5 cm diameter
                G

£120

This plate and another in the same shape with a landscape centre are illustrated in Lockett & Godden.

W. H. GOSS
(1858–1939)

William Henry Goss served an apprenticeship in the London retail offices of W. T. Copeland. He then went to Stoke to gain experience of potting, serving under John Mountford, who claimed to be the inventor of Parian. Goss learned well, for in 1858 he established his own firm for the manufacture of Parian, producing some models which were nearly identical to those of Copeland! Goss continued to produce Parian busts, figures and tablewares until c.1890. Today the firm is best remembered for their glazed Parian Heraldic Ware (see chapter 20).

Nicholas Pine has divided the production of the Goss factory into three periods, and they have been generally adopted by collectors. During the First Period (1858–87) William Henry Goss owned and ran the pottery, and most of the unglazed Parian wares were made. During the Second Period (1881–1930) the firm was managed by his three sons Adolphus, Victor and William Huntley Goss, and the chief product was Heraldic Porcelain. During the Third Period (1930–9), the firm was owned and managed by Cauldon Potteries, and earthenwares were introduced, although cheap crested china was still made.

Further Reading

Nicholas Pine. *Goss and Crested China* (Shire Publications, Aylesbury, 1984).
Nicholas Pine. *William Henry Goss* (Milestone Publications, Horndean, 1987).
Nicholas Pine. *The Concise Encyclopaedia and Price Guide to Goss China* (Milestone Publications, Horndean, 1992).

Goss glazed Parian covered jar decorated with turquoise enamel and gilding with modelled flower knop.

c.1860–85. Printed Goshawk mark. 8 cm height   CCC

£320

This jar may be found in plain white, with green enamelling or with a plain knop.

Goss glazed Parian three-handled tyg inscribed with verse by Adolphus Goss.

c.1890–20. Printed Goshawk mark. 11.7 cm height   CCC

£75

GRAINGER'S WORCESTER
(c.1805–1902)

George Grainger (& Co.) succeeded Grainger, Lee & Co. c.1839. They made a wide range of porcelains including Parian. The factory was bought by Royal Worcester in 1889 but continued as a separate operation until 1902. The approximate dates of introduction of pattern numbers 1831–45 are:

Pattern numbers	Date of introduction
396x – 1229x	1831–40
$1244x - 2008x; \frac{2}{1} - \frac{2}{680}$	1840–45
$\frac{2}{682}$	1845–

For earlier Grainger porcelains see chapter 16.

Further Reading

Henry and John Sandon. *Grainger's Worcester Porcelain* (Barrie & Jenkins, 1989).

George Grainger (& Co.) semi-porcelain plate with gadroon rim, celeste ground, painted in polychrome enamels and gilded.

c.1850. Chip to reverse. Impressed mark 'SP/GGW'. 24 cm diameter   G

£120

The impressed mark 'SP/GGW' or 'GGW/SP' was used c.1848–60 on the special 'Semi Porcelain' body.

Pair of George Grainger (& Co.) porcelain 'Hawthorn tapers'.

c.1897. Printed shield mark with 'G & Co/ESTAB-LISHED/1801' within shield;'ROYAL CHINA WORKS WOR-CESTER' in a circle around it; shape number 98; date code G (1897). 8.5 cm height   JM

£58

George Grainger (& Co.) reticulated porcelain vase.

c.1891–1902. Printed shield mark with 'G & Co/ESTAB-LISHED/1801' within shield; 'ROYAL CHINA WORKS WORCESTER' in a circle around it; 24 cm height   HBW

£265

During the second half of the 19th century Grainger made a speciality of reticulated porcelain, although they never approached the artistry of George Owen (see p. 486). Sandon & Sandon illustrate a number of these wares.

George Grainger (& Co.) porcelain frog ornamental container.

c.1897. Impressed shape number 330; date code 'G' (1897). 16 cm length   V

£170

George Grainger (& Co.) glazed Parian butter dish with gilding.

c.1860. Star crack to inside of lid. Painted mark 'G. Grainger Worcester'. 20.5 cm diameter of base   JM

£125

Grainger made a few Parian figures in the 1840s and 1850s. The Shinns note in *Victorian Parian China* (Barrie & Jenkins, 1971): 'Much later Grainger ware of the 1870s and 1880s is really a glazed Parian body, but it is not generally accepted as such.'

LOCKE & CO
(1896–1915)

The independent Worcester firm of Locke & Co. is relatively unknown, although they produced some good quality porcelains over a period of nearly two decades. Edward Locke had worked at Grainger's and Royal Worcester and in the Staffordshire Potteries. It is thought that Locke, who had advanced to foreman, was unhappy when Grainger's was taken over by Royal Worcester in 1889. In 1895 he resigned to establish his own factory.

Locke & Co. specialised in smaller ornamental porcelains. More than 1,000 shape numbers have been recorded to date. Although Locke stated that his designs were all original, it is not surprising that his products resemble those of the other two Worcester factories. In the early 20th century Locke also made crested china.

Further Reading

L. H. Harris and T. Willis. *An Exhibition of Porcelain Manufactured by* E. *Locke & Co, Worcester* (Dyson Perrins Museum, Worcester, 1989).

Locke & Co. porcelain vase with mirror image pattern.

c.1900. Printed Locke mark. 8.5 cm height   TV

£80

Locke & Co. porcelain bamboo triple vase.

c.1900. Painted pattern number 363. 19 cm height   TV

£145

Locke & Co. *pâte-sur-pâte* jar with green ground and gilding.

c.1900. Printed mark 'Locke & Co./Ltd/WORCESTER/ ENGLAND. 13.5 cm height   HBW

£225

MINTON
(c.1793 to the present day)

At the beginning of this period Minton suffered a seemingly great blow. Thomas Minton died in 1836, and his son Herbert went into partnership with Zachariah Boyle. However, only five years later Boyle left the partnership and Herbert Minton came into his own. During this period Minton produced the finest of porcelains, often with magnificent gilding and hand-painting. By the time of the Great Exhibition in 1851, Minton was on its way to establishing its reputation as the premier porcelain manufacturer of the Victorian period. Many of the later wares were marked, in distinct contrast to the earlier period. From 1842 Minton used an impressed date cipher as shown in the table below.

1842	1843	1844	1845	1846	1847	1848	1849
1850	1851	1852	1853	1854	1855	1856	1857
1858	1859	1860	1861	1862	1863	1864	1865
1866	1867	1868	1869	1870	1871	1872	1873
1874	1875	1876	1877	1878	1879	1880	1881
1882	1883	1884	1885	1886	1887	1888	1889
1890	1891	1892	1893	1894	1895	1896	1897
1898	1899	1900	1901	1902	1903	1904	1905
1906	1907	1908	1909	1910	1911	1912	1913
1914	1915	1916	1917	1918	1919	1920	1921
1922	1923	1924	1925	1926	1927	1928	1929
1930	1931	1932	1933	1934	1935	1936	1937
1938	1939	1940	1941	1942			

407

Painted pattern numbers appear on most porcelains after the early period, as follows:

Pattern numbers	Date of introduction
1–2865	c.1824–35
2865–6518	c.1835–44
6518–9999	c.1844–8
A1+	c.1848–68 tablewares
O1+	c.1848–96 ornamental wares

For earlier Minton wares see chapter 16.

Further Reading

Elizabeth Aslin and Paul Atterbury. *Minton 1798–1910* (Victoria & Albert Museum, 1976).
Paul Atterbury and Maureen Batkin. *The Dictionary of Minton* (Antique Collectors' Club, Woodbridge, 1990).
Geoffrey Godden. *Minton Pottery & Porcelain of the First Period, 1793–1850* (Barrie & Jenkins, 1968).
Geoffrey Godden. 'The Minton porcelains, 1793 to the present day', *Staffordshire Porcelain* (Granada, 1983).

Christopher Dresser was a distinguished botanical scholar, who is best known today for his avant-garde industrial designs. His designs were produced by Minton and several other manufacturers. Any ceramics which can be identified as having been designed by Dresser increase in value dramatically.

Minton porcelain vase with turquoise ground painted in polychrome enamels and gilded, possibly designed by Christopher Dresser.

c.1874. Impressed shape number 1717; printed Mintons globe mark in pink. 28 cm height AD

£320

A vase in this shape was illustrated in the catalogue of the exhibition *Christopher Dresser 1834–1905* (The Fine Art Society and Haslam & Whiteway Ltd, 1990).

Minton porcelain plate in polychrome raised paste enamels and platinum and gilded, designed by Christopher Dresser.

c.1882. Pink printed MINTONS mark. Diameter 24 cm AD

£250

Minton porcelain cup and saucer painted in polychrome enamels and gilded, designed by Christopher Dresser.

c.1875. Impressed mark MINTON/0/RB; painted pattern number in red G591. Cup 6.8 cm height; saucer 14 cm diameter WG

£40

A cup and saucer in this shape decorated with another of Dresser's patterns is illustrated in Widar Halen's *Christopher Dresser* (Phaidon/Christie's, Oxford, 1990). The G prefixed pattern numbers were used at Minton 1868–1900.

Minton porcelain butterfly-handle cup and saucer.

c.1869. Impressed mark MINTONS. Painted pattern number B251. Impressed diamond registration mark on cup for 7 April 1869. Cup 5.3 cm height; saucer 14 cm diameter JJB

£135

Minton porcelain 'Dresden Match Pot' with painted landscape in polychrome enamels and gilded.

c.1830–5. 12 cm height TV

£300

Godden 1968 illustrates the drawing of the Dresden Match Pot from the factory pattern books, as well as a photograph of a floral encrusted version.

Minton porcelain dessert dish with bat-prints.

c.1830–40. 25.4 cm length   AF

£11

One of these bat-prints appears on a 'Dresden embossed' shape bowl illustrated in Godden 1968. Minton used bat-prints from c.1805, reusing many of these on bone china tablewares of the 1830s and 1840s, such as the dish shown here. Unlike most other firms, Minton continued to use bat-printing into the 20th century. The normal cost of a dish like this one could be about £60.

One of a pair of Minton porcelain comports painted in polychrome enamels and gilded.

c.1847. Painted pattern number 9306. 23.3 cm diameter; 12 cm height   JJB

£375 the pair.

Minton had been working on their *pâte-sur-pâte* since the 1850s when in 1870 they brought M. L. Solon from France, where he had been using the technique for some time. He trained a number of other Minton artists in this technique, some of whom subsequently left Minton, bringing the technique to other firms. The body of these wares is Parian, usually tinted, with the cameo type design built-up with layers of slip. The technique was very time-consuming and costly.

Minton *pâte-sur-pâte* vase and cover with teal ground and gilding.

c.1893. Printed gold mark 'MINTONS/Manufactured for Philadelphia Caldwells'; impressed '2969/MINTONS'. Indistinct date cipher for 1893(?). 36 cm height   LM

£1,800

410

Reverse.

One of a pair of Minton *pâte-sur-pâte* plates gilded.

c.1893. Painted monogram MLS for Marc Louis Solon. Printed mark of globe with British and American flags, and A. B. Daniel & SONS/40 WIGMORE ST., LONDON'. Probably made for the Columbian Exhibition, Chicago 1893. 24 cm diameter   LM

£420 each

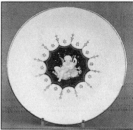

Rare mark on reverse.

A. B. Daniel, under various styles, was a London retailer whose mark is also found on Coalport wares. The firm closed in 1917.

JOHN RIDGWAY
(1830–54)

After dissolving his partnership with his brother William in 1830, John Ridgway continued alone. The firm specialised in fine quality tea and dessert wares, many of which have exceptional enamel painting and gilding. Few of these wares bear factory marks, but most will have distinctive painted fractional pattern numbers. The pattern numbers and their approximate dates of introduction follow: note that tea wares, dessert wares and ornamental wares each have their own runs of pattern numbers. This is important, because if you find a teapot with a pattern number of 6/4242, for example, it cannot be Ridgway, but must be the product of another factory. There is a tendency to assume that every piece of porcelain with a fractional pattern number is Ridgway, but other firms used fractional pattern numbers.

Tea ware pattern numbers	Date of introduction
$\dfrac{2}{2500} - \dfrac{2}{3800}$	1830–40
$\dfrac{2}{3800} - \dfrac{2}{9999}$	1840–9
$\dfrac{5}{\text{XXXX}}$	1850+

Dessert ware pattern numbers	Date of introduction
2000–5000	1830–40
5000–9014	1840–c.1848
$\dfrac{6}{\text{XXXX}} - \dfrac{6}{4000}$	c.1849–52
$\dfrac{6}{4000} - \dfrac{6}{7926}$	c.1852–c.1855
$\dfrac{6}{7926} +$	1855+

Ornamental pattern numbers	Date of introduction
$\dfrac{3}{700} - \dfrac{3}{1000}$	c.1820–40

For information on earlier Ridgway porcelains see chapter 16.

Further Reading

Geoffrey A. Godden. *Ridgway Porcelains*, 2nd edn (Antique Collectors' Club, Woodbridge, 1985).

Geoffrey Godden. 'The Ridgway porcelains, 1808–1856', *Staffordshire Porcelain* (Granada, 1983).

John Ridgway porcelain sucrier painted with green enamel and gilded.

c.1843–5. Pattern number $\dfrac{2}{2007}$. 14 cm height excluding knop   W

£195

Although this pattern number was introduced c.1830, the shape is c.1843–5. A covered bowl and stand with the same knop and handles illustrated in Godden 1985 also has an earlier pattern number $\dfrac{2}{2785}$. This is a good example of how it is *imperative* to look carefully at the shapes of the wares as well as the pattern numbers!

One of a pair of John Ridgway porcelain dishes painted in polychrome enamels and gilded.

c.1840. Painted pattern number in red $\frac{2}{4163}$. 26 cm length

G

£450 the pair

The wonderful gilding and fine flower-painting on these dishes shows John Ridgway's porcelains at their best.

One of a pair of John Ridgway porcelain plates with painted floral centre in polychrome enamels and gilded.

c.1845. Transfer-printed Royal Arms mark with 'JR'. Painted pattern number 7544. 26 cm diameter

JJB

£375 the pair

ROCKINGHAM
(c.1825–42)

The Bramelds at the Rockingham Works at Swinton began producing porcelains c.1825. As the firm shut down in 1842, it is not surprising that the wares are quite rare. However, because they were so well known in the 19th century, many wares have been wrongly attributed to the factory. Study of many of the contemporaries of the Rockingham works have resulted in the reattribution of many of these wares.

Further Reading

Alwyn Cox and Angela Cox. *Rockingham Pottery & Porcelain* 1745–1842 (Faber & Faber, 1983).
Arthur A. Eaglestone and Terence A. Lockett. *The Rockingham Pottery*, revised edn (David & Charles, Newton Abbot, 1973).
D. G. Rice. *Rockingham Ornamental Porcelain* (Adam Publishing Co., 1965).
D. G. Rice. *The Illustrated Guide to Rockingham Pottery & Porcelain* (Barrie & Jenkins, 1971).

Rockingham porcelain botanical plate painted in polychrome enamels and gilded.

c.1826–30. Small crack in footrim and chip. Written on reverse 'Noble Liverwort'. 25 cm diameter

AD

£460

A very similar plate is illustrated by Cox & Cox.

KERR & BINNS
(1851–62)
WORCESTER ROYAL PORCELAIN CO.
(1862–1976)

Kerr & Binns (c.1851–62) took over the works of Chamberlain & Co. at Worcester. When William Kerr left in 1862 the firm was restyled Royal Worcester Porcelain Co. Since 1976 the title has been Royal Worcester Spode. The firm made some of the finest porcelains of the Victorian era, vying with Minton for the Grands Prix at the international exhibitions.

A visit to the Worcester factory and the Dyson Perrins Museum on the factory grounds is a must for anyone interested in pottery and porcelain. Reservations for factory tours should be made in advance: (0905) 23221.

Further Reading

Derek Shirley. *A Guide to the Dating of Royal Worcester Porcelain Marks from 1862* (D. B. Shirley, 1982). Henry Sandon. *Royal Worcester Porcelain from 1862 to the Present Day*, 3rd edn (Barrie & Jenkins, 1978).

Kerr & Binns porcelain vase painted by James Bradley senior. Named scene 'On the Scheld' (Holland).

c.1853. Green ground with raised gilding. Printed uncrowned Worcester mark with '51' in centre. 17.5 cm height
TV

£255

James Bradley senior worked for Kerr & Binns c.1852–60s. His son James Bradley junior also worked as a painter for the factory.

Kerr & Binns porcelain vase with green ground and raised chased gilding, painted scene 'Arctic Snowy Owl and Prey' by Luke Wells.

Dated 1862. Printed Kerr & Binns shield mark with artist's initials in lower left hand corner. Slight restoration to rim. 23 cm height
TV

£1,200

This is probably the work of Luke Wells senior who worked at Worcester c.1852–65. His son Luke Wells junior also worked as a painter in the 1860s and 1870s. Kerr & Binns used this shield mark on their finest specimens 1854–62. The artist's initials are usually found in the lower left hand corner of the shield. This beautifully painted vase is quite rare, hence its value.

Royal Worcester porcelain shell on coral wall pocket.

c.1868. Impressed Royal Worcester mark and diamond registration mark for 25 March 1868, parcel 8. 28 cm length
TA

£88

This wall pocket is shown lying on its side, though it would have been hung vertically on the wall, with its pair.

One of a pair of Royal Worcester Vitreous Ware porcelain plates painted with a Cantonese subject in polychrome enamels and gilded by Po-Hing in a *famille rose* palette.

c.1870. Impressed Royal Worcester mark. 23.5 cm diameter
JJB

£575 the pair

Po-Hing is the probable name of a Cantonese painter who worked at Royal Worcester c.1870. A similar plate is illustrated in Sandon, colour plate V.

Pair of Royal Worcester porcelain candlesticks painted in blue enamel.

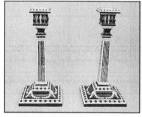

c.1875. Restored. Impressed shape number 488; printed Royal Worcester mark. 26.5 cm height
AD

£685

Shape number 488 ('tall square candlestick, pierced nozzle') was introduced in 1875.

Royal Worcester porcelain *Bamboo flower holder* with blue glaze decoration.

c.1877. Printed Royal Worcester mark; indistinct impressed diamond registration mark for 1877; incised shape number 631. 16 cm height
G

£75

This shape, introduced and registered in 1877, was a popular one. It is one of the many Worcester designs influenced by the *japonisme* of the 1870s and 1880s.

Royal Worcester porcelain relief-moulded naturalistic coffee cup and saucer painted in polychrome enamels.

c.1875. Impressed Royal Worcester mark. Cup 6.8 cm height; saucer 14 cm diameter   JJB

£45

Many manufacturers made tea wares in these naturalistic shapes during the 1870s. See Powell & Bishop example on p. 418.

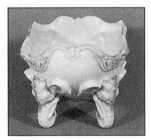

Royal Worcester Parian vase with glazed interior and black and orange enamel painting.

c.1880. Printed mark. 18 cm height   GCC

£200

For more about Royal Worcester Parian wares see chapter 19.

Pair of Royal Worcester ivory finish porcelain square bowls with elephant head feet, gilded.

c.1884. Registered number 5032. Impressed shape number 1019. 11 cm height   TV

£235

Shape 1019, 'square bowl with four elephant head feet', was introduced and registered in 1884.

Royal Worcester porcelain 'Tusk Ice Jug' painted in polychrome enamels with raised gilding.

c.1886. Printed Royal Worcester mark with date code for 1886. Impressed shape number 1116. 23 cm height   TV

£500

A very popular shape introduced in 1885, probably designed for iced water.

Royal Worcester ivory finish porcelain pierced 'Honeycomb vase' with landscape scenes painted in polychrome enamels with raised gilding.

c.1888. Small damage to piercing. Printed Royal Worcester mark with a 'Z' beneath (date code for 1888). Painted 'HP' in gold; gilder's mark '7' in red. 16 cm height   LM

£600

This vase is shape 1074 (introduced in 1885), and another with similar painting by Harry Bright is illustrated in Sandon.

Royal Worcester porcelain dessert plate painted in polychrome enamels and gilded.

c.1875. Impressed Royal Worcester mark. 23 cm diameter   JJB

£65

OTHER MANUFACTURERS

Porcelain tray, with painted landscape, peach ground, blue bands and raised paste gilding.

c.1875. 30 cm length   AD

£87

Staffordshire porcelain two-handled jug with painting in polychrome enamels of 'The improved holstein Dutch Breed', gilded.

c.1835. 19 cm height, excluding handle and spouts.   AD

£1,250

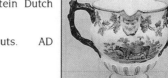

417

Wedgwood bone china cabaret tray with gold print.

c.1880. Printed Portland Vase mark. 32 cm length   TV

£200

Powell & Bishop porcelain relief-moulded teacup and saucer painted in turquoise enamel and gilded.

c.1871. Painted pattern number $\frac{3}{1525}$. Diamond registration mark for 15 February 1871. Cup 6.6 cm height; saucer 14.2 cm diameter   JJB

£48

This is typical of the naturalistic designs of the 1880s, see p. 416 for a similar Royal Worcester cup and saucer. Powell & Bishop (c.1866–78), who made porcelains for the cheaper end of the market, were succeeded by Powell, Bishop & Stonier.

Porcelain plate with pale green ground, raised enamel border and painted floral centre in polychrome enamels and gilded.

c.1875. Painted pattern number 212. 23 cm diameter   TA

£45

E. J. D. Bodley porcelain dessert plate painted in polychrome enamels, signed by A. J. Capey and gilded.

c.1890. Blue printed mark 'TRADEMARK/EJBD/BURSLEM'. 22 cm diameter   TA

£38

Celeste ground porcelain comport with polychrome enamel painted scene and gilding.

c.1870. Painted pattern number 1723. 27.2 cm diameter
TA

£85

Red ground porcelain plate with floral painting in polychrome enamels and raised paste gilding.

c.1860. Painted pattern number 1769. 22.7 cm diameter
JJB

£45

One of a pair of Brownfield porcelain vases, with lavender blue tinted body, applied modelled flowers and pierced decoration.

c.1875. One lid damaged. 24.8 cm height
G

£220

Copeland bone china plate with green ground with yellow swags and painting in polychrome enamels of 'Goodwood House'.

c.1850. Printed mark in green with interlaced script 'C's with 'COPELAND' beneath. 23.5 cm diameter
G

£145

Hill Pottery Co. porcelain sucrier painted in tan and brown enamels and gilded.

c.1865. 17.5 cm length   G

£70

Derby Crown Porcelain plate with 'Peacock' blue transfer-print.

c.1877–90. Blue transfer-printed mark with monogram below crown. DERBY impressed. 23.5 cm height   JJB

£48

'Peacock' was one of Derby Crown Porcelain's most popular prints, remaining in production until 1945.

Doulton Burslem Plate, hand-painted with raised gilding over matt glaze.

c.1887. Printed Doulton Burslem mark with crown; painted pattern number c1178 and painter's monogram TP; printed registration number 72067 (1887). 23 cm diameter   G

£120

For more information about Doulton Burslem, see chapter 21.

Marks on reverse.

18 PORCELAIN FIGURES BEFORE 1900

Successful figure models were often repeated by factories over many decades. However, a number of changes were likely to be made with the passage of time. Some changes in figures can be generalised, but just when and to what degree these changes took place at any given factory is variable. There are three main parts to a figure, the base or plinth, the support and the figure itself. The figure may be made up from many separately moulded parts, e.g. head, arms, hands, hats, accessories. In general at the end of the 18th century and during the 19th century the factories reduced labour costs by casting the figures in fewer parts. For example, what had been an individually modelled arm held aloft became a relief-moulded arm resting on the lap or held across the breast, so that it could be made part of the body mould. Accessories were eliminated or again were relief-moulded against the body or the base.

Early models often have simple pad bases, bases moulded to look like rocks, or in the better class of early figures often C-scroll rococo bases. Later in the 18th century these were frequently replaced with neo-classical plinths, often with vertical moulding.

The greatest challenge for the figure modeller is to design a figure which will not collapse in the kiln. In order to do this successfully, it is necessary to integrate a support into the design. It is easier to do this with seated figures, which can have a chair, bench or rock as a support. Standing figures may lean against a column or a tree. A bocage is a tree support, often decorated with applied modelled leaves and flowers, or in some cases with tiny pieces of clay which have been forced through a sieve.

While some figures, particularly those of domestic or farmyard animals, were probably modelled from life, many figures were modelled after sculptures or engravings (see the Derby Shakespeare figure).

As a rule I have avoided including damaged pieces. However, in the case of early figures, it would be impossible to present a wide selection if all damaged or restored figures were excluded. The damage or restoration in each case is noted.

Further Reading

Paul Atterbury, ed. *The History of Porcelain* (William Morrow, New York, 1982).

Peter Bradshaw. *18th Century Porcelain Figures 1745–1795* (Antique Collectors' Club, Woodbridge, 1981).

Geoffrey Godden. *English China* (Barrie & Jenkins, 1985).

Geoffrey Godden. *Eighteenth-century English Porcelain* (Granada, 1985).

Geoffrey Godden. *Encyclopaedia of British Porcelain Manufacturers* (Barrie & Jenkins, 1988).

Julia Poole. *Plagiarism Personified? European Pottery and Porcelain Figures* (Fitzwilliam Museum, Cambridge, 1986).

D. G. Rice. *English Porcelain Animals of the Nineteenth Century* (Antique Collectors' Club, Woodbridge, 1989).

John Sandon. *English Porcelain of the 18th and 19th Centuries* (Merehurst Press, 1989).

SAMUEL ALCOCK
(c.1826–59)

Samuel Alcock started as a potter at Burslem and Cobridge c.1826. He produced china, Parian and earthenwares at Burslem until 1859 and at Cobridge until 1853. Although the wares were not as a group of the quality made at some of the major factories, some of the wares were very fine. The firm's figures are charming, and often amusing.

For other Alcock porcelains see chapter 17.

Further Reading

Dr Geoffrey and Mrs Alma Barnes. 'The Samuel Alcock porcelains, c.1822–1859' in G. Godden, ed., *Staffordshire Porcelain* (Granada, 1983).

Alcock type figure of a drunken man and barrel with spill vase painted in polychrome enamels and gilded.

c.1835. Very slightly damaged. 10 cm height   G

£140

Rare and amusing Samuel Alcock figure of a begging dog.

c.1840. Impressed model mark 329 and 10 painted in red. 11.3 cm height   G

£400

The extreme rarity of this attractive model makes it more valuable than the preceding figure.

BOW
(c.1748–74)

Bow figures fall into two groups, those made before 1765 and those made afterward. The earlier figures are more finely modelled and generally of a higher standard. During the second period, many earlier models were revived, but often with elaborate rococo bases, as opposed to the simple rectangular or pad bases used on the earlier models.

Over 530 models of figures and groups have been recorded. Some of these were modelled after Meissen figures, others perhaps after contemporary English porcelain figures. Actors and actresses or political figures may have been taken from contemporary engravings.

For more information on the Bow porcelain factory see chapter 15.

Further Reading

Elizabeth Adams and David Redstone. *Bow Porcelain*, 2nd edn revised (Faber & Faber, 1991).
Peter Bradshaw. *Bow Porcelain Figures* (Barrie & Jenkins, 1992).
Anton Gabszewicz. *Bow Porcelain: The Collection formed by Geoffrey Freeman* (Lund Humphries, 1982).

Bow undecorated porcelain figure of a seated num.

c.1755. Restored. Mark '7' incised. 15.5 cm height   V

£290

This figure was after a Meissen prototype c.1744 modelled by J. J. Kändler. Bradshaw 1981 illustrates an example with just a little polychrome enamel decoration. The figure occurs with both hands on the book, one hand on the leg (as shown here) or with one hand poised in the air ready to turn the page. This shape was copied by Chaffers at Liverpool, probably from a mould made from a Bow original, as the Chaffers example is smaller (12.7 cm height). The Chaffers example has less fine detail, possibly because of the method of mould making, and also because the glaze is thicker, obscuring details.

Rare pair of Bow porcelain cooks painted in polychrome enamels.

c.1756. No restoration. Woman 17.5 cm height; man 18 cm height

£7,550 the pair

These figures may have been modelled after larger Chelsea examples, or from the original source, a book of engravings *Études prises dans le bas peuple, ou les cris de Paris*, published in five sets between 1737 and 1747. See Peter Bradshaw, 'Two Bow Cooks and the Cries of Paris', *Northern Ceramic Society Newsletter*, No. 84, December 1991. These figures have always been popular models with collectors and it is unusual to find them in unrestored condition.

Bow porcelain Nun and Fryer figures painted in polychrome enamels and gilded.

c.1755. Height of both 11 cm   D

£1,500

Adams & Redstone note that Nun and Fryer figures were among items which were sent to Richard Dyer for decoration outside the factory.

Bow made several series of figures to represent the Four Seasons. A list of these can be found in Bradshaw 1981 appendices H and I.

Bow porcelain figure of Winter painted in polychrome enamels and gilded.

c.1760–4. Some leaves in bocage restored. 16.5 cm height
                                                              BG

£1,275

An earlier version c.1755 with a simple pad base and without bocage (which is typical of the 1760s) is illustrated in Gabszewicz.

Porcelain figure of Winter, possibly Bow.

c.1757–60. Hand repaired. 14 cm height   BG

£500

Pair of Bow porcelain musician figures painted in polychrome enamels and gilded.

c.1770. Restoration to hands and instruments and lady's ribbon. 18.4 cm height   KK

£5,000 the pair.

Bow made many musician figures, usually issued in pairs. These are freely based on Meissen originals. Earlier Bow figures usually had plain flat or rectangular bases; the elaborate rococo footed bases shown here are more typical of the 1760s.

CHAMBERLAIN'S WORCESTER
(c.1791–1851)

Robert Chamberlain was the head of the decorating department at the Worcester Porcelain Company before he established his own china decorating studio c.1786 (see chapter 16). At first the firm decorated blanks from the Caughley Porcelain Works, but by c.1791 Chamberlain's had begun to manufacture *some* of their own porcelains. The first wares were hybrid hard-paste porcelains with a hard, glassy glaze. An enormous range of fine quality porcelains were manufactured over the next six decades.

A visit to the Worcester factory, still on the site of the Chamberlain works, and the impressive Dyson Perrins Museum on the factory grounds is a must for anyone interested in pottery and porcelain. Reservations for factory tours should be made in advance: (0905) 23221.

Further Reading

Geoffrey A. Godden. *Chamberlain-Worcester Porcelain 1788–1852.* (Barrie & Jenkins, 1982).

Chamberlain's porcelain foxhound with pink base painted in red and yellow enamels.

c.1820–40. Painted mark in red 'Chamberlain's Worcester'. 7 cm height   D

£485

Another example of this figure is illustrated in Rice.

Chamberlain's porcelain peacock with dry blue ground base painted in enamels and gilded.

c.1820–40. Painted mark 'Chamberlain's Worcester'. 8.5 cm height   HBW

£575

Chamberlain's made both peacocks and peahens. These were sometimes supplied with glass shades. They are thought to have been made in larger sizes. A very similar example is illustrated in Rice.

CHELSEA
(c.1744–69)

The Chelsea porcelain factory was founded by Nicholas Sprimont, a Huguenot silver-smith. The factory was patronised by courtiers and aristocrats, but declined when Sprimont's health failed. In 1769 the factory was taken over by William Duesbury I (see Derby below, and chapter 15).

Further Reading

Elizabeth Adams. *Chelsea Porcelain* (Barrie & Jenkins, 1987).

Chelsea porcelain flautist painted in polychrome enamels.

c.1752–8. Red anchor mark. Repaired. 15 cm height   BG

£590

Large Chelsea porcelain figure of a musician painted in polychrome enamels and gilded.

c.1760. 28 cm height   D

£2,250

DERBY
(c.1756–1848)

William Duesbury's ceramic career may have started as a decorator in London and his account book of the 1751–3 period has been preserved. He seemingly moved to Stafford-shire and it is assumed that he was working with William Littler at the Longton Hall fac-tory in about 1754 before he moved to Derby c.1756. The porcelains of the Derby factory are of a uniformly high quality. Fine tablewares, ornamental wares and figures were produced. In 1769 he purchased the Chelsea factory, which he ran until 1784, when all staff and materials were moved to Derby. Upon his death in 1786, the firm was continued by his son William Duesbury II who continued alone until 1795. He then took Michael Kean into partnership and they operated under the style Duesbury & Kean until 1811. The firm was then controlled by Robert Bloor and his executors until 1848.

Derby made a large number of exceptionally fine figures and groups. Many of the early models were continued in slightly altered forms well into the Bloor Derby period. Some were reissued at the subsequent King Street factory.

Further Reading

Gilbert Bradley. *Derby Porcelain 1750–1798* (Thomas Heneage, 1990).
Peter Bradshaw. *Derby Porcelain Figures 1750–1848* (Faber & Faber, 1990).
John Twitchett. *Derby Porcelain* (Barrie & Jenkins 1980).

WILLIAM DUESBURY I (c.1756–86)

Derby porcelain 'Horned Ewe and Ram, Recumbent' painted in polychrome enamels.

c.1765. Ewe with ears and tail restored; ram with ears restored. Ewe 12.5 cm length; ram 11 cm length   D

£575

A similar pair are illustrated in Bradshaw 1990.

These Derby porcelain *Mars* figures portray him as a Roman centurion. They were originally paired with a *Minerva* figure. The model imitates a Meissen example modelled by Kändler, as did a later Gold Anchor period Chelsea model. The Derby *Mars* figures were popular and continued in production for a long time.

Early Derby porcelain *Mars* figure painted in polychrome enamels and gilded.

c.1758–60. Head restored. 35 cm height   KK

£825

This larger figure is more valuable than the smaller version which follows.

Derby porcelain *Mars* figure painted in polychrome enamels and gilded.

c.1750–65. Restored. 18 cm height   KK

£500

Derby porcelain *Mars* figure candlestick painted in polychrome enamels and gilded.

c.1758. 25 cm height   KK

£350

The Derby *Mars* candlestick was originally paired with *Venus with a Cupid*. A single figure is quite acceptable, but a single candlestick looks odd, explaining the difference in price between this candlestick and the figure above.

Two Derby porcelain *Negress* figures painted in polychrome enamels and gilded.

c.1760–9. 22 cm height   LM

£1,200 for the two.

These are not a pair; they would have originally paired with *Blackamoor* figures, each one also carrying a shell. A pair is illustrated in Twitchett.

Derby porcelain *Welch Life* figure painted in polychrome enamels and gilded.

c.1780. Incised mark 'No 116' with a dot in a circle. Damage to base. 14.5 cm height   HBW

£425

The *Welch Tailor and his Wife* are adapted from Meissen figures modelled by Kändler (1737) and Eberlein (1740) respectively. The adjective Welch comes from the German for 'who' in the title for the figures 'Schneider, welcher auf einem Ziegenbock reutet' (Tailor, who rides on a goat). The model number should be '62' rather than '116'.

These figures remained in production into the Bloor Derby period. The later versions have rococo bases with weaker lines. The figures are enamelled in stronger colours and the modelling is thicker, particularly in the goat's leg, and the lady's arms. In the earlier version shown here, the goat's head is tilted at a winsome angle, whereas the Bloor Derby goat looks ahead sternly.

The figures were still being produced at the King Street factory (see below) in the 20th century. These figures (which appeared in the 1934–5 catalogue) are very highly coloured, and the modelling has degenerated still further.

Derby porcelain *Andromache weeping over the ashes of Hector* figure painted in polychrome enamels and gilded.

c.1775–80. Firing cracks in base. Incised mark 'N 100'; '2G'. 23 cm height   HBW

£550

This figure was inspired by an engraving by Thomas Burke after a painting by Angelica Kauffmann. Note the neo-classical elements of the design – the Greek Key border on the plinth and the urn upon which the figure rests. The Leeds Pottery copied this figure in enamelled pearlware.

WILLIAM DUESBURY II (1786–95)

Derby porcelain *Diana with a Hunting-Dog* figure painted in polychrome enamels and gilding.

c.1790–5. Restored head, dog's ear and tail. Incised mark 'N 65'; '2' with a line over it. 20.5 cm height   HBW

£250

An early Derby *Diana* c.1765 (after a Meissen original by J. F. Eberlein) is much more finely modelled with one leg and one arm posed in the air, holding a bow in her left hand, her dog seated at her feet and the base with rococo 'C' scrolls (illustrated in Twitchett). The version here has obviously been simplified to reduce the number of pieces needing to be separately moulded. This version was made in two sizes (16.5 and 20.5 cm height) c.1772–95. The neo-classical plinth on the figure shown here helps to date the figure at the end of this period.

Derby. porcelain figure of Shakespeare painted in polychrome enamels and gilded.

c.1790. 24.5 cm height   W

£365

This model is after the statue of William Shakespeare by Peter Scheemakers (1740) which is in Poet's Corner in Westminster Abbey. The English antiquarian and engraver George Vertue wrote of Scheemakers's rivalry with the sculptor John Michael Rysbrake: 'At length by taking object Shakespeare (the publick favourite of all English playwrights), tossed this sculptor [Scheemakers] above on the summit of the wheel, and so became the admiration of the publick, immediately brought him into considerable employments of profit and honour and joynd to that some subtiltys nature had given to Scheemakers in the management of his affairs boldness and also alwayes underworking the other's price, added to his success.'

Scheemakers's presentation of the thoughtful poet standing and leaning on a plinth upon which rest books and a scroll, became a popular pose employed by engravers, sculptors and porcelain makers for portraying contemporary nobles. The Shakespeare statue is known in enamelled earthenware and salt-glazed stoneware. Derby made a Milton figure (also made at Chelsea) with which the Shakespeare was paired.

The Shakespeare figure with less enamel decoration and a rococo base is illustrated by Twitchett. The figure was very popular and continued in production for many years. It was much copied elsewhere even in the Victorian period. The neo-classical base in this example dates it to c.1790.

ROBERT BLOOR, DERBY (c.1811–48)

Robert Bloor took over at Derby c.1811. In 1828 his mental health deteriorated so badly that the management of the firm was assumed by James Thomson. In 1844, Bloor's sole surviving descendant took out a statute of lunacy on Bloor, and managed the firm herself until 1848. Much of the equipment was sold to Robert Boyle in Fenton, and some of the moulds then passed to Copeland. For other Bloor Derby porcelains see chapter 16.

Bloor Derby porcelain figure group of cow and calf painted in polychrome enamels with bocage.

c.1811–15. Horns restored. Painted mark in red 25, in pink 13. 15.5 cm height   V

£485

A similar figure with the same painted marks is illustrated in Twitchett, attributed to Robert Bloor & Co. 1811–15. Twitchett mentions a similar, but earlier group illustrated in George Savage, *Englische Keramik* (Vienna, 1961). A white and gilt version c.1810–30 is illustrated in Rice.

Two Bloor Derby *French Seasons* porcelain figures painted in polychrome enamels and gilded.

c.1815–40. Restored in several places. Incised model number 'No 123'. Crown, crossed batons, dots and 'D'; mark painted in red. Boy *Winter* figure 17 cm height; girl *Summer* figure 19 cm height.   KK

£465

The *French Seasons* modelled by Pierre Stephan were first made during the 1770s after the Tournai originals modelled by N. J. F. Gavron based on designs by Boucher. These earlier versions were more elaborately modelled, and originally had pierced scroll bases (illustrated in Bradshaw). The set was remodelled by William Coffee between 1791 and 1795 (illustrated in Twitchett). The Bloor Derby versions shown here are inferior to either of the earlier versions. The design has obviously been simplified to reduce the number of pieces needing to be separately moulded.

Bloor Derby *English Shepherdess* porcelain figure painted in polychrome enamels and gilded.

c.1815–40. 18 cm height   TA

£170

This figure was originally paired with the English Shepherd. The pair were still being produced in the 20th century at the King Street Derby factory, and are illustrated in the firm's catalogue for 1934–5.

KING STREET DERBY (1848–1935)

Locker & Co. succeeded the Robert Bloor firm at King Street, Derby. The firm underwent several changes of style until it was purchased by Royal Crown Derby in 1935.

Locker & Co.	1848–59
Stevenson, Sharp & Co.	1859–66
Stevenson & Hancock	1863–6
Sampson Hancock	1866–1935

The firm continued many of the old Derby figures, as shown by a 1934–5 catalogue which is reproduced in Twitchett 1988. As the firm used the same mark ('S' and 'H') 1863–1935 it can be difficult to date the figures within that period. The mark was also occasionally used after Royal Crown Derby had taken over the works. As the figures were not made for export the word 'England' does not appear in the mark.

The standard was high, and the wares should not be considered inferior to those made by their competitors at the Derby Crown Porcelain Co., subsequently Royal Crown Derby Porcelain Co.

Further Reading

John Twitchett, *Royal Crown Derby*, revised edn (Antique Collectors' Club, Woodbridge, 1988).

King Street Derby undecorated porcelain candelabra with figure.

c.1865. Crown, crossed batons, dots and 'D' mark with 'S' and 'H' painted in red. 22 cm height   G

£120

King Street Derby *Billy Waters* figure painted in polychrome enamels and gilded.

1863–1935. Crown, crossed batons, dots and 'D' mark with 'S' and 'H' painted in red. 10 cm height   HBW

£265

Billy Waters was a black man who had lost a leg in His Majesty's service. He earned a living playing the fiddle in London's West End. Waters appeared in some illustrations of colourful London characters by Cruikshank published in 1821. Another Derby figure from these Cruikshank drawings is *Black Sall*. The original models are attributed to Samuel Keys junior working at Derby c.1815–30. Billy Waters figures are also known in Staffordshire earthenware. The pair were still being produced in the 20th century, and are illustrated in the firm's catalogue for 1934–5.

OTHER MANUFACTURERS

Pair of rare Longton Hall porcelain figures.

c.1755. Restored. 13 cm height   KK

£5,500

For more information about the Longton Hall factory see chapter 15.

Plymouth hard-paste porcelain figure of Bacchus painted in polychrome enamels.

c.1768–70. Repairs. 14 cm height   D

£395

William Cookworthy set up the short-lived Plymouth Porcelain Manufactory (c.1768–70), which was the first British firm to produce hard-paste porcelain. He experienced considerable technical difficulties, and commonly found faults in the wares include smoke stains, discoloration and warping. Figures had a tendency to lean or show open firing cracks in the thicker parts.

433

A pair of Minton porcelain candlesticks decorated with applied flowers, polychrome enamels and gilding.

c.1835–6. Excellent condition. 22.5 cm height   BG

£2,500

An identical pair of candlesticks, and another pair with different bases, along with a drawing from the Minton pattern books is illustrated in Geoffrey Godden's *Minton Pottery & Porcelain of the First Period* 1793–1850 (Barrie & Jenkins, 1978).

Bisque figure possibly Rockingham.

c.1826–42. 13.5 cm height   HBW

£260

Figures with the impressed Brameld mark are more valuable. For more about the Rockingham factory see chapter 17.

Enoch Wood was a celebrated modeller and manufacturer at Burslem whose firm traded under various styles c.1784–1846.

Porcelain bust of Venus, decorated in the Enoch Wood style.

c.1810. 20 cm height   T

£300

434

Porcelain bust painted in polychrome enamels in the Enoch Wood style with lustre base.

c.1810. Damage at neck. 19 cm height   G

£600

Bisque figure of a flute player and his dog.

c.1826–42. 16.5 cm height   V

£275

Pair of Staffordshire porcelain figures with children (thought to be two of Queen Victoria's children) seated on goats, painted in polychrome enamels.

c.1845. 13 cm height   JM

£300 the pair

These are almost certainly of Staffordshire origin, but porcelains of this general type were often attributed to the Rockingham factory in error.

Rare Staffordshire porcelain group inscribed 'Happy Married Life' decorated with polychrome enamels and gilded.

c.1830. 14 cm height   BG

£675

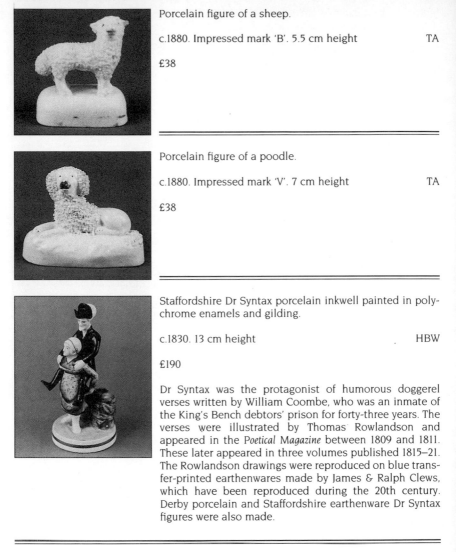

Porcelain figure of a sheep.

c.1880. Impressed mark 'B'. 5.5 cm height   TA

£38

Porcelain figure of a poodle.

c.1880. Impressed mark 'V'. 7 cm height   TA

£38

Staffordshire Dr Syntax porcelain inkwell painted in polychrome enamels and gilding.

c.1830. 13 cm height   .   HBW

£190

Dr Syntax was the protagonist of humorous doggerel verses written by William Coombe, who was an inmate of the King's Bench debtors' prison for forty-three years. The verses were illustrated by Thomas Rowlandson and appeared in the *Poetical Magazine* between 1809 and 1811. These later appeared in three volumes published 1815–21. The Rowlandson drawings were reproduced on blue transfer-printed earthenwares made by James & Ralph Clews, which have been reproduced during the 20th century. Derby porcelain and Staffordshire earthenware Dr Syntax figures were also made.

19 PARIAN BUSTS AND FIGURES

Parian, also known as Carrara or statuary porcelain, is a highly vitrified, often unglazed, fine-grained feldspathic porcelain which was first introduced by Copeland & Garrett and by Minton in 1844. They were soon followed by many other manufacturers, who produced Parian in great quantities. There was a great dispute at the time as to who was the inventor of Parian, and this question has not yet been answered; the name itself was a trade name of Minton referring to the famous Greek marble. Parian is unrelated to bisque or biscuit porcelains which had been used for figures since the 18th century. Biscuit porcelain was slightly porous since it did not have to be fired to vitrification temperature, and was easily stained, even by dust. It was also impossible to hide imperfections by glazes and other decoration, so fewer pieces were passed for sale, which made them quite expensive.

Originally used for reduced copies of sculptures, the Parian wares were a way of bringing fine art into the middle-class home. The Art Unions, which were formed for this purpose, commissioned a number of Parian figures for distribution to their members: such figures may sometimes bear special marks. The Victorian period was a golden age for sculptors. With the enormous growth of the cities, and immense building projects, came a demand for sculptures to grace parks, squares and buildings, which has never been repeated. The arts press, led by the *Art Journal* and the *Magazine of Art*, regularly reported on these sculptures, often reproducing them in engravings. Sculptors became household names, in a way which they have never been since. The demand for works such as John Bell's *Dorothea* (see below) was such that the figures were popular for decades.

Later Parian came to be used for relief-moulded jugs and incidental tablewares such as butter dishes (see chapter 23). Some manufacturers, most notably Belleek, Grainger and W. H. Goss produced very finely glazed Parian wares (these are included in chapter 17). Much crested china was also produced with a Parian body and glazed before decoration (see next chapter).

Parian is possibly at its best when left undecorated, but the Victorian love for embellishment soon prevailed. Some wares were painted with enamels, and relief-moulded wares sometimes have enamelled grounds. Gilding was also employed at times. A few manufacturers including W. T. Copeland applied majolica glazes. The body itself was stained by a few manufacturers, the most common colours being lavender, celadon green and terracotta.

The collector should look for quality, both in the artistry of the original model and in the potter's rendering. Fine, crisply modelled detail is paramount. The body should be flawless and creamy or white (unless deliberately stained with colour). Items other than figures and busts should be very translucent when held to the light. The earlier finely finished Parian wares made by manufacturers such as Minton, Copeland, Wedgwood and Worcester are in general of a superior quality to those of later manufacturers such as Robinson & Leadbeater, who mass-produced busts and figures.

Parian figures may have the name of the original sculptor or the modeller, sometimes dated. This information is very useful, and wares so marked are preferable. Many unmarked wares may be identified from the illustrations in Atterbury (see below).

Further Reading

Paul Atterbury, ed. *The Parian Phenomenon* (Richard Dennis, 1989).
Dennis Barker. *Parian Ware* (Shire Publications, Aylesbury, 1985).
Geoffrey Godden. *Victorian Porcelain* (Herbert Jenkins, 1961).
Geoffrey Godden. *Encyclopaedia of British Porcelain Manufacturers* (Barrie & Jenkins, 1988).
Nicholas Pine. *The Price Guide to Crested China* (Milestone Publications, Horndean, 1992).

Julia Pool. *Plagiarism Personified? European Pottery and Porcelain Figures* (Fitzwilliam Museum, Cambridge, 1986).

Charles and Dorrie Shinn. *The Illustrated Guide to Victorian Parian China* (Barrie & Jenkins, 1971).

MINTON
(c.1793 to the present day)

Thomas Minton had worked as an engraver for the Caughley factory, and blue transfer-printed earthenwares were among his earliest productions. From the time that Thomas Minton founded this firm c.1793 until 1884, the firm went under a number of styles, passing through various Minton partnerships.

Minton's first Parian (their trade name which has subsequently been adopted as a generic name) was probably produced in 1845. It seems that in their case the busts and figures followed production of useful wares in the Parian body. Many Parian figures and busts were shown by Minton at the Great Exhibition of 1851. The *Art Journal* commented: 'Of these many from original sources; some after eminent foreign sculptors, but chiefly from the leading artists of our own school.'

Minton's Parian wares are of exceptionally fine quality. The firm also produced tinted Parians, whose bodies are related to those used for *pâte-sur-pâte* wares (see p. 410).

Further Reading

Elizabeth Aslin and Paul Atterbury. *Minton 1798–1910* (Victoria & Albert Museum, 1976).

Paul Atterbury and Maureen Batkin. *The Dictionary of Minton* (Antique Collectors' Club, Woodbridge, 1990).

Geoffrey Godden. *Minton Pottery & Porcelain of the First Period, 1793–1850* (Barrie & Jenkins, 1968).

Geoffrey Godden. 'The Minton porcelains, 1793 to the present day', *Staffordshire Porcelain* (Granada, 1983).

Minton Parian figure *Dorothea*, designed by John Bell.

c.1850. Incised mark on base 456/5-50 (5-50 is probably a date code for May 1850). Impressed diamond registration mark for 4 October 1847. Moulded mark with 'JOHN BELL'. 33.5 cm height   TA

£165

This figure is after Bell's full-size marble made for Lord Lansdowne in 1844. The subject was taken from Cervantes's *Don Quixote*. The Parian *Dorothea* was advertised by Summerly's Art Manufactures in 1847, and then for the Art Union of London. It was shown by Minton at the Great Exhibition 1851. *Dorothea* was a best seller, remaining in production 1848–90. A companion figure *Clorinda* was also designed by John Bell. Bell (1812–95) was an important Victorian sculptor. His best known statues are *Queen Victoria* (1841) and his *America* group (1864) for the Albert Memorial. His designs were produced by Minton and Wedgwood.

COPELAND & GARRETT
(1833–47)

W. T. COPELAND & SONS
(1847–1970)

Copeland & Garrett (late Spode) introduced their Statuary Porcelain by the end of 1845. The succeeding firm W. T. Copeland considerably expanded production. By 1848 the production was so large that the firm was able to issue an entire catalogue of Parian wares. In the 1930s Copeland attempted to revive production, but this was not successful. Limited edition Parian figures were made by Spode Ltd in the 1970s, but again the revival was not very successful.

There is, as mentioned above, considerable confusion about the invention of Parian, but John Mountford claimed to have invented it while he was working at Copeland's. He had previously been a modeller for Derby.

Exceptionally large Copeland Parian bust of Juno.

c.1851. Impressed mark 'COPELAND T 28'; 'Copyright'.
59 cm height   S

£3,300

An example of this bust, modelled by William Theed the younger (1804–91) after the antique original, was shown at the Great Exhibition of 1851, where the firm exhibited some forty Parian statuettes. The original is in the Museo Nazionale in Rome. A smaller Minton version modelled by L. A. Malempré (c.1865) is illustrated in Atterbury.

Exceptionally large Copeland Parian bust of a maiden.

c.1865–70. Restored chip. Impressed mark 'COPELAND L 84'; 'Copyright'. 59 cm height   S

£2,420

A Minton example of this bust is illustrated in Atterbury.

Copeland Parian bust of Sir Robert Peel.

c.1850. Moulded mark 'James S. Westmacott sculpt Published Augt. 18th 1850'. 27 cm height   T

£195

One of these busts was exhibited by W. T. Copeland at the Great Exhibition in 1851. An earlier Copeland bust of Sir Robert Peel was included in their list of Statuary Porcelain for 1848. James Sherwood Westmacott (1823–88), successful Victorian sculptor, made a number of Parian models for Copeland.

    Sir Robert Peel (1788–1850) was Prime Minister 1834–5 and 1841–6. He died from injuries sustained when his horse threw him in 1850.

WORCESTER ROYAL PORCELAIN CO.
(1862–1976)

Royal Worcester made a wide variety of busts, figures, ornamental and useful wares in their 'Ivory Porcelain' Parian body. This was sometimes glazed and/or enamelled and gilded (see chapter 17).

Further Reading

Henry Sandon. *Royal Worcester Porcelain from 1862 to the Present Day*, 3rd edn (Barrie & Jenkins, 1978).

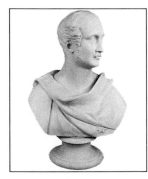

Kerr & Binns or Royal Worcester Parian bust of Prince Albert.

c.1862. 36 cm height   CCC

£300

Busts of Prince Albert were shapes number 2 and 3 in the firm's list of shapes: this is number 2, the larger model. The busts were modelled by E. J. Jones, as were many other Worcester busts and figures.

    Prince Albert, the younger of the two sons of the Duke of Saxe-Coburg and Gotha married Queen Victoria in 1840. Albert was a talented man with many interests, and played a large part in the organisation of the Great Exhibition in 1851. Their happy marriage ended on his death in 1861.

WEDGWOOD
(c.1759 to the present day)

Carrara (after the fine marble found in that district of Italy) was Wedgwood's trade name for Parian or statuary porcelain, introduced c.1846. Some of the earlier Carrara productions were made from existing moulds previously used for black basalt. Later models were sometimes produced in both Carrara and basalt.

Further Reading

Robin Reilly and George Savage. *The Dictionary of Wedgwood* (Antique Collectors' Club, Woodbridge, 1980).

Wedgwood Carrara bust of Lord Zetland.

c.1868. Marked 'WEDGWOOD/23/11TH DECEMBER/1868/ EDGE'. 48 cm height   CCC

£1,950

Thomas 2nd Earl of Zetland (1795–1873) was MP for Richmond and York. He was Lord-Lieutenant of West Riding of Yorkshire and Grand Master of Freemasons of England 1843–69.

W. H. GOSS
(1858–1939)

William Henry Goss served an apprenticeship in the London retail offices of W. T. Copeland. He then went to Stoke to gain experience of potting, serving under John Mountford, who claimed to be the inventor of Parian. Goss learned well, for in 1858 he established his own firm for the manufacture of Parian, producing some models which were nearly identical to those of Copeland! Goss continued to produce Parian busts, figures and tablewares until c.1890. Today the firm is best remembered for their glazed Parian Heraldic Ware (see chapter 20).

Nicholas Pine has divided the production of the Goss factory into three periods, and these have been generally adopted by collectors. During the First Period (1858–87) William Henry Goss owned and ran the pottery, and most of the unglazed Parian wares were made. During the Second Period (1881–1934) the firm was managed by his three sons Adolphus, Victor and William Huntley Goss and the chief product was Heraldic Porcelain. During the Third Period (1930–9), the firm was owned and managed by Cauldon Potteries, and earthenwares were introduced, although cheap crested china was still made.

Further Reading

Nicholas Pine. *Goss and Crested China* (Shire Publications, Aylesbury, 1984).
Nicholas Pine. *William Henry Goss* (Milestone Publications, Horndean, 1987).
Nicholas Pine. *The Concise Encyclopaedia and Price Guide to Goss China* (Milestone Publications, Horndean, 1992).

Goss Parian bust of Sir Walter Scott.

c.1870. 13.8 cm height   TV

£55

Sir Walter Scott (1771–1832) was a popular subject for the potters. Minton, W. T. Copeland, Wedgwood and Royal Worcester all made Parian busts of the poet and novelist. This very common bust is most similar to the Minton bust, a drawing of which is illustrated in Atterbury: the principal difference seems to be that the brooch on Scott's left breast is missing from the Minton version. The two may have been taken from the same source. The Goss bust of Scott is illustrated in Pine 1992 and in Atterbury.

A less common version with Scott wearing a jacket and cravat are worth considerably more than the bust shown here, as are the larger sizes of both versions.

Goss Pallas Athena Parian bust.

c.1860–85. 35.5 cm height   CCC

£550

This fine large bust is uncommon, and is desirable as a decorative piece as well as a collector's item.

Rare bullock and sheep group.

c.1882. Printed mark 'Copyright as The Act Directs/W.H. GOSS/STOKE-ON-TRENT/1st September 1882'. 14.8 cm height; length of base 19.6 cm   CCC

£1,200

This model was commissioned by Albert Loring Murdock to promote his Murdock's Liquid Food, a potion to cure pernicious anaemia. It usually appears with the slogan inscribed on the side of the bullock: 'Murdock's Liquid Food is Condensed Beef, Mutton & Fruits' (illustrated in Pine 1992). The high price reflects the large number of Goss collectors, to whom this group would be highly desirable.

Pair of Goss classical figures with enamel decoration.

c.1860–85. 34.5 cm height   CCC

£375

ROBINSON & LEADBEATER
(1864–1924)

By the 1870s many manufacturers included Parian among their wares, and of these Robinson & Leadbeater were among the best. Although a late entrant into the market, Robinson & Leadbeater devoted themselves exclusively to the manufacture of Parian busts and figures. As might be expected, the designs were imitations of pioneers such as Copeland, Minton and Wedgwood. Robinson & Leadbeater took over the machinery and moulds which had been used by Giovanni Melli, who had been a free-lance modeller before establishing his own works in 1852, and so some of the pieces attributed to Melli may actually have been manufactured by Robinson & Leadbeater.

The firm specialised in busts and hired as their designer Rowland James Morris. Morris had achieved success as a modeller of both Wedgwood and Moore Bros majolica. He had also modelled the façade of the Wedgwood Institute at Burslem. Later in life he modelled for Thomas Bevington.

Robinson & Leadbeater Parian bust of Paderewski.

c.1919. Incised 'RaL'. 20.5 cm height   CCC

£160

Robinson & Leadbeater's mark is usually 'R&L'. Ignace Jan Paderewski (1860–1941) was a pianist and in 1919 first Prime Minister of independent Poland.

Parian bust of a girl, possibly one of Queen Victoria's daughters.

c.1864–80s. Incised mark R&L. 27 cm height   TA

£78

Parian figure of Red Riding Hood.

c.1880. Hand restored. 29 cm height   CCC

£160

Robinson & Leadbeater Parian figures of Scotland and England painted in polychrome enamels.

c.1890. Incised mark on Scotland 'R. & L'. 15.9 cm height
CCC

£175 each

These figures without enamel decoration are illustrated in Atterbury.

Robinson & Leadbeater Parian bust of Beethoven.

c.1890–1910. 29 cm height   HBW

£175

Robinson & Leadbeater Parian bust of J. T. W. Mitchell.

c.1895. Incised mark R&L. 18.5 cm height CCC

£180

J. T. W. Mitchell (1828–1895) was the President of the Co-operative Wholesale Society from 1874.

Robinson & Leadbeater Parian bust of Lord Roberts.

c.1900 Moulded mark 'LORD ROBERTS/W C LAWTON SCUPT/COPYRIGHT/Jan. 1900'; incised mark 'R&L'. 20 cm height GCC

£220

After a long and distinguished career including campaigns and service in India, Abyssinia, Afghanistan and Ireland, Lord Roberts of Kandahar (1832–1914) was Commander-in-Chief in South Africa for most of the Boer War. He returned to England in 1901 to assume the rank of Commander-In-Chief and was made an earl.

Lawton also sculpted a full figure of Lord Roberts which was produced in Parian by Robinson & Leadbeater (illustrated in Atterbury).

OTHER MANUFACTURERS

Podmore China Parian bust of John Bunyan with crest of the City of Lincoln.

1921–41. Moulded and printed marks 'PODMORE CHINA CO.' 14 cm height CCC

£75

This is one of the three unglazed Parian busts known to have been made by Podmore China Co. (1921–41) who are better known for their tablewares and crested china.

Hewitt & Leadbeater Parian bust of Sir Walter Scott with Edinburgh Arms.

1905–19. Incised mark H&L; printed mark 'Caledonia Heraldic China'. 14.5 cm height   CCC

£36

Caledonia Heraldic China was produced for a Scottish wholesaler by Birks, Rawlins & Co., Wiltshaw & Robinson and Hewitt & Leadbeater. This bust was made by Hewitt & Leadbeater (1905–19), a partnership between Edwin Leadbeater (son of the senior partner in the firm of Robinson & Leadbeater, see above) and his brother-in-law Arthur Hewitt. The firm specialised in crested china, which they produced under the trade name Willow Art (see chapter 20).

A. B. Jones & Sons Parian bust of Lloyd George with glazed base with Yeovil Arms.

c.1916–22. Moulded mark "LLOYD GEORGE REGD. NO. 659418'; A B J & SONS/ENGLAND' in a Staffordshire knot. 13 cm height   GCC

£55

A. B. Jones & Sons manufactured porcelain and earthenware at Longton c.1900–72. David Lloyd George, 1st Earl (1863–1945) was a pacifist during the Boer War, but changed his opinions when Belgium was threatened by the Germans. He was coalition Prime Minister 1916–22.

Birks Rawlins & Co. Parian bust of King Albert of Belgium.

c.1914. Printed mark 'SAVOY CHINA'; 'W. H. COOPER, Sculptor'; 'Belgium invaded by Germany Aug. 4th 1914. Capital occupied Aug. 20th 1914.' 15 cm height   CCC

£85

The plight of Belgium in 1914 mobilised many in Britain to raise funds for her aid. *King Albert's Book* published by the *Daily Telegraph* in 1914 in aid of the Daily Telegraph Belgian Fund said: 'No more woeful and terrible spectacle of a country in utter desolation ever came from earthquake, eruption or other convulsion of Nature in her wrath than has been produced by the hand of man. A complete nation is in ruins. A whole country is in ashes. An entire people are destitute, homeless and on the roads. A little kingdom, dedicated to liberty, has "kept the pledge and died for it".'

Parian bust of 'Queen Mary/Born May 26th 1867'.

c.1910. Printed circular mark with globe and crown 'A & S/STOKE-ON-TRENT/ARCADIAN'. 12.5 cm height   CCC

£55

Princess Mary of Teck married the Duke of York in 1893 and became Queen in 1910. Arkinstall & Sons was a manufacturer at Stoke c.1904–24.

Arkinstall & Sons Parian bust with glazed base with transfer-printed and enamelled arms of Boulogne-sur-Mer.

c.1914. Moulded mark 'LORD ROBERTS SVC/BY W C LAWTON SCULPT/COPYRIGHT'. Printed circular mark with globe 'A & S/STOKE ON TRENT/PORCELAINE ARCADIENNE'. 14.5 cm height   GCC

£125

After a long and distinguished career including campaigns and service in India, Abyssinia, Afghanistan and Ireland, Lord Roberts of Kandahar (1832–1914) was appointed Commander-in-Chief in South Africa in the Boer War. He returned to England in 1901 to assume the rank of Commander-in-Chief and was made an earl.

Lawton also sculpted a full figure of Lord Roberts which was produced in Parian by Robinson & Leadbeater, illustrated in Atterbury.

Two Parian busts.

c.1860. Left: Shakespeare, 20 cm height. Right: Milton, 19 cm height.   AD

£250

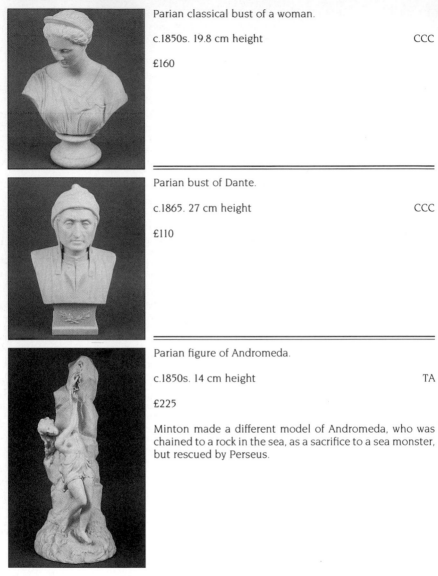

Parian classical bust of a woman.

c.1850s. 19.8 cm height   CCC

£160

Parian bust of Dante.

c.1865. 27 cm height   CCC

£110

Parian figure of Andromeda.

c.1850s. 14 cm height   TA

£225

Minton made a different model of Andromeda, who was chained to a rock in the sea, as a sacrifice to a sea monster, but rescued by Perseus.

20 CRESTED CHINA

C RESTED china is porcelain or occasionally earthenware decorated with coats of arms. Heraldic Porcelain, first introduced by W. H. Goss c.1880, was soon copied by many other china manufacturers, mainly in Longton: indeed after 1900 there were over 100 firms producing crested ware in Britain, and numerous imports from Germany and Czechoslovakia. Many of these are of quite poor quality, but none the less collectable. The wares reached the peak of their popularity around the time of the First World War, and production had almost ceased by the end of the 1920s.

All the items below, unless otherwise mentioned, are made of porcelain. The Goss items are made of a very fine glazed Parian. Each piece is decorated with arms, often of a place for which it is a souvenir. When a piece bears matching arms, e.g. the arms for the place which relates to the subject matter of the figure or model, it is more desirable, and hence the value is greater. The arms are usually transfer-printed and filled in with enamels. Some cheaper models, especially German ones, have lithographed arms. Commemorative crested wares are included in chapter 24.

Crested china can be found in many antique shops and at fairs. Although crested china has increased considerably in value during the past decade, there are still bargains to be found for the informed collector. Two firms sell crested china by mail order, with illustrated catalogues: The Goss & Crested China Club, 62 Murray Road, Horndean, Hants, PO8 9JL and The Crested China Company, Driffield, North Humberside. Nicholas Pine, founder of the Goss & Crested China Club, publishes the definitive standard catalogues on the subject and is largely responsible for repopularising heraldic porcelain in recent years.

Further Reading

Sandy Andrews. *Crested China* (Milestone Publications, Horndean, 1980).
Nicholas Pine. *The Price Guide to Crested China* (Milestone Publications, Horndean, 1992).

W. H. GOSS
(1858–1939)

William Henry Goss served an apprenticeship in the London retail offices of W. T. Copeland. He then went to Stoke to gain experience of potting, serving under John Mountford, who claimed to be the inventor of Parian (see chapter 19). Goss learned well, for in 1858 he established his own firm for the manufacture of Parian, producing some models which were nearly identical to those of Copeland!

There is some dispute as to whether it was Goss or his son Adolphus who invented Heraldic Porcelain. However, the material fact is that both were actively engaged in the design and manufacture of the early wares. Goss was a great collector of antiquities, and so it is not surprising that he took great care that his models were carefully produced after authentic artifacts. Until 1883, wares were only produced with their matching arms; afterwards, due to pressure from the retailers, shapes could be ordered with any arms desired. These were sold by agents, whose printed marks may appear on the items. By 1900 there were 481 of these agencies. In that year the first Goss Record, compiled by J. J. Jarvis, was published, listing all available models of Goss Heraldic Porcelain and their agencies. Eight subsequent editions (1901–21) carried items of interest to collectors. Jarvis established the National League of Goss Collectors in 1904.

In the words of Nicholas Pine: 'The collecting of Goss china became a craze that swept the nation and it is thought that in Edwardian times some 90% of all homes contained Goss porcelain miniatures, a higher incidence than telephones or television sets enjoy today. After the craze died in the 1920s, the nation spent the next forty years throwing crested china away.'

Nicholas Pine has divided the production of the Goss factory into three periods, and these have been generally adopted by collectors. During the First Period (1858–87) William Henry Goss owned and ran the pottery, and most of the unglazed Parian wares were made. During the Second Period (1881–1934) the firm was managed by his three sons Adolphus, Victor and William Huntley Goss and the chief product was Heraldic Porcelain. Early during the Third Period (1930–9), the firm was taken over by Cauldon Potteries and earthenwares were introduced, although inexpensive crested china was still made.

The first Heraldic Porcelain was made by Goss late in the First Period. Some items span the periods, as with any manufacturer, but many wares distinguish the three.

Although Heraldic Porcelain was the principal product of the Goss factory during the Second Period, the firm made many other interesting wares, which are shown elsewhere in this book.

Further Reading

Nicholas Pine. *Goss and Crested China* (Shire Publications, Aylesbury, 1984).

Nicholas Pine. *William Henry Goss* (Milestone Publications, Horndean, 1987).

Nicholas Pine. *The Concise Encyclopaedia and Price Guide to Goss China* (Milestone Publications, Horndean, 1992).

Nicholas Pine. *The Price Guide to Arms and Decorations on Goss China* (Milestone Publications, Horndean, 1992).

Goss Heraldic Porcelain *Bagware* sugar bowl and cream jug with turquoise enamelled cord and gilded tassels. Inscribed 'ARMS FOR BURNS', with arms, crest and mottoes 'WOOD NOTES WILD'; 'BETTER A WEE BUSH THAN NAE BIELD'.

c.1881–1930. Printed Goshawk mark. Sugar bowl 10 cm diameter; cream jug 8 cm height   GCC

£65 the pair.

This is part of the *Bagware* tea service made during the First and Second Periods.

Goss Heraldic Porcelain Manx legs sugar bowl, legs glazed in yellow and gilded. County of Stirling arms.

c.1890. Printed mark 'PUB. BY W. MIDDLETON/WALLACE MONUMENT/STIRLING RD. NO. 149157.' (1890); printed Goshawk mark. Sugar bowl 7 cm height   GCC

£25

A matching teapot was also made. Some examples have white legs.

Goss Heraldic Porcelain *Viking Model of Norwegian Dragon-shaped beer bowl,* painted in polychrome enamels and gilded. Arms for Littlehampton with banner reading 'PROGRESS'.

c.1908. Design registration number 526,382 (1908). Printed Goshawk mark. 15.5 cm length   CCC

£36

This model is worth more with matching Norwegian Arms and most valuable with inscription in Norwegian.

Goss Heraldic Porcelain *Model of covered urn found near site of Walden Abbey in* 1878 painted in polychrome enamels and gilded with Eastbourne arms and motto 'MELIORA SEQUI-MUR',

c.1913. Printed Goshawk mark; impressed mark W. H. GOSS. 12.1 cm height   CCC

£38

This model is more valuable with Saffron Walden Arms or any Egyptian Arms (as the model is of a canopic jar). It was made in two sizes, of which this is the larger.

Goss Heraldic Porcelain *Model of Sedan Chair used by the Countess of Boulogne XVII Century* painted in polychrome enamels and gilded. Arms for Brighton with motto 'IN DEO FIDE-MUS'.

c.1909. Printed Goshawk mark; 'Rd. No. 539423' (1909). 'Published by Diplock/29 Western Rd., Hove.' 7 cm height   CCC

£48

The matching arms for this item are those of Boulogne, which would greatly increase the value. A turquoise enamelled version is most highly sought after.

Goss Heraldic Porcelain *Model of Ancient Lamp found at Lake Clay Pits, Hamworthy, Poole* painted in polychrome enamels and gilded. Arms of Weymouth and Melcombe-Regis.

c.1906. Printed mark 'Rd. no. 489479' (1906). 10 cm length   CCC

£14.50

This is more valuable with the matching arms for Poole.

Goss Heraldic Porcelain hippopotamus painted in polychrome enamels and gilded. Arms for Ealing.

c.1881–1930. Printed Goshawk mark. 12.7 cm length   CCC

£470

The matching arms for this figure are B. E. E. Wembley. This model continued in production during the Third Period.

Goss Heraldic Porcelain *Durham Abbey Knocker Cup* painted in polychrome enamels and gilded. Matching Arms of the City of Durham on reverse.

c.1894. Printed Goshawk mark; registration number '245459' (1894); 'Pub. by Mrs Sharpe, Sadler St., Durham'. 8 cm height   GCC

£99

The Durham Abbey Knocker is also found on wall pockets and night-lights. These may be found in brown Parian.

Goss Heraldic Porcelain *Salisbury Kettle* painted in polychrome enamels and gilded. Matching Arms of See of Salisbury.

c.1913. 'Model of Old Kettle in Salisbury Museum/ Published by Watson & Co./The Halle of John Halle Salisbury'. Printed Goshawk mark. 14 cm height   GCC

£30

A smaller version may also be found. Doulton made a stoneware version of this at Lambeth for a local retailer.

452

Goss Heraldic Porcelain *Beachy Head Light House* with brown band painted in polychrome enamels and gilded. Arms for Brighton with motto 'IN DEO FIDEMUS'.

c.1913. Printed mark 'Cheesman & Co./169 North St./Brighton/Rd. No. 622475' (1913). 12.6 cm height   GCC

£50

Goss Heraldic Porcelain William Henry Goss glazed Parian tyg with his portrait in profile painted in polychrome enamels and gilded.

c.1906. Ribbon inscribed 'W. H. Goss F. G. S. F. R. MET. SOC.' Goss arms with motto 'SE INSERIT ASTRIS' and Stoke-on-Trent arms with motto 'VIS UNITA FORTIOR'. Goshawk mark. 11 cm height   GCC

£185

This was produced upon Goss's death in 1906.

Goss Heraldic Porcelain brown tinted Parian 'Model of Ancient Cross St. Columb Major Churchyard'.

c.1911. Printed Goshawk mark;'Rd. No. 589060' (1911). 9.3 cm height   CCC

£160

Goss produced a series of monumental crosses in unglazed brown Parian. These were sometimes also made in white glazed or unglazed Parian. Arms may appear on the white versions. The St Columb Major cross here sometimes has the Blackpool arms, which halves its value.

453

Goss Heraldic Porcelain lidded *St. Martin's Church font, Canterbury* in unglazed Parian. Inscribed 'Model of Font (Restored) in which King Ethelbert was Baptized by St. Augustine in St. Martin's Church Canterbury'.

c.1913. Printed Goshawk mark. 7.4 cm height   GCC

£90

This was one of twelve models of fonts produced by Goss. This particular model was also produced during the First Period. It may be found in lidded, dished or open models made in white (glazed or unglazed) or brown Parian bodies. The dished or open models may have arms; the matching arms are the City or See of Canterbury.

Goss Heraldic Porcelain glazed Parian beaker painted in polychrome enamels and gilded. Blackpool crest on reverse with motto 'PROGRESS'.

c.1901–20. Printed Goshawk mark. 11.2 cm height   CCC

£60

Goss Heraldic Porcelain teapot stand with black transfer-printed verse written by Adolphus Goss painted in polychrome enamls and gilded. Arms for Morecambe, Lancashire and England.

c.1881–1930. Printed Goshawk mark. 14.5 cm square   GCC

£30

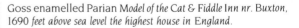

Goss enamelled Parian *Model of the Cat & Fiddle Inn nr. Buxton, 1690 feet above sea level the highest house in England.*

c.1925. Printed Goshawk mark. 6 cm height   CCC

£275

Nicholas Pine tells how Noel Goss and a workman measured the Cat and Fiddle Inn to ensure the faithfulness of this replica in his *Concise Encyclopaedia and Price Guide to Goss China.*

Goss glazed Parian *First & Last House in England, Lands End* with cream roof.

c.1908. Printed Goshawk mark; Rd. No. 521,645 (1908).
6.5 cm length   GCC

£140

Goss Parian *Model of Oven in which Goss porcelain is fired*, decorated with red, brown and green enamels.

c.1921. Printed Goshawk mark; 'copyright'. 7.6 cm length
                                                                GCC

£380

The oven is still standing in Sturgess Street, Stoke.

Goss Parian *Model of Shakespeare's House* decorated with red and brown enamels.

c.1894–1930. Printed mark: 'Model of Shakespeare's House Rd. No 225833' (1894); printed Goshawk mark. 14 cm length
                                                                GCC

£100

There are many variations in this, the most common Goss cottage.

Goss Parian *Black Mammy* ashtray painted in polychrome enamels with the arms of Clevedon.

c.1930–9. Printed Goshawk mark. 8 cm length   GCC

£150

Goss Parian model (glazed base) of a racehorse and jockey with the arms of Newmarket painted in polychrome enamels and gilded.

c.1930–9. Printed Goshawk mark; 'Pretty & Co./High St., Newmarket/Sowen Racehorse'. 10 cm height   GCC

£125

Goss Art Deco glazed Parian 'Toucan' ashtray painted in polychrome enamels and gilded. Bournemouth arms with motto 'PULCHRITUDO ET SALUBRITAS'.

c.1930–9. Printed black Goshawk mark. 9 cm length   GCC

£95

ARKINSTALL & SONS
(ARCADIAN CHINA)
(1903–25)

Harold Taylor Robinson formed Arkinstall & Sons at Stoke in 1903, with the intention of producing crested china. The trade name Arcadian was used from 1904. This was the beginning of his empire, which was to collapse with disastrous repercussions in 1932. By this time Robinson had gained control of some of the largest pottery and porcelain manufacturers in England and he was director of thirty-two companies, all of whom suffered when he was declared bankrupt. Arkinstall was merged with Robinson & Leadbeater in 1908. Subsequently it became a part of A. J. Robinson & Sons, later of Cauldon Potteries (1925). The Arcadian mark was used into the 1930s, although they shared moulds with others owned by Robinson. Early models may have model numbers 1–800.

Arkinstall was the largest manufacturer of crested china, although its quality was not very good compared with Goss Heraldic Wares. Arcadian China was successfully aimed at the lower end of the market. The firm also produced coloured figures and unglazed Parian busts, some of which were made from Robinson & Leadbeater models.

For other Arkinstall wares see chapter 21.

Arcadian China fireplace painted in coloured enamels with a lithographic transfer poppy.

c.1904–12. Inscription 'From Torquay'. Printed mark 'ARCA-DIAN/A&S'. 11.5 cm height   CCC

£28

Compare this model with the Wiltshaw & Robinson hob shown below. The Arcadian model has relief-moulded decoration, but the finer Wiltshaw & Robinson model has separately moulded and applied ornament. There is another version of the Arcadian model with bold relief; both versions came in two sizes. Floral lithographic transfers are rarely found on Arcadian China, the poppy most often.

Arcadian China glazed Parian statue of King Alfred the Great with matching City of Winchester arms painted in polychrome enamels and gilded.

c.1908. Printed mark 'A&S/STOKE ON TRENT/ARCADIAN CHINA'; 'Rd. No. 521701' (1908). 17 cm height   CCC

£65

This is a model of a statue by Sir (William) Hamo Thornycroft (1850–1925). Commissioned by the Mayor of Winchester, Alfred Bowker, in 1901, the statue still stands in the centre of Winchester.

Nicholas Pine has noted that the registration numbers on Arcadian models are 'notoriously unreliable and are often found not to be the number that the piece was actually registered under.' Checking against reference works is advised!

Arcadian China model of St Paul's Cathedral with matching City of London Arms painted in polychrome enamels and gilded.

c.1905. Printed mark 'A&S/STOKE ON TRENT/ARCADIAN CHINA'. 13.3 cm height   CCC

£38

This model (number 114) was available in three sizes, of which this is the largest.

Arcadian China goat with Bedlington arms painted in polychrome enamels and gilded.

c.1904–30. Printed mark 'A&S/STOKE ON TRENT/ARCADIAN CHINA'. 11.7 cm height   CCC

£110

Arcadian China orange lustre bulldog with 'Lucky Black Cat' transfer.

c.1930. Printed mark 'A&S/STOKE ON TRENT/ARCADIAN CHINA'. 8 cm height   CCC

£42

A white version of this figure would be valued at about £25.

Arcadian China Scottish terrier with blue enamelled tam-o'-shanter.

c.1904–30. Printed mark 'A&S/STOKE ON TRENT/ARCA-DIAN CHINA'. 8.2 cm height   CCC

£14.50

This model with an uncoloured tam-o'-shanter appreciates by about 50%.

Arcadian China scallop shell with Bexhill-on-Sea Arms painted in polychrome enamels and gilded.

c.1904–30. Printed mark 'A&S/STOKE ON TRENT/ARCA-DIAN CHINA'. 9 cm length   GCC

£4

Shell shapes were popular as seaside souvenirs, and are usually found with the arms of seaside resorts.

Arcadian China lifeboat with Stevenage Arms painted in polychrome enamels and gilded.

c.1904–30. Printed mark 'A&S/STOKE ON TRENT/ARCA-DIAN CHINA'. 12 cm length   GCC

£24

Arcadian China *Cock O' the North*, usually thus inscribed, painted in polychrome enamels. Unidentified arms.

c.1904–30. Printed mark 'A&S/STOKE ON TRENT/ARCADIAN CHINA'. 10 cm height   GCC
£20

HEWITT & LEADBEATER
(WILLOW ART CHINA)
(1905–19)
HEWITT BROS
(1919–c.1925)
WILLOW POTTERIES
(c.1925–30)

Edwin Leadbeater (son of the senior partner of Robinson & Leadbeater, Parian manufacturers) and his brother-in-law Arthur Hewitt formed a partnership at the Willow Pottery, Longton in 1905. Apart from their Willow Art Heraldic Ware they made Parian figures and busts marked 'H&L'. The early wares were of fine quality, but in later years under Harold Taylor Robinson's control the quality deteriorated, and eventually the wares were made alongside Swan China and Arcadian China at Arkinstall & Sons' Arcadian Works at Stoke-on-Trent (see preceding section).

When Edwin Leadbeater left the partnership in 1919 it continued under the style Hewitt Bros, which became Willow Potteries, a branch of Cauldon Potteries.

Willow Art China sunburst with Windsor Arms painted in polychrome enamels and gilded.

c.1925–30. Printed mark 'Willow Art/MADE IN ENGLAND/CHINA/STOKE ON TRENT' with willow tree. 10 cm height   CCC

£55

Willow Art China Ruskin Memorial, Friars Crag with Keswick Arms painted in polychrome enamels and gilded. Inscribed 'JOHN RUSKIN/MDCCCXIX–MDCCCC/THE FIRST THING WHICH I REMEMBER AS AN EVENT IN LIFE WAS BEING TAKEN BY MY NURSE TO THE EDGE OF FRIAR'S CRAG ON DERWENT WATER/RUSKIN MEMORIAL FRIARS CRAG'.

c.1905. Attributed to Willow Art. 18.2 cm height   GCC

£22

John Ruskin (1819–1900) was the most influential writer on the arts during the Victorian period. This Memorial was made in two sizes.

Willow Art China model inscribed 'MODEL OF BURNS COTTAGE. ROBERT BURNS, THE` AYRSHIRE BARD, WAS BORN AT ALLOWAY NEAR AYR ON THE 25TH JANUARY, 1759. HE DIED, ON THE 21ST JULY, 1796, AT DUMFRIES WHERE HE WAS BURIED'. Painted in polychrome enamels.

c.1925–30. Printed mark with willow tree, 'WILLOW/MADE IN ENGLAND/STOKE-ON-TRENT'. 10.6 cm length   CCC

£65

Willow Art also made a model of the house where Burns lived 1793–6.

Willow Art China model inscribed 'MODEL OF THE HOUSE IN EDINBURGH WHERE JOHN KNOX THE SCOTTISH REFORMER DIED 24TH NOV 1572' painted in polychrome enamels.

c.1907–25. Printed mark with willow tree, 'WILLOW/ART/ CHINA.LONGTON'. 10.2 cm length   CCC

£150

Willow Art China model inscribed 'FAMOUS OLD BLACK-SMITHS SHOP AND MARRIAGE ROOM, GRETNA GREEN' painted in polychrome enamels and gilded.

c.1907–25. Printed mark with willow tree 'WILLOW/ART/CHINA/LONGTON'. 8.8 cm length   GCC

£45

Willow Art China model inscribed 'ANN HATHAWAY'S COTTAGE', unglazed porcelain with polychrome enamel decoration, and gilded, attributed to Willow Art.

c.1905–30. 13 cm length   GCC

£45

ALFRED B. JONES & SONS
(GRAFTON CHINA)
(1880–1972)

Alfred B. Jones of Longton made a wide range of china tablewares, as well as china novelty wares (see chapter 21). The firm now trades as Crown Lynn Ceramics Ltd using the trade name Royal Grafton.

Grafton China Glanford Brigg War Memorial with matching Glanford Arms painted in polychrome enamels.

c.1920. Printed mark 'GRAFTON CHINA' with 'ABJ' in Staffordshire knot with '& SONS/ENGLAND' below. 11.4 cm height   CCC

£185

Grafton China camel with Brighton Arms painted in polychrome enamels.

c.1915–33. Printed mark 'GRAFTON CHINA' with 'ABJ' in Staffordshire knot with '& SONS/ENGLAND' below. 13 cm height   CCC

£48

Grafton China Parian model inscribed 'The Old Maids Cottage Lee, Ilfracombe' decorated with coloured glazes.

c.1915–33. Grafton China printed mark of Staffordshire knot with 'ABJ & SONS/ENGLAND'. 7 cm length   GCC

£85

WILTSHAW & ROBINSON
(CARLTON CHINA)
(1890–1957)

Established in 1890 as an earthenware manufacturer at Stoke, Wiltshaw & Robinson began to produce Carlton Heraldic China in 1902. The firm went into receivership in 1931 and merged with Birks, Rawlins & Co. Ltd following year.

Renamed Carlton Ware Ltd in 1957, the firm was purchased by Arthur Wood & Son (Longport) in 1966. The firm was then purchased by County Potteries Plc in 1987 operating under the style Carlton & Kent, going into receivership in 1989. The trade name, pattern books and some moulds were purchased by Grosvenor Ceramic Hardware Ltd in 1989, and the trade name was relaunched in 1990. For more information about Carlton Ware see chapter 14.

Carlton Heraldic China ashtray inscribed 'Horsey keep your tail up' with hair tail, lustre and polychrome enamel decoration and Scarborough Arms.

c.1920s. Printed mark with swallow 'W&R/STOKE ON TRENT/CARLTON CHINA'. 10 cm height   CCC

£75

Carlton Heraldic China hob with separately modelled and applied kettle and teapot painted in polychrome enamels and gilded. Arms of Richmond, Yorkshire and inscription 'East or West, Home is best/The Kettle on the fire is singing/The Old Clock ticks, And the Teapot is on the hob/Sure it's a good Old Home/Sweet Home'.

c.1902–30. Printed mark with swallow 'W&R/STOKE ON TRENT/CARLTON CHINA'. 9.5 cm length   CCC

£28

Compare this with the Arcadian model above. The Arcadian model has relief-moulded decoration, but the finer Wiltshaw & Robinson model has separately modelled and applied ornament.

Carlton Heraldic China *Jenny Jones figure* with Milford Haven Arms painted in polychrome enamels.

c.1902–30. Printed mark with swallow 'W&R/STOKE ON TRENT/CARLTON CHINA'. 15 cm height   CCC

£48

There are two varieties of this Welsh lady: the other, which is smaller and has no basket, is worth about £90.

Carlton Heraldic China motorcyclist with sidecar with Folkestone Arms painted in polychrome enamels and gilded.

c.1915. Printed mark with swallow 'W&R/STOKE ON TRENT/ CARLTON CHINA'. 11 cm height   CCC

£110

Heraldic China Scottish terrier wearing tam-o'-shanter painted in polychrome enamels and gilded, attributed to Wiltshaw & Robinson.

c.1902–30. 8 cm height   GCC

£10

OTHER MANUFACTURERS

Swan China *Ancient Font in Tideswell* with matching arms of Tideswell painted in polychrome enamels and gilded.

c.1909. Printed Swan mark with monogram 'CF'; 'SWAN CHINA/ENGLAND'; 'Rd. No. 535941' (1909); 'F. CHAFFNER. FANCY DEPOT/TIDESWELL'; 'MODEL OF ANCIENT FONT IN TIDESWELL CHURCH/DATED BACK TO THE 6TH CENTURY/COPYRIGHT'. 9 cm height   CCC

£75

Charles Ford (1871–1925) originally made some good quality tablewares and ornamental porcelains at Hanley. In 1904 shortly after Ford introduced the manufacture of crested china, the firm was acquired by Harold Taylor Robinson. The firm continued to use its own style and trade name after it was merged with another of Robinson's acquisitions Robinson & Beresford. Production was transferred to J. A. Robinson's works in 1910. J. A. Robinson was incorporated in Harold Robinson's Cauldon Potteries in the 1920s; the Charles Ford style disappeared c.1925.

Royal Worcester porcelain sugar bowl and cream jug painted in polychrome enamels and gilded. Arms of the City of Edinburgh with motto 'NISI DOMINUS FRUSTRA'.

c.1903. Printed Royal Worcester mark with twelve dots (date cipher for 1903). Painted pattern number 340/G. Bowl 9 cm diameter; jug 13 cm height   CCC

£60

Coronet Ware china whelk shell painted in polychrome enamels and gilded. Marlborough Arms with motto 'UBI NUNC SAPIENTIS OSSA MERLINI'.

c.1921–4. Printed mark 'THE CORONET WARE' with crown; 'MADE IN ENGLAND'. 10 cm length   GCC

£5

It is believed that Coronet Ware china was manufactured at Longton by Taylor & Kent or J. A. Robinson & Sons. The mark appears with the initials 'F. P. & S' 1917–21 and with 'F. LTD' 1921–c.1924. It is thought that these might be the initials of a retailer.

Savoy China Monnow Gate with Monmouth Arms painted in polychrome enamels.

c.1910–32. Circular printed mark with crown 'BR & C/STOKE-ON-TRENT/ENGLAND/SAVOY CHINA'; '368K'. 11 cm height   GCC

£40

Birks, Rawlins & Co. (1900–32) produced Savoy China, including crested novelties from 1910. They also made a number of interesting porcelains (see chapter 21).

Victoria China teddy bear with Colwyn Bay Arms painted in polychrome enamels and gilded.

c.1910–24. Printed mark 'ENGLAND/VICTORIA CHINA/J R & Co'. 9 cm height   GCC

£35

This is a mystery mark abut which several conjectures have been made, but none with adequate documentation.

Alexandra China sitting polar bear with 'Lucky Black Cat' transfer probably by Hewitt Bros.

c.1919–25. Printed circular mark 'ALEXANDRA CHINA' with 'CEBL' in the centre. Impressed mark '398'. 10 cm height   CCC

£45

Wares marked Alexandra China form a problem group. Several manufacturers including Sampson Hancock & Sons and Hewitt Bros used this mark when manufacturing wares for retailers. The initials 'CEBL' sometimes found on the marks may refer to such a retailer.

Taylor & Kent Florentine China model of an 18th-century lady's shoe with arms for Richmond, Yorkshire painted in polychrome enamels and gilded.

c.1920s. Printed circular mark with wings: 'FLORENTINE CHINA/MADE IN ENGLAND'. 10.5 cm length   CCC

£6.50

Taylor & Kent (1867–1983) made a wide range of table, fancy and heraldic ware. Their trade name was Florentine China. The firm has operated under the style Elizabethan Fine Bone China since 1983. The firm made four other shoe models.

Two Wedgwood bone china handled vases painted in polychrome enamels and gilded. Left with Westminster Arms; right with figure 'EILAND MARKEN'.

c.1900. Printed marks 'WEDGWOOD/ENGLAND'. Left 6 cm height; right 7 cm height   CCC

£32

Wedgwood made a few miniature bone china vases with painted arms c.1900. Three shapes have been recorded.

China model inscribed 'The Little Tea House, Church Shetham', painted in polychrome enamels, attributed to Leadbeater Art China.

c.1919–24. 12 cm length   GCC

£75

Edwin Leadbeater formerly of Hewitt & Leadbeater (see above), operated his own pottery 1919–24.

Rare Shelley China *Marianne* figure painted in polychrome enamels and gilded. Lancaster Arms and motto 'LUCK TO LUYNE'.

c.1923. Inscribed 'Vive La Femme'. Printed mark 'SHELLEY CHINA/406'. 11.2 cm height   CCC

£135

Wileman & Co. made crested china at Longton c.1903–23. Examples may be marked Foley China, or after c.1910 Shelley or Shelley China. Model numbers are printed on every piece.

21 20TH-CENTURY PORCELAIN

Iᴛ is a maxim (not without exceptions) that in dating tablewares of the 18th and early 19th century, there exists a hierarchy. A new style first appeared in silver (the most expensive medium), imitations then appeared in porcelain and finally in pottery. By the 20th-century this was entirely reversed. Perhaps this was due to the rise of the middle classes. In the 18th century, the small upper class could afford silver and porcelain in the latest fashion, without caring how soon it must be replaced. By the 20th century the porcelain industry was dependent upon the middle classes, where it had become traditional for brides to choose a porcelain pattern which would serve for life. Even to this day, the porcelain industry must depend on revivals of classic patterns which the purchasers feel to be timeless, patterns which they may choose at twenty and still place upon the table with pride fifty years later. It was the cheaper earthenwares which for the most part became the leaders of fashion. Crockery for everyday use was not expected to last for more than a few years, and then could easily be replaced with the prevailing fashion.

The 20th-century porcelains of greatest interest to the collector are the ornamental wares. Here the designers and potters could follow the latest trends, or even set them. Innovative design and new technology made possible remarkable wares such as Wedgwood's Fairyland Lustre and the high-fired glazed wares by Bernard Moore and Doulton at Burslem.

Although reproductions of 18th-century figures remained popular in the present century, porcelain manufacturers produced many stylish new figures, especially in the 1930s. Some of these reflected modern fashion, and are highly valued today. Also widely collected are the many figures with 'old-fashioned' dress: ladies in crinolines or with long skirts, bonnets and muffs. The most attractive of these portray a figure in motion, as opposed to one stiffly posed.

Further Reading

Geoffrey Godden, ed. *Staffordshire Porcelain* (Granada, 1983).
Geoffrey Godden. *Encyclopaedia of British Porcelain Manufacturers* (Barrie & Jenkins, 1988).
Kathy Niblett. *Dynamic Design. The British Pottery Industry 1940–90* (City Museum & Art Gallery, Stoke-on-Trent, 1990).
Judy Spours. *Art Deco Tableware* (Ward Lock, 1988).

ARKINSTALL & SONS
(ARCADIAN CHINA; ARCADIA WARE)
(1903–25)

Harold Taylor Robinson formed Arkinstall & Sons at Stoke in 1903, with the intention of producing crested china (see chapter 20). Other ornamental wares for the cheaper end of the market were also produced. These are collected by crested china enthusiasts, inflating their value above similar items made by other manufacturers.

Further Reading

Nicholas Pine. *The Price Guide to Crested China* (Milestone Publications, Horndean, 1992).

Three Arcadia Ware *Arabia* porcelain vases.

c.1920–5. All with circular printed mark 'A&S/STOKE ON TRENT' with a globe and crown 'ARABIA/ARCADIA WARE'. Left to right: 251 pattern number, 10 cm height, £55; 8.5 cm height, £45; painted pattern number 150, 9.7 cm height, £55

CCC

Two Arcadia Ware porcelain vases with blue ground, transfer-printed, filled in with polychrome enamels and gilded.

c.1920–5. Circular printed mark 'A&S/STOKE ON TRENT' with a globe and crown; 'Arcadia Ware'. Left: 'Blue Lagoon'; right: 'MIKADO'. Both 10 cm height   GCC

£95 each.

Blue Lagoon was produced in earthenware by Cauldon Potteries (see p. 258).

Arcadian China candlestick decorated with commercial purple lustre.

c.1910s. Circular printed mark 'A&S/STOKE ON TRENT/ARCADIAN' with a globe and crown. 12.2 cm height   CCC

£40

Arcadian China vase decorated with commercial pink lustre.

c.1910s. Printed circular mark with crown 'ARCADIAN/A&S/STOKE-ON-TRENT'. 20.8 cm height   CCC

£35

Arcadian China turkey decorated with orange commercial lustre.

c.1910s. Printed mark 'ARCADIAN/A&S/STOKE-ON-TRENT'.
7.5 cm height   CCC

£45

BIRKS, RAWLINS & CO.
(SAVOY CHINA)
(1900–1932)

Birks, Rawlins & Co. of Stoke (formerly L. A. Birks & Co.) made a number of interesting art porcelains. Managing director Lawrence A. Birks specialised in *pâte-sur-pâte*. He and Frederick Alfred Rhead served their apprenticeship together under M. L. Solon at Minton. At the International Exhibition, Turin in 1911, Birks exhibited *pâte-sur-pâte* decoration by F. A. Rhead and by himself, as well as tube-lined porcelain vases decorated by Charlotte Rhead and her sister Dollie. Lustre and flambé wares were also shown. The Rheads' work was also shown at the Universal Exhibition, Ghent in 1913, and Parian wares at the British Empire Exhibition of 1915. At the British and Key Industries Exhibition 1918 Birks 'had a case containing a miscellaneous assortment of badge ware, floating flower bowls, birds and butterflies, figures and busts, pierced ware, grotesques and other decorative goods' (*Pottery Gazette*, November 1918).

The firm also produced Savoy China crested novelties (see chapter 20).

Further Reading

Bernard Bumpus. *Charlotte Rhead, Potter & Designer* (Kevin Francis, 1987).
Nicholas Pine. *The Price Guide to Crested China* (Milestone Publications, Horndean, 1992).

Three Birks, Rawlins & Co. *Persindo* porcelain vases with Persian inspired enamel design of red, green and blue.

c.1911. Printed marks 'BR & Co/STOKE-ON-TRENT/ENGLAND'; painted mark '1YO/1Y/N'. Left to right: Small vase 7 cm height, cracked, £45; tall two-handled vase, 25 cm height, some damage to enamel, £180; vase, 13 cm height, £110   GCC

Persindo porcelain was shown at the International Exhibition, Turin in 1911.

Birks, Rawlins & Co. porcelain milkmaid figure painted in polychrome enamels and gilded.

c.1920. Printed circular mark with crown 'SAVOY CHINA/ STOKE-ON-TRENT/ENGLAND'. 23 cm height   CCC

£250

Birks, Rawlins & Co. porcelain bust of a girl painted in polychrome enamels.

c.1930. Printed mark 'BIRKS RAWLINS/STOKE ON TRENT'. 10 cm height   CCC

£75

Pierced double-walled porcelain jar with raised enamel decoration and gilded, possibly by Birks, Rawlins & Co.

1915. Crack in lid. Incised mark 'M. J. DECON/Potter/1915/ B&R/ STOKE'. 15 cm height   CCC

£295

Nothing is known about M. J. Decon, but this piece may have been made for the British Empire Exhibition in 1915.

COALPORT
(c.1790s and continued in The Potteries to the present day)

Cauldon Potteries purchased the firm in 1924, moving production to Shelton in 1926. Ten years later production was moved to Stoke, where the firm shared George Jones & Co.'s Crescent Pottery. In 1958 E. Brain & Co. took over the Coalport concern and production was moved to Fenton, where they continue to operate, since 1967 as a part of the Wedgwood Group.

470

In the present century the firm has specialised in high quality bone china tablewares, although they are well known for their Coalbrookdale type floral encrusted ornamental wares.

Coalport porcelain plate with green ground and raised paste gilding. Centre painted in polychrome enamels 'Trout' signed by P. Simpson.

c.1901–20. 'Z841' painted pattern number. Impressed mark 12KH. Printed mark with crown 'ENGLAND/COALPORT/AD 1750'. Retailer's mark 'T. GOODE'. 23 cm diameter   TA

£70

Percy Simpson worked at Coalport 1901–56 as a painter. He was their finest painter of fish and game subjects, eventually becoming the firm's art director. Two examples of his work are illustrated in Godden.

Coalport porcelain figures painted in polychrome enamels, *Peggy* and *June*.

c.1935–9. Printed mark 'MADE IN ENGLAND/COAL-PORT/A.D. 1750' with crown; 'Pors Ringer'. 12.5 cm height
CCC

Peggy £125; June £85.

These figures are reproductions of W. H. Goss Flower Girls (see below). Coalport was purchased by Cauldon Potteries in 1924 and W. H. Goss by Cauldon in the early 1930s. Obviously Cauldon transferred production of these models to Coalport sometime afterwards.

W. T. COPELAND & SONS
(1847–1970)

W. T. Copeland continued many of the shapes and patterns used by Copeland & Garrett (1833–47), and by Spode, who preceded Copeland & Garrett. The firm made both earthenwares and porcelains. Copeland is one of the exceptions to the rule that period designs are most desirable, as some of their finest pieces were reproductions of earlier shapes and designs. Copeland used a series of impressed and printed marks. They also introduced a system of impressed date codes in 1870, in which the last two digits of the year are surmounted by a letter for the month. The system was used on bone china until 1963. The company has continued since 1970 under the style Spode Ltd.

Further Reading

Robert Copeland. 'Spode porcelains, c.1797–1833, and the succeeding firms', *Staffordshire Porcelain* (Granada, 1983).
The Spode Society. *Recorder & Review* (1986 to the present day).

Copeland bone china pot-pourri decorated with polychrome enamels and gilding.

c.1910. Butterfly restored. Painted pattern number R3827. Printed mark 'SPODE'S/B233/Rd No 553455/SPODE/COPELAND'S CHINA/ENGLAND'. 16 cm height   HBW

£150

This is an example of one of their many revivals of Spode (1770–1833) wares. For a Spode example of this shape see p. 382.

One of a pair of Copeland bone china plates painted in polychrome enamels and gilded.

c.1930. Printed marks 'SPODE/COPELAND'S CHINA/ENGLAND'; 'T. GOODE & CO/LONDON'. Painted pattern number C/2024. 23 cm diameter   JJB

£165 the pair.

The C-prefix pattern numbers were a special series for the retailer Thomas Goode. Pattern C/2024 was introduced in 1930.

CROWN STAFFORDSHIRE PORCELAIN CO.
(1889–1948)

This firm was established in 1833 by Thomas Green and remained in the Green family until 1964. The style was changed to Crown Staffordshire Porcelain Co. in 1889. Crown Staffordshire made a wide variety of interesting bone china tablewares, figures and fancies. It was the first Longton china firm to introduce realistic floral fancies with moulded applied flowers, although floral encrusted porcelains had been made elsewhere since the 18th century, and set up a 'flower' workshop in 1910. This has remained the greatest speciality. Geoffrey Godden has said that it is a neglected factory, whose wares are undervalued. The firm changed its name to Crown Staffordshire China Co. in 1948. It is now part of the Wedgwood Group.

An article in the *Pottery Gazette and Glass Trade Review* in October 1952 mentions miniature tea sets with trays, which were exact replicas of full-size factory productions. David Queensberry designed tableware patterns and a famous set of nursery ware for Crown Staffordshire in the late 1950s. The nursery ware was controversial, because many people thought that it would frighten children, the animals not being cute enough. Today one can not see anything alarming in the designs, which would be worth looking out for.

Crown Staffordshire Chinese style bone china lamp base decorated with polychrome enamels.

c.1920s. 21 cm length of base   CCC

£200

Crown Staffordshire bone china figures after wooden models painted in polychrome enamels.

c.1930s. Printed mark with impressed crown. Left to right: Wife, 9 cm height, £80; Little wife, 6.8 cm height, £80; Witch, 9 cm height, £150; Lady, 10.5 cm height, £80.   CCC

Crown Staffordshire bone china figure of Punch after a wooden model painted in polychrome enamels.

c.1930s. Printed mark with impressed crown. 12.8 cm height
CCC

£200

Crown Staffordshire bone china figure of Old Peasant painted in polychrome enamels.

c.1930s. Printed mark with impressed crown. 16 cm height
CCC

£100

473

Crown Staffordshire bone china figure of Falstaff painted in polychrome enamels.

c.1930s. Printed mark with impressed crown. 11 cm height

CCC

£100

DOULTON & CO.,BURSLEM
(1882 to the present day)

Henry Doulton bought a controlling interest in the Nile Street Pottery of Pinder, Bourne & Co. in 1877 and took complete control in 1882. The success of the firm was largely brought about by the combined talents of John C. Bailey, who was engaged as general manager, John Slater as art director, and C. J. Noke as chief designer. Bone china was introduced in 1884 and from that time the better-quality wares were made in that body.

When J. C. Bailey joined Doulton in 1900, Charles Noke and John Slater had been trying to perfect a reduction rouge flambé glaze for some time. Bailey continued these experiments, but the results remained inconsistent. In 1902, Doulton appointed Bernard Moore as consultant to assist in developing their rouge flambé wares. Moore had devoted many years to reduction rouge flambé glazes (see p. 490). With the help of Charles Noke, Bailey and Moore perfected the Doulton flambé glaze, which was exhibited at the Louisiana Purchase Exhibition in St Louis in 1904. The animal models were particularly popular and after a break during the Second World War, their production has been successfully revived.

Although Doulton have continued many traditional patterns throughout the 20th century, they made stylish tablewares in the 1920s and 1930s.

A fine collection of Doulton wares may be seen at the Henry Doulton Gallery at the Royal Doulton works, Nile Street, Burslem, Stoke-on-Trent.

Further Reading

Paul Atterbury and Louise Irvine. *The Doulton Story* (Royal Doulton Tableware, 1987).
Desmond Eyles. *Doulton Burslem Ware* (Barrie & Jenkins, 1980).
Desmond Eyles, Richard Dennis and Louise Irvine. *Royal Doulton Figures* (Richard Dennis, 1987).
Jocelyn Lukin. *Doulton Flambé Animals* (M. P. E., Yelverton, n.d.).
Royal Doulton Figures (Doulton & Co. Ltd, n.d.)
Mike Yewman. *Lyle Price Guide to Doulton* (Lyle Publications, 1990).

One of a set of six Royal Doulton bone china demitasse cups and saucers painted in polychrome enamels and gilded.

c.1926. Printed mark in green with lion and crown 'ROYAL DOULTON ENGLAND'; painted pattern number H2718. Cup 5.8 cm height; saucer 10.8 cm diameter   AF

£90

Royal Doulton Titanian porcelain bowl with blue ground, painted daffodils and gold edge signed H. Allen.

c.1920. Printed mark 'ROYAL DOULTON/OBORON/ TITA-NIAN/ENGLAND'; painted pattern number 822; 105 incised. 8 cm diameter   G

£220

The Titanian process, produced 1916–c.1933, was developed by Charles J. Noke. A new, light, exceptionally translucent body, a new glaze and new blends of pigments were developed. Titanian ware's characteristic smoky blue colour comes from titanium oxide. The overall effect is similar to wares that Royal Copenhagen had been making since the turn of the century.

Some of Titanian wares, such as the bowl shown here, are beautifully painted, while others depend on glaze effects which Desmond Eyles describes as 'tender veils of colour enveloping the simple shapes.' A combination of underglaze printing and painting was also employed. Tablewares were made as well as ornamental wares.

Harry Allen was one of Doulton's best artists, working 1900–50. Pattern number 822 (H series) was introduced in 1919.

Royal Doulton flambé glazed porcelain rabbit.

c.1923–7+. Ear restored. Printed lion mark without crown with 'MADE IN ENGLAND'. 9.6 cm height   TV

£60

This rabbit model was produced 1912–62 and has since been returned to production.

Royal Doulton flambé porcelain cat.

c.1950+. Printed lion and crown mark with 'MADE IN ENGLAND'. 13.6 cm height   TV

£125

This cat model has been continuously produced since 1950.

Royal Doulton *Autumn Breezes* porcelain figure modelled by Leslie Harradine.

Dated 1939. 20 cm height   TV

£135

Royal Doulton has a long history of making fine quality figures. Leslie Harradine was apprenticed at the Doulton Lambeth factory 1902–12. He designed for Doulton Burslem on a free-lance basis 1920–60. Other important figure modellers at Royal Doulton include Harry Tittensor (1914–21) and Peggy Davis (1939–80s). More than 200 models remain in production. This figure was made 1939–76.

These Royal Doulton figures have been exhaustively covered in a number of price guides. As these list prices for nearly every model, they effectively determine the values for the figures. A dealer acquiring one of these figures just checks the price in the guide and voilà! This is possible because there are so many of these figures around and they are so well marked. The quality is consistent and colour variations have been documented. The period of production is also known, with figures only produced for a brief period at a premium, and the more popular models, produced for decades, valued much lower.

W. H. GOSS
(1858–1939)

W. H. Goss is best known today for their crested china (see chapter 20) but they also produced fine Parian wares (see chapter 19).

Nicholas Pine has divided the production of the Goss factory into three periods, and these have been generally adopted by collectors. During the First Period (1858–87) William Henry Goss owned and ran the pottery, and most of the unglazed Parian wares were made. During the Second Period (1881–1934) the firm was managed by his three sons

Adolphus, Victor and William Huntley Goss and the chief product was Heraldic Porcelain. Sometime during the early years of the Third Period (c.1930–9), the firm was taken over by Cauldon Potteries, and earthenwares were introduced, although cheap crested china was still made.

Third Period Goss figures are sought after by collectors although the quality is not as good as Royal Worcester or Doulton. The subjects of many of these were obviously inspired by Royal Doulton. However, the models were designed so as to minimise the number of separately cast pieces. Thus, we see that Goss figure arms nearly always rest against the dress or body, and are never separated or extended, as is often found in the Royal Doulton figures.

Further Reading

Nicholas Pine. *Goss and Crested China* (Shire Publications, Aylesbury, 1984).
Nicholas Pine. *William Henry Goss* (Milestone Publications, Horndean, 1987).
Nicholas Pine. *The Concise Encyclopaedia and Price Guide to Goss China* (Milestone Publications, Horndean, 1992).

Goss glazed Parian preserve jar and lid with cherry knop, decorated with transfer-print coloured in with enamels.

c.1890–1920. Printed Goshawk mark. 11 cm height   CCC

£65

These jam jars are in imitation of Wemyss Ware, which was earthenware and hand-painted. Pine has recorded some thirteen floral or fruit patterns. The matching fruit knop adds about £10 to the value of the jar.

Goss Parian 'Welsh Lady' teapot, glazed and enamelled.

c.1930s. Printed Goshawk mark; 'ENGLAND'. 15.8 cm height
CCC

£95

Goss glazed Parian 'Flower Girl' figures painted with polychrome enamels.

c.1930–9. Printed Goshawk mark; 'ENGLAND'. All 13 cm height   GCC

Peggy £165; Bridesmaid £65; Gwenda £255.

Three of a range of thirty 'Flower Girl' figures.It is interesting to note that Royal Doulton issued figures named Peggy, Bridesmaid and Gwendolyn during the 1930s of

477

which the Goss figures are loose imitations. The 'Flower Girls' were individually decorated by paintresses, who often signed their initials on the bases. Some of these figures (especially the smaller models) may only be marked 'ENGLAND'. Some time after Goss was purchased by Cauldon Potteries in the early 1930s, production of the 'Flower Girls' was transferred to Coalport, another Cauldon subsidiary. The prices of these vary considerably depending on rarity.

Goss glazed Parian 'Balloon Seller'.

c.1930s. Printed mark 'W. H. GOSS'. 9 cm height   GCC

£175

Balloon Seller figures modelled by Leslie Harradine were first manufactured by Royal Doulton in 1921. Goss's imitation is a poor one, with the balloons all lumped together.

ALFRED B. JONES & SONS
(GRAFTON CHINA)
(1880–1972)

Alfred B. Jones made a wide range of china. The firm now trades as Crown Lynn Ceramics Ltd using the trade name Royal Grafton. They were major manufacturers of crested china from c.1900 (see chapter 20).

Grafton China porcelain demitasse cup and saucer decorated with polychrome enamel and gilding.

c.1930s. Printed mark 'GRAFTON CHINA' with 'ABJ' in Staffordshire knot with '& SONS/ENGLAND' below. Cup 5.2 cm height; saucer 11 cm diameter   CCC

£30

Grafton China porcelain elephant with matt blue glaze.

c.1930. Printed mark 'GRAFTON CHINA' with 'ABJ' in Staffordshire knot with '& SONS/ENGLAND' below; painted pattern number 437. 9 cm height   GCC

£45

Grafton China porcelain monkey with orange glaze.

c.1930. Printed mark 'GRAFTON CHINA' with 'ABJ' in Staffordshire knot with '& SONS/ENGLAND' below. 8 cm height
CCC

£45

R. H. & S. L. PLANT
(TUSCAN CHINA)
(1898 to the present day)

Best known for its Tuscan China tablewares, this Longton firm also produced china figures and novelties. An article in the *Pottery Gazette and Glass Trade Review* in May 1919 explained that the firm divided their wares into three categories: '(1) Tea and breakfast services, the pre-eminent and staple trade of the "Tuscan" Works; (2) vases, and (3) birds, animals and fancies.' They made Tuscan Faience after the First World War (see p. 283) and introduced their Ploverine Ware 'drawing room vases' with 'an all-over treatment reminiscent of veined and figured marble, over which hangs a delicate sheen of purple lustre.'

The firm became part of the Wedgwood Group in 1966 and was named Royal Tuscan in 1971. In 1976 Tuscan China Holdings was formed from R. H. & S. L. Plant and Susie Cooper, under the style Wedgwood hotelware. The factory was renamed Royal Tuscan in 1989.

Tuscan China bone china garden scene ornament painted in polychrome enamels.

c.1930s. Hairline crack on base. TUSCAN CHINA/R. H. & S. L. PLANT/ENGLAND' with winged crown. Painted mark 'No. 2AB'. 13 cm height   AF

£90

Tuscan China bone china figure painted in polychrome enamels.

c.1930s. 'East of Suez/No. 75/Potted by Plant' painted in orange. 'PLANT/TUSCAN CHINA/MADE IN ENGLAND' printed in green with an eagle. 14 cm height   CCC

£135

Tuscan China bone china ornament portraying a garden scene with pond painted in polychrome enamels.

c.1930s. Hairline crack in base. 'PLANT/TUSCAN CHINA/ENGLAND' with winged crown. 12 cm height   AF

£80

ROYAL CROWN DERBY PORCELAIN CO.
(1890–1975)

This new porcelain factory was established at Derby by Edward Phillips and William Litherland, specialising in very fine quality porcelains. Like other major porcelain manufacturers, many of their 20th-century designs were revivals of earlier styles. Most of these wares are marked, and many carry impressed date ciphers. Pattern numbers may also assist but only in so far as they tell us the approximate date of introduction, since many of these patterns continued in production for years. The Royal Crown Derby factory is now part of Royal Doulton Tablewares Ltd. The factory museum is open to the public, and tours of the factory are available.

Pattern numbers	Date of introduction	Pattern numbers	Date of introduction
6100–6750	c.1900–1	8400–8700	c.1909–10
6750–7000	c.1902	8700–9100	c.1911–13
7000–7350	c.1903	9100–9600	c.1914–25
7350–7500	c.1904	c.9600–9999	c.1926
7500–7750	c.1905	A1–A.1213	c.1926–59
7750–8000	c.1906	A.1215–A.1318	c.1959–88
8000–8400	c.1907–8		

Further Reading

John Twitchett and Betty Bailey. *Royal Crown Derby*, revised edn (Antique Collectors' Club, Woodbridge, 1988).

Royal Crown Derby is perhaps best known for its Japan patterns: introduced by many factories during the 1810s, these patterns enjoyed a great revival in the 1870s, and are still popular today. The most common of them used at Derby is the Witches pattern, no. 6299.

Royal Crown Derby Japan pattern porcelain muffin dish painted in polychrome enamels and gilded.

c.1917. Printed mark with crown 'ROYAL CROWN DERBY'. year cipher for 1917. 21 cm diameter   JM

£250

Toy or miniature shapes were introduced in 1904 and have been very popular with collectors ever since, which is reflected in the high prices for these wares. Production of toys had largely ceased by 1940.

Royal Crown Derby porcelain toys in Witches pattern number 6299 painted in polychrome enamels and gilded.

Printed marks with crown 'ROYAL CROWN DERBY'. Cauldron impressed shape number 1480, year cipher for 1917, 6.7 cm height, £235. Kettle (shape 1479), year cipher for 1911, 6.4 cm height, £425.   TV

Two Royal Crown Derby Japan patterned miniature porcelain vases painted in polychrome enamels and gilded.

Printed marks with crown 'ROYAL CROWN DERBY'. Left: pattern number 1128, shape 465, year cipher for 1916, 8 cm height, £215. Right: Witches pattern, number 6299, shape 1453, year cipher for 1928, 8.5 cm height, £215.   TV

One of a pair of Royal Crown Derby porcelain plates with green ground, painted in polychrome enamels and gilded, signed by A. Gregory.

c.1920. Printed mark with crown 'ROYAL CROWN DERBY/ MADE IN ENGLAND'. Painted pattern number 9441. 23 cm diameter   JJB

£295 the pair.

Albert Gregory is best known for the 'Gregory' rose featured in this plate: a similar example is illustrated in Twitchett & Bailey. Gregory worked at Derby from the 1890s until the 1940s.

WEDGWOOD
(c.1759 to the present day)

The early years of the 20th century were difficult for Wedgwood. Apart from the recession at the turn of the century, they suffered the absence of senior management during the Boer War and a lawsuit against a mining firm over subsidence damage to the Etruria pottery.

During the second decade of the century Wedgwood developed ornamental bone china for the first time. Fairyland Lustre was made 1916–41 under the direction of Susanna Margaretta 'Daisy' Makeig-Jones. The manufacture of these wares was complex and expensive. First the pot was biscuit-fired, then transfer-printed before being painted with underglaze colours. The colour was then hardened on in a muffle kiln, dipped in a clear lead glaze and glost-fired. A commercial, liquid lustre was then painted on and fired at a low temperature (this process sometimes being repeated for a second time). The pot was then transfer-printed with a paste of mercuric oxide and oil. Gold powder was dusted over the print, where it adhered to the paste (known as pluck-and-dust printing), and liquid gold was painted on the rim. This was fired and the gilding polished with silver sand. In some cases enamel decoration was then added, and fired again. One must keep in mind that each stage and its attendant firing increased the risk of damage. As these lustre wares underwent five or six firings, they were extremely difficult to produce. In 1929 during a rationalisation of the factory production, twenty-three of the 100 Fairyland Lustre patterns were cancelled, fourteen were retained and the remainder were available only by special order. Other lustre wares with less complex designs were also made featuring dragons, butterflies, fish or birds. The Fairyland Lustres are today extremely costly, and forgeries do exist.

Most Wedgwood wares are well marked. The prefix 'Z' was used for china fancies, including Fairyland Lustre (first pattern number Z4823).

A fine collection of Wedgwood wares may be seen at the Wedgwood Museum at Barlaston, Staffordshire.

Further Reading

Maureen Batkin. *Wedgwood Ceramics, 1846–1959* (Richard Dennis, 1982).
Una des Fontaines. *Wedgwood Fairyland Lustre* (Sotheby Parke Bernet, 1975).
Una des Fontaines, Lionel Lambourne and Ann Eatwell. *Miss Jones and her Fairyland* (Victoria & Albert Museum, 1990).
Geoffrey Godden and Michael Gibson. *Collecting Lustreware* (Barrie & Jenkins, 1991).
Robin Reilly. *Wedgwood*, vol. II (Macmillan, 1989).

Wedgwood Fairyland Lustre Imperial shape bone china bowl.

c.1916–29. Printed Portland Vase mark (Wedgwood trademark). Painted pattern number Z4968. 6.8 cm height   T

£295

This pattern number Z4968 was used for at least forty-five different complex patterns.

Wedgwood Lustre bone china covered jar.

c.1916–41. Gold printed mark 'WEDGWOOD/ETRURIA'; Portland Vase mark (Wedgwood trademark); impressed mark '2410'; painted mark 'Z4829'. 25 cm height with lid
G

£450

This dragon pattern was used on many shapes, and remained in production 1916–41.

Wedgwood bone china demitasse cup and saucer decorated in silver lustre and orange enamel by Thérèse Lessore.

c.1930–5. Crack to cup. Printed brown Portland Vase mark with 'MADE IN ENGLAND'. Signed with 'TL' monogram. Cup 5.6 cm height; saucer 10.8 cm diameter
G

£80

Thérèse Lessore (1883–1944) was the granddaughter of the painter Émile Lessore who had been employed by Wedgwood for many years (see p. 143). Originally a painter, Thérèse was probably introduced to pottery decoration by Alfred and Louise Powell.

She worked as an independent decorator using Wedgwood blanks. Unlike the Powells, most of her subject matter seems to have been contemporary, often using figures in modern dress in modern settings. A selection of wares painted by Thérèse Lessore are illustrated in Batkin.

WILTSHAW & ROBINSON
(CARLTON CHINA; MOTHER SHIPTON CHINA)
(1890–1957)

Established in 1890 as an earthenware manufacturer, Wiltshaw & Robinson began to produce Carlton Heraldic China, in competition with W. H. Goss, in 1902 (see chapter 20). The firm went into receivership in 1931 and merged with Birks, Rawlins & Co. the following year. It was during the 1930s that these china figures were produced.

Further Reading

Nicholas Pine. *The Price Guide to Crested China* (Milestone Publications, Horndean, 1992).

Carlton China porcelain *Grandma* figure painted in polychrome enamels.

c.1930s. Printed mark 'CARLTON CHINA/'Grandma'/MADE IN ENGLAND'. Painted pattern number 4276. 19 cm height
CCC

£125

Mother Shipton China porcelain figure painted in polychrome enamels.

c.1930s. Printed mark 'MOTHER SHIPTON CHINA' with picture of Mother Shipton. 11 cm height
CCC

£125

Mother Shipton was used by Wiltshaw & Robinson for the retailer J. W. Simpson, Dropping Well, Knaresborough.

WORCESTER ROYAL PORCELAIN CO.
(1862–1976)

Throughout the 20th century, Royal Worcester (continuing as Royal Worcester Spode Ltd from 1976) has excelled in producing traditional tableware. Their clientele have come to expect the sumptuous coloured ground, gilding and fine painting typical of the firm's Victorian tablewares, although the firm has produced modern lines, such as Art Deco tea sets and Contemporary style tablewares. It is mainly in the production of ornamental wares that the firm has continued to introduce new wares and contemporary designs. In the early years of the century, many of their finest designers and artists were carried over from the Victorian period (see chapter 17), and hence the wares produced were much like those produced in the previous century (for example the George Owen pierced vase and Sabrina Ware below).

Further Reading

Derek Shirley. *A Guide to the Dating of Royal Worcester Porcelain Marks from 1862* (D.B. Shirley, 1982).

Henry Sandon. *Royal Worcester Porcelain from 1862 to the Present Day*, 3rd edn (Barrie & Jenkins, 1978).

Royal Worcester porcelain armorial bowl with blue and brown transfer-prints decorated with enamels and gilding.

c.1903. Printed mark with date code for 1903. Impressed mark 10A. 17 cm diameter   JJB

£65

Royal Worcester porcelain blush biscuit barrel painted in polychrome enamels and gilded.

c.1903. Printed Royal Worcester mark with twelve dots (date code for 1903). Printed registration number 101230 (1888); painted pattern number 1236. 14 cm height   JM

£245

Royal Worcester porcelain plate painted in polychrome enamels signed by G. H. Cole and gilded.

c.1910. Printed Royal Worcester mark with date code for 1910. Painted pattern number 9134. 22.8 cm diameter   JJB

£345

George H. Cole (d. 1912) was a fine painter of roses and other flowers, as well as scenes of Malvern.

One of a pair of Royal Worcester porcelain plates, painted in polychrome enamels with flowers by Richard Sebright and gilded by William Phipps.

Dated 1905. 'B10' impressed. Pattern number W6934. 23 cm diameter   TV

£380 the pair.

Richard (Dick) Sebright (1868–1951) is best known for his fine paintings of fruit, which he pursued at Worcester from c.1890 to the late 1940s. He was also a skilled painter of flowers. William Phipps (1885–1960) specialised in raised paste gilding and aerographing. He was foreman gilder

485

1938–45, retiring in 1950. Pattern W6934 was introduced in 1903. The clay mark (impressed) B indicates that the plate was made in 1904, a year before it was decorated.

Royal Worcester reticulated porcelain vase by George Owen.

c.1909. Incised signature George Owen; printed Royal Worcester mark with 18 dots (date code for 1909). 28 cm height
B

£5,000

George Owen often produced these reticulated wares in his own time. These were then sold by the firm to collectors, and Owen would be paid. Finely reticulated wares could take months to complete, and were not economical for normal factory production. The piercing was done when the pot was still in a green state, before biscuit firing. As clay dries out rapidly the pot was stored in a metal-lined box with damp rags until the work was completed. The work was painstaking, and the slightest error was irreparable. Most of George Owen's later work was signed G. Owen, and unsigned pieces may be assumed to be the work of other reticulators. Other George Owen wares are illustrated in Sandon.

Royal Worcester blush vellum glaze porcelain jug painted in polychrome enamels and gilded.

c.1909. Printed Royal Worcester mark with eighteen dots (date code for 1909). Painted mark 24/11. Printed mark 1094. 11 cm height
TA

£120

This is a common shape, which was made in various sizes.

Royal Worcester porcelain plate with green ground, raised paste gilding and polychrome enamel decoration signed by F. Roberts.

c.1917. Painted pattern number C1411 RS; printed Royal Worcester mark for 1917. 22.2 cm diameter
JJB

£375

Frank Roberts (1857–1920) worked at Royal Worcester 1872–1920, painting fruit and flowers, and doing traced and raised gold work. C pattern numbers began in 1913.

Royal Worcester Sabrina Ware Parian vase decorated in blue and green, signed by Walter Harold Austin.

Dated 1926. Impressed shape number 2368. Printed 'Sabrina Porcelain'; Royal Worcester mark. 30 cm height
TV

£585

Sabrina Ware was produced 1897–1930. The subtle effects were obtained by the use of metallic salts, the reaction of these in the kiln not being entirely controllable. As a result some examples have a muddy appearance with the decoration badly obscured. However, at its best, as in this example, the ware is fascinating, with the decoration shimmering in the depths. Although Sabrina Wares had a Parian body, the decorative treatment renders the wares opaque. Sabrina Ware is almost always marked 'Sabrina'. Shape number 2368 was introduced in 1904 for use with Sabrina decoration. Other Sabrina Wares are illustrated in Sandon.
    Walter Harold Austin (1891–1971) specialised in the painting of fruit, flowers and birds. His pastime, angling, is reflected in this painting. He left Worcester in 1930.

Royal Worcester porcelain plate with blue ground and gilding, signed H. Everett.

Dated 1926. Registration number 651926 (1915). Printed Royal Worcester mark with 'MADE IN ENGLAND'. 27 cm diameter
TV

£265

Miss Hilda Everett was primarily a painter of flowers, working at Worcester from the 1920s to the early 1930s.

Royal Worcester porcelain vase with scene painted in polychrome enamels inscribed 'Ripple', signed by Raymond Rushton and gilded.

Dated 1929. Royal Worcester printed mark with G42. 22.2 cm height
TV

£1,150

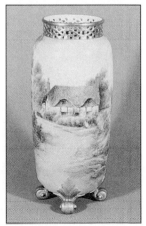

Raymond Rushton (1886–1956) painted landscapes and gardens, specialising in pictures of cottages, manor houses and castles. He retired in 1953.

Royal Worcester porcelain plate with mazarine ground and gilding, printed and coloured scene of 'Ventnor' signed by J. Walters.

c.1928. Printed Royal Worcester mark with 'MADE IN ENGLAND'. Painted pattern number Z/285. 'Painted by Hand'. 26.5 cm diameter   TA

£95

Walter Sedgeley, who worked at Royal Worcester 1889–1929, specialised in flower painting and Italian garden scenes. He used the pseudonyms Seeley and J. Walters on printed and coloured pieces. Z pattern numbers began in 1928 and are used to the present day.

WILEMAN & CO.
(SHELLEY; FOLEY)
(1892 to the present day)

Formerly Wileman & Co., this firm was incorporated as Shelley Potteries Ltd in 1928. Their trade names were Foley and Shelley. The name was changed to Shelley China in 1965. It was taken over the following year by Allied English Potteries, and is now part of Royal Doulton Tablewares Group. Today the firm's wares are widely collected, most especially their Art Deco china tea wares. After the second World War the firm, like many other china manufacturers, increasingly devoted production to traditional shapes and patterns. They did not introduce coupe shape dinner ware until 1957 (four years after Midwinter had introduced their first coupe shaped earthenwares), and these do not seem to have been a great success. As interest in Contemporary style tablewares grows and Art Deco Shelley wares become prohibitively expensive, these coupe shape tablewares are likely to attract the notice of collectors. The firm also made china fancies, such as figures, and crested ware.

The trade name Foley was also used by E. Brain & Co. Old Foley was the trade name of James Kent.

Further Reading

C. Watkins, W. Harvey and R. Senft. *Shelley Potteries* (Barrie & Jenkins, 1980).
Susan Hill. *The Shelley Style* (Jazz Publications, 1990).

Cup and saucer from Shelley bone china trio in Queen Anne shape with 'Cottage 2' pattern painted in polychrome enamels over transfer-print.

c.1930. Printed mark 'Shelley/ENGLAND/Rd 723404 (1926); painted pattern number 31621/4. Cup 6.7 cm height; saucer 13.5 cm diameter; tea plate 16.4 cm diameter   HA

£48 for the trio.

Shelley Regent style bone china jug and bowl painted in polychrome enamels.

c.1933. Printed mark 'Shelley/ENGLAND'; 'IDEAL CHINA No.' followed by painted pattern number W.R.074; 'REG NO 781613' (1933). Bowl 13.7 cm diameter; jug 9 cm height
HA

£25

Shelley bone china morning set painted in polychrome enamels, including teapot, two cups and saucers, biscuit plate, cream jug and sugar bowl.

c.1930. Painted pattern number U 119895/E. Printed mark 'Shelley/ENGLAND'. Printed retailer's mark 'LAWLEY'S/ REGENT ST/ESTD PHILLIPS 1760'. Teapot 11 cm height
HA

£225

Shelley bone china Queen Anne shape morning set painted with Vase of Flowers pattern in polychrome enamels over transfer-print, including teapot, two cups and saucers, biscuit plate, cream jug and sugar bowl.

c.1930. Pattern number 11445/D. Printed mark 'Shelley/ENGLAND/Rd. 723404' (1926). Teapot 12 cm height   HA

£265

OTHER MANUFACTURERS

Royal Venton Ming ware porcelain vase with a crackled mutton fat glaze dripping down over a uranium orange glaze.

c.1930s. Impressed mark 'ROYAL VENTON WARE/Ming/ ENGLAND'. 20 cm height   AF

£2

Royal Venton was a trade name used by John Steventon & Sons (1923 to the present day). Steventon made table and novelty wares typical of the 1930s. The Royal Venton Ware mark was used 1931–40. They now make tiles and sanitary wares. The Ming wares were probably inspired by Doulton's much more expensive Chang glazes. A more realistic price for this vase would probably be £10–12, and they are likely to increase in value considerably over the next decade.

Bernard Moore rouge flambé porcelain vase.

c.1905–15. Incised mark 'BERNARD MOORE' with wavy line beneath. 23 cm height   HBW

£175

Bernard Moore (1850–1935) began art pottery production after he was forced to sell his family's pottery at Longton, Moore Bros, in 1905. Moore had been experimenting with *sang-de-bœuf* and rouge flambé glazes for some years. Certainly he had perfected the techniques by 1902, when he presented some fine examples to the British Museum. His wares were highly praised and shown at all of the major International Exhibitions of the period. Some wares were decorated with only glazes, but others were painted by one of several fine ceramic artists in Moore's employ. See Aileen Dawson, *Bernard Moore Master Potter 1850–1935* (Richard Dennis, 1982).

Large rouge flambé porcelain vase.

c.1912. Mark incised in the glaze 'HOWSONS/1912'. 26 cm height   G

£95

G. Howson & Sons (Ltd) (1865–1966) were sanitary ware manufacturers at Hanley. George Howson's youngest son, Richard, decided to join the great revival of high-temperature flambé wares. He may have been inspired by the success of his cousin, William Howson Taylor. As Richard lacked technical expertise, he hired Edward Wilkes in 1910. Wilkes had been working with Bernard Moore since 1905, and apparently felt that he had not been given sufficient credit for his part in developing the flambé technique. Howson's flambé wares were produced 1911–16. The glaze scratches quite easily.

Porcelain plate with raised paste gilded border and painted centre.

c.1910. Painted pattern number 9311. 22.5 cm diameter JJB

£165

Part of a Susie Cooper coffee set, including coffee pot, six cups, six saucers, and six tea plates.

c.1957. Printed mark of facsimile signature 'Susie Cooper'; 'BONE CHINA/ENGLAND.' Coffee pot 21 cm height.   MB

£135 the set.

Susie Cooper has been in the forefront of ceramic design for five decades. She worked for Gray's Pottery 1922–9. In 1929 she established her own decorating studio, from which these pieces would have come. For Susie Cooper earthenwares see chapter 14.

22 LUSTREWARE

THE most commonly found lustrewares are a uniquely English invention c.1805. These are items completely coated with pigments containing minute amounts of gold (for a copper or pink lustre) or platinum (for a silver lustre) and fired in a low-temperature oxidising atmosphere. Copper lustre is most successful when applied to a brown earthenware body. A thin gold solution on a white body produces a pink lustre.

Initially the intention may have been to imitate silver, but soon the merits and potentials of the lustres were recognised and they were used as decoration on their own or in conjunction with coloured enamels. Lustre occurs on a wide variety of wares, from the best quality porcelains to the cheapest earthenwares.

The main centres of production were Staffordshire, Sunderland, Swansea, Newcastle and Leeds.

For more about other types of lustres see p. 19.

Further Reading

John C. Baker. *Sunderland Pottery*, revised edn (Tyne and Wear County Council Museums, 1983).

Geoffrey Godden and Michael Gibson. *Collecting Lustreware* (Barrie & Jenkins, 1991).

Patrick McVeigh. *Scottish East Coast Potteries* (John Donald Publishers, Edinburgh, 1979).

Philip Miller and Michael Berthoud. *An Anthology of British Teapots* (Micawber Publications, Broseley, 1985).

Noël Riley. *Gifts for Good Children* (Richard Dennis, Ilminster, 1991).

John A. Shuman III. *The Collector's Encyclopaedia of Gaudy Dutch & Welsh* (Collector Books, Paducah, Ky, 1991).

Yellow glaze earthenware jug decorated with silver lustre and bat-prints of *Hope* and *Faith*.

c.1808–20. 12 cm height   BG

£345

These wares are sometimes called Canary Yellow. Godden & Gibson illustrate a third print in the series, *Application*.

Reverse.

Rare New Hall porcelain teapot and stand painted in Japan pattern (number 446) over underglaze blue transfer-print with platinum lustre.

c.1810. Some rubbing. Teapot with lid 15 cm height; stand 16.8 cm length   G

£285

The New Hall pottery was operated by a series of five partnerships c.1782–1835. Pattern 446 is ordinarily found with gilding, rather than platinum lustre. Geoffrey Godden has noted that these platinum lustre pots do not have pattern numbers. For more about New Hall porcelains see chapter 16.

Factory Z porcelain teapot with polychrome enamel and platinum lustre decoration.

c.1810. Hairline cracks. 14.5 cm height including lid, excluding handle and spout.   T

£118

Factory Z (c.1800–20 or earlier) is a name assigned by scholars to a group of porcelains which appear to have been made by one manufacturer, whose identity remains uncertain. There have been a number of suggestions, and it now seems possible that the group were manufactured by the Wolfe & Hamilton partnership.

An example of this teapot is in the Norwich Museum. Despite the damage, the fine quality of potting and decoration, with the naïve painting of the lion, make this a desirable pot.

Silver lustre earthenware allegorical figure of a woman dressed in classical robes.

c.1810–30. 18 cm height   HBW

£170

A similar figure representing Plenty is illustrated in Godden & Gibson.

493

A rare cream coloured earthenware porridge bowl of 'lug-gie' shape painted in pink lustre and polychrome enamels, probably from Rathbone's Portobello Pottery.

c.1815. Inscribed 'Mathew Aicken Bruce'. 12 cm diameter

D

£350

A similar bowl is illustrated in McVeigh.

Silver resist decoration as seen on the following two jugs is created by painting the parts of the design to be left without lustre with a 'resist' of wax or grease to which the lustre will not adhere. The effect is very decorative, and the wares are highly valued by collectors.

Pink lustre earthenware jug with silver resist decoration.

c.1815–25. Chip. 12 cm height   HBW

£120

This jug is of a standard shape made by many manu-facturers. Godden & Gibson illustrate a similar example with the rare impressed mark 'Boardman'.

Silver resist lustre earthenware jug.

c.1815–25. 15 cm height   HBW

£245

Splashed pink lustre earthenware cat, press-moulded with glazed white hollow interior.

c.1820. 16 cm height   S

£5,500

This is an exceedingly rare figure, and figures of cats have always been most popular with collectors. Delftware examples in shapes similar to this figure have been recorded from the 17th century. For an example decorated with coloured oxides underglaze see p. 153.

Staffordshire porcelain cream jug with pink lustre decoration and on-glaze black transfer-prints of *Hope* and *Faith*.

c.1820. Some staining. 10 cm height excluding handle   T

£75

Lustre goblets were usually sold in pairs, often with a matching jug. These would have been popular at a time when the tax on glass was high. Copper lustre examples are often decorated with sprigging or painted with polychrome enamels. Be wary of examples with inscriptions, dates or names, as some forgeries have been recorded.

Silver lustre earthenware goblet with copper lustre interior.

c.1820. 12.5 cm height   G

£60

A simple classical form which lends itself well to lustre decoration. The silver exterior and copper lustre interior is unusual and attractive.

Staffordshire copper lustre earthenware goblet, with polychrome enamel and lustre band.

c.1820. 10.5 cm height   G

£60

A pink splashed lustre earthenware goblet.

c.1820. 11.5 cm height   HBW

£90

These splashed lustres are sometimes referred to as Sunderland lustre, but in fact this technique was used at all pottery centres.

Earthenware cow creamer with lustre decoration.

c.1825. 14 cm height at head   V

£498

Cow creamers have been popular since the late 18th century, and have been made in earthenware with a wide variety of decorations to the present day. The largest collection of cow creamers in the world can be seen at the City Museum & Art Gallery, Stoke-on-Trent. Other examples may be seen on pp. 147-8 and 294.

Enoch Wood type copper lustre earthenware jug with red transfer-prints washed with enamels signed by J. Kennedy and a band of enamel decoration at the neck.

c.1830+. Flaw in lustre on front. 28 cm height   G

£650

Godden & Gibson illustrate a similar jug which links with Enoch Wood's deposit of 1828. Enoch Wood & Sons operated the Fountain Place works at Burslem from 1818–46. Some of their lustre wares are marked. The firm deposited articles in the foundations of St Paul's Church, Burslem in 1828, which have since aided scholars in identifying the firm's wares.

The shape of the next two jugs preceded the tall-form shapes illustrated below. Note the rounded shoulder of the earlier shape, compared with the angled shoulder of the tall-form jugs.

Copper lustre earthenware jug with band of blue ground which has sprigged decoration painted in pink, green and brown enamels.

c.1830. 9 cm height   TA

£42

Staffordshire copper lustre earthenware jug with pink and copper lustre decorated band.

c.1830. 10.8 cm height   G

£75

These tall-form jugs are typical of the post-1837 period. A number of decorative techniques were employed including sprigging, painting in polychrome enamels and resists. Examples are illustrated in Godden & Gibson.

Staffordshire lustre earthenware jug with sprigging painted in polychrome enamels and beaded edges.

c.1837–45. Slight chip at base. 15.9 cm height   G

£95

Staffordshire copper lustre earthenware jug with relief-moulded decoration painted in polychrome enamels.

c.1837–45. Slight chips. 11.5 cm height   G

£65

This jug is less expensive than the example shown above because it is smaller and less carefully decorated.

Rare lustre earthenware mug with green, orange, brown, blue and white agate effect decoration.

c.1840. 12 cm height   G

£160

497

Staffordshire porcelain jug with pink lustre and poly-chrome enamel decoration.

c.1840. 17 cm height   G

£75

Rare Davenport pink lustre teapot, with polychrome dec-oration.

c.1840+. 19.7 cm height   G

£140

Copper lustre earthenware salt-cellar with blue and yellow bands and pink lustre stripe.

c.1840. 6 cm height   TA

£14

The shape of the following teapots reflects the neo-rococo style which first became popu-lar in the 1830s. A number of teapots in similar shapes are illustrated in Miller & Berthoud. These would have been fairly common when originally produced. However, as they were used on a regular basis, relatively few have survived, and they are now quite valuable.

Typical Staffordshire copper lustre earthenware pear-shaped teapot on rococo moulded feet painted in yellow, blue and white enamels.

c.1840–50. 18.5 cm height   G

£185

Staffordshire silver lustre earthenware teapot.

c.1845. Some minor scratches. 16 cm height   G

£95

Apart from minor scratches, this silver lustre teapot is less desirable than the copper lustre teapot above, as it is undecorated.

Polka pattern relief-moulded earthenware jug, with blue enamel and copper lustre.

c.1852–60. 14.5 cm height   G

£40

This shape was registered by the modeller George Ray on 11 April 1852. The jugs are very common and may be found in many sizes and with many types of decoration, including all-over lustres. The shape was popular and has been copied many times since. Other examples are illustrated in Godden & Gibson.

Earthenware jug decorated with transfer-prints, enamels and lustre, inscribed 'To William Williams Salt Brook Inn 1864'.

c.1864. 23 cm height   BG

£575

These large jugs with children's animal prints were once relatively common. This is a very fine jug and the inscription and date add to its value. Two similar jugs are illustrated in Riley.

Sunderland lustre earthenware plaque.

c.1840–65. Impressed mark 'DIXON, PHILLIPS & CO.' surrounding an anchor. 22 cm length   HBW

£85

Sunderland lustre is an oil spot lustre, that is the lustre was splashed with oil to create the characteristic mottled appearance. Although it was made in quantities at Sunderland, it was also made at Liverpool, Bristol and Stafford-

499

shire. Wedgwood made a version known as variegated lustre, sometimes erroneously called Moonlight Lustre.

These plaques were a speciality of the Sunderland Pottery which operated under various partnerships during the 19th century. The motto 'Prepare to meet thy God' is probably one of the most commonly found. Commemoratives or those with unusual mottoes are more valuable. A comprehensive list of mottoes, many of which are quaint or humorous, found on these plaques is given in Baker. There are many reproductions of these plaques so it is best to familiarise yourself with genuine examples before embarking on a collection.

23 RELIEF-MOULDED STONEWARE AND PARIAN

RELIEF-MOULDED stonewares and Parian are one of the many fascinating developments in Victorian pottery. Little appreciated a decade ago, the publication of R. K. Henrywood's fine book has brought these wares to the attention of a wide section of the collecting public. Three more books and major exhibitions in London and Salisbury have ensued. Many of the jugs with scenes have sources in contemporary engravings, sometimes after well-known paintings. Henrywood has researched these extensively and the sources given here are all taken from his book, where many of the original engravings are illustrated along with the jugs.

The relief-moulded stonewares derive their colour from a body stained with metallic oxides. The high temperature required to fire stonewares restricted the palette considerably. The most commonly found colours are white, blue, drab (buff) and sage green. The interiors were fully glazed to render them watertight, but the exteriors were covered only with a light smear-glaze; either brushed on or created by encouraging vapour in the kiln by the use of chemicals.

The relief-moulded Parian wares are porcelainous, that is they are usually translucent. The best way to see this is to look into the jug, with the base close to an electric light bulb. The Parian body was occasionally tinted, and quite often the ground is enamelled to set off the moulded decoration. For more about Parian see chapter 19.

Occasionally the wares were enamelled, lustred or gilded over the glaze. Today's collectors often prefer undecorated examples. The extent to which the decoration affects the value of the piece depends on three factors: the condition of the enamelling or gilding, the neatness of the decoration (which can sometimes appear sloppy) and the colours used (which can sometimes appear very gaudy). Relief-moulded stonewares were occasionally decorated with majolica glazes (W. T. Copeland did this), but most majolica wares were earthenware.

The vast majority of relief-moulded stonewares are jugs. This is largely because the demand was enormous in the Victorian era, when jugs were taken to the pub or the dairy and filled for use at home. Many jugs will be found with impressed or moulded size marks. Most often the largest size was 2, which denoted a size of six pints in the 'potters count'. This was followed by 3, 6, 9, 12 (nominally one pint), 18, 24, 30, 36 and 42 (usually the smallest, although even smaller sizes of 54 and 60 have been recorded), but some factories used other systems.

Many of these jugs have (or had) Britannia metal lids. Probably because the fixing pins had rusted, these have often been removed, leaving tell-tale holes along the rim. A jug thus marred is considerably lessened in value.

Many of these pots are marked, which increases their value, but many more can be identified by shape. Some marks are moulded and some are impressed. Many of the designs were protected against copying, and elaborate moulded publication marks can be found on some pots dating before 1842. From 1842–83, the design registration diamond was used. As these diamond registration marks were often part of the mould, they can sometimes be illegible. Hughes 1991 contains a digest of some of the registered designs illustrated with drawings and photographs from the Patent Office records.

These multifarious wares are widely available, some for less than £20 and many for less than £50. Commemoratives, because they are collected by more than one group of collector, are at a premium (see chapter 24).

As with all relief-moulded wares, look for crisp moulding and avoid those which look as though they had scrambled eggs thrown on the sides. Detailed patterns with figures are the most valued, but this author prefers the simple floral and foliage designs, in which James Dudson excelled. The collector will also find numerous wares which suffered in the firing. Usually this takes the form of dark specks caused by ash in the kiln. Occasionally there will be bare spots, which the glaze does not cover. Either of these faults, which would have made the wares 'seconds', should be reflected in the price. Blue stoneware in particular is often found with brown specks in the body. This only affects the value to the extent that it is disfiguring.

Further Reading

R. K. Henrywood, *Relief-Moulded Jugs* 1820–1900 (Antique Collectors' Club, Woodbridge, 1984).

Kathy Hughes, *A Collector's Guide to Nineteenth-century Jugs* (Routledge & Kegan Paul, 1985).

Kathy Hughes, *A Collector's Guide to Nineteenth-century Jugs*, vol. II (Taylor Publishing Co., Dallas, 1991).

Jill Rumsey, *Victorian Relief-moulded Jugs* (Richard Dennis, 1987).

JAMES DUDSON
(1838–88)
J. T. DUDSON
(1888–98)
DUDSON BROS
(1898 to the present day)

Dudson's first design for a relief-moulded jug was registered in 1855. The jugs became one of the Hanley firm's specialities. Most Dudson jugs had pleasant floral and foliage decoration, but a great variety of designs can be found. The shapes are simple and the wares always well potted.

The jugs are often unmarked, but when found the mark was 'DUDSON' impressed, with 'ENGLAND' from 1891. After 1898, the firm used the mark 'DUDSON BROS.'

Further Reading

Audrey Dudson. *Dudson* (Dudson Publications, Hanley, 1985).

Dudson *Fern Fronds* blue relief-moulded stoneware jug.

c.1865. 17 cm height   AF

£20

This shape was registered by Wood & Sale in 1864. The moulds were transferred to James Dudson in 1865.

Dudson *Cactus* white relief-moulded stoneware jug, painted in blue enamel.

c.1860s–96. Impressed mark X. 22.5 cm height   AF

£38

Dudson illustrates a white *Cactus* jug without enamelling and with a Britannia metal lid.

Dudson *Vine Leaf* blue relief-moulded stoneware jug.

c.1890s. Impressed size mark '24'. 19 cm height   AF

£25

This jug was discontinued in 1900. Its date of introduction is unknown, but it was probably designed in the late 1880s. The *art nouveau* influence can be seen in the sinuous lines of the tendrils and even in the shape of the spout (compare with the shape of the other Dudson jugs).

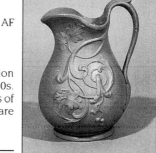

Dudson *Tulip* blue relief-moulded stoneware jug.

c.1840–1900. 18.5 cm height   AF

£20

This is the most common of Dudson shapes, found in many colours, with coloured enamels or even lustred. The shape was introduced in the 1840s, but remained in production until 1900. The highly decorated versions were made in the 1870s.

Some jugs in this shape of very poor quality may be found. They are always unmarked, as are many Dudson examples. However, as the quality of these jugs is inconsistent with Dudson wares, it is believed that they were made by one or more other manufacturers.

503

Dudson *Birds* blue relief-moulded stoneware jug.

c.1870–80s. 21 cm height   AF

£28

This design is inspired by the *japonisme* of the 1870s, but may have remained in production afterwards. Another shape named *Birds* (or alternatively *Robin*) is illustrated in Dudson.

'Fig' blue relief-moulded stoneware jug, possibly Dudson.

c.1890s. 22 cm height at spout   G

£48

W. H. GOSS
(1858–1939)

William Henry Goss served an apprenticeship in the London retail offices of W. T. Copeland. He then went to Stoke to gain experience of potting, serving under John Mountford, who claimed to be the inventor of Parian. Goss learned well, for in 1858 he established his own firm for the manufacture of Parian, producing some models which were nearly identical to those of Copeland! Goss continued to produce Parian busts, figures (see chapter 19) and tablewares until c.1890. Today the firm is best remembered for their glazed Parian Heraldic Ware (see chapter 20) produced from c.1881 onwards.

Decorated Goss 20th-century Parian useful wares may be found in chapter 21.

Further Reading

Nicholas Pine. *Goss and Crested China* (Shire Publications, Aylesbury, 1984).
Nicholas Pine. *William Henry Goss* (Milestone Publications, Horndean, 1987).
Nicholas Pine. *The Concise Encyclopaedia and Price Guide to Goss China* (Milestone Publications, Horndean, 1992).

Goss Parian bread tray.

c.1860–85. 35 cm diameter — GCC

£110

An enamelled version of this bread tray is illustrated in Pine 1992.

Goss Parian bread tray.

c.1860–85. 31.5 cm length — CCC

£175

An enamelled version of this bread tray is illustrated in Pine 1992.

Goss Parian charger with turquoise and pink enamel decoration.

c.1860–85. Some damage to enamel. 31 cm diameter GCC

£200

An oval version of this bread tray is illustrated in Pine 1992.

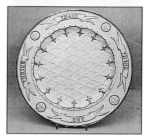

WILLIAM RIDGWAY
(1830–60)

William Ridgway began to pot on his own account in 1830. The first designs to appear in the firm's pattern books were relief-moulded stonewares, of which William Ridgway was one of the earliest manufacturers. Many of these early, unmarked Ridgway wares can be positively identified from the pattern book drawings. Ridgway's stonewares are fine-grained and have a lovely satin feel. The William Ridgway partnerships (all of which made relief-moulded stonewares) for the period 1830–60 are as follows:

W. Ridgway, Son & Co.	1830–8
W. Ridgway & Co.	1838–45
Ridgway & Abington	1845–60

Further Reading

Geoffrey Godden. *Ridgway Porcelains*, 2nd edn (Antique Collectors' Club, Woodbridge, 1985).

William Ridgway 'Acorns and Berries' drab-coloured relief-moulded stoneware jug.

c.1830s. 19 cm height   AF

£70

This is shape no. 24 in the William Ridgway pattern book.

William Ridgway blue relief-moulded stoneware *Tam O'Shanter* jug with Britannia metal lid.

c.1835. Impressed mark 'Published by W. Ridgway & Co., Hanley, October 1, 1835'. 21 cm height   HBW

£65

This design is after engravings by Slader and J. Thompson of Thomas Landseer's illustrations for Marsh & Miller's 1830 edition of Robert Burns's *Tam O'Shanter*. (These engravings are illustrated in Henrywood.) The shape was very popular and these jugs are still relatively common. This shape was also made with the narrative scene replaced by linen fold decoration.

   Machin & Potts produced a Burns jug (illustrated in Henrywood) which used other illustrations from *Tam O'Shanter*.

William Ridgway & Co. *Pan* drab-coloured relief-moulded stoneware jug.

c.1830. Moulded urn and anchor mark with 'W. RIDGWAY & CO.' 18.5 cm height   HBW

£75

This jug is pattern no. 1 in the William Ridgway pattern book. The jug was also produced by the succeeding partnerships. It was made as late as 1846 by Ridgway & Abington when it was illustrated in the *Art-Union*. The design was also used for a mustard pot. The jug is illustrated in Henrywood.

Large Ridgway & Abington *Sylvan* blue relief-moulded stoneware jug.

c.1849. Moulded diamond registration mark for 16 February 1849, parcel 11; impressed size number 6. 27 cm height AF

£85

This was a popular shape, and is fairly common today. However, the size of this example makes it unusual and desirable.

William Ridgway drab-coloured relief-moulded stoneware candlestick.

c.1835. 20 cm height   AF

£85

This candlestick appears as no. 7 in the William Ridgway pattern book (illustrated in Godden).

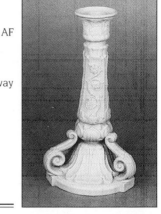

William Ridgway blue relief-moulded stoneware dessert plate.

c.1835. 22 cm diameter   AF

£20

This plate appears as shape no. 30 in William Ridgway's pattern book. The plates are relatively common, and were made in drab and sage as well as blue. The elaborate footed fruit basket and one of the dessert service dishes (illustrated in Godden, along with the relevant page from the pattern book) are not commonly found.

OTHER MANUFACTURERS

Copeland & Garrett blue relief-moulded stoneware *The Vintage* jug.

c.1845. Pad mark 'The Vintage/Copeland & Garrett'. 20 cm height   HBW

£95

This jug was illustrated in the *Art-Union* in November 1844. The jug may also found with a later Copeland mark dating from 1847 and afterwards. The jug and the mark are illustrated in Henrywood.

Stephen Hughes sage relief-moulded stoneware 'Stag' jug.

c.1835–55. Impressed mark 'S. Hughes & Co.' 22.5 cm height   HBW

£95

Stephen Hughes operated at Cobridge 1835–c.1855.

Relief-moulded stoneware with white glaze Tam O'Shanter jug.

c.1830s. 22.5 cm height   TA

£58

This jug is illustrated in Henrywood along with the statues of Tam O'Shanter and Souter Johnnie now at the Burns Monument, Alloway from which this design was taken. The statues were sculpted by James Thom (1802–50) and toured Britain in 1829. The protruding arm would have been separately cast and attached before biscuit firing. A table-based figure group with the same subject is illustrated on p. 168, and a William Ridgway Tam O'Shanter jug is illustrated above.

Reverse portraying Souter Johnnie.

White relief-moulded stoneware teapot with turquoise enamelled spout, knop and handle.

c.1870s. 19 cm height   CCC

£75

This teapot can be dated from the Japanese influence seen in the imitation of a wicker handle and 'bamboo' spout, although the pattern on the body is quite Western.

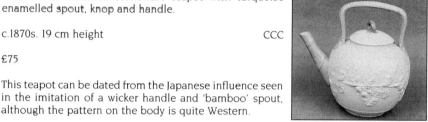

Relief-moulded buff stoneware mustard pot with Britannia metal lid.

c.1880s. 8 cm height without lid   JJB

£55

The geranium was a popular pattern for green-glazed, relief-moulded dessert wares in the 1880s.

Charles Meigh Parian 'Bacchanalian Dance' mug with blue enamelled ground.

c.1850. Star crack. Printed mark reading 'THE SOCIETY OF ARTS MEDAL PRESENTED TO CHARLES MEIGH FOR THE BEST MODEL OF A MUG ORNAMENTED IN RELIEF'. 12 cm height excluding handle   G

£90

Charles Meigh (& Son) of Hanley (1835–61) made relief-moulded stoneware jugs as early as 1839. The 'Bacchanalian Dance' was adapted from Nicholas Poussin's painting

509

Bacchanalian Revel Before a Herm of Pan (illustrated in Henrywood). The medal referred to in the mark was awarded in
1847. Originally made in stoneware, the later Parian
examples are only rarely found with an enamelled blue
ground. A two-handled loving cup and a jug were also
made with this pattern. The jugs have an applied mark including a diamond registration mark for 1844 (illustrated in
Henrywood). Meigh also made Parian busts, figures and
ornamental vases.

Base.

Brownfield Parian Swiss jug.

c.1871. Hairline crack. Moulded Staffordshire knot mark
with 'WB' and 'SWISS'. 18.3 cm height   TA

£25

William Brownfield (& Son(s)) (1850–92) made a wide range
of stoneware and Parian relief-moulded jugs. These are
almost always marked, often including the name of the
design. An enamelled stoneware Swiss jug with a Britannia
metal lid is illustrated in Hughes 1985. Brownfield also
made Parian busts, figures and vases.

Samuel Alcock Parian jug painted in enamels and gilded.

c.1854. Impressed size mark 30. 15.5 cm height   CCC

£180

Samuel Alcock & Co. potted at Burslem c.1826–59, as well
as at Cobridge. A drab stoneware version of this jug with a
diamond registration mark for 30 January 1854 is illustrated
in Hughes 1985.

Minton Parian relief-moulded jug with enamelled blue ground.

c.1843. Cracked and riveted. Impressed shape number 884; date cipher for 1843. 23 cm height   AF

£20

This shape has been made by Minton in other bodies. The very fine modelling of the figures makes it a striking decorative object and a highly desirable piece. A perfect example of this size could well cost anything up to £200.

T. J. & J. Mayer Parian 'Paul and Virginia' relief-moulded jug with blue enamelled ground.

c.1850. Printed royal arms mark 'T. J. and J. MAYER'S/DALE HALL POTTERY/LONGPORT with 'PATENT' in ribbon; registration mark for 2 July 1850 parcel 2; moulded pad mark of a ribbon reading 'No. 97/18' (97 the model number; 18 the size). 22.5 cm height   AF

£45

Thomas, John and Joseph Mayer operated the Furlong Works and Dale Hall Pottery 1843–55, making a number of fine quality Parian relief-moulded jugs. This design is now known to show Paul and Virginia from the popular novel *Paul et Virginie* originally written in French by Bernardin de St. Pierre.

This shape is fairly common and the factory is not one which is generally collected, but the exquisite modelling makes it a highly desirable piece. It also appears in plain white, or with brown or green grounds (this last being rare). The shape was copied by the Bennington Pottery in the USA, and although these pieces are not as well modelled, the demand for American pottery of the 19th century makes these copies more valuable than the originals.

511

24 COMMEMORATIVES

COMMEMORATIVES are a genre of their own. They have been made in all types of bodies and with all types of decoration. Early examples include slipware and delftware dishes commemorating Charles I (reigned 1625–49), Charles II (reigned 1649–85), and James II of England and VII of Scotland (reigned 1685–9). These include some seven recorded examples of Thomas Toft slipware dishes decorated with the royal coat of arms, and thought to commemorate the restoration of Charles II. During the 18th century mass production techniques of potting and decoration, especially transfer-printing, made commemoratives affordable for working-class families, and many of these can still be found quite reasonably. Large numbers of later commemoratives are still extant, as they were, after all, meant as souvenirs, not useful wares. John and Jennifer May also point out that the increased dissemination of news increased the market for commemoratives: 'People could scarcely be expected cheerfully to purchase a pot commemorating an event they didn't know had happened!'

Not surprisingly, a great many commemoratives are associated with royal events: births (rarely), promotions, accessions, coronations, marriages and deaths. It is sometimes difficult to distinguish between accession and coronation souvenirs. These events were often nearly a year apart and some potters used the same design for both events.

The value of commemoratives rests largely on the popularity of the person or cause portrayed. The wares are not only collected by pot collectors, but by those who are interested in a particular subject, collecting ephemera and commemoratives in all manner of media. For this reason, a well potted, well decorated pot commemorating a forgotten or little-known event could conceivably command a lower price than a poorly potted and badly decorated piece commemorating a more popular event.

For Parian figures and busts of celebrated persons see chapter 19.

Further Reading

There are not many works dealing with commemoratives, but nearly every book on ceramics of any type, period or manufacturer will include a few. The best volume at present is John and Jennifer May, *Commemorative Pottery 1780–1900* (Heinemann, 1972).

WILLIAM III & MARY II

William III (1650–1702), Stadtholder of Holland from 1672, ruled as king of Great Britain and Ireland 1689–1702. He was invited to invade England and depose James II, whose Catholic preference was leading to civil war, and became king through his marriage to Mary, eldest daughter of James II, who ruled jointly as Mary II. After her death in 1694, his rule was weakened, but he maintained his position until his death from a riding accident.

London delftware plate painted in blue portraying William and Mary.

c.1690. Crazed, rim chips. 22 cm diameter   JH

£1,950

London polychrome delftware blue dash charger depicting William III.

c.1690. Restored. 33 cm diameter   JH

£9,000

The foliage formed of looped lines filled in with a colour wash is typical of London delftware potters of this period.

GEORGE I

George I (reigned 1714–27) was the first Hanoverian king of Great Britain and Ireland, succeeding Queen Anne in accordance with the Act of Settlement (1701). His close cooperation with the ruling oligarchy made his reign relatively uneventful.

One of a pair of Bristol delftware plates painted in in-glaze blue.

c.1720. Rim chips. 19.8 cm diameter   JH

£3,300 the pair.

GEORGE II

George II (reigned 1727–60) was the last British monarch to take part in battle, taking the field as commander of the British Army at Dettingen in 1743. Although Sir Robert Walpole, his principal minister, pursued a peace policy, the country was almost continually at war during George's reign. There was the Spanish War in 1737, the War of Austrian Succession (1742–8) and the British involvement in the Seven Years War (1756–63). The Jacobite uprising in 1745 ended with a victory at Culloden, where the troops were led by George's second son William Augustus, the Duke of Cumberland. All of these events doubtless inspired commemoratives, but few have survived.

Worcester soft-paste porcelain tankard, with on-glaze black transfer-print of George II.

c.1757–60. Crack. 15 cm height   KK

£550

Staffordshire salt-glazed stoneware bowl with sprigged decoration, inscribed 'THE BRITISH GLORY REVIV'D BY ADMIRAL VERNON'; 'HE TOOK PORTOBELLO WITH SIX SHIPS ONLY'; 'NOV YE 22 1739'.

c.1740. Major cracks repaired. 24.5 cm diameter   AS

£2,900

Admiral Vernon captured Porto Bello, Panama, base of Spanish revenue vessels, in 1739. This inspired a number of salt-glazed stoneware commemoratives. A mug with identical sprigging is illustrated in Peter Walton's *Creamware and other English Pottery at Temple Newsam House Leeds*. A white salt-glazed stoneware teapot commemorating the same event is illustrated in Jonathan Horne, *A Collection of Early English Pottery* (Jonathan Horne, 1982–92), vol. VI.

THE SEVEN YEARS WAR

Britain became involved in the Seven Years War (1756–63) chiefly to defend Hanover, but benefited considerably from its successes outside of Europe. Robert Clive's victory at Plassey in India in 1757 helped to lay the foundations of the British Empire, and General Wolfe's victory at Quebec in 1759 established British supremacy in North America. Frederick II, King of Prussia (reigned 1740–86) was Britain's ally in the Seven Years War.

Worcester soft-paste porcelain mug with on-glaze transfer-print of the King of Prussia.

c.1760. Two cracks. 12 cm height   KK

£225 (perfect example LM £500)

Some of Worcester's King of Prussia prints were dated 1757. See Henry Sandon's *Worcester Porcelain 1751–1793*.

Creamware jug with King of Prussia Rex, painted in polychrome enamels on a black and white ground.

c.1790. A bit missing off bottom of handle, beak noticeably askew. 10.6 cm height   AS

£2,600

Bristol delftware bowl painted with chinoiserie fence and flowers on exterior in in-glaze blue, interior inscribed 'To Granby the Brave'.

c.1760. 22 cm diameter   JJM

£1,450

John Manners, Marquess of Granby (1721–70) was Commander-in-Chief 1766–70. This bowl commemorates the Battle of Warburg 1760, where he led his cavalry to a spectacular victory.

Large creamware jug with black on-glaze print depicting the death of Wolfe at Quebec.

c.1759. 28 cm height   JJM

£1,200

Major-General James Wolfe (1727–59) commanded the British capture of Quebec in 1759. Both Wolfe and Montcalm, commander of the defending French forces, were killed in the battle.

Reverse.

GEORGE III

George III's coronation in 1760, his first recovery from madness in 1789, his jubilee in 1810 and, of course, his death in 1820 all occasioned commemoratives. There were also many other major events during his reign. The Seven Years War was brought to a conclusion in 1763 by an unpopular peace treaty with France and Spain. The repeated attempts to tax the American colonies resulted in the American Declaration of Independence in 1776 and defeat for the British in 1781. The Union with Ireland was effected in 1801. From 1811 the Prince of Wales was Prince Regent due to George's insanity.

Further Reading

David Drakard. *Printed English Pottery, History and Humour in the Reign of George* III 1760–1820 (Jonathan Horne, 1992).

Red stoneware teapot with sprigged decoration commemorating George III and Queen Charlotte.

c.1760. 13 cm height   JJM

£1,650

This style of sprigging on red stoneware was typical of the period 1760–75.

Creamware jug with brown on-glaze transfer-print coloured with enamels, inscribed 'Georgius III Rex/Charlotte Regina' with a print of the Duke of York on the reverse.

c.1790. 12.5 cm height   JH

£1,350

This jug may commemorate the recovery of George III from madness in 1789 or the promotion of the Duke of York to Field Marshal in 1795. This is not a particularly finely crafted pot, but its rarity as a commemorative item makes it extremely valuable.

Reverse.

Pearlware jug with underglaze blue transfer-print of the Royal Arms, inscribed on reverse 'MAY BRITONS TRUE THEIR RIGHTS PURSUE AND E'ER ESPOUSE THE CAUSE OF CHURCH AND KING AND EV'RY THING THAT CONSTITUTES THEIR LAWS'.

c.1793. 17 cm height   JJM

£675

This jug was occasioned by the attack on Britain by Revolutionary France in 1793.

Prattware mug with George III on one side and Queen Charlotte on the reverse.

c.1810. 15 cm height   JJM

£1,280

Reverse.

Earthenware spill vase with underglaze transfer-print inscribed 'To The Memory of Her Royal Highness the Princess Charlotte of Wales and Saxe Coburg who died Nov. 6th 1817'. A portrait of the Duke of Wellington is on the reverse.

c.1817. Hairline crack. 11.5 cm height   JJM

£425

As Princess Charlotte was the only legitimate child of the Regent, the future George IV, she was his heir presumptive. She died giving birth to a stillborn son in 1817.

Reverse.

Relief-moulded pearlware plate with underglaze blue transfer-print inscribed 'Sacred to the Memory of George III/Who died 29 Jany. 1820'.

c.1820. 12 cm diameter, excluding handle   LR

£500

This print appears on a plate with a different relief-moulded border illustrated in Noël Riley's *Gifts for Good Children* (Richard Dennis, 1992).

Davenport pearlware plate with blue transfer-print of George III.

c.1809 or 1820. Impressed anchor mark with 'W. DAVEN-PORT'. 24.5 cm diameter   JJM

£525

London delftware plate with feather border and scene painted in blue, except for polychrome balloon.

c.1784. 20 cm diameter   JH

£780

Many commemoratives were made of the first balloon ascent from London by Vincenzo Lunardi in 1784. Other pots were made in commemoration of Jean-Pierre Blanchard's several flights the following year.

The painted feather border and swags are typical of London delftwares of the period, and are also found on pearlwares, which will have a moulded feather border.

ADMIRAL LORD NELSON

The famous naval hero (1758–1805) started his career in 1770. He served in the West Indies and in the Arctic expedition of 1773. He returned to the West Indies where he commanded the naval expedition against San Juan in 1780. At the outbreak of the French revolutionary wars he was given a command in the Mediterranean, and destroyed Napoleon's fleet at Aboukir in 1798. In 1801 he was promoted to vice-admiral and made second in command in the Baltic expedition. He was made commander in the Mediterranean in 1803, and was killed in the decisive engagement with the French and Spanish at Trafalgar in 1805. Nelson remained a popular figure throughout the 19th century, and commemoratives continued to be issued long after his death.

Sunderland earthenware frog mug with black on-glaze transfer-print inscribed 'England Expects EVERYMAN TO DO his DUTY/TRAFALGAR VICTORY'.

c.1805. 13 cm height   JH

£385

Prattware pipe with Admiral Nelson bowl, impressed 'Nelson FOREVER'.

c.1805. Restored mouthpiece. 24 cm length   LR

£1,100

Creamware plate with underglaze black print mourning the death of Nelson, inscribed 'NELSON/D. 1805' on a tombstone in one cartouche.

c.1805. 21 cm diameter   JJM

£550

519

Pearlware jug portraying Admiral Nelson painted in poly-chrome enamels over a transfer-print with an anchor on reverse.

c.1805. 17.5 cm height   JJM

£875

Creamware frog mug with overglaze print mourning the death of Nelson.

c.1805. 11.8 cm height   JJM

£680

Very rare biscuit porcelain figure of Nelson.

c.1810. 32 cm height   JJM

£1,000

Lambeth brown salt-glazed stoneware jug with a bust of Nelson wearing medal reading 'NILE 1798/TRAFALGAR 1805'.

c.1845. 26 cm height   CCC

£200

Doulton & Watts brown salt-glazed stoneware jug portraying Nelson.

c.1830. Cracks on bottom and handle; damaged hat. Impressed mark 'DOULTON & WATTS/LAMBETH POTTERY/ LONDON'. 19.5 cm height   TA

£95

FREDERICK AUGUSTUS, DUKE OF YORK

Frederick Augustus (1763–1827), second son of George III, was commemorated frequently for his military successes, particularly at Valenciennes in 1793. He attained the rank of Lieutenant-General in 1789, and Field Marshal in 1795. Since Princess Charlotte had died in 1817, the Duke of York became heir presumptive to George IV, but predeceased him.

Prattware type Duke of York flask.

c.1793. Chip restored. 14 cm length   AD

£525

MRS MARY ANNE CLARKE

The actress Mrs Mary Anne Clarke (1776–1852) was the mistress of Frederick Augustus, Duke of York, 1803–7. She trafficked in commissions and was exposed in the House of Commons in 1809. The House eventually decided that the Duke was not guilty of personal corruption, but he was obliged to resign his official appointments.

Creamware jug with on-glaze transfer-print captioned 'I have a small list of promotions I wish to be fill'd up immediately My dearest' / 'It shall be Done my Darling'.

c.1809. 11.5 cm height   JJM

£1,000

Earthenware jug commemorating the death of Mrs Clarke with black underglaze transfer-print and lustre decoration. Inscribed 'My dear little Angel Charm of my Soul'/ 'MRS. CLARKE/ THE LATE FAVOURITE LADY OF HIS ROYAL HIGHNESS THE DUKE OF YORK'. Painted in lustre 'SARAH WEILDER 1852'. Verse on reverse.

c.1852. 14 cm height   JJM

£1,450

Reverse.

PRINCE REGENT; GEORGE IV

George IV (1762–1830) reigned 1820–30, but had effectively ruled the country as Prince Regent since 1811. In 1795 he married his cousin Caroline of Brunswick. The couple found each other mutually repellent, and for most of the next twenty-five years lived apart. Given the Prince of Wales's reputation for gluttony, drink and womanising, the Princess was the object of much sympathy.

At George IV's accession in 1820, he offered Caroline an annuity of £50,000 if she would renounce the title of Queen and live abroad. When she refused, the government instituted a Bill of Pains and Penalties to deprive her of the royal title and annul her marriage. Public sympathy and Lord Brougham's spirited defence prevailed and the ministry gave up the Bill. Caroline made a triumphal entry into London to claim her rights as Queen, but was turned away from George's coronation a few days before her death.

Pearlware plate with blue transfer-print painted in enamels, commemorating the Regency.

c.1811. 24.5 cm diameter   JJM

£490

Relief-moulded pearlware plate painted in polychrome enamels.

c.1820. Inscribed 'KING GEORGE IIII'. 21.5 cm height   JJM

£685

This plate may have been made at the Bankfoot Pottery, Prestonpans. Robert Gordon and his son George took over the pottery c.1795.

These two plates portraying Queen Caroline, which seem innocuous today, were actually inflammatory at the time they were made. The many commemoratives with her portrait and the inscription 'Queen Caroline' are evidence of the great public sympathy for her. Quite a few were made in Scotland, where feelings were particularly high. In an effort to assuage the Scots, George IV made a visit to Edinburgh in 1822, which was also duly commemorated by the Scottish East Coast potteries.

Pearlware plate with relief-moulded emblems of the thistle and rose, with Queen Caroline in the centre painted in polychrome enamels and purple lustre, probably by Rathbone's Portobello Pottery, inscribed 'Queen Caroline'.

c.1820. Small rim chip. 19 cm diameter   LR

£400

Pearlware plate with Queen Caroline brown transfer-print, inscribed 'HER MAJESTY/QUEEN CAROLINE OF ENGLAND'.

c.1820. Star crack. 17 cm diameter   JJM

£385

LORD BROUGHAM

Henry Brougham (1778–1868) and Thomas Denman defended Queen Caroline in 1820, for which they enjoyed considerable popularity. Brougham was also a fierce opponent of slavery, introducing the Felony Act in 1811. He was raised to the peerage in 1830, and later served as Lord Chancellor.

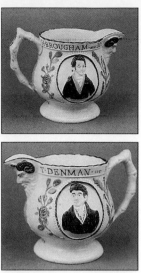

Relief-moulded earthenware jug painted in polychrome enamels, probably made by one of the Scottish East Coast potteries.

c.1820. Inscribed 'H. P. Brougham Esq. MP; T. Denman Esq. MP'. 12 cm height JJM

£485

Reverse.

Earthenware inkstand of Lord Brougham painted in red, green and black enamels, possibly made at Portobello Pottery.

c.1820. 7.6 cm length of base. BG

£750

LORD CANNING

George Canning (1770–1827) was Treasurer of the Navy under Pitt and Foreign Secretary in the Portland ministry. He supported the Liverpool ministry until 1820, when he resigned over the government's action against Queen Caroline. On Liverpool's resignation in 1827 he helped to form an administration with the help of the Whigs, but died the same year.

Alcock porcelain bust of Lord Canning decorated with unburnished gold.

c.1830–5. Printed mark 'Improved Porcelain/Samuel Alcock/Cobridge/Staffordshire'. 21 cm height JJM

£485

Illustrated in Geoffrey Godden's *Encyclopaedia of British Porcelain Manufacturers* (Barrie & Jenkins, 1988). Samuel Alcock potted at Cobridge c.1826–53.

METHODISM

Prattware type bust of John Wesley.

c.1820. 12 cm height   AD

£520

John Wesley (1703–91) was the founder of Methodism, originally a movement within the Church of England. He founded the first Methodist chapel in 1739.

An earthenware plate with black transfer-print.

c.1832. Inscribed 'HE THAT BELIEVETH SHALL BE SAVED/ ADAM CLARKE, L.L.D.E.S.A./WESLEYAN MINISTER'. JJM

£185

Adam Clarke (1762–1832) was a Wesleyan divine and author of the eight-volume *Biographical Dictionary* (1802–6) and an eight-volume edition of the Holy Scripture (1810–26).

WILLIAM IV

As he was the third son of George III, it was not expected that William Henry, Duke of Clarence (1765–1837) would ever succeed to the throne. At thirteen he became a midshipman in the Navy, formally advancing through the ranks until he became Admiral of the Fleet in 1811. From 1790 to 1811, William lived with the actress Dorothea Jordan, who bore him ten children. However on the death of Princess Charlotte, heir presumptive to the Prince Regent in 1817, it seemed more likely that William might one day be king, and there was pressure on him to marry and produce legitimate heirs. He married Adelaide of Saxe-Coburg-Meiningen (1792–1849) in 1818. Described as 'worthy but dull', she bore William two children, both of whom died in infancy.

In 1827 upon the death of the Duke of York, William became heir presumptive to the throne and he was given the honorific post of High Admiral of England. Upon the death of George IV in 1830, William acceded to the throne, but the coronation did not take place until the following year.

William was known as the 'sailor king' and many of the commemoratives of his reign incorporate naval motifs. William's relatively short reign was marked by the upheavals over the Reform Bill, which he initially opposed.

Very rare William IV and Adelaide pearlware coronation plate, relief-moulded with ships' ropes, and painted in polychrome enamels, inscribed 'CORONATION/W & A/AT WESTMINSTER SEPTEMBER 1831'.

c.1831. 17.5 cm diameter   LR

£500

William IV and Queen Adelaide purple transfer-printed mug, inscribed 'OUR BELOVED KING WILLIAM 4TH'; 'OUR AMIABLE QUEEN ADELAIDE'.

c.1831. Royal arms transfer-printed mark. 9.5 cm height
JJM

£415

Reverse.

Minton relief-moulded stoneware jug with grey body and white sprigging including portraits of William IV and Queen Adelaide.

c.1831. Sprigged mark 'No. 13'. 20 cm height   JJM

£385

Earthenware bust of William IV painted in polychrome enamels with purple lustre band.

c.1830–1. Some flaking to enamel. 25.4 cm height   LR

£5,000

ABOLITION OF SLAVERY

The slave trade was outlawed in Britain in 1807, but slavery continued in the colonies. The first measures of the bill abolishing slavery took effect on 1 August 1834, but the final freedom did not come until 1838.

Earthenware plate with blue transfer-print, inscribed 'Freedom First of August 1838'.

c.1838. 26.5 cm diameter   JJM

£785

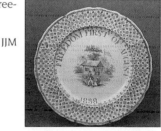

REFORM BILL

The shifts of population which occurred as a result of enclosures and the industrial revolution left certain boroughs nearly uninhabited, and new centres of population without adequate representation. Some boroughs had only a few dozen inhabitants, and these sold their votes freely or under duress, meaning that seats in Parliament could actually be bought. The first Reform Bill was introduced to the Commons in 1831 and passed the following year. It disenfranchised some of the 'rotten boroughs' and enfranchised new boroughs, but as it made sure not to upset the balance of party power, some rotten boroughs remained.

527

Earthenware mug with purple transfer-print.

c.1831. Inscribed 'LORD ALTHORP'; 'EARL GREY'; 'UNION IS STRENGTH'. 9.5 cm height   AD

£250

Earl Grey was Prime Minister 1830–4. John Charles Spencer, Viscount Althorp and 3rd Earl Spencer (1782–1845) was Grey's Chancellor of the Exchequer and served in the same capacity for Melbourne's brief government in 1834. Althorp shared the burden of debates on the Reform Bill with Grey.

Relief-moulded Reform Bill earthenware plate with on-glaze black transfer-print painted in polychrome enamels.

c.1831. Black transfer-printed mark 'C&R' probably for Chetham & Robinson (1822–37). 16 cm diameter   JJM

£285

Mark.

Reform Bill earthenware jug with blue transfer-print.

c.1831. 15.5 cm height   JJM

£250

Earthenware mug painted in polychrome enamels and pink and copper lustres, probably by Rathbone's Portobello Pottery.

c.1831. 12 cm height   JJM

£345

An identical mug with the word Reform on the base of the crown is illustrated in Patrick McVeigh's *Scottish East Coast Potteries* (John Donald Publishers, Edinburgh, 1979).

Bourne's brown salt-glazed stoneware bottle shaped like a man sitting on a barrel.

c.1833. Impressed on the front of the base 'SUCCESS TO REFORM'. Impressed mark on reverse 'DENBY & CODNOR PARK/BOURNES/POTTERIES/DERBYSHIRE'.   20.5   cm height   HBW

£200

Joseph Bourne acquired the Denby pottery in 1812, but did not take over the Codnor Park pottery until 1833. A similar bottle made by Oldfield & Co., Brampton, Derbyshire is illustrated in Robin Hildyard's *Browne Muggs* (Victoria & Albert Museum, 1985).

Reverse.

DUKE OF WELLINGTON

During his long career as a soldier and later as a statesman, there were several occasions on which commemoratives of Arthur Wellesley, 1st Duke of Wellington (1769–1852) were manufactured. After making a name for himself in India, he became an MP 1806–9, becoming Irish Secretary in 1807. He returned to military service briefly in 1808, and then from 1809–14. After Napoleon abdicated in 1914 he was created Duke of Wellington. However, Napoleon escaped from Elba, only to be beaten by Wellington's forces at the Battle of Waterloo (1815). There followed a long and distinguished career as a statesman until his retirement in 1846. Wellington was Prime Minister 1828–30 and Foreign Secretary 1834–45. His death in 1852 occasioned a great many commemoratives.

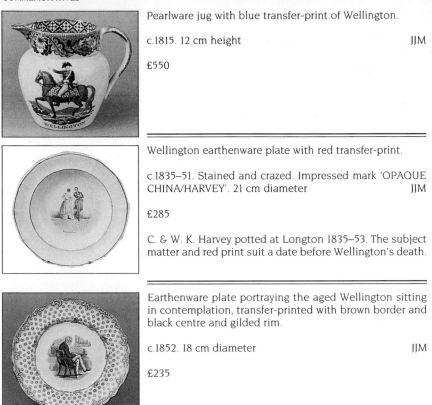

Pearlware jug with blue transfer-print of Wellington.

c.1815. 12 cm height   JJM

£550

Wellington earthenware plate with red transfer-print.

c.1835–51. Stained and crazed. Impressed mark 'OPAQUE CHINA/HARVEY'. 21 cm diameter   JJM

£285

C. & W. K. Harvey potted at Longton 1835–53. The subject matter and red print suit a date before Wellington's death.

Earthenware plate portraying the aged Wellington sitting in contemplation, transfer-printed with brown border and black centre and gilded rim.

c.1852. 18 cm diameter   JJM

£235

NAPOLEON I

Napoleon Bonaparte (1769–1821) became a popular figure in the 1850s, when France under his nephew Napoleon III was Britain's ally in the Crimean War.

Staffordshire earthenware figure painted in polychrome enamels and gilded.

c.1850s. 25 cm height   HBW

£225

This and a number of other Napoleon figures are illustrated in P. D. Gordon Pugh's *Staffordshire Portrait Figures of the Victorian Era* (Antique Collectors' Club, Woodbridge, 1987).

VICTORIA

Victoria (reigned 1837–1901) was a popular monarch whose long reign occasioned many commemoratives. These include her accession, coronation, marriage, the births of her nine children, the death of Prince Albert, her Golden and Diamond Jubilees and her death. The Princes and Princesses were also much portrayed both in childhood and upon their marriages. Although commemoratives of Victoria's reign are plentiful, they are much collected, and so relatively expensive.

Further Reading

John May. *Victoria Remembered* (Heinemann, 1983).

Brown salt-glazed stoneware bottle celebrating the accession of Queen Victoria. The Duchess of Kent, who was Victoria's mother and Regent, is portrayed on the reverse.

c.1837. 26 cm height   JJM

£270

A very similar example is shown in Robin Hildyard's *Browne Muggs* (Victoria & Albert Museum, 1985), attributed to Brampton, Derby, which with Denby led the stoneware market in the earlier part of the 19th century. There were a number of stoneware potteries at Brampton, and so it is used as a generic attribution. Another similar bottle, but bearing portraits of Queen Victoria and Prince Albert, is illustrated in May.

Reverse.

Brown salt-glazed stoneware bottle portraying Queen Victoria.

c.1837. 19 cm height   HBW

£90

Similar bottles (without relief-moulding of cherubs) made by Oldfield & Co., Brampton, Derby are illustrated in Robin Hildyard's *Browne Muggs* and in May.

Brown salt-glazed stoneware plant pot with relief-moulded portraits of the Duchess of Kent and Queen Victoria.

c.1839. In typesetters' print on side 'J. & E. Longson 1839'. 13 cm height   JJM

£250

The Duchess of Kent, Victoria's mother, had been appointed Regent in the event of William IV's death before Victoria came of age. Her portrait is after a miniature by William Ross, which was also the basis of a transfer-print.

Other views.

Davenport earthenware mug with blue transfer-print celebrating Queen Victoria's coronation for the citizens of Preston.

c.1837. 8 cm height   JJM

£1,250

Swansea earthenware plate with relief-moulded border, transfer-printed centre celebrating Queen Victoria's coronation.

c.1837. Impressed mark 'DILLWYN SWANSEA'. 16 cm diameter   JJM

£585

A Swansea mug bearing this print, and another similar Staffordshire print are illustrated in May. Lewis Llewellyn Dillwyn was proprietor of the Cambrian Pottery from 1836–50, previously operated by his father.

Brown salt-glazed stoneware bottle modelled as Queen Victoria.

c.1837. 23 cm height   JJM

£445

Queen Victoria married Prince Albert, the younger of the two sons of the Duke of Saxe-Coburg-Gotha in 1840. Albert was a talented man with many interests. He played a large part in the organisation of the Great Exhibition in 1851. Their happy marriage ended with his death in 1861.

Staffordshire blue-glazed relief-moulded earthenware jug portraying Prince Albert.

c.1840. Small chip. 18 cm height at spout.   AD

£370

These are sometimes found with Queen Victoria on the reverse.

Relief-moulded earthenware plate with brown transfer-print commemorating the death of Prince Albert with the London Exhibition 1862 in the background.

c.1862. 16 cm diameter   JJM

£380

This plate is illustrated in May. The print also appears on a jug, which has a print on the reverse illustrating the Great Exhibition of 1851.

Earthenware plate with blue transfer-print of Prince Albert.

c.1840–50s. Transfer-printed mark of crown with 'UNION'. 23 cm length   JJM

£245

This plate and a matching one portraying Queen Victoria are illustrated in May, who believes it to have been made in Scotland, but Coysh & Henrywood, The Dictionary of Blue and White Printed Pottery 1780–1880 (Antique Collectors' Club, Woodbridge, 1982), suggest that 'UNION' may refer to the Royal marriage or to the Southwick Union Pottery, Sunderland or the Operative Union Pottery, Burslem.

Mark on reverse.

Brown salt-glazed stoneware relief-moulded jug commemorating the wedding of Queen Victoria and Prince Albert.

c.1840. Applied pad mark 'STEPHEN GREEN LAMBETH'. 24 cm height   JJM

£300

Illustrated in Robin Hildyard, Browne Muggs (Victoria & Albert Museum, 1985), where he suggests that F. Wetherill may have been responsible for the mould. For more about Stephen Green see p. 74.

Other views.

Diamond Jubilee pottery mug, lithograph print with gold rim.

c.1897. Heavily crazed. 9 cm height   G

£15

SIR ROBERT PEEL

Sir Robert Peel (1788–1850) entered Parliament as Tory MP in 1809. He was Secretary for Ireland 1812–18, and became Home Secretary in 1822. Peel established the Metropolitan (London) police force. He was Prime Minister 1834–5 and 1841–6. He died from injuries sustained when his horse threw him in 1850.

535

Earthenware plate with unusual black underglaze print and relief-moulded border commemorating the death of Sir Robert Peel. inscribed 'SIR ROBT. PEEL/BORN 5TH FEBY 1788/DIED JULY 2ND 1850' with small inscriptions at the sides 'CATHOLIC EMANCIPATION'; 'REPEAL CORN LAW 1846'; . . . |METROPOLI|TAN POLICE'; 'IRISH . . .'.

c.1850. 18 cm diameter   JJM

£320

This transfer is after an engraving from the Illustrated London News, illustrated in J. & J. May.

CRIMEAN WAR

Many events and personalities connected with the Crimean War (1854–6) were subjects of commemoratives. There were also many figures of anonymous soliders and sailors.

Rockingham glazed earthenware·watch stand portraying two Turkish soldiers seated in front of a mosque.

c.1855. 22 cm height; 15.5 cm base length   JJM

£80

This non-portrait figure group is also found with polychrome enamel decoration and without the adaptation for the watch. See P. D. Gordon Pugh, Staffordshire Portrait Figures of the Victorian Era (Antique Collectors' Club, Woodbridge, 1987).

Goodwin & Bullock porcelain jug celebrating the alliance with France in the Crimean War with a black transfer-print, red enamel and gilding. 'THE UNION OF ENGLAND & FRANCE IS STRENGTH'; 'MAY ENGLAND FOR EVER SUCH UNITY BOAST!' Inscribed in gold 'Ch. Jones 1857'.

c.1857. Printed Staffordshire knot mark with 'G&B'; 'ALLIANCE JUG'. 17 cm height   JJM

£240

Two successive partnerships under the style Goodwin & Bullock operated in Longton 1852–9. An identical jug with a print of the Charge of the Light Brigade at Balaclava is illustrated in May.

Sir Colin Campbell and his Highlanders from the 93rd, probably at Alma, portrayed on a relief-moulded jug with white glaze.

c.1854. 20 cm height   /   JJM

£100

There were a number of commemoratives of the Battle of Alma.

Victorian earthenware flatback figure *Britain's Glory*, painted in blue, orange, yellow and black enamels and gilded.

c.1854. Gilding slightly rubbed. Some restoration to base. 28 cm height   WA

£640

This Crimean War figure is paired with *Scotland's Pride*. Such figures would have been popular with the families of men who were fighting.

Rare Victorian flatback earthenware figure *Ready and Willing* painted in black, blue, yellow and orange enamels.

c.1854. 30 cm height   WA

£980

This figure is identical to *Britain's Glory* above except for the decoration and the title on the base. Just this difference in the lettering on the base is responsible for a more than 50% increase in value.

Rare Victorian flatback earthenware figure *The Wounded Soldier*, painted in polychrome enamels.

c.1855. 33 cm height   WA

£960

This figure is based on an engraving 'Landing of the invalided and the wounded from the Crimea' which appeared in *Cassell's Illustrated Family Paper* on 7 April 1855. See P. D. Gordon Pugh's *Staffordshire Portrait Figures of the Victorian Era* (Antique Collectors' Club, Woodbridge, 1987).

Staffordshire earthenware Crimean group, 'Turkey/England/France', painted in underglaze blue with polychrome enamels and gilded.

c.1854. 28.5 cm height   BG

£450

Sultan Abd-ul-Medjid is on the left, Queen Victoria in the centre and Napoleon III on her right. The source of the design was a medal struck by A. A. Caque to celebrate the triple alliance, an engraving of which was printed in *The Illustrated London News*, 9 September 1854. A similar but rare figure is recorded with the order of the figures reversed.

SIR HENRY HAVELOCK

Sir Henry Havelock (1795–1857), after a long and distinguished career in the military, became a great hero in the Indian Mutiny 1857. During the conflict he died of dysentry.

Earthenware Staffordshire portrait figure *Havelock*, painted in polychrome enamels and gilded.

c.1857. 23 cm height   BG

£350

The matching figure is of Sir Colin Campbell, who relieved Havelock at Lucknow.

OTHER VICTORIAN COMMEMORATIVES

Earthenware plate with brown transfer-print inscribed 'In Commemoration of the Viscount Clive Attaining his Majority November 5th 1839'.

c.1839. Chip to back and other tiny rim chips. Transfer-printed mark 'J. Clementson, Broad St., Shelton, Staffs'. 26.5 cm diameter   V

£64

Joseph Clementson potted at the Phoenix Works, Shelton c.1839–64. Many of his transfer-prints were in colours other than blue.

Copeland earthenware plate decorated with a transfer-print painted in polychrome enamels. Inscribed 'Presented to S. H. Cheetham for his services to the Stockport Corporation'.

c.1857. Painted pattern number D133. Printed mark in green 'COPELAND LATE SPODE'. 28 cm diameter   JJM

£185

Earthenware plate with willow border blue transfer-print and brown transfer-printed centre portraying Albert Smith.

c.1850. Printed mark 'COPELAND LATE SPODE/160 New Bond Street/LONDON'. Impressed crown mark. 23 cm diameter   JJM

£95

Albert Smith (1816–60) was a flamboyant playwright and writer for *Punch*. He made an historic ascent of Mont Blanc with three companions, sixteen guides, twenty porters and great provisions, including some ninety bottles of wine! Afterwards he rented the Egyptian Hall at Piccadilly where his illustrated lecture (including two chamois, several St Bernards and an assortment of Swiss barmaids) ran for some six years. He sold these transfer-printed plates as souvenirs at the lectures. Queen Victoria attended as a command performance, and afterwards received Smith as well as the barmaids and dogs (but not the chamois). Later, after Smith's visit to China he sold souvenir plates, again with his portrait, but with a Chinese fan pattern border.

These plates are fairly common, but are still expensive because they were made by Copeland and the combination of brown and blue prints is unusual.

Earthenware plate with relief-moulded border painted in polychrome enamels and red transfer-print, inscribed 'GREAT WESTERN STEAM SHIP/Length 236 feet Breadth 58 ⅓ feet'.

c.1838. 15.5 cm diameter   JJM

£525

Isambard Kingdom Brunel designed the *Great Western*, which was the first steam ship to cross the Atlantic (1838). Twenty years later Brunel's *Great Eastern* was launched, the first steamship capable of making a non-stop voyage to Australia: commemoratives of this ship may also be found.

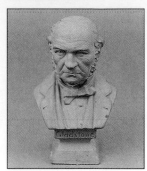

Watcombe Terra-Cotta Co. terracotta bust of Gladstone, modelled by A. Bruce Joy after the head of a statue in the East End, London.

c.1880s. 13 cm height   BK

£65

William Ewart Gladstone (1809–98) was leader of the Liberal Party and Prime Minister (1868–74, 1880–5, 1886, 1892–4). For more about Watcombe Terra-Cotta Co. see pp. 236-8.

Earthenware jug with transfer-prints painted in orange and green enamels, inscribed 'PLIMSOLL SAILORS FRIEND', 'THE SAILORS RETURN'.

c.1876. 15.5 cm height   CCC

£180

Samuel Plimsoll (1824–98) was known as the Sailors' Friend. He published *Our Seamen* (1873) and was an active campaigner for the Merchant Shipping Act (1876), which prevented ship owners from dangerously overloading their vessels. Staffordshire flatback figures with the subject of 'The Sailors Return' (dating to the Crimean War) may also be found.

Reverse.

Goss small glazed Parian urn in remembrance of Emperor Frederick. Inscribed 'GOTT MIT UNS 1870'; 'IN MEMORY OF THE HEROIC EMPEROR FREDERICK. DIED JUNE 15TH 1888.'

c.1888. Printed Goshawk mark, 'Urn found at Old Windsor, from original in Museum.' 8.5 cm height   CCC

£180

Frederick III (1831–88) King of Prussia and German Emperor, was the husband of Victoria, Princess Royal, Queen Victoria's eldest daughter. He died shortly after his accession to the throne in 1888.

Sampson Smith Victorian flatback earthenware figures of Moody and Sankey painted in polychrome enamels and gilded.

c.1873–83. 30.5 cm height   HBW

£275 the pair.

Dwight Lyman Moody and Ira David Sankey were American evangelists who made popular tours of Britain in 1873 and 1883. A mould of the Moody figure has been discovered on the site of the Sampson Smith factory. However, reproduction Moody and Sankey figures are known to have been made by William Kent c.1910–20.

Goss Parian vase.

c.1875. Inscribed ' "Dew-drops"/copyright/Published as the Act directs (see 54 Geo III, C.56)/W H Goss Stoke-on-Trent/5th Nov 1875.' 12 cm height   GCC

£200

'Dew-drop' was one Dr Edward Vaughan Hyde Kenealy (1819–80) who was a controversial and unpopular character. In 1850 he was sentenced to a month in gaol for punishing his son with undue severity (given the level of corporal punishment thought proper at the time, he must have beaten the child to within an inch of his life). After a trial in 1873 in which he was defence counsel, he was disbarred for his behaviour and indiscretions. Despite this he became an Independent MP for Stoke (1874–80). When he took his seat in Parliament, no member could be found who would introduce him.

William Henry Goss despised Kenealy, and also designed a full figure spill vase portraying him. In the case of both vases, the figure is empty-headed. The caricature is after a cartoon of Kenealy by George Bernascuni. The spill vase and cartoon are illustrated in Nicholas Pine's *William Henry Goss* (Milestone Publications, Horndean, 1987).

EDWARD VII

Queen Victoria's eldest son was sixty years old by the time he acceded to the throne. The Queen did not consider him to be very responsible and he was a prominent figure in European café society. He had several mistresses and was cited as a witness in a divorce suit in 1870. In 1863 he married Alexandra, eldest daughter of King Christian IX of Denmark.

Doulton salt-glazed brown stoneware jug with applied Prince of Wales feathers.

c.1858–90. Impressed mark '3927/DOULTON/LAMBETH'. 14.2 cm height   TA

£28

Pair of Victorian earthenware flatback figures 'Pr of Wales' and 'Pr Alfred', painted in polychrome enamels and gilded.

c.1858. 27 cm height   WA

£1,900

The Prince of Wales and Prince Alfred received their first commissions in 1858.

Earthenware jug with brown transfer-printed Prince and Princess of Wales (later King Edward VII and Queen Alexandra) probably commemorating their marriage in 1863.

Transfer-printed mark 'DM & SS', possibly for David Methven & Sons. 19 cm height   JJM

£140

Reverse.

FIRST WORLD WAR

There were an enormous number of First World War (1914–1918) commemoratives. Small items made by the manufacturers of crested china were particularly popular.

Crown Staffordshire porcelain bust of Kaiser Wilhelm, 'WHICH'LL HE BE?'.

c.1916. Printed 'Rd. No. 654090' (1916); in capitals 'Five per cent of cost of all "Which'll" articles sold goes to the leading funds for disabled heroes. The Kaiser caused the War, so make use of him to provide comforts for our wounded soldiers and sailors.' 15.5 cm height   CCC

£550

Collingwood Bros earthenware jug with black transfer-print commemorating the surrender of the German fleet, 21 November 1918.

c.1918. Printed mark 'Manufactured by Collingwood Bros. Ltd/St George's Works/Longton'. 16 cm height   CCC

£450

Alternative views.

Wiltshaw & Robinson Carlton China model with transfer-printed and enamelled Wolverhampton Arms, inscribed 'Model of British Anti-aircraft and Motor'; 'The Victory of Justice, Armistice of the Great War signed Nov. 11th 1918'.

c.1918. Printed circular mark with swallow 'W&R/STOKE ON TRENT/CARLTON CHINA'. 11.7 cm length   CCC

£195

Wiltshaw & Robinson Carlton China figure of a telegraph operator, 'LISTENING IN', with transfer-printed and enamelled Lancaster Arms.

c.1914–18. Printed circular mark with swallow 'W&R/STOKE ON TRENT/CARLTON CHINA'. 8.5 cm height   CCC

£140

Arkinstall & Sons Arcadian China Cenotaph with City of London Arms transfer-printed and enamelled.

c.1920. Printed circular mark with globe and crown 'A&S/ STOKE-ON-TRENT/ARCADIAN. 14 cm height   GCC

£45

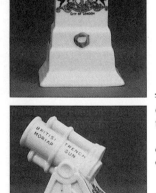

Caledonia China model of a British 'Trench Mortar' with transfer-printed and enamelled Brighton Arms.

c.1914–18. Printed circular mark with lion rampant and crown 'CR & Co/GLASGOW/Caledonia China. 9.3 cm height   GCC

£50

Caledonia China was a trademark used by Taylor & Kent, Longton for a Glasgow retailer: the firm's usual mark was Florentine China.

Wiltshaw & Robinson Carlton China 'HMS Anglia' with transfer-printed and enamelled Arms of Aberdare. Inscribed 'Great War 1914–18/The German Fleet surrendered 74 warships Nov. 21st 1918'.

c.1918. Printed mark Crown China with crown. 17 cm length
GCC

£35

Crown China was a trade mark used by Wiltshaw & Robinson up until the 1920s.

Arkinstall & Sons Arcadian China model of a pair of field glasses with transfer-printed and enamelled Borough of Reading Arms.

c.1914–18. Printed circular mark with globe and crown, 'A&S/STOKE-ON-TRENT/ARCADIAN CHINA. 6.5 cm height
GCC

£21

EDWARD VIII

Edward VIII (1894–1972) succeeded to the throne in 1936, but abdicated later the same year, before his coronation, because Parliament would not sanction his marriage to Mrs Wallis Simpson, an American divorcée. Nevertheless, a large number of coronation souvenirs had already been made, and are commonly found, along with those which were made for the abdication.

Aller Vale two-handled mug, red earthenware body dipped in white slip with sgraffito decoration in a variation of the pottery's Q1 pattern: 'Prince Edward of York 1894/ Bright be the stars on the eve of St. John. Luckie the babe that is born there on'.

c.1894. Cracked. 19 cm height   JJM

£485

Commemorating the birth of Prince Edward of York, later Edward VIII.

Reverse.

Earthenware ashtray commemorating the coronation of Edward VIII.

c.1936. 10 cm diameter   AF

£15

Earthenware tankard inscribed 'Coronation Edward VIII. May 12th 1937'.

c.1936. Impressed mark 'ENGLAND'; stamped mark 'MADE IN ENGLAND'. 13.4 cm height   GCC

£23

Earthenware souvenir mug of the abdication of Edward VIII, with lithographs and gilding.

c.1936. Printed mark 'Made in England by Bovey Pottery Devon'. 9 cm height   G

£25

GEORGE VI

George VI (1895–1952) acceded to the throne in 1936 when his elder brother Edward VIII abdicated. There are relatively few commemoratives of his reign as restrictions on the production of decorated pottery and porcelain for the home market were imposed during the Second World War and continued until 1952.

Beaker inscribed 'George VI and Queen Elizabeth./C.F.O. Graham Mayor/Official design of the British Pottery Manufacturers Federation.'

c.1937. 11 cm height   GCC

£15

CANADA JUBILEE

Canada Diamond Jubilee plate with brown and blue transfer-prints. Inscribed 'DIAMOND JUBILEE 1867 1927'.

c.1927. Printed mark 'DOMINION OF CANADA/COAT OF ARMS/ADOPTED 1822'; 'MANUFACTURED BY/JOSIAH WEDGWOOD & SONS LTD/ETRURIA ENGLAND'; 'IMPORTED BY NERLICH & CO. TORONTO'; 'Rd. No. 696982 (1923). 26.5 cm diameter   CCC

£65

EXHIBITIONS

The Great Exhibition at the Crystal Palace in 1851 was the first of many such international exhibitions held throughout the world. These were often commemorated on pots which could be sold as souvenirs at the exhibitions. Exhibition pieces which displayed the highest pinnacle of the potter's art were made by many manufacturers. These may be actual commemoratives, or may only bear special marks indicating that they were made for a specific exhibition.

Earthenware plate with brown transfer-print depicting the Crystal Palace for the Great Exhibition 1851.

c.1851. Badly crazed. 24 cm diameter   JJM

£200

Earthenware mug commemorating the Great Exhibition with transfer-print, inscribed 'A View on the Road from Hyde Park Corner'; 'The Building for the Exhibition in 1851/ The Works of Industry of All Nations'.

c.1851. Marked 'GREENS LONDON 75883' with diamond registration mark for 20 January 1851, parcel 4, a design registered by James Green, a London retailer. 7 cm height
JM

£150

Doulton salt-glazed stoneware jug with cobalt and brown decoration, portraits of Christopher Columbus and George Washington, commemorating the Columbian Exposition, Chicago 1893.

c.1893. Impressed Doulton rosette mark with 'ENGLAND', and shape number 1748. 19 cm height   CCC

£650

Arthur J. Wilkinson flow blue earthenware transfer-printed plate portraying the Virginia Building at the Jamestown Exposition, 1907.

c.1907. Printed mark 'ROYAL STAFFORDSHIRE POTTERY/ BURSLEM'; printed retailer's mark 'NUSBARUM BOOK & ART Co./100 & 102 CRANBY ST./NORFOLK, VA.' 26.5 cm diameter   CCC

£110

British Empire Exhibition souvenir ashtray with tube-lined decoration.

c.1924. Printed retailer's mark 'NORMAN W. FRANCIS LTD/ CHEPSTOW PLACE W2/COTTAGE POTTERY'. 12 cm diameter   MH

£65

25 TILES

THE tiles shown here fall into four major groups. The first comprise the medieval *encaustic* tiles, which were floor tiles used for the most part in churches and abbeys or royal buildings. Those which have survived are usually *in situ*, for example at Winchester Cathedral, the largest extant medieval floor in Europe. During the 16th and 17th centuries a small number of tin-glazed floor tiles were made in London, but in the 18th century *tin-glazed delftware* wall tiles for fireplace surrounds were made principally in London, Bristol and Liverpool. The Victorian era saw a great renaissance in the use of encaustic tiles for flooring (often copied from medieval designs), and the development of *glazed wall tiles*, which were reasonable enough to be used for whole rooms, though most often for entrances. With the 20th century we have seen the increasing use of *plain tiles*, most often for use in kitchens and bathrooms.

There are interesting collections of tiles at the Gladstone Pottery Museum, Uttoxeter Road, Longton, Stoke-on-Trent, at the Jackfield Tile Museum, which is part of the Ironbridge Gorge Museum in Shropshire and at Leighton House, Kensington.

The Tiles and Architectural Ceramics Society publishes a regular Newsletter, the magazine *Glazed Expressions* and a *Journal*, as well as a wide variety of related publications. The society's meetings often include trips to sites of historical interest and the premises of tile manufacturers. Enquiries about the society should be addressed to Hans van Lemmen, Faculty of Cultural and Education Studies, Leeds Polytechnic, City Campus, Leeds LS1 3HE.

Further Reading

J. and B. Austwick. *The Decorated Tile* (Pitman House, 1980).
Fired Earth, 1000 Years of Tiles in Europe (Richard Dennis and Tiles and Architectural Ceramics Society, 1991).
Jonathan Horne. *A Collection of Early English Pottery*, Parts I–XII (Jonathan Horne, 1982–92).
Jonathan Horne. *English Tin-glazed Tiles* (Jonathan Horne, 1989).
Hans van Lemmen. *Tiles: A Collector's Guide*, revised edn (Souvenir Press, 1990).

ENCAUSTIC TILES

Encaustic tiles were in common use from c.1350. The method of manufacture was quite simple: a thin layer of white clay was laid on an unfired red clay tile, which was deeply impressed with a stamped pattern. The surface was then scraped off, leaving the white clay pressed into the pattern. During the third and fourth decades of the 16th century, the dissolution of the monasteries brought church building to a virtual standstill, and tin-glazed paving tiles began to be imported from Antwerp. These two factors led to the decline of the encaustic tile industry.

Medieval encaustic tiles can still be seen in some churches today. The Abbey at Malvern has a fine collection. The medieval tiles are often covered up by carpets, and as can be seen by the examples below, will have become damaged with centuries of wear.

The early part of Victoria's reign saw the Gothic revival. Architects, the most famous of whom was A. W. N. Pugin (1812–52), designed neo-Gothic churches and, of course, they wanted to pave them with encaustic tiles. The secret of manufacture had long been lost, but in 1830 Samuel Wright patented a process for reproducing them. He was unsuccessful in marketing the tiles, and in 1835 sold his moulds and equipment to Herbert Minton. However, he retained the patent and licensed Minton and later Chamberlain also to produce the tiles in return for a 10% royalty. The Minton firm experimented with Wright's methods for several years, and by 1841 was able to accept their first large commission for the tiles. Many other firms followed them into this burgeoning industry.

Wright's method was different from that of the medieval manufacturers. The Victorian encaustics were moulded in red clay with the design in relief. The surface was then covered with white clay, and when scraped level, the design in red clay was exposed, the remainder of the tile being filled in white clay. Additional colours were sometimes added by making indentations in the surface of the tile and inlaying coloured clays.

The tiles were used in the new Gothic revival churches, as well as for the refurbishment of medieval churches. Pugin and other architects designed many of these tiles, others being direct copies of medieval designs.

Further Reading

Kenneth Beaulah. *Church Tiles of the nineteenth century* (Shire Publications, Aylesbury, 1987).
Elizabeth Eames. *English Medieval Tiles* (British Museum Publications, 1985).
J. M. Lewis. *Welsh Medieval Paving Tiles* (National Museum of Wales, Cardiff, 1976).
Hans van Lemmen, 'Encaustic Tiles', *Minton Tiles* (Stoke-on-Trent City Museum & Art Gallery, 1984, reprinted 1992).

A collection of eight medieval encaustic tiles mounted in a frame. Top left from Buldwas Abbey, others Croxden Abbey.
JH

£780

Prices for individual medieval encaustic tiles are in the range of £50–200 as opposed to £5–50 for Victorian encaustic tiles.

Early Chamberlain encaustic tile with brown and buff clays, clear glazed.

c.1836–40. Impressed marks 'CHAMBERLAIN/AND CO/ WORCESTER. 15.2 cm square   AF

£15

Walter Chamberlain at Chamberlain's Worcester Porcelain began the manufacture of encaustic tiles in 1836, encouraged by his friend Harvey Eginton, antiquary and architect, who designed some of the tiles. From 1840, G. Barr and Fleming St John continued production, jointly purchasing Wright's patent with Minton in 1844 when it was due for renewal. They ceased production in 1848 and sold their equipment to J. H. Maw in 1850.

This design is based on a medieval original. Note the cracks in the inlay caused by differential contraction in the kiln.

Early Minton encaustic tile with yellow majolica glaze painted over white inlay, designed by A. W. N. Pugin after a medieval original.

c.1842. Irregular stab holes in back. 15.2 cm square   AF

£20

A. W. N. Pugin, a personal friend of Herbert Minton, produced a number of designs for Minton for majolica tiles and tablewares. Many of these designs continued in production after Pugin's death in 1852. He is best known as the architect of the interior of the Houses of Parliament.

Minton encaustic tile from St Edwards Church, Corfe Castle, laid in 1848 and lifted in 1948, brown and buff with strong blue vitrified inlay, unglazed.

c.1848. Impressed 'MINTON & Co./PATENT/STOKE UPON TRENT'. 15.2 cm square   AF

£15

Later Minton encaustic tile for domestic rather than ecclesiastical use, buff white and black, clear glaze.

c.1870. Impressed 'MINTON & Co/PATENT/STOKE UPON TRENT'. 15.2 cm square   AF

£12

Malkin, Edge & Co. later dust-pressed encaustic tile in brown, buff, blue, green, black and white.

c.1885. 15.2 cm square   AF

£7

Malkin, Edge & Co. was the tile manufacturing subsidiary of Edge, Malkin & Co. They used the Boulton and Worthington screw press for encaustic tile production.

TIN-GLAZED TILES (DELFTWARE)

Delftware was first made in Britain by immigrant potters from Antwerp at Norwich c.1571 (see chapter 2). The first English tin-glazed tiles were paving tiles, some of which date to the second half of the 16th century. Wall tiles, which are thinner and were prone to warping in the kiln, were not made in England until the third quarter of the 17th century. A ban on the import of Dutch delftware in 1672 boosted potters in England, but Dutch tiles continued to be imported. There were no specialist factories for tin-glazed tile production in England: tiles were made alongside delftware pots. It is known that there were technical difficulties in English tin-glazed wall tile manufacture from 1680 to 1700, and few tiles can be confidently attributed to that period. These early tiles would be difficult to distinguish from contemporary Dutch delft tiles.

Tiles were shaped in moulds and after drying to a leather-hard state were trimmed and fired. Most tin-glazed tiles are painted in blue on a dried but unfired white glaze. This was a very difficult process, because the dried glaze was powdery and easily disturbed. It was also impossible to correct mistakes as the pigment was absorbed by the glaze. The patterns were usually 'pounced' on to the tile, that is, powdered charcoal was sprinkled over a stencil with tiny holes outlining the design, so that when the stencil was lifted, the painter could follow the faint outline of charcoal dots. However, some tiles were painted freehand. When fired the colour sunk into the glaze. Polychrome painting is uncommon, and so such tiles are more valuable. Manganese, which creates a brown or mauve colour, was sometimes used for painting, or more commonly as a powdered pigment to create a mauve ground.

The techniques and subjects used by delftware potters in the early 18th century varied little; however, as a general rule, the later tiles are thinner. When the Dutch East India Company began to import Chinese porcelains in the early 17th century most of the delftware potteries copied these attractive designs, which are now generically known as chinoiserie patterns. They remained popular throughout the 18th century, and were used by English as well as Dutch tile makers, but European subjects on tiles seemed to be more popular. As the English tile industry grew in the first half of the 18th century, they copied many Dutch designs, but their style of painting is distinctive and more humorous. More interesting designs and techniques were introduced during the second half of the 18th century, particularly in Liverpool.

Corner motifs can be used in identifying tin-glazed tiles, but should not be used as the sole guide, as these were often copied. It is sometimes possible to notice that the corner motifs are not as well-painted as the central designs, for the corners were often painted by apprentices.

Tin-glazed tiles are relatively easy to find, but to the beginner it seems impossible to distinguish between the Dutch and English tiles, let alone between the three major areas of English delftware production, London, Bristol and Liverpool. As a general rule, the Dutch tiles are whiter, the blues and manganese are more intense and the tin glaze has a tendency to craze. The design on English tiles has a tendency to sink into the glaze, causing slight depressions. The Dutch body is more open and sandy than the English body which is harder and denser.

Tin-glazed tiles, despite the fact that they have been well-documented by Jonathan Horne, are still relatively cheap, and examples can be found for around £35. However, these will be found in the stock of the general antique dealer, and if the collector wants to rely on such sources, he must make a serious study of the wares, so as to be sure of his purchase. Dutch delft tiles, while certainly attractive and collectable, are more numerous and the common subjects are less valuable than the English tin-glazed examples. Subjects, styles of painting and corner motifs are all important in identifying the date and origin of a tin-glazed tile. Other indicators such as the thickness and uniformity of the glaze and the thickness of the tile itself can only be judged from the experience of handling various examples.

As the tiles were embedded in fireplaces and walls, single examples will have suffered some damage on being prised from their original homes. When this has been done properly, the damage will be limited to small chips to the edges, but it is not uncommon to find tiles for sale partly embedded in great chunks of plaster or mortar. It is advisable to take expert advice before attempting to remove mounted or encrusted tiles.

Further Reading

Frank Britton. *London Delftware* (Jonathan Horne, 1987).
Jonathan Horne. *English Tin-glazed Tiles* (Jonathan Horne, 1989).
Jonathan Horne. *A Collection of Early English Pottery*, Parts I–XII (Jonathan Horne, 1982–92).
Hans van Lemmen. *Delftware Tiles* (Shire Publications, Aylesbury, 1986).
Anthony Ray. *English Delftware Tiles* (Faber & Faber, 1972).

EARLY ON-GLAZE PAINTED TILES

London

Delftware paving tiles were made in England from the second half of the 16th century, these are *very* rare and not easy to distinguish from Antwerp examples. Delftware wall tiles were made in London from as early as 1676, when Jan Ariens Van Hamme, a potter from Delft, obtained a patent for their manufacture. There is evidence that during the late 17th century, wall tile makers continued to experience technical difficulties.

Rare Southwark tin-glazed 'galley paving tile', with blue, manganese-purple, green and orange painting, possibly from Pickleherring Quay, Southwark, London.

Early 17th century. 12.7 cm square   AF

£450

As these were floor tiles they will show considerable wear.

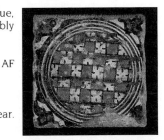

London tin-glazed tile painted in blue with scene of Abraham Dismissing Hagar, with 'barred ox-head corners'.

c.1730–50. 11.8 cm square   JH

£70

Biblical subjects are more commonly found on Dutch delftware tiles than English. Jonathan Horne has recorded 130 different religious subjects used by the London tile makers in the first half of the 18th century, whereas over 500 religious subjects on Dutch tiles have been recorded.

Horne illustrates two other versions of this scene, one of which is very similar (although in reverse) to the one illustrated here.

London tin-glazed tile painted in blue with European landscape with 'Diaper' corners.

c.1775. 13 cm square   JH

£65

The landscape was another popular subject among the London delftware potters, and these European landscape scenes were used for much of the 18th century. The 'Diaper' corner motif on this tile has been excavated in London at the site of a delftware potter, and appears only on late London tiles. This tile is thinner and more evenly made than the previous tile, hence a late date of attribution.

London tin-glazed tile painted in blue with flower vase.

c.1780. 12.5 cm square   JH

£60

Floral decoration was another popular subject for the London delftware potters. This type of corner was excavated at Lambeth. The design is also known in polychrome.

London tin-glazed tile painted in blue with European landscape scene, powdered manganese border with carnation corners.

c.1740s. 12.4 cm square   JH

£95

Decoration by sprinkling powdered manganese on the dried glaze before firing was popular on delftware during the first half of the 17th century. In England it then went out of fashion until a revival in the late 17th and early 18th century. The Dutch made many of these tiles, but did not use the powdered blue ground which may sometimes be found on English tiles. Powdered red and green ground are also known on English delftware tiles, but are extremely rare.

These carnation corners have been excavated in London, but they were also used in Bristol.

Bristol

The Bristol tiles are often slightly larger than the London examples, and are in general more finely made. Their backs are usually smoother.

Bristol tin-glazed tile painted in blue with European landscape scene.

c.1750–60. 13.1 cm square   JH

£85

The sketchy trees here are typical of Bristol.

Bristol *bianco sopra bianco* tin-glazed tile painted in blue with chinoiserie landscape.

c.1760. 13 cm square   JH

£85

Bianco sopra bianco is a white decoration on a pale blue ground. For an example of this technique on a delftware dish see p. 40.

Liverpool

Liverpool introduced onto tiles the new technique of transfer-printing (see below) and also a varied range of complicated hand-painted designs, which during the second half of the 18th century were more interesting than those being produced by the Dutch.

Liverpool tin-glazed tile polychrome painted with figure of a Chinaman with 'Michaelmas daisy' corners.

c.1765. Restored. 12.4 cm square   JH

£75

Polychrome delftware tiles are uncommon, hence the relatively high price for this example, despite the restoration. The 'Michaelmas Daisy' corners are typical of Liverpool and usually found on chinoiserie subjects. When four of these tiles are assembled the corners make complete flowers.

Liverpool tin-glazed tile painted in blue with European landscape scene, with 'Louis XV Border, with diaper corners'.

c.1765. 12.2 cm square   JH

£45

The 'Louis XV Border' reflects the influence of French design in the later 18th century. This complicated hand-painted border design was copied by Sadler of Liverpool when he first introduced his transfer-printed tiles in 1756. These could be produced more quickly and cheaply than hand-painted examples.

ON-GLAZE TRANSFER-PRINTED TILES

In 1756 the process of transfer-printing was first applied to tin-glazed tiles, with whose flat surfaces it was easy to work. The technique was considered a great advance as John Sadler and Guy Green were able to print more than 1200 tiles in six hours, which was more than 100 skilled pot painters could have painted in that time. The tiles were used for walls and hearths. These tiles are rarely found today.

Liverpool tin-glazed tile with Sadler & Green transfer-print.

c.1765. 12.7 cm square   JH

£185

This tile depicts the contemporary dancer Miss Nancy Dawson as shown in *The Ladies Amusement*, a book of engravings from which many transfer-prints were taken.

Liverpool delftware tile, transfer-printed in black by Guy Green, with stencilled green enamel decoration.

c.1775–80. 12.8 cm square   AF

£90

This design was taken from an engraving by J. S. Muller illustrating an edition of Horace published by William Sandby in 1749.

SALT-GLAZED TILES

Extremely rare Whieldon salt-glaze press-moulded tile.

c.1755–65. One corner repaired. 12.4 cm square   JH

£3,500

This tile is similar to four others of different subjects that are reputed to have come from the mantel shelf in a house tenanted by Thomas Whieldon. Fragments of similar earthenware (not stoneware) tiles have been found at Whieldon's Fenton Vivian factory site. A similar tile is illustrated in Horne, vol. VIII.

VICTORIAN TILES

Britain's tile industry was revolutionised by Richard Prosser, a Birmingham engineer, when he patented a method of dust-pressing buttons in June 1840. Herbert Minton saw its potential for tesserae (for mosaics) and ultimately tiles. The clay was ground into a fine powder with a fixed moisture content, before being pressed into shape and fired. This minimised warping and the speed (up to 1800 tiles per machine per day) and simplicity of this technique made for cheap tiles. Moreover, they were of consistently good quality. By the end of the 19th century Britain had the largest tile industry in the world.

In September 1878 *Pottery and Glass Trade Review* exclaimed:

> To what use cannot tiles be put? Cornices and chair-mouldings, door-frames and windows are set with them; hearths outlined or made wholly from them; doors inlaid, and staircases decorated with tiles let into the ends of stairs or laid as steps themselves; summer houses are gay with them, and summer vestibules, for the tile is always fresh and cool-looking in its bright designs, while nothing is warmer or more admirable for winter rooms than the dark earth-coloured ones.

Tiles were also used in furniture, especially wash stands and hall stands, flower stands and jardinières. Tiles were durable, easy to clean and, for the first time in history, highly decorated tiles were reasonably priced.

Once the technical difficulties of mass-producing tiles were overcome, the manufacturers devoted themselves to developing new techniques and designs for decoration. Architects, designers and graphic artists of great talent were employed by the tile manufacturers, often on a free-lance basis. Among the best known of these designers were A. W. N. Pugin, Lewis F. Day, Walter Crane, J. Moyr Smith and Owen Gibbons.

557

Further Reading

Maureen Batkin. *Wedgwood Ceramics, 1846–1959* (Richard Dennis, 1982).
Victoria Bergesen. *Majolica* (Barrie & Jenkins, 1989).
Victoria Bergesen. *Encyclopaedia of British Art Pottery* (Barrie & Jenkins, 1991).
Julian Bernard. *Victorian Ceramic Tiles* (Studio Vista, 1972).
Terence A. Lockett. *Collecting Victorian Tiles* (Antique Collectors' Club, Woodbridge, 1979).
Noël Riley. *Tile Art* (Apple Press, Baldock, 1987).
Deborah Skinner and Hans van Lemmen, eds. *Minton Tiles 1835–1935* (City of Stoke-on-Trent Museum & Art Gallery, 1984, reprinted 1992).
Hans van Lemmen. *Victorian Tiles* (Shire Publications, Aylesbury, 1981).
Hans van Lemmen. *Tiled Furniture* (Shire Publications, Aylesbury, 1989).

UNDERGLAZE TRANSFER-PRINTED TILES

Sherwin & Cotton tile with underglaze transfer-printed and hand-coloured decoration in brown, gold and green.

c.1880. Typical moulded back with Staffordshire knot (illustrated in Austwick figure 124). Transfer-printed marks: design registration diamond for 31 December 1880, parcel no. 4; pattern numbers S701 and S819 (partly visible; an alternative colourway). 15.2 cm square　　　　　RS

£9.50

The partnership trading under the style Sherwin & Cotton operated at several locations in Hanley 1876–c.1930. They made a wide variety of tiles using several decorative techniques.

Decorative Art Tile Co. *Chrysanthemum* tile with underglaze transfer-printed and hand-coloured decoration in brown, pink, yellow and green.

c.1884. Transfer-printed marks on reverse 'No R' (pattern number) and 'Rd No 19686 CHRYSANTHEMUM c 4th 12 1884'. 15.2 cm square　　　　　RS

£9.50

This was one of the first designs registered by the Decorative Art Tile Co., Hanley. As this company decorated only blanks obtained from other firms, their work could be wrongly attributed to these firms. Fortunately the company registered some 195 designs between 1881 and 1904. The registration numbers which appear on the tile backs, can be used to attribute the decoration of these tiles to the correct firm. The design on the tile shown here was printed and coloured on a blank manufactured by T. & R. Boote.

Wedgwood tile with underglaze red sheet transfer-print.

c.1895. Moulded marks on reverse of Portland Vase (trade-mark of Wedgwood) and transfer-printed pattern number T505; 'WEDGWOOD ETRURIA ENGLAND'. 15.2 cm square
RS

£6.50

Tiles with sheet patterns (uniform all-over design) are much less desirable than those with integral designs.

PICTURE TILES

Picture tiles are more desirable and so more valuable than other designs. They were often issued in series, and the tile collector's ambition is to complete a series, much more valuable than the sum of the individual tiles. Although the tiles would usually have been mounted as a complete series, these have often been broken up during demolition or by the antiques trade in the years before tile collecting became popular.

Malkin, Edge & Co. tile with black underglaze transfer-print.

c.1885. 15.2 cm square   RS

£20

This is one of a set of twelve *Medieval Sports & Pastimes* manu-factured by Malkin Edge & Co., Burslem. Two other designs in the series are illustrated in Lockett.

Wedgwood tile with underglaze blue transfer-print.

c.1878. Moulded mark 'JOSIAH/WEDGWOOD/& SONS/ETRURIA'. 15.2 cm square   JM

£30

The months and the seasons were popular subjects for tile series. This is *March* from the *Old English* or *Early English* series, designed by Helen J. A. Miles. This is one of the best known and most collected tile series. Although quite com-mon, the Wedgwood name makes them more costly than similar tiles by less desirable manufacturers. The version transfer-printed in brown is less common, but not neces-sarily more valuable, as many people find the blue version more attractive. A larger version (20.3 cm) was also pro-duced with an additional *Harebell* border. Underglaze hand-tinted versions are also known (illustrated in Batkin).

Maw & Co. tile with transfer-print designed by Owen Gibbons, signed 'OG'.

c.1881. Moulded marks "MAW & Co/BENTHALL WORKS/ BROSELEY/SALOP'. 20.5 cm square   AF

£70

Owen Gibbons, Headmaster of the Coalbrookdale School of Art, designed a number of tiles for Maw & Co. In 1885 he established Gibbons, Hinton & Co., tile manufacturers, with his brother Francis (also a designer) and his brother-in-law W. J. Hinton.

Copeland plastic clay tile, transfer-printed and hand-painted.

c.1878. Impressed mark 'COPELAND'; date code for May 1878. 15.2 cm square   AF

£55

This tile is from Copeland's *Hunting* series. A water-colour design for another in the series is illustrated in Lockett.

BLOCK-PRINTED TILES

F. W. M. Collins and Alfred Reynolds patented a new method of lithographic or block printing for tiles in 1848. The earliest examples were on-glaze, but soon the decoration was underglaze. The design was transferred from a flat stone surface or zinc plate. A multicolour print could be obtained by using a succession of blocks, each inked up with a different colour.

Early Minton dust-pressed tile with Collins & Reynolds patent green on-glaze block-printed design by A. W. N. Pugin, on buff clay.

c.1850. Moulded mark 'MINTON & Co./PROSSER'S PATENT/STOKE ON TRENT/No 2'. 15.2 cm square   AF

£12

Pugin (1812–52) made early use of this new process for his designs.

T. & R. Boote *Summer* tile with underglaze brown block-print.

c.1880. 15.2 cm square   TV

£35

T. & R. Boote were large tile manufacturers at Burslem c.1842–1963. This tile is from their *Four Seasons* series.

Craven Dunnill & Co. *February* tile with underglaze brown block-printed design.

c.1890. Moulded mark on reverse 'CRAVEN DUNNILL & CO/ JACKFIELD SALOP/102'. 15.2 cm square   RS

£24

Earlier versions of this series of *Months* tiles occur with 'COPYRIGHT' printed on the face, and without any writing, on Webb & Co. Tileries (Worcester) blanks.

Minton, Hollins & Co. tile with underglaze brown block-printed design.

c.1880. Moulded marks on reverse 'MINTON HOLLINS & CO/PATENT TILE WORKS/STOKE ON TRENT/EWB'. 15.2 cm square   RS

£16

In 1845, the production of Minton's encaustic tiles was taken over by Minton, Hollins & Co., a partnership between Herbert Minton and his nephew, Michael Daintry Hollins, who ran the firm. After the death of Herbert Minton, several changes of partnership and a protracted law suit over the use of the Minton name, Hollins received £30,000 compensation, which he invested in a new factory, which produced all types of tiles. One of a series of eight *Classical Female Heads*, this tile is pattern number 1332H.

Minton's China Works block-printed tile designed by J. Moyr Smith.

c.1880. Moulded marks 'MINTON'S/CHINA WORKS/ STOKE-ON-TRENT; and trademark. 20.5 cm square   AF

£35

Minton's China Works began large-scale production of decorative wall tiles c.1868, continuing the lines previously produced at Minton. This tile is one of twelve designs in J. Moyr Smith's *Waverley Novels* series, introduced at the Paris Exhibition of 1878. Smith was the leading designer of printed pictorial literary scenes. He also produced designs for Minton Hollins, Burmantofts, W. B. Simpson and others.

RELIEF-MOULDED MAJOLICA TILES

Not long after the introduction of majolica by Minton at the Great Exhibition in 1851, tile manufacturers realised the potential of relief-moulded tiles with majolica glazes. These soon became a standard product made by many large tile manufacturers. For the most part, they were more subdued than other majolica wares, and as such survived well into the 20th century. Monochrome majolica tiles increasingly found favour towards the end of the 19th century.

Majolica tiles are usually relief-moulded, most often in low relief, but sometimes in dramatic high relief. Some were tube-lined, but more often one discovers tiles moulded to appear tube-lined, in order to reduce costs.

Majolica tiles suited the warm and cosy look sought so often by the Victorians in their homes. In 1885 *The Pottery and Glassware Reporter* explained the success of majolica tiles: 'Now . . . the use of coloured glazes is general, and the chilliness of appearance is reduced to the reflecting surface of the glaze. This is also in measure overcome by the employment of uneven surfaces of different grains which blunt and diffuse the light . . .'

The introduction of art nouveau design at the end of the 19th century revitalised the demand for majolica tiles, as the sinuous lines of the designs were easily produced by tube-lining or relief-moulding and the areas between filled with the coloured majolica glazes. These tiles were immensely popular and are quite easy to find today. They are probably the only field open to the art nouveau collector with limited resources.

Minton Hollins dust-pressed relief-moulded tile decorated with polychrome majolica glazes.

c.1855. Moulded marks 'MINTON & Co./STOKE ON TRENT'. 15.2 cm square   AF

£20

Minton Hollins dust-pressed relief-moulded tile decorated with polychrome majolica glazes.

c.1880. Moulded marks 'MINTON/HOLLINS & Co/PATENT TILE WORKS/STOKE ON TRENT'. 15.2 cm square   AF

£12

Maw & Co. dust-pressed tile with high relief-moulding and white, yellow and mottled blue opaque majolica glazes on buff body.

c.1860. Moulded marks 'MAW & CO/BENTHALL/WORKS/ BROSELEY/SALOP'. 15.2 cm square   AF

£13

Maw & Co. tile with sprigged design of leaves in white clay on buff body under deep blue majolica glaze.

c.1865. Moulded marks 'MAW & CO/BROSELEY/SALOP'. 15.2 cm square   AF

£30

Ruabon relief-moulded tile with pink, blue and brown translucent majolica glazes.

c.1890. Moulded marks on reverse. 'RUABON GLAZED BRICK AND FIRE CLAY CO. LD. PANT WORKS RUABON NO. 3'. 15.2 cm square   RS

£9.50

This tile was made by a small company taken over by William Pen Dennis at Ruabon in the 1890s. Similar tiles were formerly on the walls of his offices at Ruabon, North Wales. This firm should not be confused with the much larger tile works at Ruabon owned by J. C. Edwards.

J. H. Barrett & Co. relief-moulded tile with green and pink translucent majolica glazes.

c.1910. 15.2 cm square   RS

£12

T. & R. Boote moulded tile with turquoise majolica glaze ground and relief-moulded art nouveau design highlighted in pink, green and yellow majolica glazes.

c.1905. Moulded mark on reverse 'ENGLAND'. 15.2 cm square   RS

£9.50

Maw & Co. relief-moulded tile with green majolica glaze.

c.1883. 15.2 cm square   TV

£44

This is one of a set of at least eight tiles depicting scenes from Longfellow's *Hanging of the Crane*. It is pattern no. 1380 in Maw's catalogue of 1883.

ARTS AND CRAFTS TILES

The Arts and Crafts movement urged potters to abandon the mass-production which had been so painstakingly achieved during the past century. The movement hoped to convince tile makers to abandon the dust-pressing method, but as even the most ardent advocate of this, William De Morgan, soon discovered, hand-made tiles have two major drawbacks. The first is the tendency to warp in the kiln, which had plagued the tile makers of the 17th and early 18th centuries. The second is the inevitable variation in size. The individualities which make hand-made tiles charming, also makes them more difficult to use. As a result, most art potters settled for applying hand-painted decoration to blanks made by the industrial tile manufacturers.

Initially William De Morgan (1839–1917) decorated blank tiles made by the Architectural Pottery at Poole and others. In 1876 he began to make his own tiles, as he was unhappy with the performance of dust-pressed tiles in his decorating kilns. Inspired by the use of tiles on the exteriors of houses which he saw in the Mediterranean, he experimented until he perfected a frost-resistant tile. De Morgan tile panels are very desirable; single tiles from De Morgan panels or runs are still quite reasonable, if you can find them!

As the Arts and Crafts style (if not the ideology) became more popular, many tile manufacturers installed studios for hand-painting, although the printed and glazed tiles continued to prove popular. Reduction lustre, which was 'rediscovered' by William De Morgan, was also used by a number of industrial potters. These include Maw & Co., Craven Dunnill and J. C. Edwards of Ruabon. De Morgan also introduced Persian designs and colours painted underglaze. These were also made by several industrial manufacturers, particularly Maw & Co.

Further Reading

A. J. Cross. *Pilkington's Royal Lancastrian Pottery and Tiles* (Richard Dennis, 1980).
William Gaunt and M. D. E. Clayton-Stamm. *William De Morgan* (Studio Vista, 1971).
John Catleugh. *William De Morgan Tiles* (Trefoil, 1983, reprinted Richard Dennis, 1991).
Martin Greenwood, *The Designs of William De Morgan* (Richard Dennis and William E. Wiltshire III, Ilminster, 1989).

William De Morgan tile hand-painted in underglaze Persian colours.

c.1888–97. Impressed Merton Abbey mark. 15.2 cm square
AF

£75

Part of a three-tile vertical repeat *Chrysanthemum Panel*.

William De Morgan tile hand-painted in underglaze Persian colours.

c.1882–8. Impressed Merton Abbey Mark. 15.2 cm square
AF

£60

Part of a two-tile vertical repeat *Mongolian* design.

Pilkingtons lustre (copper, gold and platinum) and iridescent tile with design hand-painted over raised engobe surface, probably designed by Lewis F. Day.

c.1905. Impressed mark P. 15.2 cm square
AF

£60

Pilkingtons Tile and Pottery Co. was established as a purpose-built tile factory, beginning production in 1893. Manager William Burton had worked as a ceramic chemist for Wedgwood, and he devoted himself to discovering new and exciting glaze effects for tiles. They are best remembered today for their lustre, which was also used for art pottery.

Lewis Foreman Day designed tiles for Maw & Co., Wedgwood, Craven Dunnill and J. C. Edwards. From 1899 he had an exclusive contract with Pilkingtons, and this is one of the designs included in Pilkingtons' stand at the 1908 Franco-British Exhibition.

PHOTOGRAPHIC TILES

Photo-Decorated Tile Co. photographic tile of 'Lion's Face Rock, Dovedale 56'.

c.1900. 15.2 cm square   AF

£48

Henry Grundy and George Arthur Lingard, photographers, first produced photographic tiles in 1895. They were granted a patent to protect their methods in 1897. Their Photo-Decorated Tile Co. made these tiles for a short time, before Grundy sold the patent to the Royal Castle Flint Glassworks who continued their manufacture until c.1902.

J. H. Barrett & Co. portrait tile, 'Portrait of Field Marshal Sir Douglas Haig, modelled by George Cartlidge after a photograph by Elliott & Fry Ltd'.

c.1917. 15.2 by 22.8 cm   AF

£110

These portrait tiles are different from the Photo-Decorated Tile Co.'s in that the image is reproduced in relief. The means by which these tiles were produced was long a mystery, but the Tile Heritage Foundation in the United States recently uncovered an article in the *Bulletin of the American Society of Ceramics*, which describes the method.

George Cartlidge appears to have discovered this method and introduced it while art director at Sherwin & Cotton. He was later partner in the firm Adams & Cartlidge, which also produced portrait tiles, and spent some time in the United States, where portrait tiles were produced by several manufacturers. Cartlidge's portrait tiles were also produced by J. H. Barrett & Co.

Douglas Haig (1861–1928) became Commander-in-Chief of the British forces in 1915. His successful offensive in August 1918 led to the German surrender, and he was created 1st Earl Haig of Bemersyde.

20TH-CENTURY TILES

Collectors have so far ignored most 20th century tiles. Those by makers such as Carter, Stabler & Adams may be quite expensive, but many fine examples of 20th century design are not. However, be warned that the tiles are not easy to find. Tiles are usually manufactured for use in decoration and come to the collector's market only when they are freed from their installations in kitchens or bathrooms. There is a wide recognition in the demolition and building trades that it is worth preserving old tiles, but until a strong market is established for them, many 20th-century tiles are being put on the tip. If you have tiles of the type shown below and are redecorating, do consider leaving them alone. They may, before too long, become a selling point for your home!

Maw tube-lined tile with eggshell glazes.

c.1925. Moulded mark 'MAW LTD/ENGLAND'. 10.2 cm square   AF

£24

Matt glazes were introduced by many firms in the 1920s. It soon became popular to cover complete fireplaces including the mantelpiece with these tiles. The picture tiles were generally scattered among plain coloured tiles.

Carter, Stabler & Adams pressed plastic clay tile, hand-painted with design by Dora Batty.

c.1925. Moulded marks 'CARTER/79/ENGLAND'. 15.2 cm square   AF

£55

Carter, Stabler & Adams are well known for their hand-painted pottery, but the principal production of the firm has always been tiles. Although most of their tiles were plain, in-glaze picture tiles were one of their specialities, and these are highly collectable today. This tile is from the *Nursery Toys* series designed by Dora Batty.

Dunsmore Tiles stencilled and aerographed tile from the *Farmyard* series.

c.1936. Endorsed mark 'DUNSMORE TILES'. 15.2 cm square
AF

£10

Dunsmore Tiles was a London decorating studio which produced very interesting and amusing designs. They are known to have used Minton and Henry Richards blanks. This is a little known firm, but their designs are strong and distinctive, well worth looking for!

E. Rosalind Ord and Sylvia Packard were art teachers at the Royal School Bath, for which Miss Ord designed a tile mural in the late 1920s. This led to other small commissions and in 1936 they established a formal partnership, Packard & Ord, with premises in Marlborough. They shut down in 1940, and Miss Packard retired after the war. Her share was purchased by Hugh Robb, and the business recommenced in 1946, styled Ord & Robb. These later tiles were signed 'OR' on the face. The firm expanded rapidly, and by 1947 employed fifteen painters. In late 1949 they introduced a range of pottery.

The earlier tiles were painted in-glaze or underglaze, but from mid 1954 they shifted to enamel painting and by 1957 underglaze painting was abandoned. In 1972 the firm turned to screen-printing, but hand-painted tiles are still made. Marlborough Ceramic Tiles, as it is known, is one of five main producers of decorated ceramic tiles in Britain.

Packard & Ord dust-pressed tile designed and painted in-glaze by E. Rosalind Ord.

c.1935. Signed on reverse 'RO'. Rhodes Tile Co. blank. 15.2 cm square   AF

£40

This tile is from the *Wild Animals* series designed and painted by E. Rosalind Ord.

Packard & Ord dust-pressed tile designed and painted underglaze by E. Rosalind Ord.

c.1935. Signed on reverse 'RO'. Pilkingtons blank with date code for 1935. 15.2 cm square   AF

£40

This tile is from the *Spring Flowers* series designed and painted by E. Rosalind Ord.

Ord & Robb dust-pressed tile painted overglaze. Designed by Sylvia Packard.

c.1955. Painted monogram 'OR' on face; 'CH 4/735' painted on reverse. H. & G. Thynne blank with date code for 1955. 15.2 cm square   AF

£26

This tile is from the *Cocks and Hens* series designed by Sylvia Packard.

26 STUDIO CERAMICS

Studio pottery embraces a wide range of 20th-century ceramics, from simple tablewares to ceramic sculptures. Stoneware, earthenware and porcelain are all used, and the potters have used many traditional modes of decoration, as well as developing new styles and techniques. The thread which ties these diverse wares together is their mode of production. The studio pottery is a small non-industrial pottery which allows the potter (or potters) to experiment with new ideas. The early studio potters usually followed the tenets of the Arts and Crafts movement, which required the digging of their own clay, throwing the pots and firing them in wood-burning kilns, preferably built with their own hands. Modern studio potters tend to use prepared clays and electric or gas kilns, which they feel frees them to concentrate on the art of actually creating and decorating a pot.

Studio pottery offers one of the most exciting areas for the collector. The works of contemporary studio potters can be acquired in craft shops, craft shows, art galleries and best of all from the potters themselves – there is something very special about meeting a potter at his pottery and talking about his work. In many cases special orders can be placed, a guarantee that your pot will be unique. However, if you should decide to visit a potter remember that you may be interrupting work. Be sure to call ahead and arrange a convenient time and date.

Try to save all documentation that may accompany a pot, such as the sales receipt and any pamphlets or postcards produced by the potter. Leave any paper labels intact. If possible sit down for a few moments after a visit and write down your impressions of the potter, the pottery, potting techniques and the equipment and materials employed. If permitted, take some photos of the pottery, the showroom, and the potter. All of these preserved in a scrapbook will add to your enjoyment of the collection and its value in future years.

It is much more difficult to fix a value for studio pots than other ceramics. Some of the pots shown here have never been sold at auction and have seldom changed hands. Therefore, in this section estimated prices, rather than actual retail prices have been given in most cases.

Studio ceramics can be seen in the collections of many museums. Rice & Gowing list 61 important collections in the UK, some of which have active programmes for the purchase of studio pottery.

Further Reading

Ian Bennett. *British 20th Century Studio Ceramics* (Christopher Wood Gallery, 1980).
Tony Birks and Cornelia Wingfield Digby. *Bernard Leach, Hamada and their Circle* (Phaidon/ Christie's, 1990).
Ceramic Review (Craftsmen Potters Association of Great Britain, 1970 to the present day).
Emmanuel Cooper and Ellen Lewenstein, eds. *Potters*, 8th edn (Craftsmen Potters Association of Great Britain, 1989). This is a useful book for anyone wanting to buy from or visit contemporary studio potters. Each potter's work is illustrated and described with addresses, telephone numbers and opening hours. The ninth edition will be available by 1993.
Bernard Leach, ed. David Outerbridge. *The Potter's Challenge* (Souvenir Press, 1975).
Paul Rice and Christopher Gowing. *British Studio Ceramics* (Barrie & Jenkins, 1989).
Sarah Riddick. *Pioneer Studio Pottery, The Milner White Collection* (Lund Humphries and York City Art Gallery, 1990).
Muriel Rose. *Artist Potters in England*, 2nd edn (Faber & Faber, 1970).
Oliver Watson. *British Studio Pottery, The Victoria and Albert Museum Collection* (Phaidon/Christie's, 1990).

BERNARD LEACH AND SHOJI HAMADA

It is impossible to exaggerate the importance of Bernard Leach (1897–1979). Leach began potting after attending a Raku tea ceremony in Japan in 1911, and is best known for the Japanese influence which he brought to English studio pottery, but he also took an interest in slipwares. He established his pottery at St Ives in Cornwall in 1921 with the assistance of Japanese potter Shoji Hamada. Many of the studio potters of the first half of the 20th century studied with Leach including Michael Cardew, Katherine Pleydell-Bouverie and Norah Braden. Leach founded a pottery dynasty of sorts and his sons David and Michael and grandson John have all become important studio potters. Apart from his teaching at St Ives, Leach also wrote several books, the most important of which was A *Potter's Book* (first edition 1940), which served as a guide at a time when little published advice was available to the aspiring studio potter.

Shoji Hamada (1894–1978) met Bernard Leach in Japan in 1918, working with him at Abiko in 1919. He accompanied Leach to England in 1920, where he helped to build the now famous climbing kiln, based on a traditional Japanese design. He left England in 1923 and eventually returned to Japan, where he continued a distinguished potting career. He was declared a National Living Treasure by the Japanese government in 1955.

Bernard Leach stoneware vase, brown glaze with slip dot decoration.

c.1960s. Impressed St Ives Pottery mark with impressed monogram BL. 10 cm height   AF

c.£400

Bernard Leach brown stoneware vase with oatmeal glaze.

c.1950s. Impressed St Ives Pottery mark with impressed monogram BL. 29 cm height   AF

c.£4,000

Bernard Leach stoneware vase, craquelé glaze with painted iron decoration.

Late 1920s. Chip repaired, not restored. Impressed St Ives Pottery mark with impressed monogram BL. 15 cm height   AF

c.£1000 if perfect

Shoji Hamada red stoneware vase with dripping olive green ash glaze.

c.1950s. 23.8 cm height   AF

c.£4,000

MICHAEL CARDEW

Michael Cardew (1901–83) first studied pottery under William Fishley Holland at the Braunton Pottery (1921–2). He worked with Bernard Leach at St Ives 1923–6, and took over a derelict pottery at Winchcombe in 1926. In 1939 he left Winchcombe (since run by Ray Finch who had joined Cardew in 1936), and established a pottery at Wenford Bridge. He worked as a pottery instructor in Ghana (1942–4) and established a pottery at Vumé on the Volta River (1946–8). He continued to spend most of his time in Africa, potting at Wenford Bridge for a few months each year until 1965.

Further Reading

Michael Cardew. *Michael Cardew, A Pioneer Potter* (Collins, 1988).

Michael Cardew Winchcombe Pottery slip-trailed red earthenware dish.

c.1938. Impressed marks 'CM'; 'WP' (for Winchcombe Pottery). 30.5 cm length   RS

£600

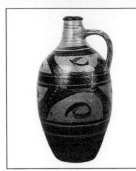

Michael Cardew large red earthenware bottle with honey glaze and brown decoration.

c.1930s. Impressed marks 'CM'; 'WP' (for Winchcombe Pottery). 33.5 cm height   AF

c.£800

Michael Cardew stoneware bowl with brown and blue painted decoration.

c.1970s. Impressed mark 'CM'; seal mark for Wenford Bridge. 25.3 cm diameter   AF

c.£500

WILLIAM STAITE MURRAY

William Staite Murray (1881–1962) studied at the Camberwell School of Arts and Crafts c.1909–12. He established his own pottery at Rotherhithe where he worked 1919–24, working in London 1924–9. He worked at Bray, Berkshire 1929–39. Thereafter he settled in Rhodesia, and ceased potting. Staite Murray considered himself to be an artist first, and potter second. His influence as head of the Royal College of Art pottery department was enormous, but was greatly eclipsed during the years of his retirement in Africa.

Further Reading

Malcolm Haslam. *William Staite Murray* (Cleveland County Museum Service, 1984).

William Staite Murray stoneware bowl with grey glaze.

c.1930s. Impressed mark M with two dots. 20.8 cm diameter   AF

c.£400

William Staite Murray stoneware bottle with grey glaze.

Mid 1920s. Impressed mark. 26.5 cm height — AF

c.£700

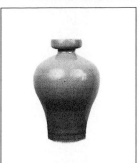

William Staite Murray stoneware vase with white glaze and incised decoration highlighted with brown glazes.

Early 1930s. Impressed mark. 26.5 cm height — AF

c.£1,500–2,000

KATHERINE PLEYDELL-BOUVERIE

Katherine Pleydell-Bouverie (1895–1985) studied with Bernard Leach in 1924, setting up her own pottery at Coleshill, Berkshire the same year, where she was joined by Norah Braden 1928–36. She is best known for her experiments with wood ash glazes on stoneware.

Katherine Pleydell-Bouverie stoneware bottle with black and red ash glaze.

c.1970. Impressed 'KPB' monogram. 10.5 cm height — AF

c.£200

Katherine Pleydell-Bouverie stoneware vase with craquelé ash glaze.

c.1928. Impressed 'KPB' monogram. 20.5 cm height — AF

c.£1,500

LUCIE RIE

In 1938 Lucie Rie (b.1902) came to Britain from Vienna where she had studied pottery at the Kunstgewerbeschule. Her work had been shown at international exhibitions in Paris, Brussels and Milan 1925–37. She established a workshop in London in 1939, where she continues to pot today. Hans Coper shared her workshop 1947–58, which experience influenced both potters' work. Her distinctive shapes and decoration have made her one of the most important potters in post-war Britain.

Lucie Rie porcelain vase with black manganese glaze and bands of red and black decoration.

c.1978. Impressed LR monogram. 23 cm height   AF

c.£12,000

Lucie Rie stoneware bowl.

Late 1970s. 17.5 cm diameter   AF

c.£1,000

Lucie Rie porcelain bowl with manganese glaze.

c.1960. 17.5 cm diameter   AF

c.£2,000

EWEN HENDERSON

Ewen Henderson (b.1934) studied at the Camberwell School of Art and has potted in London since. His hand-built pots derive their colours and textures from combinations of different clays.

Ewen Henderson tea bowl decorated in pink and green.

c.1980s. 8.5 cm height   AF

c.£250

Ewen Henderson hand-built vase made from a mixture of different clays with white glaze.

Early 1980s. 38 cm height   AF

c.£1,000–1,500

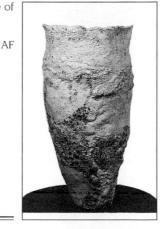

Ewen Henderson hand-built vase made from a mixture of different clays with copper green glazes.

Early 1980s. 34 cm height   AF

c.£1,000–1,500

OTHER STUDIO POTTERS

Norah Braden stoneware pot with celadon crackle glaze and brown painted decoration including crayfish.

c.1930s. Painted monogram. 10.5 cm height   AF

c.£400

This is a unique pot and nothing similar has ever been on the market. Norah Braden joined the Leach Pottery in St Ives as a pupil in 1925. Three years later she joined Katherine Pleydell-Bouverie at Coleshill, where she continued to pot until 1939.

W. B. Dalton stoneware vase with brown glazes.

c.1920. Incised 'WBD' monogram. 13 cm height   AF

c.£300

William Bower Dalton (1868–1965) was one of the early students at the Camberwell School of Arts and Crafts. He established a workshop at Longfield, Kent, where he worked 1909–41. He moved to the United States in 1941, where he potted until his return to England shortly before his death. His pieces very seldom show up on the market, so this price is conjectural. It is difficult to assess the demand for Dalton's work. So little of it is available that there is not a large group of Dalton collectors, and so the demand would come from those who would like an example of his work in a general collection.

David Leach stoneware vase with manganese glaze.

c.1970s. Impressed LD monogram. 24 cm height   AF

c.£300

David Leach joined his father's pottery at St Ives in 1930. He established his own pottery at Lowerdown, Bovey Tracey in 1958. His technical training at Stoke (1934–6) was instrumental for developments which enabled the St Ives Pottery to survive as a commercially viable operation.

James Tower press-moulded earthenware charger decorated with white and black tin glazes.

Late 1970s. Signature mark 'James Tower'. 49.8 cm length
AF

c.£1,500

This press-moulded and tin-glazed charger is typical of the wares made by James Tower (1919–88) in the 1970s. It was first covered with a black tin glaze and then with a white layer. The pattern was created by drawing through the top glaze, revealing the black beneath.

Geoffrey Swindell porcelain covered bowl with crackle glaze top and lustre and mottled glazes on base.

c.1980s. Impressed mark S. 11 cm height   AF

c.£200

Geoffrey Swindell (b.1945) makes small precisely potted porcelain pots, which have been acclaimed since the 1970s.

Ian Auld slab-built stoneware bottle decorated with impressed seals.

c.1960s. Impressed mark in square 'IA'. 45 cm height   AF

c.£400

Ian Auld (b.1926) specialised in the slab-building technique for nearly twenty years, particularly in the making of rectangular bottles like the one shown here.

Mary Rogers porcelain bowl.

Early 1980s. Impressed mark 'MER'. 10.6 cm height   AF

c.£400

Mary Rogers (b.1929) made coiled stoneware pots during the 1960s, but turned to delicate porcelain pinched pots based on natural forms in the 1970s. Her style has been copied widely, particularly after the publication of her book *Mary Rogers on Pottery and Porcelain*.

Charles Vyse stoneware vase with grey glaze and iron decoration.

c.1930s. Incised mark 'C VYSE/CHELSEA'. 16 cm height AF

c.£400

Charles Vyse (1882–1971) and his wife Nell, who was a skilled ceramic chemist, are well known for their figure models, but they also made an interesting range of stonewares with Tenmoku, Chun, celadon and other glazes. See Richard Dennis, *Charles Vyse* (Richard Dennis/Fine Art Society, 1974)

Janet Leach stoneware vase with brown glazes decorated with impressed pattern.

c.1960s. Impressed St Ives Pottery mark and 'JL'. 22.5 cm height   AF

c.£200–300

Janet Leach (b.1916) became the third wife of Bernard Leach in 1956. She has been potting since 1947, at first in the United States and later in Japan and St Ives. This pattern was probably made by impressing a coarse weave fabric into the soft clay, which would burn off during the biscuit firing, leaving the design behind.

Large William Marshall stoneware bottle with white, green and brown glazes.

c.1970s. Incised mark in square 'MW'. 36 cm height   AF

c.£400

William Marshall (b.1923) worked at the St Ives Pottery in 1938, and remained for nearly forty years. Much of his work is in the style of Bernard Leach and Shoji Hamada. Marshall's large rectangular bottles, such as the one shown here, are quite distinctive. He set up his own pottery at Lelant, not far from St Ives, in 1977.

Denise Wren hand-built salt-glazed stoneware vase with scored decoration.

c.1960. Incised mark 'DKW Oxshott'. 26 cm height   AF

c.£150

Denise Wren (1891–1979) began to pot at Oxshott in 1920. Her husband Henry Wren and daughter Rosemary also potted there. She is best known for her hand-built stoneware pots.

Bernard Rooke hand-built stoneware vase with incised decoration.

c.1960s. 20 cm height   AF

c.£300

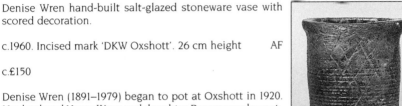

Angus Suttie hand-built stoneware 'jug' with polychrome decoration.

c.1985. Signed 'SUTTIE'. 28.5 cm length   AF

c.£800

Angus Suttie (b.1946) treats useful shapes playfully to create sculptural forms. His earlier wares were occasionally marked 'ANGUS MADE ME' or 'ANGUS'. Since 1985 the wares have the incised mark 'SUTTIE'.

Poh Chap Yeap stoneware bottle with oatmeal and brown decoration.

c.1970s. signed 'Yeap'. 35 cm height   AF

c.£300

Poh Chap Yeap makes stonewares and porcelain in the Chinese tradition.

Rare Same Haile white stoneware vase with white glaze and painted iron decoration.

c.1935. Incised monogram. 27 cm height   AF

c.£300

Thomas Sam Haile (1909–48) trained as a painter, switching to pottery under William Staite Murray. He potted and taught until his departure for the United States in 1939, where he potted until 1943. He was killed in a motor accident in 1948.

Reverse.

Ruth Duckworth stoneware bowl with blue-green glazed interior.

c.1960s. Impressed mark 'RBD'. 25.7 cm diameter   AF

c.£1,500

Ruth Duckworth (b.1919) was a sculptor before she studied pottery at the Central School of Art 1956–8. She designed tablewares, but her most influential work was the sculptural hand-built pottery such as this piece. She has lived in the United States since the mid 1960s.

C. D. Nowell stoneware bowl with green hare fur interior and streaky blue exterior, glazed base.

1950s. Incised signature 'C. D. Nowell' with 'PRESTBURY'; 'R'. 12.7 cm diameter   CG

£15

C. D. Nowell potted at Prestbury c.1951–9. His wares are beautifully potted and have lovely and interesting glazes.

Large Harry Juniper 'Great Torrington Cavalier' slipware jug. Inscribed 'A World Record for *Ferrets in the Pants* 1972'; 'Held by Terry Davey of Winkleigh, Time 36 min'.

1972. 30 cm height   TPCS

£115

Harry Juniper combines traditional North Devon techniques with contemporary subjects. The size and humorous subject of this jug add to its value.

Reverse

Chelsea Pottery earthenware wall plaque with sgraffito decoration painted in polychrome enamels by Mary Lieberman.

c.1954. Incised mark 'Chelsea Potteries' with Yin and Yang symbol. Painted initials ML. 30 cm diameter   SG

£45

The Chelsea Pottery was one of several communal workshops for potters established by David Rawnsley. Mary Lieberman's work was exhibited in 1954,

BIBLIOGRAPHY

Elizabeth Adams. *Chelsea Porcelain* (Barrie & Jenkins, 1987).

Elizabeth Adams and David Redstone. *Bow Porcelain*, 2nd edn (Faber & Faber, 1991).

Sandy Andrews. *Crested China* (Milestone Publications, Horndean, 1980).

Michael Archer and Brian Morgan. *Fair as China Dishes, English Delftware* (International Exhibitions Foundation, 1977).

Elizabeth Aslin and Paul Atterbury. *Minton 1798–1910* (Victoria & Albert Museum, 1976).

Paul Atterbury, *Moorcroft*, revised edn (Richard Dennis and Hugh Edwards, Shepton Beauchamp, 1990).

Paul Atterbury, ed. *The History of Porcelain* (William Morrow & Co., New York, 1982).

Paul Atterbury, ed. *The Parian Phenomenon* (Richard Dennis, 1989).

Paul Atterbury and Louise Irvine. *The Doulton Story* (Royal Doulton Tableware, 1987).

Paul Atterbury and Maureen Batkin. *The Dictionary of Minton* (Antique Collectors' Club, Woodbridge, 1990).

J. and B. Austwick. *The Decorated Tile* (Pitman House, 1980).

John C. Baker. *Sunderland Pottery*, revised edn (Tyne and Wear County Council Museums, Newcastle upon Tyne, 1983).

A. Ball. *The Price Guide to Pot Lids* (Antique Collectors' Club, Woodbridge, 1980).

David Barker. *William Greatbatch a Staffordshire Potter* (Jonathan Horne, 1991).

David Barker and Pat Halfpenny. *Unearthing Staffordshire* (Stoke-on-Trent City Museum & Art Gallery, 1990).

Dennis Barker. *Parian Ware* (Shire Publications, Aylesbury, 1985).

Ray Barker. *The Crown Devon Story* (Warwick Printing Co., Warwick, 1991).

K. J. Barton. *Pottery in England from 3500BC–AD 1730* (David & Charles, Newton Abbot, 1975).

Maureen Batkin. *Wedgwood Ceramics, 1846–1959* (Richard Dennis, 1982).

Kenneth Beaulah. *Church Tiles of the nineteenth century* (Shire Publications, Aylesbury, 1987).

John Bedford. *Toby Jugs* (Cassell, 1968).

Ian Bennett. *British 20th Century Studio Ceramics* (Christopher Wood Gallery, 1980).

Julian Bernard. *Victorian Ceramic Tiles* (Studio Vista, 1972).

Victoria Bergesen. *Majolica* (Barrie & Jenkins, 1989).

Victoria Bergesen. *Encyclopaedia of British Art Pottery* (Barrie & Jenkins, 1991).

Michael Berthoud. H. & R. *Daniel* (Micawber Publications, Wingham, 1980).

Michael Berthoud. *The Daniel Tableware Patterns* (Micawber Publications, Wingham, 1982).

Michael Berthoud. A *Compendium of British Cups* (Micawber Publications, Bridgnorth, 1990).

David Bindman, ed. *John Flaxman* (Thames & Hudson, 1979).

Tony Birks and Cornelia Wingfield Digby. *Bernard Leach, Hamada & their Circle* (Phaidon/Christie's, 1990).

Gilbert Bradley. *Derby Porcelain 1750–1798* (Thomas Heneage & Co., 1990)

Peter Bradshaw. *18th Century Porcelain Figures 1745–1795* (Antique Collectors' Club, Woodbridge, 1981).

Peter Bradshaw. *Derby Porcelain Figures 1750–1848* (Faber & Faber, 1990).

Lawrence Branyan, Neal French and John Sandon. *Worcester Blue & White Porcelain 1751–1790*, 2nd edn (Barrie & Jenkins, 1989).

Virginia Brisco. *Torquay Mottowares* (The Torquay Pottery Collectors' Society, 1989).

Virginia Brisco. *Torquay Commemoratives and Advertising Wares* (The Torquay Pottery Collectors' Society, 1991).

Bristol Fine Wares 1670–1970 (City of Bristol Museum & Art Gallery, 1979).

Frank Britton. *English Delftware in the Bristol Collection* (Sotheby Publications, 1982).

Frank Britton. *London Delftware* (Jonathan Horne, 1987).

Cheryl Buckley. *Potters and Paintresses. Women Designers in the Pottery Industry 1870–1955* (The Women's Press, 1990).

Bernard Bumpus. *Charlotte Rhead, Potter & Designer* (Kevin Francis, 1987).
Elizabeth Cameron. *Encyclopaedia of Pottery and Porcelain. The Nineteenth and Twentieth Centuries* (Faber & Faber, 1986).
Michael Cardew. *Michael Cardew, A Pioneer Potter* (Collins, 1988).
John Catleugh. *William De Morgan Tiles* (Trefoil, 1983).
Victoria Cecil. *Minton 'Majolica'* (Jeremy Cooper, 1982).
Ceramic Review. (Craftsmen Potters Association of Britain, 1970 to the present day).
G. Coke. *In Search of James Giles* (Micawber Publications, Wingham Kent, 1983).
Emmanuel Cooper and Ellen Lewenstein, eds. *Potters*, 8th edn (The Craftsmen Potters Association of Great Britain, 1989). The ninth edition will be available by 1993.
R. G. Cooper. *English Slipware Dishes* (Tiranti, 1968).
Robert Copeland. *Blue and White Transfer-printed Pottery* (Shire Publications, Aylesbury, 1982).
Robert Copeland. *Spode's Willow Pattern & other designs after the Chinese* (Studio Vista, 1980).
A. W. Coysh. *Blue Printed Earthenware 1800–1850* (David & Charles, Newton Abbot, 1972).
A. W. Coysh. *Blue and White Transfer Ware 1780–1840*, 2nd edn (David & Charles, Newton Abbot, 1974).
A. W. Coysh and R. K. Henrywood. *The Dictionary of Blue and White Printed Pottery 1780–1880* (Antique Collectors' Club, Woodbridge, 1982).
A. W. Coysh and R. K. Henrywood. *The Dictionary of Blue and White Printed Pottery 1780–1880*, vol. II (Antique Collectors' Club, Woodbridge, 1989).
Alwyn Cox and Angela Cox. *Rockingham Pottery & Porcelain 1745–1842* (Faber & Faber, 1983).
A. J. Cross. *Pilkington's Royal Lancastrian Pottery and Tiles* (Richard Dennis, 1980).
Graeme Cruickshank. *Scottish Saltglaze* (Scottish Pottery Studies, 2, Edinburgh, 1982).
N. Robert Cumming. *Minton Bone China in the Early Years* (N. Robert Cumming, 1988).
John Cushion. *Handbook of Pottery & Porcelain Marks*, 4th edn (Faber & Faber, 1980).
Peter Davey. *Buckley Pottery* (Buckley Clay Industries Research Committee, Chester, 1975).
Nicholas M. Dawes. *Majolica* (Crown Publishers, New York, 1990).
Aileen Dawson. *Bernard Moore Master Potter 1850–1935* (Richard Dennis, 1982).
Decorative Art, The Studio Yearbook, 1949.
Richard Dennis. *Doulton Stoneware Pottery 1870–1925* (Richard Dennis, 1971).
Richard Dennis. *Charles Vyse* (Richard Dennis/Fine Art Society, 1974).
A. de Saye Hutton. *A Guide to New Hall Porcelain Patterns* (Barrie & Jenkins, 1990).
Una des Fontaines. *Wedgwood Fairyland Lustre* (1975).
Una des Fontaines, Lionel Lambourne and Ann Eatwell. *Miss Jones and her Fairyland* (Victoria & Albert Museum, 1990).
Lawrie Dex. *Hornsea Pottery, a Collectors Guide, 1949–1967* (L. Dex, 1989).
Don Pottery Pattern Book (Doncaster Library Service, 1983).
David Drakard. *The Castleford Pottery Pattern Book 1796* (EP Publishing, Wakefield, 1973).
David Drakard. *Printed English Pottery. History and Humour in the reign of George III 1760–1820* (Jonathan Horne, 1992).
David Drakard and Paul Holdway. *Spode Printed Ware* (Longman, 1983).
Audrey Dudson. *Dudson* (Dudson Publications, Hanley, 1985).
Arthur A. Eaglestone and Terence A. Lockett. *The Rockingham Pottery*, 2nd edn (David & Charles, Newton Abbot, 1973).
Elizabeth Eames. *English Medieval Tiles* (British Museum Publications, 1985).
Ann Eatwell. *Susie Cooper Productions* (Victoria & Albert Museum, 1987).
Diana Edwards. *Neale Pottery and Porcelain* (Barrie & Jenkins, 1987).
Rhoda Edwards. *Lambeth Stoneware. The Woolley Collection including Doulton Ware and the products of other British Potters* (Borough of Lambeth, 1973).
Robin Emmerson. *British Teapots & Tea Drinking.* (HMSO, 1992).
Desmond Eyles. *The Doulton Lambeth Wares* (Hutchinson, 1975).
Desmond Eyles. *Doulton Burslem Ware* (Barrie & Jenkins, 1980).
Desmond Eyles, Richard Dennis and Louise Irvine. *Royal Doulton Figures* (Richard Dennis, 1987).

Fired Earth, 1000 Years of Tiles in Europe (Richard Dennis and Tiles and Architectural Ceramics Society, 1991).

Gordon Forsyth. Twentieth Century Ceramics (The Studio Ltd, 1950).

Friends of Blue. Bulletin (1973 to the present day).

Anton Gabszewicz. Bow Porcelain. The Collection formed by Geoffrey Freeman (Lund Humphries, 1982).

William Gaunt and M. D. E. Clayton-Stamm. William De Morgan (Studio Vista, 1971).

Glazed Expressions (Tiles and Architectural Ceramics Society, 1981 to the present day).

Geoffrey Godden. Victorian Porcelain (Herbert Jenkins, 1961).

Geoffrey Godden. Minton Pottery and Porcelain of the First Period, 1793–1850 (Barrie & Jenkins, 1968).

Geoffrey Godden. Jewitt's Ceramic Art of Great Britain 1800–1900 (Barrie & Jenkins, 1972).

Geoffrey Godden. British Porcelain, an Illustrated Guide (Barrie & Jenkins, 1974).

Geoffrey Godden. British Pottery, an Illustrated Guide (Barrie & Jenkins, 1974).

Geoffrey Godden. An Illustrated Encyclopaedia of British Pottery and Porcelain, 2nd edn (Barrie & Jenkins, 1980).

Geoffrey Godden. Caughley and Worcester Porcelains 1755–1800, 2nd edn (Antique Collectors' Club, Woodbridge, 1981).

Geoffrey Godden. Coalport & Coalbrookdale Porcelains, 2nd edn (Antique Collectors' Club, Woodbridge, 1981).

Geoffrey Godden. Chamberlain-Worcester Porcelain 1788–1852 (Barrie & Jenkins, 1982).

Geoffrey Godden. Eighteenth-century English Porcelain (Granada, 1985).

Geoffrey Godden. English China (Barrie & Jenkins, 1985).

Geoffrey Godden, Lowestoft Porcelains (Antique Collectors' Club, Woodbridge, 1985).

Geoffrey Godden. Ridgway Porcelains, 2nd edn (Antique Collectors' Club, Woodbridge, 1985).

Geoffrey Godden. Encyclopaedia of British Porcelain Manufacturers (Barrie & Jenkins, 1988).

Geoffrey Godden. The Concise Guide to British Pottery and Porcelain (Barrie & Jenkins, 1990).

Geoffrey Godden. Mason's China and the Ironstone Wares, 3rd edn (Antique Collectors' Club, Woodbridge, 1991).

Geoffrey Godden. Encyclopaedia of British Pottery and Porcelain Marks, revised edn (Barrie & Jenkins, 1992).

Geoffrey Godden, ed. Staffordshire Porcelain (Granada, 1983).

Geoffrey Godden and Michael Gibson. Collecting Lustreware (Barrie & Jenkins, 1991).

Miranda Goodby, Oriental Expressions: The Influence of the Orient on British Ceramics (Northern Ceramic Society, 1989).

Edmund Gosse. Sir Henry Doulton (Hutchinson, 1970).

M. H. Grant. Makers of Black Basalt (W. Blackwood & Sons, 1910, new edn Holland Press, 1967).

Martin Greenwood. The Designs of William De Morgan (Richard Dennis and William E. Wiltshire III, Ilminster, 1989).

Leonard Griffin and Louis K. and Susan Pear Meisel. Clarice Cliff, The Bizarre Affair (Thames & Hudson, 1988).

Reginald Haggar and Elizabeth Adams. Mason Porcelain & Ironstone, 1796–1953 (Faber & Faber, 1977).

Reginald G. Haggar. English Pottery figures 1660–1860 (John Tiranti, 1947).

Pat Halfpenny. English Earthenware Figures 1740–1840 (Antique Collectors' Club, Woodbridge, 1991).

Pat Halfpenny. English Earthenware Figures 1740–1940 (City of Stoke-on-Trent Museum & Art Gallery, 1991).

Patricia A. Halfpenny and Stella Beddoe. Circus & Sport, English Earthenware Figures 1780–1840. (The JBSpeed Art Museum, Louisville, Kentucky, 1990).

Frances Hannah. Ceramics, Twentieth Century Design (E. P. Dutton, New York, 1986).

L. H. Harris and T. Willis. An Exhibition of Porcelain Manufactured by E. Locke & Co. Worcester

(Dyson Perrins Museum, Worcester, 1989).

Clive W. Hart. *Linthorpe Art Pottery* (Aisling Publications, Cleveland, n.d.).

Dorothy Hartley. *Made in England* (Century 1939, reprinted 1987).

Dennis Haselgrove and John Murray. *John Dwight's Fulham Pottery, 1672–1978, a Collection of Documentary Sources* (Journal of Ceramic History, 11, Stoke-on-Trent City Museums, 1979).

Jeremy Haslam. *Medieval Pottery* (Shire Publications, Aylesbury, 1984).

Malcolm Haslam. *English Art Pottery 1865–1915* (London Antique Dealers' Club, 1975).

Malcolm Haslam. *The Martin Brothers* (Richard Dennis, 1978).

Malcolm Haslam. *William Staite Murray* (Crafts Council, Cleveland County Museum Service, 1984).

Jennifer Hawkins. *The Poole Potteries* (Barrie & Jenkins, 1980).

R. K. Henrywood. *Relief-moulded Jugs 1820–1900* (Antique Collectors' Club, Woodbridge, 1984).

R. K. Henrywood. *Bristol Potters 1775–1906* (Redcliffe, Bristol, 1992).

Robin Hildyard. *Browne Muggs* (Victoria & Albert Museum, 1985).

Susan Hill. *The Shelley Style* (Jazz Publications, 1990).

Bevis Hillier. *Master Potters of the Industrial Revolution. The Turners of Lane End* (Cory, Adams & Mackay, 1965).

R. L. Hobson. *Catalogue of the Frank Lloyd Collection of Worcester Porcelain of the Wall Period* (Victoria & Albert Museum, 1923).

Malcolm and Judith Hodkinson. *Sherratt? A Natural Family of Staffordshire Figures* (Chisquare, 1991).

David Holgate. *New Hall Porcelain* (Faber & Faber, 1987).

Irene and Gordon Hopwood. *The Shorter Connection* (Richard Dennis, 1992).

Jonathan Horne. *A Catalogue of English Brown Stoneware from the 17th and 18th centuries* (Jonathan Horne, 1985).

Jonathan Horne. *A Collection of Early English Pottery*, Parts I–XII (Jonathan Horne, 1982–92).

Jonathan Horne, *English Tin-glazed Tiles* (Jonathan Horne, 1989).

Kathy Hughes, *A Collector's Guide to Nineteenth-century Jugs* (Routldge & Kegan Paul, 1985).

Kathy Hughes, *A Collector's Guide to Nineteenth-century Jugs*, vol. II (Taylor Publishing Co., Dallas, 1991).

Llewellyn Jewitt. *The Ceramic Art of Great Britain*, 2 vols (Virtue & Co., 1878; 2nd edn 1883). Facsimile reprints are available (New Orchard Editions, Poole, 1985).

Marilyn G. Karmison with Joan B. Stacke. *Majolica, a Complete History and Illustrated Survey* (Harry N. Abrams, New York, 1989).

Alison Kelly. *Wedgwood Ware* (Ward Lock, 1970).

Jana Kybalová. *European Creamware* (Hamlyn, 1989).

Heather Lawrence. *Yorkshire Pots and Potteries* (David & Charles, Newton Abbot, 1974).

Bernard Leach, ed. David Outerbridge. *The Potter's Challenge* (Souvenir Press, 1975).

Sarah Levitt. *Pountneys, the Bristol Pottery at Fishponds 1905–1969* (Redcliffe, Bristol, 1990).

Griselda Lewis. *A Collector's History of English Pottery*, 3rd edn (Antique Collectors' Club, Woodbridge, 1985).

J. M. Lewis. *Welsh Medieval Paving Tiles* (National Museum of Wales, Cardiff, 1976).

J. M. Lewis. *The Ewenny Potteries* (National Museum of Wales, Cardiff, 1982).

Louis Lipski, ed. Michael Archer. *Dated English Delftware Tin Glazed Earthenware 1600–1800* (Sotheby Publications, 1984).

W. I. Little. *Staffordshire Blue* (B. T. Batsford, 1969, reprinted 1987).

Terence A. Lockett. *Davenport Pottery and Porcelain, 1794–1887* (David & Charles, 1972).

Terence A. Lockett. *Collecting Victorian Tiles* (Antique Collectors' Club, Woodbridge, 1979).

Terence A. Lockett and Geoffrey A. Godden. *Davenport China, Earthenware, Glass* (Barrie & Jenkins, 1989).

T. A. Lockett and P. A. Halfpenny, eds. *Stonewares & Stone china of Northern England to 1851* (Stoke-on-Trent City Museum & Art Gallery, 1982).

T. A. Lockett and P. A. Halfpenny, eds. *Creamware & Pearlware* (Stoke-on-Trent City Museum & Art Gallery, 1986).

Abraham Lomax. *Royal Lancastrian Pottery, 1900–1938* (Abraham Lomax, Bolton, 1957).

Longpark Pottery Co. Ltd. Illustrated Catalogue and Revised Price List (Torquay, c.1930s, reprinted The Torquay Pottery Collectors' Society).

Jocelyn Lukins. *Doulton Flambé Animals* (M. P. E., Yelverton, n.d.).

F. Severne Mackenna. *Chelsea Porcelain: The Triangle and Raised Anchor Wares* (F. Lewis, Leigh-on-Sea, 1948, reprinted 1969).

F. Severne Mackenna. *Chelsea Porcelain: The Red Anchor Wares* (F. Lewis, Leigh-on-Sea, 1951)

F. Severne Mackenna. *Chelsea Porcelain: The Gold Anchor Wares* (F. Lewis, Leigh-on-Sea, 1952).

Wolf Mankowitz. *Wedgwood* (Spring Books, 1966).

Mariann K. Marks. *Majolica Pottery* (Collector Books, Paducah, Ky., 1983).

Mariann K. Marks. *Majolica Pottery, Second Series* (Collector Books, Paducah, Ky., 1986).

H. Rissik Marshall. *Coloured Worcester Porcelain of the First Period* (1954; facsimile edition, Ceramic Book Co., Newport, 1977).

John May. *Victoria Remembered* (Heinemann, 1983).

John and Jennifer May. *Commemorative Pottery 1780–1900* (Heinemann, 1972).

Harvey May. *The Beswick Collectors' Handbook* (Kevin Francis Publishing, 1986).

Patrick McVeigh. *Scottish East Coast Potteries* (John Donald Publishers, Edinburgh, 1979).

Michael Messenger. *Shropshire Pottery and Porcelain* (Shrewsbury Museums, 1976).

Philip Miller and Michael Berthoud. *An Anthology of British Teapots* (Micawber Publications, Broseley, 1985).

Steven Moore and Catherine Ross. *Maling: The Trademark of Excellence!* (Tyne and Wear Museum Services, Newcastle upon Tyne, 1989).

Mostyn Art Gallery, *Buckley Pottery* (Gwynned, 1983).

Arnold R. Mountford. *The Illustrated Guide to Staffordshire Salt-glazed Stoneware* (Praeger, 1971).

Kathy Niblett. *Dynamic Design, The British Pottery Industry 1940–90* (City Museum & Art Gallery, Stoke-on-Trent, 1990).

Paul and Kathy Niblett. *Hand-painted Gray's Pottery*, 3rd edn (Stoke-on-Trent City Museum & Art Gallery, 1987).

Anthony Oliver. *Staffordshire Pottery, the Tribal Art of England* (Heinemann, 1981).

Anthony Oliver. *The Victorian Staffordshire Figure* (1971).

Adrian Oswald, R. J. C. Hildyard and R. G. Hughes. *English Brown Stoneware 1670–1900* (Faber & Faber, 1982).

Deena Patrick. *Torquay Pottery Marks Book* (The Torquay Pottery Collectors Society, St Albans, 1986).

Nicholas Pine. *Goss and Crested China* (Shire Publications, 1984).

Nicholas Pine. *William Henry Goss* (Milestone Publications, Horndean, 1987).

Nicholas Pine. *The Concise Encyclopaedia and Price Guide to Goss China* (Milestone Publications, Horndean, 1992).

Nicholas Pine. *The Price Guide to Arms and Decorations on Goss China* (Milestone Publications, Horndean, 1992).

Nicholas Pine. *The Price Guilde to Crested China* (Milestone Publications, Horndean, 1992).

Julia Poole. *Plagiarism Personified? European Pottery and Porcelain Figures* (Fitzwilliam Museum, Cambridge, 1986).

Clive Mason Pope. *A–Z of Staffordshire Dogs* (Resego AG/SA Switzerland, 1990).

J. D. Pountney. *Old Bristol Potteries, being an Account of the Old Potters and Potteries of Bristol and Brislington, between 1650 and 1850* (J. W. Arrowsmith, Bristol, 1920, reprinted by EP Publishing, Wakefield, 1972).

P. D. Gordon Pugh. *Staffordshire Portrait Figures of the Victorian Era*, revised edn (Antique Collectors' Club, Woodbridge, 1987).

Bernard Rackham and Herbert Read. *English Pottery: Its Development from Early Times to the End of the Eighteenth Century* (London, 1924, reprinted EP Publishers, Wakefield, 1973).

Anthony Ray. *English Delftware Tiles* (Faber & Faber, 1972).

Robin Reilly. Wedgwood, 2 vols (Macmillan, 1989).
Robin Reilly and George Savage. The Dictionary of Wedgwood (Antique Collectors' Club, Woodbridge, 1980).
D. G. Rice. English Porcelain Animals of the Nineteenth Century (Antique Collectors' Club, Woodbridge, 1989).
D. G. Rice. The Illustrated Guide to Rockingham Pottery & Porcelain (Barrie & Jenkins, 1971).
Paul Rice and Christopher Gowing. British Studio Ceramics (Barrie & Jenkins, 1989).
Sarah Riddick. Pioneer Studio Pottery, the Milner White Collection (Lund Humphries and York City Art Gallery, 1990).
Noël Riley. Gifts for Good Children (Richard Dennis, Ilminster, 1991).
Noël Riley. Tile Art (Chartwell Books, Secaucus, New Jersey, 1987).
Muriel Rose. Artist Potters in England, 2nd edn (Faber & Faber, 1970).
Diana Edwards Roussel. The Castleford Pottery 1790–1821 (Wakefield Historical Publications, Wakefield, 1982).
Royal Doulton Figures (Doulton & Co., n.d.).
Jill Rumsey. Victorian Relief-moulded Jugs (Richard Dennis, 1987).
James H. Ruston. Ruskin Pottery, 2nd edn (Sandwell Metropolitan Borough Council, 1990).
Henry Sandon. Worcester Porcelain 1751–1793, 2nd edn (Barrie & Jenkins, 1974).
Henry Sandon. Flight and Barr Worcester Porcelain, 1783–1940 (Antique Collectors' Club, 1978).
Henry Sandon. Royal Worcester Porcelain from 1862 to the Present Day, 3rd edn (Barrie & Jenkins, 1978).
Henry and John Sandon. Grainger's Worcester Porcelain (Barrie & Jenkins, 1989).
John Sandon. English Porcelain of the 18th and 19th Centuries (Merehurst Press, 1989).
V. Schuler. Toby Jugs (Pearson, 1986).
John A. Shuman III. The Collector's Encyclopaedia of Gaudy Dutch & Welsh (Schroeder Publishing Co., 1991).
Amoret and Christopher Scott. Staffordshire Figures of the Nineteenth Century (Shire Publications, Aylesbury, 1989).
Simeon Shaw. History of the Staffordshire Potteries (Hanley, 1829; several reprints available, e.g. Praeger, New York, 1970).
Charles and Dorrie Shinn. Victorian Parian China (Barrie & Jenkins, 1971).
Derek Shirley. A Guide to the Dating of Royal Worcester Porcelain Marks from 1862 (D. B. Shirley, 1982).
Deborah Skinner and Hans van Lemmen, eds. Minton Tiles 1835–1935 (City of Stoke-on-Trent Museum & Art Gallery, 1984).
Alan Smith. Liverpool Herculaneum Pottery (Barrie & Jenkins, 1970).
G. M. Smith. Belleek Porcelain and Pottery (Toucan Press, Guernsey, 1979).
M. L. Solon. Art of the Old English Potter, 2nd edn (1885).
The Spode Society. Recorder & Review (1986 to the present day).
Judy Spours. Art Deco Tableware (Ward Lock, 1988).
Staffordshire Portrait Figures. A Catalogue of the P. D. Gordon Pugh Collection in the City Museum and Art Gallery, Stoke-on-Trent (Stoke-on-Trent City Museum & Art Gallery, n.d.).
Lynne Sussman. Spode/Copeland Transfer-printed Patterns (Parks Canada, Ottawa, 1979).
Ross E. Taggard. The Frank P. and Harriet C. Burnap Collection of English Pottery in the William Rockhill Nelson Gallery, revised edn (Nelson Gallery/Atkins Museum, Kansas City, Missouri, 1967).
E. Lloyd Thomas. The Old Torquay Potteries (Arthur Stockwell, Ilfracombe, 1978).
E. Lloyd Thomas. Victorian Art Pottery (Guildart, 1974).
Torquay Pottery Collectors' Society Magazine.
Donald Towner. Creamware (Faber & Faber, 1978).
H. A. B. Turner. A Collector's Guide to Staffordshire Pottery Figures (Emerson Books, New York, 1971).
John Twitchett. Derby Porcelain (DJC Books, 1980).
John Twitchett and Betty Bailey. Royal Crown Derby, revised edn (Antique Collectors' Club,

Woodbridge, 1988).

Hans van Lemmen. *Victorian Tiles* (Shire Publications, Aylesbury, 1981).

Hans van Lemmen. *Delftware Tiles* (Shire Publications, Aylesbury, 1986).

Hans van Lemmen. *Tiled Furniture* (Shire Publications, Aylesbury, 1989).

Hans van Lemmen. *Tiles: A Collector's Guide*, revised edn (Souvenir Press, 1990).

Susan J. Verbeek. *The SylvaC Story* (Pottery Publications, 1989).

Susan J. Verbeek. *The SylvaC Companion* (Pottery Publications, 1991).

Peter Walton. *Creamware and Other English Pottery at Temple Newsam House Leeds* (Manningham Press, 1976).

I. Warner and M. Posgay. *The World of Wade* (c.1988).

C. Watkins, W. Harvey and R. Senft. *Shelley Potteries* (Barrie & Jenkins, 1980).

Bernard Watney. *Longton Hall Porcelain* (Faber & Faber, 1957).

Bernard Watney. *English Blue & White Porcelains of the Eighteenth Century*, revised edn (Faber & Faber, 1973).

Oliver Watson. *British Studio Pottery, The Victoria and Albert Museum Collection* (Phaidon/Christie's, 1990).

Wedgwood Illustrated Catalogue of Ornamental Shapes 1878 (Reprinted by the Wedgwood Society, 1984).

Wedgwood 1880 Illustrated Catalogue of Shapes (Reprinted by the Wedgwood Society, 1971).

Leonard Whiter. *Spode* (Barrie & Jenkins, 1970, reprinted with new colour illustrations 1989).

Sydney B. Williams. *Antique Blue and White Spode*, 3rd edn (B. T. Batsford, 1949, reprinted 1987).

Geoffrey Wills. *Wedgwood* (Country Life Books, 1980).

Mary Wondrausch. *Mary Wondrausch on Slipware* (A. & C. Black, 1986).

Mike Yewman. *Lyle Price Guide to Doulton* (Lyle Publications, 1990).

KEY TO DEALER CODES

AD	Andrew Dando
AF	MIscellaneous antique fairs, flea markets, boot fairs, or anonymous by dealer's request
AS	Alistair Sampson Antiques Ltd
B	Steppes Hill Farm Antiques
BG	Beaubush House Antiques
BK	Brenda Kimber
CCC	The Crested China Company
CD	Claire Denman
CE	Christine Evans
CG	Colin Green
D	Delomosne & Son Ltd
G	Geoffrey Godden
GCC	Goss and Crested China Ltd
HA	Martin & Shelagh Lister
HBW	H. & B. Wolfe Antiques Ltd
IGH	Irene & Gordon Hopwood
JH	Jonathan Horne Antiques
JJB	J. & J. Baker
JJM	J. & J. May
JM	Jennifer Moody
KK	Klaber & Klaber
LM	Laurence Mitchell
LR	Leonard Russell
MB	Marguerite Bond
MH	Muir Hewitt
RS	Richard Scott and Trevor Dennis Antiques
S	Sotheby's
SG	Steve Gamgee
SHA	Suffolk House Antiques
T	Red House Antiques
TA	Tilings Antiques
TPCS	Torquay Pottery Collectors Society, sales and auctions at meetings
TV	Teme Valley Antiques
V	Venners Antiques
VH	Valerie Howard
W	W. W. Warner (Antiques) Ltd
WA	Woodstock Antiques
WG	Weston Antique Gallery

PARTICIPATING DEALERS

J. and J. Baker
12–14 Water Street; 3a High Street, Lavenham, Suffolk
Telephone: (0787) 247610
Business Hours: Monday–Saturday 9 am–1 pm; 2–5.30 pm
Speciality: English porcelain

Beaubush House Antiques
95 Sandgate High Street, Folkestone, Kent CT20 3BY
Telephone: (0903) 249099
Business Hours: Monday–Saturday 9.30 am–5 pm. Closed Wednesday
Speciality: 18th and 19th-century porcelain and pottery

Marguerite Bond
Treasures Antiques, The Crossroads, Four Elms, Edenbridge, Kent
Telephone: (0732) 70363
Business Hours: Monday–Saturday 10 am–5 pm

The Crested China Co.
Station House, Driffield, North Humberside YO25 7PY
Telephone: (0377) 47042 (24 hours); (0377) 45002
Business Hours: Monday–Friday 9 am–5 pm or by appointment. Also by mail order cata-
  logue
Speciality: Goss and crested china

Andrew Dando
4 Wood Street, Queen Square, Bath
Telephone: (0225) 422702
Business Hours: Monday–Friday 9.30 am–1 pm and 2.15–5.30 pm; Saturday 10 am–1 pm;
  afternoon by appointment
Speciality: Fine quality 18th and early 19th-century porcelain and pottery

Delomosne & Son Ltd
Court Close, North Wraxall, Chippenham, Wiltshire SN14 7AD
Telephone: (0225) 891505
Business Hours: Monday–Friday 9.30 am–5.30 pm; Saturday 9.30 am–1 pm; by appoint-
  ment only.
Specialities: 18th and early 19th-century porcelain, pottery and glass

Claire Denman
Halifax Antiques Centre, Queens Road Mills, Queens Road/Gibbett Street, Halifax, West
  Yorkshire HX1 4LR
Telephone: (0422) 266657
Business Hours: Tuesday–Saturday 10 am–5 pm

Christine Evans
Treasures Antiques, The Cross Roads, Four Elms, Edenbridge, Kent
Telephone: (0732) 70363
Business Hours: Monday–Saturday 10 am–5 pm

Steve Gamgee
Telephone: (0303) 260405
Fairs: Covent Garden, Ardingly

Geoffrey Godden
at Klaber and Klaber, 2 Bedford Gardens, Kensington Church Street, London W8
Telephone: (071) 727 4573
Business Hours: Monday–Friday 10 am–1 pm and 2–5 pm; Saturday 10.30 am–4 pm
Speciality: 19th-century British pottery and porcelain

Godden of Worthing Ltd (Geoffrey Godden, chinaman), 19a Crescent Road, Worthing,
    West Sussex BN11 1RL
Telephone: (0903) 235958
Business Hours: Monday–Friday, by appointment only
Speciality: British pottery and porcelain

Goss and Crested China Ltd
62 Murray Road, Horndean, Waterlooville, Hants PO8 9JL
Telephone: Horndean (0705) 597440
Facsimile: (0705) 591975
Business Hours: Monday–Saturday 8.30 am–5.30 pm
Specialities: Goss and other crested china, good quality 20th-century pottery (Carlton
    Ware, Charlotte Rhead, Chameleon Ware etc.)

Colin Green
Rochester Antique Centre, Rochester High Street, Rochester, Kent
Telephone: (0634) 846996
Speciality: Art and studio pottery, 19th and 20th-century glass
Fairs: Covent Garden

Muir Hewitt
Halifax Antiques Centre, Queens Road Mills, Queens Road/Gibbett Street, Halifax, West
    Yorkshire HX1 4LR
Telephone: (0422) 366657
Business Hours: Tuesday–Saturday 10 am–5 pm
Speciality: Art Deco ceramics

Irene and Gordon Hopwood
Telephone: (0453) 758328
Speciality: Shorter earthenwares

Jonathan Horne Antiques
66c Kensington Church Street, London W8 4BY
Telephone: (071) 221 5658
Business Hours: Monday–Friday 9.30 am–5.30 pm.
Speciality: Early English pottery

Valerie Howard
131e Kensington Church Street, London W8 7PT
Telephone: (071) 792 9702
Business Hours: Monday–Friday 10 am–5.30 pm; Saturday 10 am–4 pm
Specialities: Mason's Ironstone, Quimper Pottery

Brenda Kimber
Bradford, Yorkshire
Telephone: (0274) 611478
Hours: by appointment only
Fairs: Newark
Speciality: Torquay pottery

Klaber and Klaber
2A Bedford Gardens, Kensington Church Street, London W8
Telephone: (071) 727 4573
Business Hours: Monday–Friday 10 am–1 pm and 2–5 pm; Saturday 10.30 am–4 pm
Speciality: 18th-century porcelain

Martin & Shelagh Lister
c/o Yew Tree Antiques Centre, Crossways, Four Elms, Edenbridge, Kent
Telephone: (0732) 70215
Business Hours: Monday–Saturday 10 am–5 pm
Specialities: Burleigh Ware, Shelley, Carlton Ware, Susie Cooper and most Art Deco china,
 glass and collectables. Some Arts and Crafts pottery

Laurence Mitchell
13 Camden Passage, Islington, London N1
Telephone: (071) 359 7579/226 1738
Business Hours: Tuesday, Thursday, Friday and Saturday 10 am–4.30 pm; Wednesday
 8.30 am–5 pm
Specialities: 18th and 19th-century porcelains

Jennifer Moody
The Antique and Craft Arcade, 77 Bridge Road, East Molesey, Surrey
Telephone: (081) 979 7954
Business Hours: Monday–Saturday 10 am–5 pm
Specialities: Blue transfer-printed earthenwares, ironstone and other 19th-century pot-
 tery

Red House Antiques
The Red House, Old High Road, Yoxford, Suffolk IP17 3HW
Telephone: (072877) 615
Business Hours: Tuesday, Thursday–Saturday 10 am–1 pm; 2–6 pm
Speciality: English pottery and porcelain

Leonard Russell
21 Kings Avenue, Denton, Newhaven, East Sussex BN9 0NB
Telephone: (0273) 515153
Business Hours: by appointment only
Speciality: Early English pottery

Alistair Sampson Antiques Ltd
156 Brompton Road, London SW3 1HW
Telephone: (071) 589 5272
Business Hours: Monday–Friday 9.30 am–5.30 pm
Speciality: Early English pottery

Richard Scott and Trevor Dennis Antiques
30 High Street, Holt, Norfolk NR25 6BH
Telephone: (0263) 712479
Business Hours: Monday–Wednesday, Friday–Saturday 11 am–5 pm
Speciality: British pottery and porcelain

Suffolk House Antiques
High Street, Yoxford, Suffolk IP17 3EP
Telephone: (072877) 8122
Business Hours: Monday–Tuesday, Thursday–Saturday 10 am–1 pm and 2.15–5.15 pm
Speciality: Early European pottery

Sotheby's
34–5 New Bond Street
London W1A 2AA
Telephone: (071) 493 8080

Steppes Hill Farm Antiques
The Hill Farm, Stockbury, Sittingbourne, Kent ME9 7RB
Telephone: (0795) 842205
Business Hours: by appointment only
Specialities: Fine English porcelains

Teme Valley Antiques
1 The Bull Ring, Ludlow, Shropshire
Telephone: (0584) 874686
Business Hours: Monday–Saturday 10 am–5.30 pm; Sunday by appointment only
Specialities: English porcelain, especially Worcester factories

Tilings Antiques
High Street, Brasted, Kent
Telephone: (0959) 64735
Business Hours: Monday–Saturday 10 am–5.30 pm
Specialities: 18th and 19th-century pottery and porcelain

Venners Antiques
7 New Cavendish Street, London W1
Telephone: (071) 935 0184
Business Hours: Monday–Friday 10.15 am–4.15 pm; Saturday 10 am–1 pm
Speciality: British pottery and porcelain, especially 18th-century English porcelain

W. W. Warner (Antiques) Ltd
The Green, Brasted, Kent
Telephone: (0959) 563698
Business Hours: Monday–Saturday 10 am–1 pm and 2–5 pm
Speciality: 18th and 19th-century porcelain

Weston Antique Gallery
Boat Lane, Weston, Stafford, Staffordshire
Telephone: (0889) 270450
Business Hours: Wednesday–Saturday 10 am–5.30 pm and by appointment
Speciality: 19th-century English pottery and porcelain

H. & B. Wolf Antiques Ltd
128 Worcester Road, Droitwich Spa, Worcestershire
Telephone: (0905) 772320
Business Hours: Friday–Saturday 9.30 am-5.30 pm; other days by appointment
Speciality: 18th and 19th-century pottery and porcelain

Woodstock Antiques
11 Market Street, Woodstock, Oxfordshire OX20 1SU
Telephone: (0993) 811494
Business Hours: Monday–Saturday 9.30 am–5.30 pm; Sundays 1–5.30 pm
Speciality: Staffordshire figures, especially dogs

INDEX

597

Half-Price entry to
WAKEFIELD CERAMICS FAIRS

Present this copy of *Bergesen's British Ceramics Price Guide* **and Wakefield Ceramics Fairs will be delighted to offer you half-price entry to the following ceramics fairs:**

1922

24th-26th September	The Pitville Pump Room, Cheltenham, Gloucestershire
17th-18th October	The Dyson Perrens Museum, Worcester, Worcestershire
24th-25th October	Worksop College, Worksop, Nottinghamshire
6th-8th November	The Crown Hotel, Harrogate, Yorkshire
27th-29th November	The Michael Herbert Hall, Wilton, Wiltshire

1993

8th-10th January	The Cumberland Hotel, Marble Arch, London
19th-21st February	Worksop College, Worksop, Nottinghamshire
26th-28th February	Margam Park, Port Talbot, Wales
12th-14th March	The Dysons Perrens Museum, Worcester
9th-11th April	Oatlands Park Hotel, Weybridge, Surrey
2nd-3rd May	The Great Danes Hotel, Hollingbourne, Kent
11th-13th June	The Cumberland Hotel, Marble Arch, London

For details of fairs taking place during the second half of 1993 please contact Fred Hynds on 0634 723461.

WAKEFIELD CERAMICS FAIRS, 1 FOUNTAIN ROAD, STROOD, ROCHESTER, KENT, ME2 3SJ

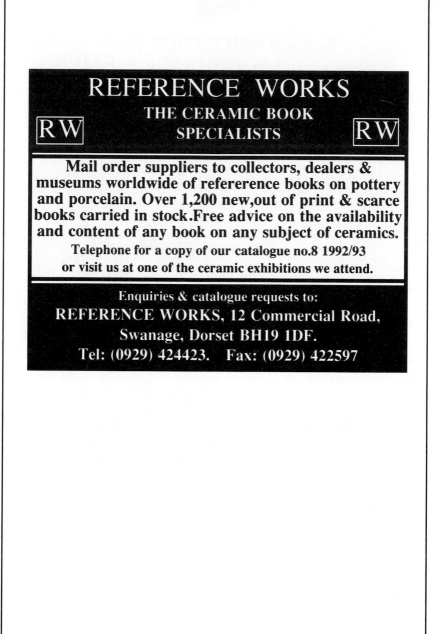

VALERIE HOWARD

Specialist in Mason's Ironstone China
and French Faience, especially Quimper

Photo: Roy Farthing

131e Kensington Church Street
London W8 7PT. Tel: 071-792 9702